A Special Message from The Globe

The Globe Pequot Press is proud to present the seventh edition of *Guide to National Park Areas: Eastern States*. This book provides detailed information about almost 200 areas east of the Mississippi, and it is written by our intrepid park experts, David and Kay Scott, who have been our park authors for more than twenty years.

But this book is special to us for another reason. Globe Pequot has been publishing books on the national parks for many years. We have helped thousands and thousands of people discover our nation's most sacred treasures. And while we are very proud of our part in this, we are also well aware that with park attendance at an all-time high, the parks themselves have suffered from excessive wear and tear. We feel that if we are going to contribute to the damage to parks by directing visitors to them, we also want to help offset that damage by directing funds to the parks.

The Globe Pequot Press will therefore donate $1.00 from the sale of each copy of this book directly to the National Parks Conservation Association, a nonprofit organization. This money will help NPCA protect parks from damaging development; monitor and inventory natural and historic resources; develop financial and transportation plans; and keep destructive and disruptive activities out of the parks.

If you would like to donate to the National Parks Conservation Association, please send a check or money order to:

National Parks Conservation Association
1776 Massachusetts Avenue, N.W.
Washington, D.C. 20036

The Globe Pequot Press is committed to helping preserve our national parks and ensuring that they will remain wonderful places to visit for generations to come.

The Staff of The Globe Pequot Press

Help Us Keep This Guide Up to Date

Every effort has been made by the authors and editors to make this guide as accurate and useful as possible. However, many changes can occur after a guide is published—establishments close, phone numbers change, hiking trails are rerouted, facilities come under new management, etc.

We would love to hear from you concerning your experiences with this guide and how you feel it could be improved and kept up to date. While we may not be able to respond to all comments and suggestions, we'll take them to heart and we'll make certain to share them with the authors. Please send your comments and suggestions to the following address:

The Globe Pequot Press
Reader Response/Editorial Department
P.O. Box 480
Guilford, CT 06437
Or you may e-mail us at: editorial@globe-pequot.com

Thanks for your input, and happy travels!

Guide to the National Park Areas:
EASTERN STATES

Seventh Edition

by
DAVID L. SCOTT *and*
KAY W. SCOTT

The
Globe
Pequot
Press

Guilford, Connecticut

Also by David L. Scott and Kay W. Scott

Guide to the National Park Areas: Western States
The Complete Guide to the National Park Lodges

Facilities and Activities chart and text photographs (unless otherwise noted) are reprinted courtesy of the National Park Service.

Cover photos by Rodger Archibald (lighthouse image) and Tom Alger (bird inset)
Cover design by Adam Schwartzman
Text and map design by Nancy Freeborn

ISSN: 1537-3320
ISBN: 0-7627-1203-1

Manufactured in the United States of America
Seventh Edition/First Printing

CONTENTS

FLORIDA

GEORGIA

ILLINOIS

INDIANA

KENTUCKY

PREFACE

Any discussion of America's national parks is likely to cause most people to automatically think of one or more well-known national parks such as Acadia, Grand Canyon, Grand Teton, Olympic, Rocky Mountain, Great Smoky Mountains (by far the most visited national park), Yellowstone, or Yosemite. These are eight of our most spectacular, visited, and photographed national parks. Literally hundreds of additional beautiful and interesting areas are operated by the National Park Service, however, even though most are not officially designated as national parks. The system of parks includes national monuments, historical parks, military parks, historic sites, reserves, seashores, lakeshores, battlefields, and recreation areas. The National Park Service administers areas that include seashores to walk, parkways to drive, rivers to float, and majestic redwoods to admire. Each area offers something special that is worth seeking. How about a visit to the fort that was the site of the first engagement of the Civil War? Have you tried camping on a pristine barrier island of the Atlantic Ocean where you can take morning strolls on the beach and pick up shells and sand dollars? Would you enjoy a visit to an old Spanish fort constructed in the 1600s? How about a stroll around the Virginia farm where George Washington was born?

Of 384 areas administered by the National Park Service, only about 15 percent are officially designated as national parks. Generally national parks are relatively large in area and contain a variety of resources. Other areas administered by the National Park Service have a more limited size and scope. The different designation doesn't make these areas any less rewarding to visit. In fact you are likely to discover that these other areas are less well known, less crowded, and offer much to see and do. On several occasions we were the only members of ranger-guided walks, and we once experienced a wonderful campfire program with only six other visitors. These experiences become a trip's most memorable events.

As these books are being revised, we have spent twenty-six summers touring the national parks. We have visited all of the states and have seen most of the parks. We have driven the length of the East Coast from Key West, Florida, to the northern tip of Newfoundland. (We did take a ferry from Nova Scotia to Newfoundland.) We walked Boston National Historical Park's Freedom Trail and Boston African-American National Historic Site's Black Heritage Trail on a beautiful Fourth of July. We have spent a day walking along the endless beach of Georgia's Cumberland Island National Seashore and several nights camping in Maine's Acadia National Park. We have driven the Blue Ridge Parkway from Great Smoky Mountains National Park in North Carolina to Shenandoah National Park in Virginia. We fought mosquitoes in Cape Hatteras National Seashore, rain at Allegheny Portage Railroad National Historic Site, and traffic at Independence National Historical Park. We have seen the sights, walked the trails, talked with the park rangers, and visited with other lovers of nature.

The idea for this series of books occurred to us during the fifth summer of our travels. Each time we headed in a new direction we found ourselves trying to decide which areas of the National Park Service to visit and, once there, attempting to determine which particular points of interest and activities held the most promise for our limited time. We discovered that we often delayed trips to areas we should have visited earlier and spent time driving to parks that were found to have little interest. In addition, after arriving at a park, we were often unsure of which campgrounds to use or what activities and facilities were available. For your own benefit, don't overlook the small park areas. Big, busy parks are out of necessity often set up to process visitors on a production-line basis, but many of the small, less frequently visited parks offer a real personal touch.

Our hope is that these books will assist others in avoiding these same pitfalls. We have tried to include enough information to allow readers to decide which parks to visit as well as how long to allow to adequately discover the major features of each park. For most areas, we have tried to provide information on why the area was set aside, a summary of the history and/or geology of the area, activities for visitors, facilities such as availability of food service and overnight accommodations, campgrounds and their facilities, and possibilities for fishermen. In the limited space allotted to each area, we believe that this is the information most useful to the majority of visitors. (If camping facilities or fishing opportunities do not exist at a site, there will not be separate headings for these activities at the end of that particular entry.)

We want to thank a great many individuals at the various National Park Service areas for reading and correcting initial drafts of the manuscript. We have tried to incorporate as many of the suggested changes as possible. The material in these books is believed to be accurate. The National Park Service, however, is constantly altering the areas under its jurisdiction, and no doubt there will be changes even before you buy this book. Budget limitations have resulted in the closing of certain facilities as funds for maintenance and personnel have been cut or, at least, have not kept up with visitation growth. In some cases, closings are temporary; in other instances, they appear permanent.

David L. Scott
Kay W. Scott
Valdosta, Georgia

The information in this guidebook was confirmed at press time. We recommend, however, that you call establishments before traveling to obtain current information.

INTRODUCTION

SOME BASICS FOR VISITING AMERICA'S NATIONAL PARKS

Preparation

Each of the 384 areas administered by the National Park Service offers something special. Learning as much as possible about what is special before you visit a park allows you to gain an appreciation for what you are likely to experience. You will also waste less of your limited time after arrival. Why wait until you arrive to find out what you will be seeing? Most park officials are good about responding to requests for information. Each of the park write-ups in this book provides a telephone number, address, and, in some cases, an e-mail address to use in requesting information. You will also find park Web site addresses that allow access to basic information including opening and closing times, facilities, and activities. If you plan to drive thousands of miles on a vacation of several weeks, take some time to bone up on what you are likely to see, both along the way and at your destination.

What to do when you arrive

The first order of business should be to stop at the park visitor center, especially when you are planning to spend a half day or less in a park area. With a short stay you need to make every minute count. Ask someone at the visitor center information desk about the activities and sights they recommend for the time you have available. Most visitor centers offer exhibits and an orientation film or slide presentation to introduce you to the park. The video presentations are generally excellent at providing a better appreciation of what you will experience in the park. Visitor centers generally operate sales areas with pamphlets and paperback guides relevant to the park and nearby areas. You may want to ask someone at the information desk which publications are likely to prove most helpful. Also check for a listing of the day's ranger-led interpretive programs. Guided walks, living history programs, and ranger presentations are nearly always worthwhile.

It is our opinion that with a limited amount of time you are better off taking time to really experience a few park areas than trying to visit as many park areas as possible. Why miss some of the worthwhile things a park has to offer when you are already there and may not return?

Fees

Most areas operated by the National Park Service levy entrance fees that range from $3.00 to $5.00 per vehicle at the low end to $20.00 per vehicle at very popular parks such as Yosemite, Grand Canyon, and Yellowstone. Separate fees apply to bikers and hikers. The initial entrance fee is generally good for several days, although this varies by park. Many individual parks also offer annual entrance passes at a higher charge. You may discover that certain activities inside a park, such as a cave tour or a guided tour of a building, will require a separate charge. Fees for entrance and activities have increased in both size and frequency in recent years. Many park areas that once offered free entrance now impose an entrance fee. In addition, nearly a hundred park areas, including most of the national recreation areas, are participating in a new program for fee demonstration areas. Most of the fees collected under this program are retained by the individual parks.

Four types of passes are available for individuals and families who expect to be visiting several parks. The National Parks Pass and Golden Eagle Passport are each valid for one year from the month of purchase. Purchase either of these passes on June 10, and the pass will be valid through the end of June in the following year. The Golden Age Passport is a lifetime pass available only for seniors, while the Golden Access Passport is a lifetime pass for the disabled. The National Parks Pass and Golden Eagle Pass each cover entrance fees but are not good for reductions on charges for facilities or tours. For example, the $8 fee charged for a home tour at Vanderbilt Mansion National Historic Site in New York is not covered by either of these passes. The Golden Age Passport and Golden Access Passport are lifetime passes that cover entrance fees and are also good for reductions on many other fees, including camping, parking, and tours. Additional information about the various passes applicable for national park entrance is available on the Internet at www.nps.gov/fees_passes.htm.

The **National Parks Pass** costs $50 and provides entrance for one year to national parks, national monuments, national historical parks, and all other areas operated by the National Park Service. For parks that charge a vehicle entrance fee, the pass provides free entrance for one private vehicle and its passengers. For parks with a per-person entrance fee, the pass provides free entrance for the pass holder, spouse, children, and parents. This pass does not cover fees charged for tours, campgrounds, shuttles, and the like. The National Parks Pass is available at most national park entrance stations and visitor centers by calling 1–888–GOPARKS, and on the Internet at www.nationalparks.org. The pass is also available by mail by sending a check or money order to National Parks Pass, 27540 Avenue Mentry, Valencia, CA 91355. A shipping charge of $3.95 applies to passes purchased by mail, phone, or via the Internet.

The **Golden Eagle Passport** costs $65 and provides one year's entrance to all federal lands, including areas operated by the National Park Service, the U.S. Forest Service, and the Bureau of Land Management. Like the National Parks Pass discussed above, the Golden Eagle Passport applies to one private vehicle and its passengers as well as to the pass holder and immediate family when a per-person fee is assessed. The $50 National Parks Pass can be upgraded for $15 at most federal areas that allow free entrance with the Golden Eagle Passport. The holder of a Golden Eagle Passport does not receive discounts on activities such as tours, parking, camping, and boat launching.

The **Golden Age Passport** costs $10 and provides lifetime entrance to all areas operated by the National Park Service. This pass is available only to citizens and permanent residents of the United States who are sixty-two years of age and older. The pass must be purchased in person and proof of age is required. The Golden Age Passport applies to one private vehicle and its occupants or to the pass holder and his or her immediate family. Unlike the National Parks Pass and Golden Eagle Passport, the Golden Age Passport also provides for a 50 percent discount on many activities, such as parking, camping, and tours. This reduction is sometimes limited to the pass holder. This pass is available at entrance stations and visitor centers of areas managed by the National Park Service. This is the best deal going if you are sixty-two or older.

The **Golden Access Passport** is a lifetime pass that is issued without charge to individuals who show proof of medically determined disability and eligibility for receiving benefits under federal law. This pass provides free entrance and a 50 percent discount for many activities, such as camping, tours, and parking. Some activities are available at a discount only to the holder of the Golden Access Passport. This pass must be obtained in person and is available only to citizens and permanent residents of the United States.

Mabry Mill on the Blue Ridge Parkway (opposite page)

Crowds

Most of America's national park areas are heavily visited, especially during summer months when the weather is good and children are out of school. If possible, try to plan your trip during the spring or fall when crowds are smaller, prices are sometimes reduced, and the weather is still enjoyable. In fact, the weather at many of the parks is delightful during the spring when flowers are blooming and the fall when leaves are turning. We had an enjoyable visit to Yosemite National Park just after Christmas when the air was crisp, the valley was covered with snow, and visitors were a fraction of the normal crowds this busy park experiences during June, July, and August.

Crowds are less of a problem at some of the smaller parks, especially in early mornings and late afternoons. Parks near urban areas are nearly always less crowded during weekdays when nearby residents are working and children are in school. Try to plan trips to eating establishments prior to or after the most popular hours.

Campgrounds

Although many National Park Service areas, especially those with primarily a historical theme, do not have campgrounds, a number of areas in the western states administered by the National Park Service do provide camping facilities. Multiple campgrounds are in the bigger national parks such as Acadia, Everglades, Shenandoah, and Great Smoky Mountains that serve as popular vacation destinations. Campgrounds are also at numerous other areas including Cape Hatteras National Seashore (NC), Gulf Islands National Seashore (FL), Sleeping Bear Dunes National Lakeshore (MI), and the Blue Ridge Parkway (NC & VA).

Most National Park Service campgrounds offer similar facilities including picnic tables, fire grates, water, a dump station, and rest rooms with flush toilets. Hookups for water, electricity, and waste disposal are generally unavailable except for a few instances when a campground is operated by a private concessioner rather than the National Park Service. Likewise, showers are not offered at most Park Service campgrounds. Concessioners sometimes provide pay showers near a visitor center or store, but this is the exception rather than the rule.

National parks with and without campgrounds are often surrounded by national forests that offer numerous camping opportunities. U.S. Forest Service campgrounds often provide relatively rustic facilities including pit toilets, although this is certainly not always the case. Many National Forest Service campgrounds are quite nice with paved parking pads and modern rest rooms. Because National Park Service campgrounds tend to be heavily utilized, you may wish to settle in at a Forest Service campground the night before entering one of the busy parks, especially if you arrive in the late afternoon.

Most National Park Service campgrounds are operated on a first-come, first-serve basis, so the earlier in the day you arrive, the more likely you are to locate a vacant campsite. Approximately two dozen park areas managed by the National Park Service have campgrounds with sites that can be reserved. Campgrounds at each of the parks listed above can be reserved through National Park Reservation Service operated by Biospherics, a publicly-held firm. Reservations (except for Yosemite that has a separate reservation service) can be made via the Internet (reservations.nps.gov), by phone (800–365–2267), or through the mail (National Park Reservation Service, P.O. Box 1600, Cumberland, MD 21501). Reservations can be made beginning on the fifth of each month (the fifteenth for Yosemite), up to five months in advance. Not all campgrounds in each of the listed parks are always subject to reservation.

Lodging

A limited number of national park areas (most of which are in the western states) offer overnight lodging facilities. Private accommodations are often available directly outside or nearby a park's entrance. Most national park lodges are owned by the federal government but operated under long-term lease by private concessioners who must have their charges approved by park superintendents. A limited number of park lodges are privately owned, including Furnace Creek Inn and Panamint Springs Resort in Death Valley National Park. Park lodging is subject to wide variation in both price and quality, from Cumberland Island National Seashore's historic Greyfield Inn at $300 to $450 per night (meals included) to the Blue Ridge Parkway's rustic Rocky Knob Cabins (without bathrooms), which rent for $52 per night. Lodging facilities generally range in price from $65 to $90 with a private bath. Park accommodations are often fully booked months in advance, so you should seek a reservation early if you plan to stay overnight at a park facility during a busy period. Reservations are easier to obtain for the off season.

National Park Service Areas in Eastern States with Campgrounds That Accept Reservations

Acadia National Park (ME)

Assateague Island National Seashore (MD)

Big South Fork National River and Recreation Area (TN/KY)

Cape Hatteras National Seashore (NC)

Everglades National Park (FL)

Great Smoky Mountains National Park (TN/NC)

Greenbelt Park (MD)

Gulf Island National Seashore (FL)

Mammoth Cave National Park (KY)

Shenandoah National Park (VA)

Sleeping Bear Dunes National Lakeshore (MI)

Facilities

Facilities available in National Park Service areas vary widely. A large and busy park such as Shenandoah National Park offers groceries, museums, restaurants, snack bars, service stations, and overnight accommodations. Smaller park areas may offer little other than a visitor center and a picnic area, one of which will generally have drinking water and rest rooms. The visitor center may even have a soft drink machine, but don't count on it. Most of these smaller park areas don't have a small store, place to eat, or vending machines. They certainly don't have a place to stay the night, except, perhaps, a campground. Plan to pick up the fixings for a picnic before you enter one of the smaller parks.

National Park Service Areas in Eastern States with Lodging Facilities

Blue Ridge Parkway (NC/VA)

Cumberland Island National Seashore (GA)

Cuyahoga Valley National Park (OH)

Everglades National Park (FL)

Isle Royale National Park (MI)

Mammoth Cave National Park (KY)

Shenandoah National Park (VA)

Virgin Islands National Park (VI)

KEY FOR
MAP SYMBOLS

———————	Roads
- - - - - - - - -	Dirt Roads
· · · · · · · · · · ·	Trails
▪▪ ▪ ▪▪▪ ▪ ▪▪▪ ▪	State Border
▬▬▬▬▬	Park Area
〰〰〰	Rivers / Water
⬠	Visitor Center
△	Camping
⊟	Lodge
▪	Building
●	Locator/Town
𝝥	Picnic Area
✗	Ruins/Historic Site (as noted on individual maps)
⬟	Parking
⌓	Overlook

Tuskegee Institute National Historic Site

ALABAMA

HORSESHOE BEND NATIONAL MILITARY PARK

11288 Horseshoe Bend Road
Daviston, AL 36256-9751
(256) 234–7111
HOBE_Administration@nps.gov
www.nps.gov/hobe/

Horseshoe Bend National Military Park preserves 2,040 acres authorized in 1956 and proclaimed by President Eisenhower in 1959 to commemorate the 1814 battlefield where General Andrew Jackson's Tennessee Army fought and defeated Chief Menawa's Red Stick or Upper Creeks in the final battle of the Creek Indian War of 1813–14. The miltary park is located in Tallapoosa County, in east-central Alabama, 12 miles north of Dadeville on State Highway 49.

On the morning of March 27, 1814, General Andrew Jackson and an army of 3,300 men, consisting of Tennessee militia, United States regulars, and both Cherokee and Lower Creek allies, attacked Chief Menawa and 1,000 Upper Creek or Red Stick warriors fortified in the "horseshoe bend" of the Tallapoosa River. To seal off the bend of the river, the Upper Creeks built an incredibly strong 40-yard-long barricade of dirt and logs. As the Cherokee and Lower Creek warriors swam the Tallapoosa and attacked from the rear, Jackson launched the militia and regular soldiers against the barricade. Facing overwhelming odds, the Red Sticks fought bravely yet ultimately lost the battle. More than 800 Upper Creeks died at Horseshoe Bend

Tuskegee Institute National Historic Site (opposite page)

defending their homeland. This was the final battle of the Creek Indian War of 1813–14, which is considered part of the War of 1812. In a peace treaty signed after the battle, both the Upper and Lower Creeks were forced to give the United States nearly 20 million acres of land in what is today Alabama and Georgia. The victory here brought Andrew Jackson national attention and helped him to be elected the seventh president of the United States in 1828.

The park visitor center offers a ten-minute slide show and a museum featuring artifacts of the battle, with exhibits detailing the Creek War, the War of 1812, and Creek Indian history. Visitors to the park may also drive a 3-mile auto tour road and/or walk a 2.8-mile nature trail in order to view the Horseshoe Bend battlefield.

Each year, during the month of March, the park hosts a living history event designed to focus attention on the participants of the battle. Authentic Indian and military camps are set up on the field behind the park visitor center. Contact the park for event information.

ENTRANCE FEE: No charge.

FACILITIES: Rest rooms, a drink machine, and water are at the visitor center. There is a large picnic area with tables, pavilions, and grills located across from the visitor center. The park maintains a boat ramp on the Tallapoosa River with a small picnic area. Food and lodging are available in Dadeville and Alexander City.

CAMPING: Camping is prohibited in the military park. There is a campground at Wind Creek State Park (25 miles southwest) near Alexander City (256–329–0845).

FISHING: Fishing from the banks of the Tallapoosa River is permitted only at the boat ramp. An Alabama fishing license is required and all state laws are in effect.

LITTLE RIVER CANYON NATIONAL PRESERVE

2141 Gault Avenue, North
Fort Payne, AL 35967-3673
(256) 845-9605
LIRI_Superintendent@nps.gov
www.nps.gov/liri/

Little River Canyon National Preserve comprises about 14,000 acres and was authorized in 1992 to protect natural, recreational, scenic, and cultural resources along a stretch of the river. The preserve is located in northeast Alabama on Lookout Mountain in Cherokee and DeKalb counties. It is best reached via State Highway 35 between the towns of the Fort Payne and Gaylesville.

The Little River has carved a deep canyon on its journey on Lookout Mountain. The area encompassing the preserve contains spectacular terrain including waterfalls, canyon rims and bluffs, sandstone cliffs, and forested uplands. The preserve provides numerous recreational opportunities for camping, hiking, fishing, kayaking, mountain biking, swimming, climbing, and hunting. Kayaking and climbing are activities for only the most experienced and skilled recreationists. Canyon Rim Drive (State Highway 176) provides access to many spectacular overlooks and some trails into the canyon. This is the most visited part of the preserve.

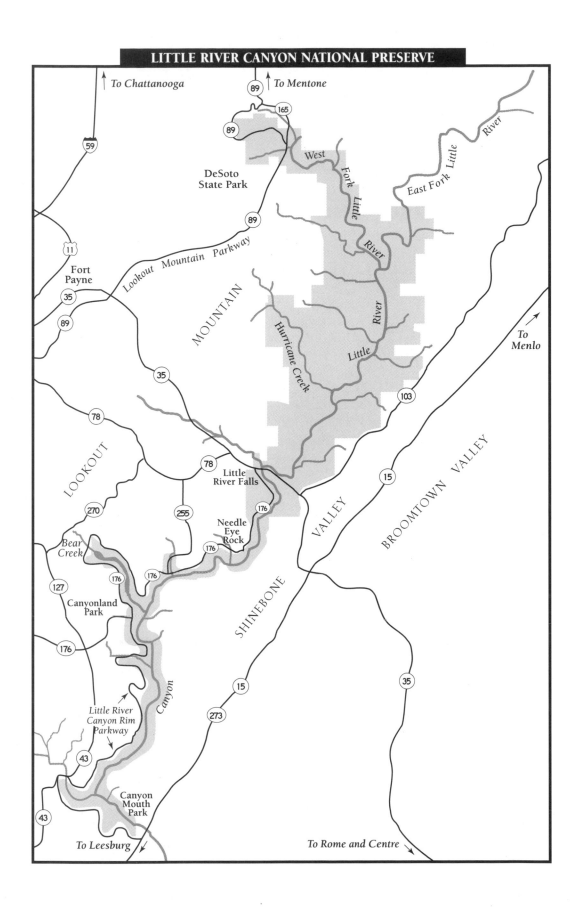

LITTLE RIVER CANYON NATIONAL PRESERVE

To Chattanooga

To Mentone

89

165

89

59

West Fork Little River

East Fork Little River

DeSoto State Park

11

89

Fort Payne

35

89

Lookout Mountain Parkway

MOUNTAIN

Hurricane Creek

Little River

35

To Menlo

103

78

Little River Falls

78

LOOKOUT

270

255

Needle Eye Rock

176

Bear Creek

176

176

176

15

SHINEBONE VALLEY

BROOMTOWN VALLEY

127

Canyonland Park

176

Canyon

15

35

Little River Canyon Rim Parkway

43

273

Canyon Mouth Park

43

To Leesburg

To Rome and Centre

ENTRANCE FEE: No charge.

FACILITIES: DeSoto State Park (256–845–0051 or 800–568–8840), at the north end of the preserve on County Highway 89, offers some facilities. These include meals, limited groceries, and lodging, including cabins and a resort lodge. Full facilities are available in surrounding communities.

CAMPING: Primitive camping is allowed by permit in the preserve. DeSoto State Park (see above) offers seventy-eight developed campsites with water and electrical hookups.

FISHING: Fishing is permitted in the Little River. Catches include mostly bass and sunfish. An Alabama fishing license is required.

RUSSELL CAVE NATIONAL MONUMENT
3729 County Road 98
Bridgeport, AL 35740-9770
(256) 495–2672
RUCA_Interpretation@nps.gov
www.nps.gov/ruca

Russell Cave's 310 acres were incorporated into the National Park System in 1961 to preserve a cave shelter revealing an archaeological record of human habitation from 7000 B.C. to about A.D. 1650. The park is located in the northeastern corner of Alabama. From U.S. 72, turn north 1 mile on County Road 75 to Mount Carmel and then right for 4 miles on County Road 98 to the entrance. The park is about 8 miles west of Bridgeport.

About 9,000 years ago, groups of nomadic Indians first began to occupy Russell Cave. These early Indians lived in the cave shelter only during the autumn and winter and subsisted by hunting game and gathering plants. Successive groups inhabited the cave until A.D. 1650.

Archaeological excavations, which first began here in 1953, have uncovered broken pottery, spear and arrow points, and animal and human skeletal remains. These items reveal the thousands of years of habitation in the cave shelter.

The visitor center, open year-round, contains exhibits to help interpret the monument. An exhibit of prehistoric lifeways is in the cave shelter, but entrance into cave passages is allowed only with written permission of the superintendent. Interpretive programs are presented in the visitor center audiovisual room upon request. Guided walks to the cave shelter and demonstrations of tools and weapons of the prehistoric Indians are available.

ENTRANCE FEE: No charge.

FACILITIES: No food or lodging is available in the park; both can be found in South Pittsburg, Tennessee; Bridgeport, Alabama; and Stevenson, Alabama. Rest rooms and drinking water are in the visitor center. A small picnic area is available, but fires are not permitted.

CAMPING: No camping is permitted in the monument. Camping is available in Stevenson. DeSoto State Park at Fort Payne, Alabama; Cloudland Canyon State Park near Trenton, Georgia; and TVA's Nickajack Dam Recreation Area are within 50 miles of Russell Cave.

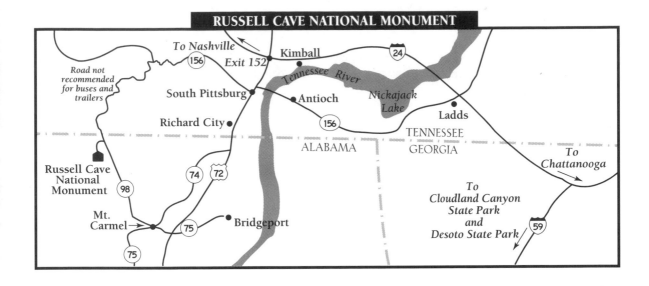

RUSSELL CAVE NATIONAL MONUMENT

TUSKEGEE INSTITUTE NATIONAL HISTORIC SITE

P.O. Drawer 10
Tuskegee Institute, AL 36087-0010
(334) 727–6390
www.nps.gov/tuin/

Tuskegee Institute National Historic Site comprises seventy-five acres and was authorized in 1974 to memorialize a famous college for black Americans founded by Booker T. Washington. The site is located in eastern Alabama in the northwest corner of the city of Tuskegee. When approaching on Interstate 85, exit on State Highway 81 South and turn right on Old Montgomery Road.

Booker T. Washington was six years old when the Civil War broke out. After gaining his freedom following the war, he held a number of jobs before graduating with honors from Hampton Institute in 1875. In 1881, he moved to Tuskegee to create Tuskegee Normal and Industrial Institute. From an initial state appropriation of $2,000 and classes in a dilapidated church, Booker T. Washington moved Tuskegee Institute through a period of growth and improvement until his death in 1915. The main campus has subsequently expanded to 161 buildings that house nearly 5,000 students, faculty, and staff. For further information on Booker T. Washington, see Booker T. Washington National Monument (Virginia) elsewhere in this book.

Information, audiovisual programs, and guide maps to the campus are available at the visitor orientation center at the George Washington Carver Museum. Many of the institute's buildings constructed during the tenure of Booker T. Washington are still standing. Most of these are built of brick made on the campus by students, and many of the historic buildings were designed by R. R. Taylor, the first black graduate of MIT and a Tuskegee faculty member. Of particular interest are the Washington family home, The Oaks (tours available), and the Carver Museum.

ENTRANCE FEE: No charge.

FACILITIES: Food service and lodging are available on campus and may also be found in the city of Tuskegee.

CAMPING: No camping is permitted at the site. Chewacla State Park is northeast of Tuskegee, near Auburn, and primitive camping is permitted at nearby Tuskegee National Forest.

CONNECTICUT

STATE TOURIST INFORMATION
(800) 282–6863
www.tourism.state.ct.us

WEIR FARM NATIONAL HISTORIC SITE

735 Nod Hill Road
Wilton, CT 06897-1309
(203) 834–1896
wefa_interpretation@nps.gov
www.nps.gov/wefa

Weir Farm National Historic Site comprises approximately sixty acres and was authorized in 1990 to preserve the home, studio, and landscape of American Impressionist painter Julian Alden Weir. The historic site is located in southwestern Connecticut between the towns of Ridgefield and Wilton. From State Highway 7, take State Highway 102 west to Old Branchville Road, to 735 Nod Hill Road. The visitor center is the red house on the right past Pelham Lane. Parking is available on the left opposite the visitor center. Nod Hill Road is steep and narrow with limited visibility. There is no turnaround or parking for RVs or large vehicles.

Julian Alden Weir (1852–1919) was one of many American art students who studied in Paris during the years following the Civil War. It was here that he made friendships and was exposed to exhibitions that would strongly influence his future work. After returning to the United States, the painter pursued his own work in portraits and still lifes while serving as an art instructor in New York City. It was not until after moving to this farm that he began to paint outdoor scenes in an impressionist style. Branchville-inspired landscapes painted by Weir and several colleagues are considered exceptional examples of the American impressionist movement.

Weir acquired the 153-acre farm in 1882 and used it as a summer home. He built a studio, enlarged the house, and eventually expanded the farm to 238 acres. He was to spend nearly four decades entertaining artist colleagues such as John Twachtman, Albert Pinkham Ryder, and Childe Hassam. Weir's daughter, Dorothy, married sculptor Mahonri Young (Brigham Young's grandson) in 1931 and Mahonri used the farm until his death in 1957.

The visitor center, located in the Burlingham House, features an introduction to the site including an exhibit of historical photographs, a video, and a computer program showing Weir's paintings. The visitor center is open Wednesday through Sunday from 8:30 A.M. to 5:00 P.M. The grounds are open daily from dawn to dusk. Scheduled tours of Weir's and Young's studios and of the grounds are available. Call for tour times. Visitors also may purchase a brochure that takes them on a self-guided walking tour of twelve historic painting sites where they can compare art reproductions with the vistas that inspired them.

ENTRANCE FEE: No charge.

FACILITIES: There are no flush toilets; portable toilets are located near the visitor center. Lodging and food are available nearby.

CAMPING: No camping is permitted at the site.

FISHING: Fishing is permitted; state regulations apply.

Weir Farm National Historic Site

DISTRICT OF COLUMBIA

The District of Columbia contains more than 300 National Park Service units comprising thousands of acres. These units consist of such diverse areas as parkways, parks, a national cemetery, and the White House. Only the more popular areas are included in this section. Chesapeake and Ohio Canal National Historical Park, which offers boat trips from Georgetown, is discussed separately in the Maryland section. The concessioner-operated Tourmobile service stops at most major points of interest with unlimited reboarding permitted on the same day a ticket is purchased (202–554–7950). Because of limited parking and long walking distances between sites in downtown Washington, the Tourmobile is a worthwhile addition to a trip, especially if it is to last only a day or two. For information on particular units, write National Capital Region, 900 Ohio Drive S.W., Washington, D.C. 20024 (202–619–7222). Entrance fees are not charged at the sights listed below, with the exception of the Sewall–Belmont House National Historic Site.

National Park Service campgrounds are available in surrounding areas. These include Catoctin Mountain Park (Maryland), Greenbelt Park (Maryland), and Prince William Forest Park (Virginia).

See maps on pages 10, 11, 13, and 14 for locations of the attractions below.

1. **Constitution Gardens:** A forty-acre park constructed during the American Revolution Bicentennial sits on what was once the site of War Department office buildings. An island in a lake in the gardens contains a memorial to the fifty-six signers of the Declaration of Independence (202–426–6841).

2. **Ford's Theatre National Historic Site** (511 Tenth Street, N.W.): This restored theater, the scene of President Abraham Lincoln's assassination, is maintained as a living memorial. A museum in the basement provides a look into the highlights of Lincoln's life, and a number of objects owned by Lincoln and his family are exhibited. Periodic talks on the assassination are presented in the theater, where visitors may view the presidential box where Lincoln was shot. Across the street is the house where Lincoln died the next morning. The

museum and house are open daily from 9:00 A.M. to 5:00 P.M. (theater closed for matinees at noon on Thursdays, and 2:00 P.M. on Sundays), and guided tours are available (202–426–6924; www.nps.gov/foth).

3. **Franklin Delano Roosevelt Memorial** (in West Potomac Park, between the Tidal Basin and the Potomac River): This was completed in May 1997 as a memorial to the thirty-second President of the United States. Made of red South Dakota granite, the memorial is divided into four outdoor galleries, one for each of the president's terms in office (202–426–6841; www.nps.gov/fdrm).

4. **Frederick Douglass National Historic Site** (1411 W Street, S.E.): Frederick Douglass was America's leading nineteenth-century black spokesman, and this restored brick house served as his home from 1877 to his death in 1895. The house is open for free guided tours daily from 9:00 A.M. to 4:00 P.M. The visitor center contains exhibits and audiovisual programs (202–426–5960). Advance reservations are required for group tours numbering ten people or more; www.nps.gov/frdo.

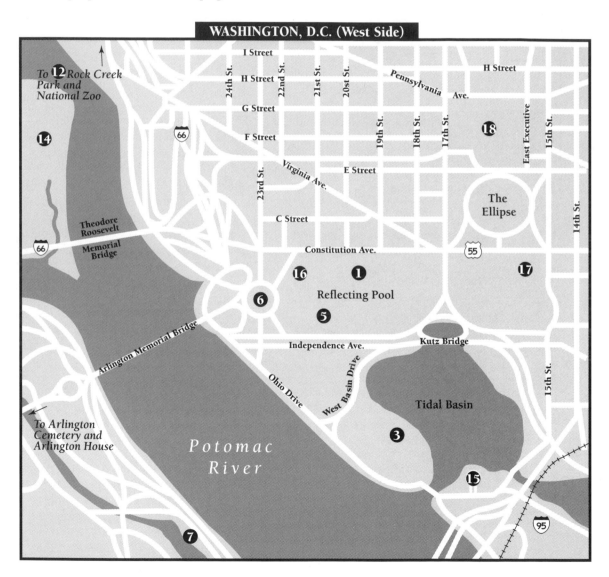

WASHINGTON, D.C. (West Side)

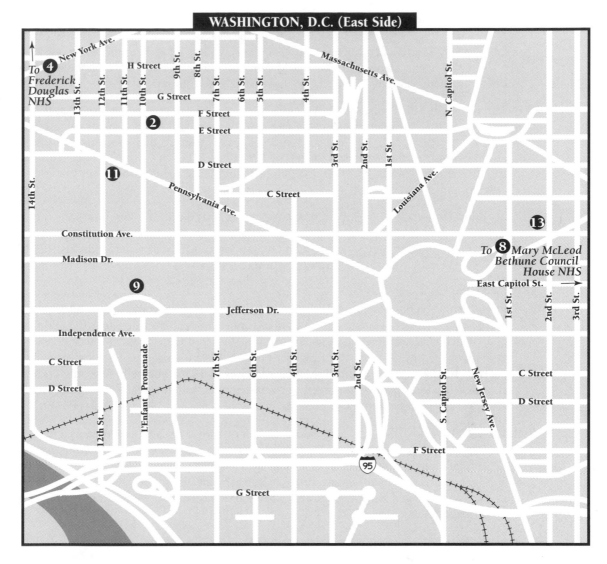

5. **Korean War Veterans Memorial** (southeast of the Lincoln Memorial on Independence Avenue): A memorial to the million-and-a-half American men and women who served in the Korean War. It includes a group of nineteen stainless-steel statues depicting a squad on patrol, a black granite wall that reflects the faces of those who served, and a Pool of Remembrance encircled by a grove of trees (202–426–6841).

6. **Lincoln Memorial** (foot of Twenty-third Street, N.W., at Arlington Memorial Bridge): Work on this huge seated figure of Abraham Lincoln commenced in 1914. The figure is surrounded by thirty-six marble columns, and Lincoln's Second Inaugural and Gettysburg addresses are inscribed on the great marble walls. Interpretive services are provided daily from 8:00 A.M. to midnight (202–426–6841; www.nps.gov/linc).

7. **Lyndon Baines Johnson Memorial Grove on the Potomac:** a seventeen-acre memorial to the thirty-sixth president located on the south side of the Potomac River overlooking the Capitol. The grove contains 500 white pines. Open dawn to dusk (703–285–2601; www.nps.gov/lyba).

8. **Mary McLeod Bethune Council House National Historic Site** (1318 Vermont Avenue, N.W.) (www.nps.gov/mamc): headquarters of the National Council on Negro Women established by Mary McLeod Bethune in 1935. Born in 1875, Ms. Bethune served as advisor to four U.S. presidents and was a leader in black women's rights movements. Open Monday through Saturday 10:00 A.M. to 4:00 P.M. Closed Sunday.

9. **National Mall:** This landscaped park with its rows of elms extends from the Capitol to the Washington Monument. Within its 146 acres visitors will find footpaths, bike trails, and refreshment stands. The mall is bordered by a number of interesting buildings, including those of the National Gallery of Art (open 10:00 A.M. to 5:00 P.M. Monday through Saturday, noon to 9:00 P.M. on Sunday) and the Smithsonian Institution (www.nps.gov.nama).

10. **Old Stone House** (3051 M Street, N.W., in Georgetown): Built in 1765, this is the oldest existing house in Washington and a fine example of pre-Revolution architecture. The site offers guided tours, living-history demonstrations, and interpretive exhibits (202–426–6851). Open Wednesday through Saturday 9:00 A.M. to 5:00 P.M. Closed Monday and Tuesday.

11. **Pennsylvania Avenue National Historic Site** (corner of Pennsylvania Avenue and Twelfth Street N.W.): The anchor site of Pennsylvania Avenue National Historic Site is the Old Post Office, which was completed in 1899. Tours of the Old Post Office tower provide an excellent view of the city from the third-highest point in Washington. The tour also goes past bells presented by Great Britain to the United States in 1976. The bells ring only on special occasions. Tours take about fifteen to twenty minutes and begin at the building's main level. A variety of restaurants and shops are inside the renovated interior (202–606–8691).

12. **Rock Creek Park:** This 1,750-acre woodland in northwest Washington contains a diverse selection of natural, historical, and recreational resources. Activities include hiking, tennis, golf, softball, picnicking, horseback riding, and bicycling. The nature center provides exhibits, a planetarium, and nature programs; nearby are self-guided nature trails. Pierce Mill is a restored gristmill built around 1820 (202–426–6829; www.nps.gov/rocr). See map on page 13.

13. **Sewall-Belmont House National Historic Site** (144 Constitution Avenue, N.E.): This house, which dates to the early 1700s, has been headquarters for the National Women's Party since 1929. The house commemorates the party's founder and women's suffrage leader, Alice Paul. The house and museum are open Tuesday through Friday 10:00 A.M. to 3:00 P.M.; Saturday noon to 4:00 P.M. They are closed Sundays, Mondays, and holidays. Call for tour hours (202–546–3989). An entrance fee of $3.00 per person is charged.

14. **Theodore Roosevelt Island:** This eighty-eight-acre island has been preserved as a wildlife sanctuary to commemorate our twenty-sixth president's devotion to conservation. No vehicles are permitted on the island, which can be reached by footbridge from a parking area on the Virginia shore. Access to the parking area is from the northbound lane only of the George Washington Memorial Parkway. The island contains trails and an impressive 23-foot-tall statue of Theodore Roosevelt; it is open from 9:30 A.M. until sundown (703–285–2601; www.nps.gov/this). See map on page 14.

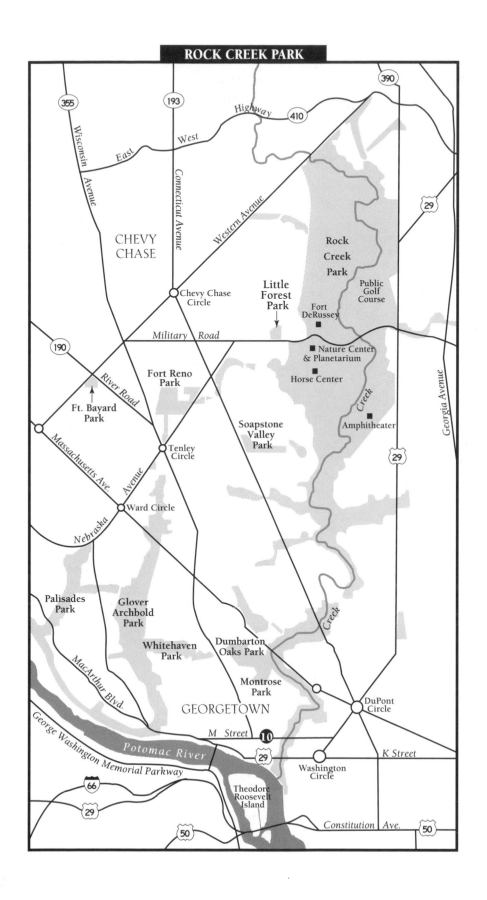

ROCK CREEK PARK

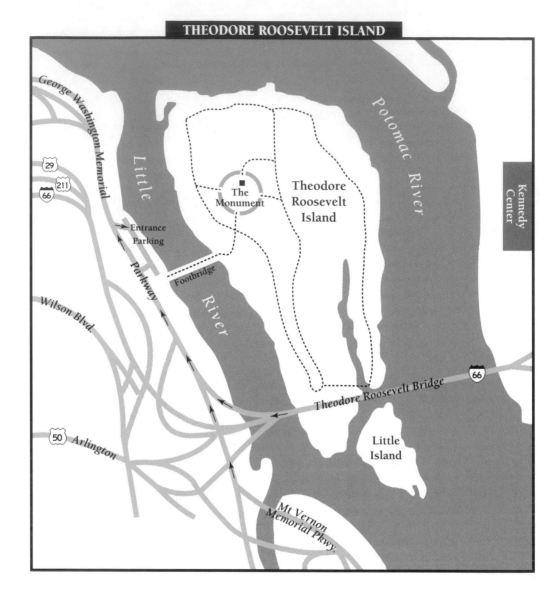

15. **Thomas Jefferson Memorial** (south bank of Tidal Basin): This circular structure, built in a style introduced in this country by Thomas Jefferson, was dedicated in 1943 as a memorial to our third president, the principal author of the Declaration of Independence. Interpretive services are available year-round from 8:00 A.M. to midnight (202–426–6841; www.nps.gov/thje).

16. **Vietnam Veterans Memorial** (Constitution Avenue and Twenty-first Street, N.W., near Lincoln Memorial): This memorial was dedicated in November 1982 as a symbol of the nation's honor and recognition of the men and women who served in the Vietnam War. It is a special tribute to and inscribed with the names of more than 58,000 individuals who died or were listed as missing in Vietnam. The memorial was built with $7 million in private funds, with its design decided through a national competition. A life-size statue of three servicemen was added in 1984, which, along with a flagstaff, forms an entrance plaza to the memorial. Directories providing the locations of individual names are available at

the memorial. The memorial is open 24 hours a day. Staff members are available at the memorial from 8:00 A.M. to midnight (202–426–6841; www.nps.gov/vive).

17. **Washington Monument** (Constitution Avenue at Fifteenth Street, N.W.): This 555-foot monument, built as a memorial to our first president, was first opened to the public in 1888. Visitors may take an elevator to the 500-foot level. The monument is open daily from 9:00 A.M. to 5:00 P.M., September through March; 8:00 A.M. to midnight, April through August. A ticket system is in effect year-round. Tickets are issued on a first-come basis starting one-half hour before opening at the ticket kiosk on Fifteenth Street (202–426–6841; www.nps.gov/wamo).

18. **White House** (1600 Pennsylvania Avenue, N.W.): The White House has been the residence of all U.S. presidents except George Washington, who selected the site upon which it stands. The house is open for tours from 10:00 A.M. to noon Tuesday through Saturday. A ticket system is in effect March through October. Tickets are issued on a first-come basis starting at 8:00 A.M. on the Ellipse. The White House is closed during official functions (202–208–1631; www.nps.gov/whho).

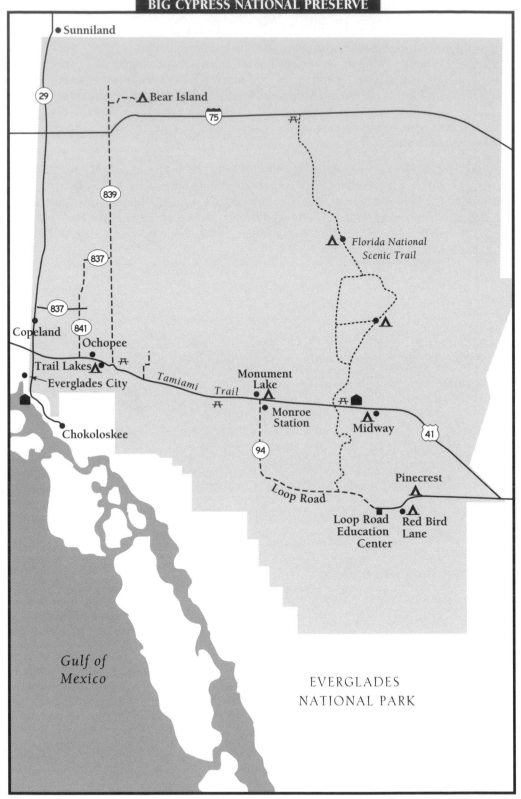

BIG CYPRESS NATIONAL PRESERVE

Sunniland

29

Bear Island

75

839

837

Florida National
Scenic Trail

837

841

Copeland

Ochopee

Trail Lakes

Everglades City

Tamiami

Trail

Monument
Lake

Monroe
Station

Midway

41

Chokoloskee

94

Pinecrest

Loop Road

Loop Road
Education
Center

Red Bird
Lane

Gulf of
Mexico

EVERGLADES
NATIONAL PARK

FLORIDA

STATE TOURIST INFORMATION
(888) 246–8728
www.flausa.com

BIG CYPRESS NATIONAL PRESERVE
HCR61, Box 110
Ochopee, FL 34141
(941) 695–2000
www.nps.gov/bicy

Big Cypress National Preserve comprises about 729,000 acres and was authorized in 1974 to preserve an area that is rich in subtropical plant and animal life as well as critical in providing fresh water to the Everglades. The preserve is located in southwestern Florida, adjoining the northwest section of Everglades National Park. Access is via U.S. Highway 41, State Highway 29, and Interstate 75.

Big Cypress Swamp is big in the sense that it encompasses 2,400 square miles in subtropical Florida. The area includes not only what is popularly considered a swamp but also sandy islands of pine, mixed hardwood islands, dry and wet prairies, and mangrove forests. Unfortunately, few giant cypress trees remain, although about one third of the swamp is covered with dwarf pond cypress. The preserve differs from many other National Park Service areas in that hunting, trapping, off-road vehicle use, oil and gas exploration, and other preexisting uses have been allowed to continue, although such uses currently require a license.

The area was opened to commercial exploitation in 1928 with the opening of the Tamiami Trail. In addition to a lumber boom in the 1930s and 1940s, Big Cypress attracted hunters, fishermen, guides, and cattlemen. Florida's first producing oil well was drilled near here in 1943. Later, in the 1960s, developers began draining the Big Cypress and selling land. A jetport was planned as Miami began to boom. It was this development and the resulting threat to the Everglades' watershed that prompted establishment of Big Cypress National Preserve.

Big Cypress contains a variety of plant life and wildlife. The latter includes herons, egrets, alligators, wild turkeys, deer, mink, bald eagles, red-cockaded woodpeckers, and the unique wood stork. Big Cypress is home to several endangered Florida panthers.

Big Cypress Visitor Center, 55 miles east of Naples on U.S. 41, is the main visitor contact station. The center has an information desk, wildlife exhibits, and a fifteen-minute-long orientation film about the preserve. It is open daily except Christmas Day from 8:30 A.M. to 4:30 P.M. Longer hours may be offered during the winter season. Primary access to the preserve is by U.S. 41. Ranger-guided activities, such as wet walks, bicycle tours, canoe trips, and campfire programs, are offered in the winter season. Information on these activities is available at the visitor center.

ENTRANCE FEE: No charge. An off-road vehicle permit has an annual fee of $50.

FACILITIES: Food service and accommodations are in Naples and Everglades City. The town of Ochopee has food service during the winter tourist season. The National Park Service offers no facilities.

CAMPING: One privately owned campground in the preserve is at Ochopee. It provides all services, including showers and a laundry. A developed campground with tables, grills, flush toilets, and showers is in Collier–Seminole State Park. Other campgrounds are in Everglades City and Naples and on Alligator Alley. The National Park Service provides primitive campgrounds on U.S. 41 and on Loop Road (Highway 94). No water or rest rooms are available, with the exception of Monument Lake Campground, which does have water and rest rooms.

FISHING: Bass, bluegills, and catfish are three of several species that may be taken from canal waters. A Florida fishing license is required.

BISCAYNE NATIONAL PARK
9700 S.W. 328th Street
Homestead, FL 33033
(305) 230–7275
BISC_Information@nps.gov
www.nps.gov/bisc

Biscayne National Park was authorized as a national monument in 1968 (redesignated as a national park in 1980) and comprises more than 172,000 acres (only about 5 percent of which is land) of reefs and water surrounding a north–south chain of more than forty islands or "keys." The park is located in extreme southeastern Florida, south of Miami and east of Homestead. The mainland section and Dante Fascell Visitor Center are reached via North Canal Drive (Southwest 328th Street) from Homestead and U.S. Highway 1.

Biscayne National Park is one of the few areas administered by the National Park Service in which the center of attraction is water and the life it supports. On the keys the tropical climate combined with extraordinarily clean, clear water produces an unusual diversity of trees, ferns, vines, flowers, shrubs, and the wildlife they support. Offshore, along Biscayne's reefs, more than

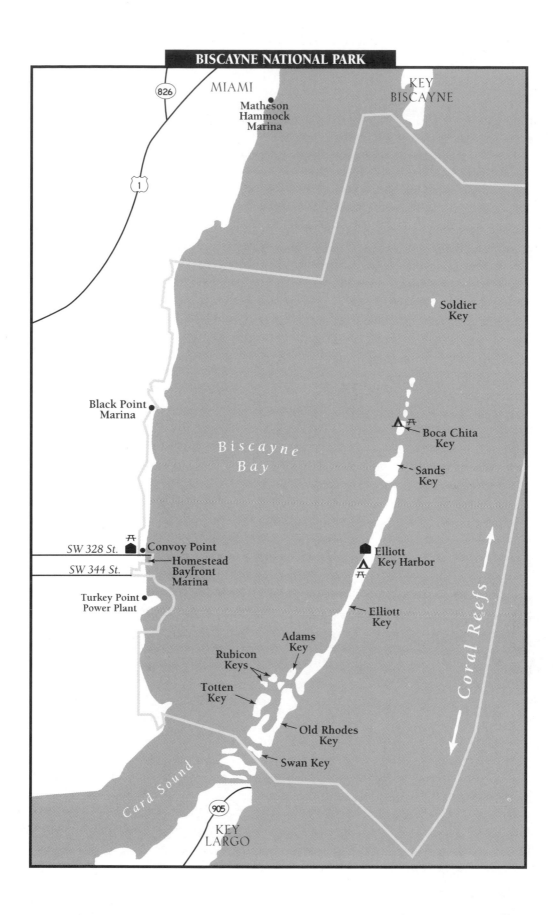

BISCAYNE NATIONAL PARK

MIAMI

KEY BISCAYNE

Matheson Hammock Marina

Soldier Key

Black Point Marina

Biscayne Bay

Boca Chita Key

Sands Key

SW 328 St.

Convoy Point

Homestead Bayfront Marina

Elliott Key Harbor

SW 344 St.

Turkey Point Power Plant

Elliott Key

Adams Key

Rubicon Keys

Totten Key

Old Rhodes Key

Swan Key

Coral Reefs

Card Sound

KEY LARGO

200 species of colorful fish can be seen. Brown pelicans, terns, and herons inhabit the bay. On the mainland, a mangrove forest provides a breeding ground for marine animals and acts as a buffer against the winds and waves of hurricanes.

Main access to the park is at Convoy Point, where park headquarters and the Dante Fascell Visitor Center are located. The visitor center, which contains exhibits and a schedule of activities, is open daily (except Christmas Day) from 8:30 A.M. to 5:00 P.M. Concessioner-operated glass-bottom boat tours depart here at 10:00 A.M. daily. Snorkeling trips to the reefs depart daily at 1:30 P.M. Call (305) 230–1100 for information or for reservations, which are recommended. Transportation for campers to Elliott Key is available with advance reservations. Reservations for scuba trips are required. Canoe and kayak rentals are also available at Convoy Point.

Offshore, Elliott Key has a nature trail, freshwater showers, drinking water, boat docks with sixty-eight boat slips (fee; first-come basis), and overnight camping. Adams Key is open for day use only and offers free docking, a picnic area, rest rooms, and a nature trail. Sands Key features a popular offshore overnight anchorage area. Boca Chita Key has docking (fee charged), picnic facilities, saltwater rest rooms, and overnight camping, but no fresh water is available.

ENTRANCE FEE: No charge. There is a $15 overnight boat docking fee for Elliott Key and Boca Chita Key Harbors, which includes one campsite.

FACILITIES: Homestead, Miami, and the Florida Keys offer a wide range of food and lodging. Snorkeling and scuba-diving gear are rented or sold in surrounding locations.

CAMPING: Elliott Key has a campground with thirty-five sites and a group campsite, each with picnic tables and grills. Drinking water, rest rooms, and showers are available. Boca Chita Key has a camping area with grills, picnic tables, and saltwater rest rooms. Docking fees are charged at both harbors. No fresh water is available. Both campgrounds are accessible by pri-

vate boat or arranged by the concessioner at Convoy Point for Elliott Key. Everglades National Park, John Pennekamp Coral Reef State Park, and other area state parks offer year-round camping.

FISHING: A variety of saltwater fish can be caught here. Florida state licensing requirements and fishing regulations apply to park waters.

CANAVERAL NATIONAL SEASHORE

308 Julia Street
Titusville, FL 32796-3521
(321) 267–1110
cana_superintendent@nps.gov
www.nps.gov/cana

Canaveral National Seashore comprises 57,627 acres and was established by Congress in 1975 to preserve one of the few remaining natural areas on Florida's Atlantic Coast. The seashore is located midway down Florida's east coast along a 24-mile stretch of beach beginning approximately 18 miles south of Daytona Beach and ending at the north end of the Kennedy Space Center.

Amid the hustle and bustle of Florida tourists and the launch area of America's space effort, Canaveral National Seashore provides a sanctuary for plants, wildlife, and man. The seashore is actually a by-product of the space program in that the National Park Service became involved in managing a portion of Merritt Island that was not being utilized for the Kennedy Space Center. Another section, Merritt Island National Wildlife Refuge, is managed by the U.S. Fish and Wildlife Service.

More than 310 species of birds have been recorded on the island, including egrets, gulls, herons, pipers, osprey, sandpipers, terns, and an occasional bald eagle. Manatees are seen in Mosquito Lagoon and Indian River; whales and dolphins can sometimes be spotted offshore. On the island are armadillos, bobcats, raccoons, and rattlesnakes. Crabs, loggerhead turtles, and green sea turtles frequent the beach.

Apollo Beach (in the North District, near New Smyrna Beach) and Playalinda Beach (in the South District, near Titusville) may be reached by State Road 44 or State Road 406 via U.S. 1 or I–95. Klondike Beach, between the two districts, is reached by foot, bicycle, or horseback and offers considerably more solitude. Ocean temperatures are relatively mild all year, but the surf can be rough; swimmers should be aware of potential rip currents and should watch for stinging jellyfish, including the Portuguese man-of-war. Mosquitoes can be a problem at certain times of the year; visitors should bring insect repellant or wear lightweight clothing to protect them from the biting insects. Boat-launching sites provide access to both Mosquito Lagoon and the Indian River Lagoon.

The seashore's headquarters is in Titusville at the intersection of Julia Street and U.S. 1, South (South Hopkins Street). The Park Information Center is in the North District at 7611 South Atlantic Avenue, New Smyrna Beach. At the Visitor Center, Headquarters, and the South

Biscayne National Park protects forested remnants of an ancient coral reef (opposite page).

CANAVERAL NATIONAL SEASHORE

44

442

Edgewater

A1A

1

95

Oak
Hill

Canaveral National
Seashore Visitor
Information Center

Apollo
Beach

Kennedy Parkway

A t l a n t i c   O c e a n

M o s q u i t o   L a g o o n

1

Klondike
Beach

46

Black Point Wildlife Drive
(One Way)

406

Playalinda
Beach

402

South
Lake

406

Merrit
Island
National
Wildlife
Refuge
Visitor Center

Titusville

50

I n d i a n
R i v e r

Kennedy
Space
Center

(Road closed to public)

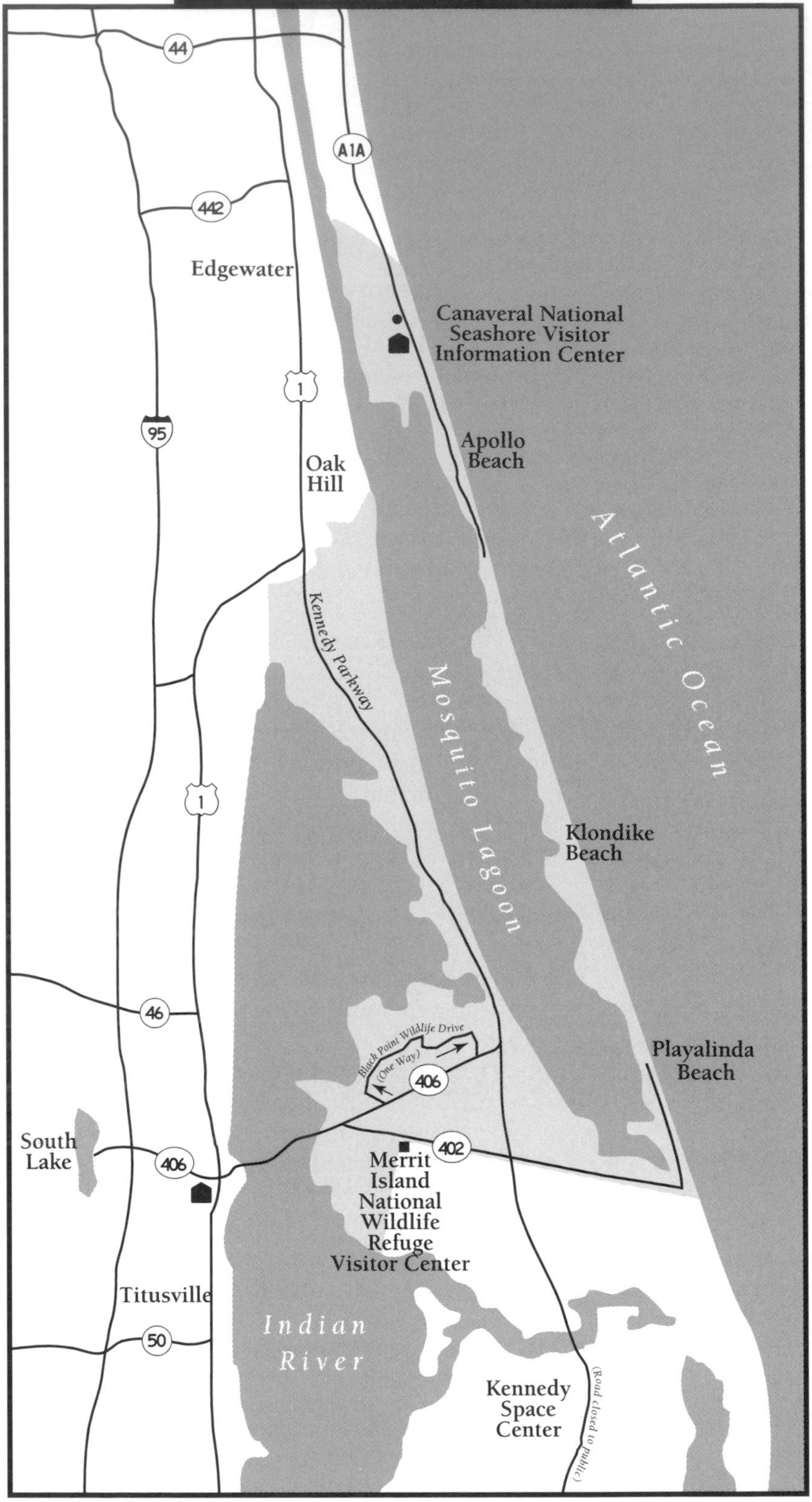

District Entrance Station visitors may obtain information on the area, including a map, a guide, and site bulletins about the wildlife, vegetation, seashells, and history of the area. Driving and hiking trails within the park provide a more intimate experience. In the North District of the park trails include Eldora, Eldora Hammock, Castle Windy, and Turtle Mound. Each trail is either historical in nature or features a look at the unique environment of a coastal barrier island habitat. Most walking trails are less than 1 mile in length. A self-guided canoe trail, 2½ miles in length, goes through Mosquito Lagoon and near backcountry campsites. The canoe trip takes about two or three hours and is especially pleasant during the fall, winter, and spring months. Visitors must provide their own canoe.

In the South District, near Titusville, the drive along the Entrance Road may be enhanced by stopping at each of the seven viewing areas, or vistas. Here visitors may observe wildlife in a coastal marsh habitat. Wildlife are not to be fed, and vehicles must be parked on paved areas. Each vista offers a different viewing experience. The South District is closed to the public three days prior to a shuttle launch. The district does not reopen until the day after a launch.

Merritt Island Wildlife Refuge also includes driving and walking trails. A visitor information center with displays and information is located off State Road 402.

ENTRANCE FEE: No charge. There is a daily user fee of $5.00 per vehicle or $1.00 per person. A backcountry camping permit is required. The cost for one to six people is $10 and $20 for more than six.

FACILITIES: The visitor center for the Seashore and the Wildlife Refuge and most parking areas have rest room facilities. Drinking water is at the visitor center only. No other drinking water is available throughout the park. Food and lodging can be found in Titusville and New Smyrna Beach.

CAMPING: Limited backcountry camping is permitted in specific beach campsites from November 1 to April 30, with access from Apollo Beach. Backcountry camping is available in Mosquito Lagoon throughout the year. A permit is required and must be obtained at the seashore's information center at Apollo Beach. A number of private campgrounds are nearby.

FISHING: The brackish water of Indian River and Mosquito Lagoon is ideal for mullet, red-fish, and trout. Freshwater impoundments in the interior of the island offer largemouth bass and bream. Surf fishing in the break zone yields bluefish, whiting, and pompano. A Florida fishing license is required for freshwater and saltwater fishing.

CASTILLO DE SAN MARCOS NATIONAL MONUMENT

1 South Castillo Drive
St. Augustine, FL 32084-3699
(904) 829–6506
casa@staug.com
www.nps.gov/casa

Castillo de San Marcos National Monument comprises twenty acres and was established in 1924 to preserve a unique relic of the Spanish presence in Florida and a specimen of military architecture and engineering developed during the Renaissance as a result of the invention of the cannon. The fort, built between 1672 and 1695 and modernized in the eighteenth century, replaced the last of

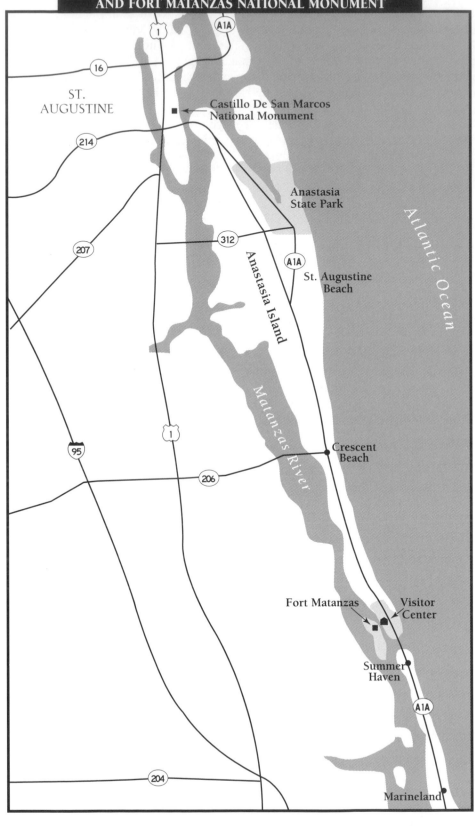

nine successive wooden forts, which, since 1565, affirmed the Spanish title to Florida and protected Spanish ships returning to Europe via the Gulf Stream. The monument is located in northeastern Florida, on the waterfront in downtown St. Augustine, adjacent to Highway A1A. (See also Fort Matanzas National Monument in this section.)

St. Augustine was settled by the Spanish in 1565. Rivalry between Spain and England resulted in attacks on St. Augustine by Sir Francis Drake in 1586 and Robert Searles (a.k.a. John Davis) in 1668. Following the latter attack, Queen Regent Marianna of Spain authorized the construction of the Castillo de San Marcos. Although the fort was never captured, it came under British rule when Spain ceded Florida to England in 1763. After being used as a British base of operations during the American Revolution, the fort reverted to Spain in 1784 before being ceded to the United States in 1821.

The fort is open daily from 8:45 A.M. to 5:15 P.M. (last admission is at 4:45 P.M.), except Christmas Day. A nominal fee is required for entrance. Talks by park rangers and living-history programs are offered periodically. After passing through the fort's entrance, begin your tour at the small museum on the left. A pleasant experience for visitors is just relaxing on one of the benches or on the large grass area surrounding the fort and watching pleasure boats sailing on the Intracoastal Waterway.

ENTRANCE FEE: $4.00 per person; visitors under sixteen (must be accompanied by an adult) are free; good for seven days.

FACILITIES: Rest rooms and water are available in the fort. In addition, souvenirs, books, and camera supplies are sold by a concessioner at a gift shop inside the fort. Food and lodging are within easy walking distance.

CAMPING: No camping is permitted within the monument grounds, and no overnight parking is allowed in the parking lot adjacent to the fort. Anastasia State Park provides campsites with tables, flush toilets, and showers a short distance south of town on A1A. A nice beach area is across the road from the state park.

FISHING: Fishing is permitted from the seawall; catches include a variety of saltwater fish. A Florida saltwater fishing license is required.

DE SOTO NATIONAL MEMORIAL

P.O. Box 15390
Bradenton, FL 34280-5390
(941) 792–0458
www.nps.gov/deso

De Soto National Memorial contains approximately twenty-five acres and was authorized in 1948 to commemorate the 1539 Florida landing of Spanish explorer Hernando De Soto. The memorial is located in west-central Florida, 5 miles west of Bradenton via Highway 64 (Manatee Avenue W.) at the north end of Seventy-fifth Street) on Tampa Bay.

In 1538 the De Soto expedition left the Spanish port of San Lucar in search of gold in the New World. After landing somewhere on the west coast of Florida, a group of more than 600 men started up the Florida peninsula on a four-year trip, which would take them through most of the southern states. In 1542 De Soto died, and the remaining members, tired of the search for gold, struck out for Mexico. Although no gold had been found and many viewed the expedition as a failure, the men learned much about the New World that was to prove useful to those who followed.

The visitor center contains exhibits and a two-minute film helps interpret the De Soto trip. From January to April park employees provide demonstrations and talks in a model encampment that represents the Indian village captured by De Soto for use as his first base camp. There is a ½-mile self-guided nature trail with signs describing the flora and fauna of the area. The park is open daily from 9:00 A.M. to 5:00 P.M.

ENTRANCE FEE: No charge.

FACILITIES: No food or lodging is available inside the park. Rest rooms and drinking water are at the visitor center.

CAMPING: No camping is permitted at the memorial. Myakka River State Park, southeast of Bradenton via U.S. 41 and Highway 72, offers campsites with tables, grills, drinking water, flush toilets, and showers. Private campgrounds are in Bradenton.

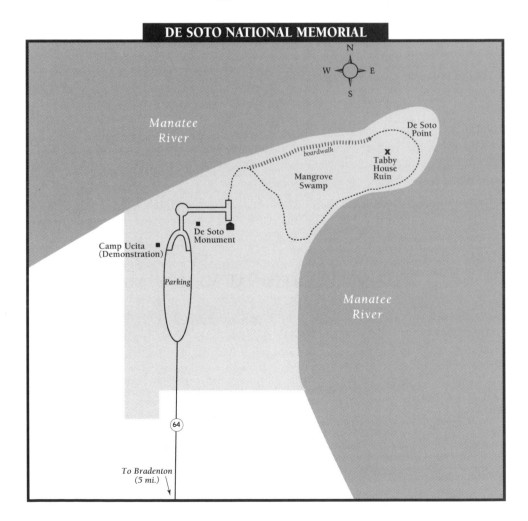

FISHING: A variety of saltwater fish may be caught in Tampa Bay from the shore or from boats. Possible catches include mackerel, cobia, snapper, grouper, sea bass, redfish, and speckled trout. A Florida fishing license is required. A copy of regulations may be picked up in the visitor center.

DRY TORTUGAS NATIONAL PARK

P.O. Box 6208
Key West, FL 33041
(305) 242–7700 (Everglades National Park)
www.nps.gov/drto

Dry Tortugas National Park contains 64,657 acres (fewer than forty acres of which are land). Initially a wildlife refuge, it was added to the National Park System in 1935 to preserve a nineteenth-century brick and masonry fort built to help control the Florida Straits and protect the Gulf Coast. The area was redesignated in 1992 as a national park to protect both the area's historical and natural features. The park is located 68 miles west of Key West in the Dry Tortugas and is accessible only by boat or seaplane, both of which are available in Key West. Private boats can obtain nautical charts at numerous locations in Key West.

Construction on the Dry Tortugas' Fort Jefferson commenced in 1846 as part of a United States program to build a chain of seacoast defenses from Maine to Louisiana. The fort's 45-foot-high and 8-foot-thick walls were designed to provide space for 420 guns around an area large enough to garrison 1,500 men. Although work continued for nearly thirty years, Fort Jefferson was never finished. During the Civil War, the structure was occupied by Federal forces and was used as a prison, but in 1874, a hurricane followed a second outbreak of yellow fever and resulted in its abandonment.

The Dry Tortugas (named for the abundant sea turtles and absence of fresh water) are in an ideal location for development of coral reefs. These reefs, in turn, support a wide variety of marine life, including multicolored sea fans, four species of sea turtles, and colorful fish. Sea birds such as magnificent frigate birds, masked boobies, and sooty and noddy terns nest in the Tortugas. Frequent droughts, storms, and a saline soil support a limited number of hardy land plants.

Fort Jefferson is open during daylight hours only. Contact the superintendent at Everglades National Park for a list of licensed operators providing transportation to the park. An orientation video program explaining the fort's significance is shown inside the visitor center. Tours of the fort are self-guided, although rangers are available to answer questions.

ENTRANCE FEE: No charge.

FACILITIES: A grass picnic area with grills and tables is available. Rest rooms are at the dock. No other facilities, including water, are provided.

CAMPING: Camping is permitted year-round in a designated area. No drinking water is available, and garbage must be carried away. Group camping requires a permit from the superintendent at Everglades National Park. Call (305) 242–7700 to obtain an application. Applications are processed by mail; allow thirty days.

FISHING: Waters within and surrounding the park contain good saltwater fishing for which a Florida saltwater fishing license is required. Fishing is permitted from the dock and shore between the north and south coaling docks. Fishing is prohibited within the moat and off of the moat wall. Fishing licenses must be obtained on the mainland.

EVERGLADES NATIONAL PARK

40001 State Road 9336
Homestead, FL 33034-6733
(305) 242–7700
ever_reception@nps.gov
www.nps.gov/ever

Everglades National Park comprises more than 1½ million acres and was established in 1947 to preserve a unique subtropical wilderness with extensive freshwater and saltwater areas, open prairies, and mangrove forests. The national park is located across the southern tip of Florida. Main access is 11 miles southwest of Homestead via State Highway 9336. Access on the west coast is off U.S. 41 at Everglades City. An additional entrance is charged at Shark Valley, also off U.S. 41, 30 miles west of Miami.

The Everglades is a fragile subtropical paradise containing a rich mixture of plants along a freshwater river that was historically 50 miles wide and from 6 inches to 2 feet deep. This river drops approximately 15 feet from its source at Lake Okeechobee to its terminus in Florida Bay at the southern tip of Florida. The park is a paradise for birdwatchers, who can view roseate spoonbills, flamingos, egrets, white herons, pelicans, cranes, hawks, and falcons. Birds are everywhere! The Everglades' most famous resident is the alligator, which is frequently seen resting beside canals and ponds. Some may seem fairly tame, but visitors should not stray too close. Walking trails and canoe trails are located throughout the park.

When entering from Homestead on the east, stop at the park's Ernest F. Coe visitor center, located just outside the entrance station. The visitor center contains exhibits, a bookstore, audiovisual presentations, and a schedule of interpretive activities throughout the park. Bathrooms and drinking water are available here. Smaller visitor centers are south of Everglades City (40 miles southeast of Naples), Shark Valley (25 miles west of the Florida Turnpike on U.S. 41), Royal Palm (a short distance inside the main entrance), and Flamingo.

From the main visitor center, a 38-mile paved road leads to Flamingo, the park's primary activity center on Florida Bay. The road passes several short hiking trails, some on elevated boardwalks, that provide visitors with intimate views of the park's land and wildlife. Included among the trails along the road to Flamingo are Anhinga Trail, which offers special exhibits and an excellent opportunity to view wildlife along a slow-moving, marshy, freshwater river; Gumbo Limbo Trail, which winds through a junglelike grove of tropical trees and small plants; Pineland Trail, which circles through pinelands on a bed of limestone; Pa-hay-okee Overlook Trail, which leads to an observation platform; Mahogany Hammock Trail, which enters a dark junglelike hardwood hammock; and West Lake Trail, which winds through mangrove trees along the edge of a large brackish lake. Eco Pond, 1 mile past the Flamingo Visitor Center, provides a good place to view alligators and wading birds.

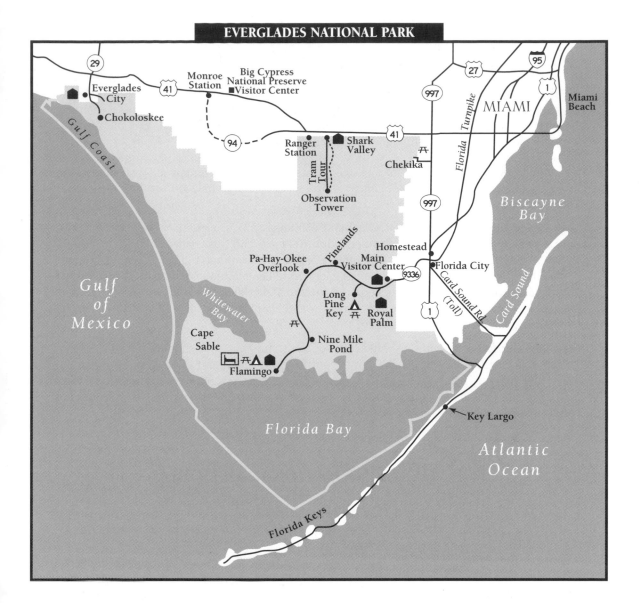

EVERGLADES NATIONAL PARK

Flamingo, at the south end of the park on Florida Bay, is the main activity center of Everglades National Park. Here you will find a small visitor center, restaurant, bar, motel, marina, gift shop, campground, and grocery. The restaurant is seasonal and is open December through March. Activities include fishing, boat tours and rentals, conducted walks (only in season, December through March), and self-guided walks. Flamingo and Long Pine Key near the entrance station are good places for bike riding. Swimming is discouraged.

On the park's north side, at Shark Valley, a wildlife-viewing tram (two hours; fee charged) travels through a sawgrass prairie into the Shark River slough. The tour includes a stop at a 65-foot tower. For reservations, call Shark Valley Tram Tours at (305) 221–8455. Bicycles can be rented if you prefer to ride the 14-mile paved loop trail. Narrated boat tours of the Ten Thousand Islands and coastal mangrove leave from Everglades City in the northwest corner of the park (800–445–7724 in Florida, 941–695–2591 outside the state).

ENTRANCE FEE: At main entrance outside of homestead, $10.00 per vehicle or $5.00 per person; good for seven days.

ENTRANCE FEE: At Shark Valley, $8.00 per vehicle or $4.00 per person.

FACILITIES: At Flamingo, the Flamingo Lodge, Marina and Outpost provides 120 motel-style rooms and twenty-four one-bedroom duplex housekeeping cottages, which include a complete kitchen. All rooms and cottages have air-conditioning. Rates are seasonal. For information, write Flamingo Lodge, #1 Flamingo Lodge Highway, Flamingo, FL 33034-6798, or call (800) 600–3813 or (941) 695–3101. Also in Flamingo are a marina, grocery store, gift shop, bar, restaurant, and gasoline (at the marina). Gifts, snacks, and canoe rentals are available on the lower level of the Gulf Coast visitor center. Some services are seasonal; contact the concessioner for availabilities.

CAMPING: Long Pine Key (107 spaces) and Flamingo (237 spaces, sixty walk-in tent sites, four group sites) offer tables, grills, water, a dump station, and flush toilets. Cold-water showers are at Flamingo. Mosquitoes can be quite a problem at Flamingo but are much less numerous at Long Pine Key. These campgrounds offer very different views of the park, so try both if you have the time. Forty-seven backcountry locations offer primitive sites for which use permits are required. Reservations for Long Pine Key and Flamingo are accepted for dates from late November to mid-April (800–365–2267).

FISHING: In bays and estuarine waters spotted sea trout, mangrove snapper, redfish, tarpon, snook, and bonefish can be caught. Largemouth bass, bluegill, and other species live in the freshwater streams, ponds, and pools. A Florida fishing license is required for both freshwater and saltwater fishing. Licenses are available at Flamingo Marina and in surrounding communities.

FORT CAROLINE NATIONAL MEMORIAL

12713 Fort Caroline Road
Jacksonville, FL 32225-1240
(904) 641–7155
www.nps.gov/foca

Fort Caroline National Memorial was authorized in 1950 to commemorate the historic French settlement of La Caroline. The park, which comprises 139 acres, is located in northeastern Florida within Jacksonville and can be reached via State Highway 10, Monument Road, and Fort Caroline Road.

In June 1564 an expedition of 300 French Huguenots anchored their three small ships in Florida's St. Johns River. Along the southern bank they established a colony named La Caroline in honor of King Charles IX of France. The colony included a triangular earth-and-wood fort. The intent was to establish a French presence in the New World and provide a Huguenot haven from the religious wars in France.

In September 1565 the Spanish established San Agustin (St. Augustine) during their effort to rid Florida of the French. In an attempt to strike first, the French set sail to attack, but caught by an untimely storm, they were shipwrecked. Taking advantage of the loosely guarded fort,

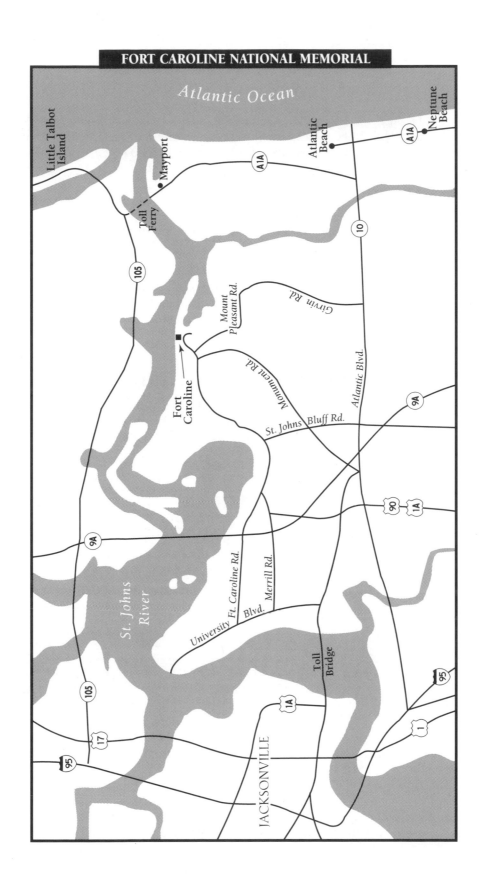

Atlantic Ocean

Little Talbot Island

Mayport

Toll Ferry

105

Mount Pleasant Rd.

Givin Rd.

Fort Caroline

Monument Rd.

St. Johns Bluff Rd.

Atlantic Blvd.

Atlantic Beach

Neptune Beach

A1A

A1A

10

9A

90

1A

9A

St. Johns River

University

Ft. Caroline Rd.

Blvd.

Merrill Rd.

Toll Bridge

105

17

95

1A

JACKSONVILLE

95

1

the Spanish attacked and claimed La Caroline for their own, renaming it San Mateo. The French massacre was avenged three years later by a force of Frenchmen and Timucuan Indians whose leader, once a Spanish galley slave, led a successful attack on San Mateo and burned it to the ground.

Although the site of the original fort has never been found, a near full-scale rendering of the structure has been built based on a sixteenth-century sketch by a French artist with the expedition. A visitor center/museum, open daily from 9:00 A.M. to 5:00 P.M., except Christmas Day, serves as the interpretive focus of the Timucuan Ecological and Historical Preserve, of which Fort Caroline is part.

ENTRANCE FEE: No charge.

FACILITIES: No food or lodging is available at the park, but drinking water and rest rooms are located in the visitor center.

CAMPING: No camping facilities are available at the memorial. Nearby camping at Little Talbot Island State Park provides forty sites with electricity, tables, flush toilets, and hot showers. This park is located northeast of Jacksonville on Highway A1A. Additional campgrounds are nearby.

FORT MATANZAS NATIONAL MONUMENT
c/o Castillo de San Marcos National Monument
1 South Castillo Drive
St. Augustine, FL 32084-3699
(904) 471–0116
www.nps.gov/foma

Fort Matanzas National Monument, comprising nearly 300 acres on Rattlesnake Island, was established in 1924 to preserve the most important auxiliary defense of St. Augustine and a specimen of military architecture and engineering originally developed during the Renaissance. The monument is located 14 miles south of St. Augustine via Highway A1A. (For an area map, see Castillo de San Marcos National Monument in this section.)

Matanzas (meaning "slaughters") Inlet received its name from the 1565 Spanish massacre of nearly 250 Frenchmen (see story of Fort Caroline National Memorial). The Spanish built a succession of wooden watchtowers there beginning in 1569 primarily to look out for enemy vessels approaching the inlet and St. Augustine. Following a British siege of St. Augustine in 1740, which included the blockade of Matanzas Inlet, Governor Manuel de Montiano decided to have a small stone fort built to guard the inlet. Fort Matanzas was completed in 1742. Twenty-one years later, in 1763 Spain ceded Frorida to the British in return for Havana, which the British had captured during the Seven Years War. In 1784 Spain recovered Florida and held the colony until it was ceded to the United States in 1821.

The park on Anastasia Island is open from 8:30 A.M. to 5:30 P.M. (except Christmas Day). The visitor center is open from 9:00 A.M. to 4:30 P.M. Here visitors will find a few exhibits explaining the history of the fort and can view an eight-minute-long video about the park. A free ferry running from 9:30 A.M. to 4:30 P.M. every hour on the half hour (weather permitting), carries passengers to the fort, where they can walk through the fort and learn of its history. A .6-mile nature trail that is handicapped accessible begins behind the rest room building. A public beach area is directly across Highway A1A. Parking for the fort is located at the visitor center. Parking for the beaches is across A1A from the entrance to the park.

ENTRANCE FEE: No charge.

FACILITIES: Rest rooms, drinking water, and a soft-drink machine are provided adjacent to the parking lot. Meals and lodging are nearby along Highway A1A.

CAMPING: No camping is permitted at the monument. Anastasia State Park, just south of St. Augustine, offers camping with tables, grills, water, flush toilets, and showers. A beautiful public beach is directly across the highway from the state park.

FISHING: The visitor center fronts the saltwater Matanzas River (a stretch of the intracoastal waterway) where fishing along the shoreline is permitted. Fishing for drum, whiting, and sheepshead is fair.

See map on page 24.

GULF ISLANDS NATIONAL SEASHORE

1801 Gulf Breeze Parkway
Gulf Breeze, FL 32561-5000
(850) 934–2600
guis_interpretation@nps.gov
www.nps.gov/guis

Gulf Islands National Seashore comprises nearly 96,000 mostly underwater acres in Florida and Mississippi and was authorized in 1971. The seashore has both mainland units and offshore islands and keys with white sand beaches and historic forts and ruins. The Florida section includes six units near Pensacola; the Mississippi section is discussed in the Mississippi chapter of this book.

Although the great glaciers of the ice ages did not cover this section of the country, some experts theorize the glaciers strongly influenced Florida's coastline. According to one theory, as large masses of ice went through phases of buildup and melting, they had the effect of raising and lowering the sea level, thus forming the barrier islands of this park.

The park's most developed area is around Fort Pickens. Tours of the early nineteenth-century fort are conducted daily at 2:00 P.M., and exhibits are available nearby at the park museum. Also in this section are nature trails, a supervised swimming beach (summer only), and fishing access. At Naval Live Oaks, visitors may walk through a heavily forested plantation of live oaks that was placed under protective management in 1828 to provide timbers used in building naval ships. The main visitor center for the national seashore in Florida is at Naval Live Oaks. On the mainland, on board the Pensacola Naval Air Station, a group of historic fortifications may be toured. A visitor contact station with exhibits, sales area, rest rooms, and a trail is located at Fort Barrancas on board NAS *Pensacola*.

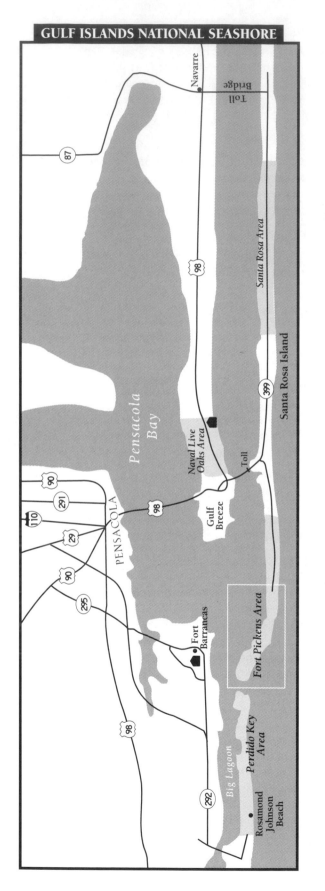

GULF ISLANDS NATIONAL SEASHORE

Navarre

Toll Bridge

87

98

Santa Rosa Area

399

Santa Rosa Island

Pensacola Bay

Naval Live Oaks Area

Toll

90

291

110

29

90

Pensacola

98

Gulf Breeze

295

Fort Barrancas

Fort Pickens Area

98

Perdido Key Area

Big Lagoon

292

Rosamond Johnson Beach

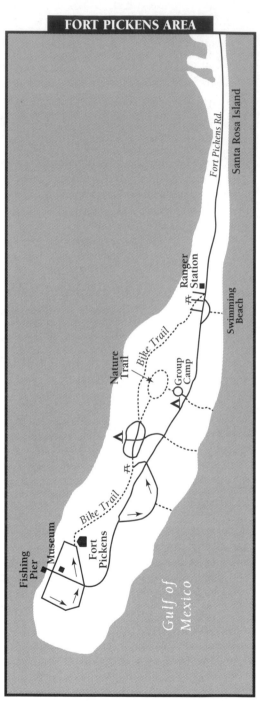

FORT PICKENS AREA

Fort Pickens Rd.

Santa Rosa Island

Ranger Station

Swimming Beach

Nature Trail

Bike Trail

Group Camp

Bike Trail

Fishing Pier

Museum

Fort Pickens

Gulf of Mexico

ENTRANCE FEE: $6.00 per vehicle or $3.00 per person; good for seven days.

FACILITIES: A store with grocery items is located in the Fort Pickens area. Rest rooms and drinking water are also available in this section. Picnic areas are at Naval Live Oaks, Fort Pickens, Santa Rosa, Okaloosa, Fort Barrancas, and Perdido Key. Snack bars are at Perdido Key and in the Fort Pickens area.

CAMPING: In the Fort Pickens area, a campground (200 sites, one group campsite) offers tables, grills, water, flush toilets, coin laundry, sanitary station, and some sites with electric hookups. Call (800) 365–CAMP to reserve a campsite.

FISHING: Surf fishing with possibilities for pompano, ling, mackerel, and sea trout is allowed along the beach where there are no swimmers. A saltwater fishing license is required in both Florida and Mississippi.

See the map on the previous page.

TIMUCUAN ECOLOGICAL AND HISTORIC PRESERVE

13165 Mount Pleasant Road
Jacksonville, FL 32225-1227
(904) 641–7155 (Fort Caroline National Memorial)
(904) 251–3537 (Kingsley Plantation)
www.nps.gov/timu

The Timucuan Ecological and Historic Preserve was established in 1988 to preserve certain wetlands and historic and prehistoric sites in the St. Johns River Valley, Florida. The park, which comprises about 46,000 acres of saltwater and freshwater wetlands and associated upland islands, is in Jacksonville, centered on the St. Johns and Nassau rivers and the Intracoastal Waterway.

One of the newest National Park Service areas in Florida, the Timucuan Preserve protects significant coastal wetlands and more than 400 years of history in northeast Florida. More than half of the preserve's acreage is wetlands. This sensitive ecological community provides a home and nursery for many varieties of fish and wildlife, stores water, helps control erosion, and serves as a natural filter for man-caused pollutants. The wetlands play host to several rare or endangered species, such as the West Indian manatee, colonial wood stork, peregrine falcon, bald eagle, and gopher tortoise.

The preserve contains significant historical sites representing important chapters in America's history. The sites include the archaeological remains of the first inhabitants of the preserve, the Timucuan Indians, for whom the preserve is named. Fort Caroline National Memorial (and main visitor center of the preserve), a separate National Park Service area within the boundaries of the preserve, commemorates early French and Spanish colonial settlement and struggles in the area.

Under continual development, the preserve also has operational areas at Kingsley Plantation, which is open daily and features a small visitor center and ranger-guided tours and programs. Kingsley is the oldest remaining plantation site in the state and includes remains of twenty-three of the original thirty-two slave quarters. The Theodore Roosevelt Area near Fort Caroline encompasses about 600 acres of Florida before development. Open daily, the area has hiking trails.

Much of the land within the boundaries of the preserve is privately owned, and federal development is limited. The management and success of this partnership park involves the assistance and cooperation of a variety of landowners. Visitors are reminded to respect private property owners' rights and to ask permission before visiting any land not designated as public.

ENTRANCE FEE: No charge.

FACILITIES: No food or lodging is available at the park. Drinking water and rest rooms are at Fort Caroline and Kingsley Plantation, and rest rooms are at the trailhead of the Theodore Roosevelt Area.

CAMPING: No camping facilities are available in the park. Nearby, Little Talbot Island State Park provides forty sites with electricity, tables, flush toilets, and hot showers. The park is located along the ocean on Highway A1A. Nearby Huguenot Memorial and Kathryn Abbey Hanna Parks, both administered by the city of Jacksonville, provide camping, swimming, picnicking, and fishing.

FISHING: Fishing is not permitted in the ponds at the Theodore Roosevelt Area but is allowed along Chicopit Bay and elsewhere in the preserve subject to state regulations.

Timucan Ecological and Historic Preserve, Kingsley Plantation, Planter's Residence

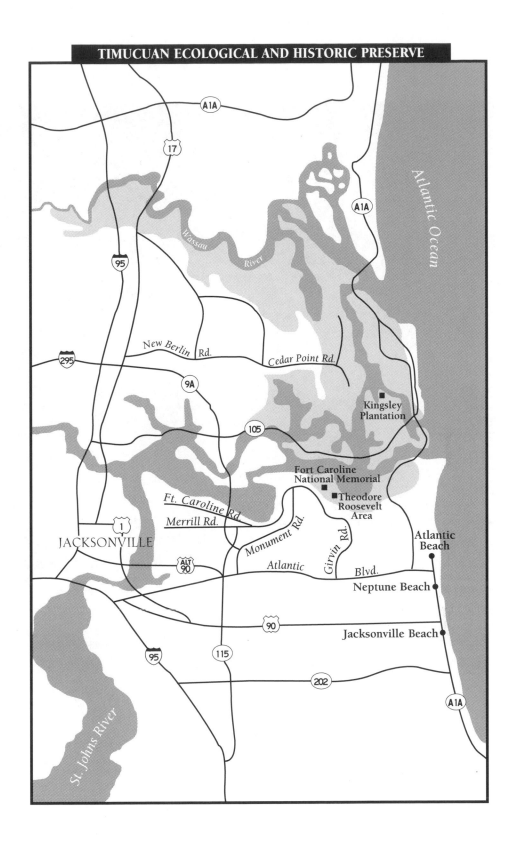

Battlefield at Chickamauga and Chattanooga National Military Park

GEORGIA

STATE TOURIST INFORMATION
(800) 847–4842
www.georgia.org

ANDERSONVILLE NATIONAL HISTORIC SITE

496 Cemetery Road
Andersonville, GA 31711-9707
(229) 924–0343
ANDE_Superintendent@nps.gov
www.nps.gov/ande

Andersonville National Historic Site comprises 495 acres and was authorized in 1970, incorporating both the national cemetery (still active) and the prison site as a unit of the National Park System. Andersonville today is a memorial to all Americans who have been prisoners of war. The site is located in southwestern Georgia, 9 miles northeast of Americus via State Highway 49. (The Jimmy Carter National Historic Site in Plains is just 21 miles southwest of Andersonville.)

Andersonville Prison (officially called Camp Sumter) was built in 1864 when Confederate leaders decided to move a large number of Federal prisoners from Richmond, Virginia, to an area of greater security and more abundant food. Although originally designed to hold 10,000 men, more than 32,000 prisoners were confined here in the summer of 1864. During fourteen months of existence, more than 12,000 men died here of disease, malnutrition, and exposure. A small structure (the "dead house") outside the prison was used to accumulate the bodies of prisoners that were to be carried by wagons to the cemetery for burial.

The park is open daily from 8:00 A.M. until 5:00 P.M. Only the grounds are open Thanksgiving, Christmas, and New Year's Days. The National Prisoner of War Museum houses exhibits and an audiovisual presentation that relates the American prisoner of war experience from the American Revolutionary War to the present. Included are databases containing the names of Andersonville prisoners and burials, as well as recent burials in Andersonville National Cemetery. Sections of the prison stockade have been reconstructed. Park interpreters are on duty to answer visitor questions. A park brochure and a cassette tape for touring by car are available at the museum.

ENTRANCE FEE: No charge.

FACILITIES: No food or lodging is at the historic site, but both are available in the vicinity. Rest rooms and drinking water are at the museum. A picnic area is available.

CAMPING: No camping is permitted at the site, but there are several local campgrounds available. Georgia Veterans Memorial State Park, between Americus and Cordele on U.S. 280, offers campsites with tables, grills, flush toilets, and showers.

CHATTAHOOCHEE RIVER NATIONAL RECREATION AREA

1978 Island Ford Parkway
Atlanta, GA 30350-3400
(770) 399–8070
www.nps.gov/chat

Chattahoochee River National Recreation Area was authorized by Congress in 1978 to preserve a series of land units along 48 miles of the Chattahoochee River for natural, scenic, recreational, and historical values. Presently, 4,243 acres are under management of the National Park Service; the proposed total acreage is 6,800. The Chattahoochee River National Recreation Area is in northern Georgia, beginning directly below Buford Dam and terminating 10 miles north of Atlanta.

The Chattahoochee River is generally cold, clear, and slow-moving as it flows 436 miles from the mountains of northern Georgia to the Gulf of Mexico. Surrounded by colorful plants and trees, the river corridor provides opportunities for fishing, hiking, floating, picnicking, and just relaxing. The banks and meadows surrounding the river support typical wildlife found in this region such as beaver, chipmunk, fox, raccoon, and squirrel.

The Chattahoochee River in the National Recreation Area is rated Class I and/or II in river difficulty. This section of the Chattahoochee has a few riffles, small waves, and rapids, with some obstructions (rocks and downed trees) that require minimum scouting and some maneuvering ability. Rafts and canoes can be rented from the park concessioner (Chattahoochee Outdoor Center at Johnson Ferry and Powers Island units) or from commercial entrepreneurs outside the park. A shuttle service for floaters is available through the park concessioner for Johnson Ferry, Powers Island, and Paces Mill units (770–395–6851).

There are a number of trails in the various units of the recreation area. In the Cochran Shoals Unit, a fitness trail has exercise stations and is a popular jogging path. In the Vickery Creek Unit, trails lead to a gorge with ruins of pre–Civil War textile mills and a dam. On the west side of the Sope Creek Unit, a loop trail leads to old homesites, a large fishing pond, and ruins of a paper mill. The park headquarters at Island Ford, exit 6 (Northridge) off GA 400 North, has trail maps. The recreation area is a daytime facility only.

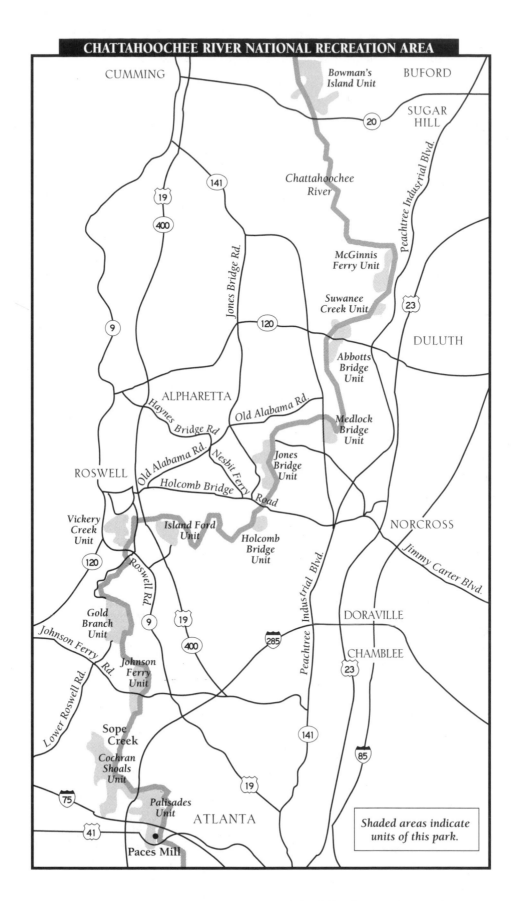

CHATTAHOOCHEE RIVER NATIONAL RECREATION AREA

CUMMING

BUFORD

Bowman's Island Unit

SUGAR HILL

20

Chattahoochee River

141

19

400

Jones Bridge Rd.

9

120

McGinnis Ferry Unit

Suwanee Creek Unit

Peachtree Indusrial Blvd.

23

DULUTH

Abbotts Bridge Unit

ALPHARETTA

Old Alabama Rd.

Medlock Bridge Unit

Haynes Bridge Rd

Old Alabama Rd.

Nesbit Ferry

Jones Bridge Unit

ROSWELL

Holcomb Bridge

Road

NORCROSS

Vickery Creek Unit

Island Ford Unit

Holcomb Bridge Unit

Jimmy Carter Blvd.

120

Roswell Rd.

Gold Branch Unit

9

19

Peachtree Industrial Blvd.

DORAVILLE

Johnson Ferry Rd.

400

285

CHAMBLEE

23

Johnson Ferry Unit

Lower Roswell Rd.

Sope Creek

141

Cochran Shoals Unit

85

75

Palisades Unit

19

ATLANTA

41

●

Paces Mill

Shaded areas indicate units of this park.

ENTRANCE FEE: No charge. There is a parking fee of $2.00 per day.

FACILITIES: Food and lodging are available in the metropolitan areas surrounding the park.

CAMPING: Overnight camping in the recreation area is not permitted. U.S. Corps of Engineers campgrounds are located around Lake Sidney Lanier. Other nearby campgrounds are located at Stone Mountain Park and Georgia state parks.

FISHING: The Chattahoochee River provides catches of bream, bass, catfish, and trout. A current Georgia fishing license with trout stamp is required.

CHICKAMAUGA AND CHATTANOOGA NATIONAL MILITARY PARK

P.O. Box 2128
Fort Oglethorpe, GA 30742-0128
(706) 866–9241
CHCH_Superintendent@nps.gov
www.nps.gov/chch

Chickamauga and Chattanooga National Military Park comprises 8,100 acres and was established in 1890 to preserve two Civil War battlefields on which Confederate troops tried to stop the Union advance toward Atlanta. The park's various separate units are located in northwestern Georgia and southern Tennessee, in and around the city of Chattanooga.

Following the battle of Stones River in January 1863, Federal forces began preparations for an attack on the Confederate rail center at Chattanooga. To avoid the entrenched Confederate army, the Union general flanked the city and forced the withdrawal of Southern troops. Upon receiving reinforcements, however, 66,000 Confederates met and defeated the Federals at Chickamauga. Two months later, with 36,000 additional men, Union troops under the command of Ulysses Grant were able to drive Confederate forces off Lookout Mountain and Missionary Ridge and take control of Chattanooga. Chattanooga then became Sherman's base for his march to Atlanta.

At Chickamauga Battlefield, a visitor center on U.S. 27 contains exhibits, a gun museum, a twenty-six-minute multimedia program (fee charged), and leaflets for a 7-mile self-guided auto tour. Tour-stop markers, monuments, and plaques are located along the road. A walking tour on Lookout Mountain will direct visitors to the most important points in this section of the park. Near Point Park (fee charged), the Ochs Museum and Overlook provides exhibits and pictures of the battle. A visitor center in this section of the park has a seven-minute audio presentation on James Walker's painting *The Battle of Lookout Mountain* and an assortment of publications. Park rangers give guided walks, historical talks, and demonstrations during summer months.

ENTRANCE FEE: No charge. There is a fee to tour Craven's House; $2.00 for adults, visitors seventeen and under are free; Point Park has a user fee of $2.00 for adults; $1.00 for seniors; visitors seventeen and under are free. There is a twenty-six-minute multimedia program at Chickamauga Battlefield that costs $3.00 for adults, $1.50 for seniors and visitors sixteen and under.

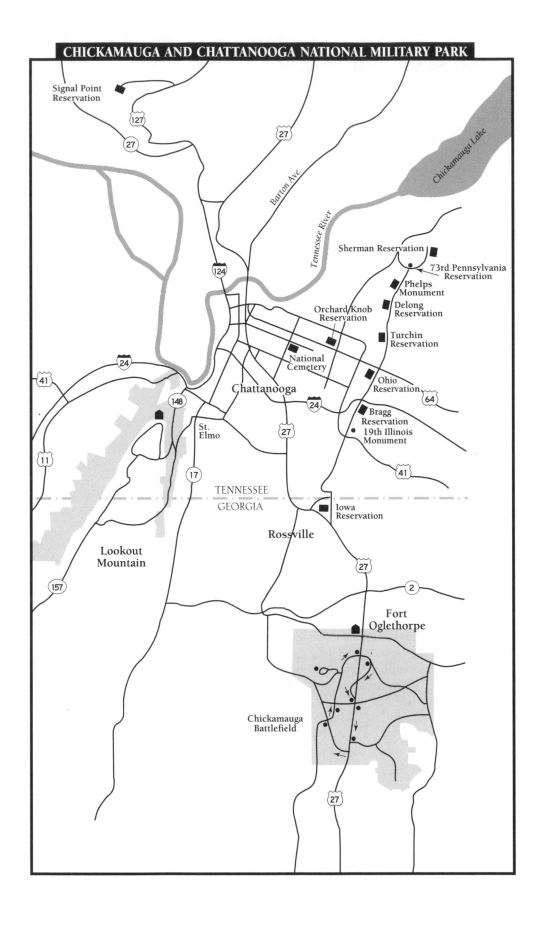

CHICKAMAUGA AND CHATTANOOGA NATIONAL MILITARY PARK

Signal Point
Reservation

127

27

27

Barton Ave.

Chickamauga Lake

Tennessee River

Sherman Reservation

73rd Pennsylvania
Reservation

124

Phelps
Monument

Orchard Knob
Reservation

Delong
Reservation

Turchin
Reservation

24

National
Cemetery

Chattanooga

Ohio
Reservation

64

41

148

24

St.
Elmo

27

Bragg
Reservation

19th Illinois
Monument

11

41

17

TENNESSEE
GEORGIA

Iowa
Reservation

Lookout
Mountain

Rossville

27

2

157

Fort
Oglethorpe

Chickamauga
Battlefield

27

FACILITIES: Food and lodging are available in Chattanooga. Rest rooms and water are in the visitor centers.

CAMPING: No camping is permitted in the park. Georgia's Cloudland Canyon State Park, approximately 20 miles southwest of Chattanooga via Interstate 59 and State Highway 136, offers camping facilities.

CUMBERLAND ISLAND NATIONAL SEASHORE

P.O. Box 806
St. Marys, GA 31558-0806
(912) 882–4335
www.nps.gov/cuis

Cumberland Island National Seashore was established in 1972 to preserve 36,545 acres of freshwater lakes, magnificent beaches and dunes, and saltwater marshes of Georgia's largest coastal island. The park is located in southeastern Georgia, approximately 30 miles north of Jacksonville, Florida, via Interstate 95 and Georgia Highway 40. Access is only by ferry from the town of St. Marys, Georgia.

Cumberland Island (named after an English duke) is a sandy island measuring 18 miles long by 3 miles wide at its widest point. The island is separated from the Georgia mainland by a mile or more of salt marsh and river. The maritime forest in the central part of the island contrasts with the white sand beaches on its eastern perimeter. The seashore contains an outstanding selection of wildlife, including deer, pelicans, and loggerhead turtles.

Headquarters for the national seashore is on the mainland in the town of St. Marys. A museum on Osborne Street houses a collection of artifacts from Cumberland Island and includes an exhibit area that is open without charge to the public. Displays depict the lives of African-Americans, the Carnegie family, and others who lived on the island. Small visitor centers are at Sea Camp Dock and Dungeness Dock on the island. Limited displays are at the Ice House Museum near Dungeness Dock. The ferry departs St. Marys at 9:00 A.M. and 11:45 A.M. daily except Tuesday and Wednesday (every day during peak season). No cars, bicycles, or pets are permitted. The ferry stops on the island at both Sea Camp and Dungeness. Return trips for the forty-five-minute ride are at 10:15 A.M. and 4:45 P.M. Reservations are strongly recommended, because the first departing and last returning runs are generally fully booked. Visitors willing to take their chances may arrive early and sign up on a standby list. For reservations call (912) 882–4335 or 1–888–817–3421. If you take the 9:00 A.M. boat, you will have about seven hours on the island. The 11:45 A.M. boat will give you about four hours on the island.

A typical trip to the island includes a short walk to the ruins of the Dungeness Mansion (built by Thomas Carnegie in the late nineteenth century), a hike along the beach (swimming allowed but no lifeguards), and a walk back to the dock. It is best to take the early boat over to the island and the late boat back to the mainland if you wish to do anything other than breeze through sights on the south end of the island.

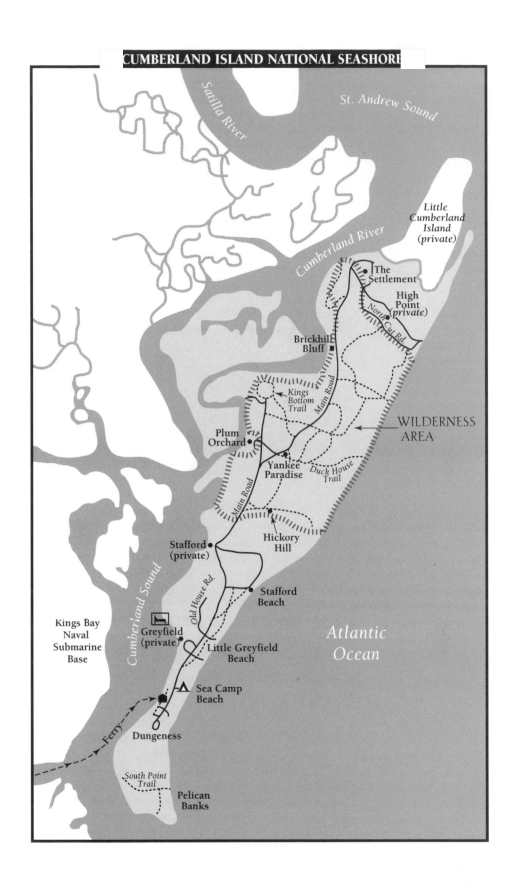

Satilla River

St. Andrew Sound

Little
Cumberland
Island
(private)

Cumberland River

The
Settlement

High
Point
(private)

North Cut Rd.

Brickhill
Bluff

Kings
Bottom
Trail

Main Road

WILDERNESS
AREA

Plum
Orchard

Yankee
Paradise

Duck House
Trail

Main Road

Hickory
Hill

Stafford
(private)

Old House Rd.

Stafford
Beach

Kings Bay
Naval
Submarine
Base

Greyfield
(private)

Little Greyfield
Beach

Atlantic
Ocean

Cumberland Sound

Sea Camp
Beach

Ferry

Dungeness

South Point
Trail

Pelican
Banks

ENTRANCE FEE: Although an entrance fee is not charged, individuals are required to pay a $4.00 per person day-use fee. Adults are charged $12 for a round trip on the concessionaire-operated ferry from St. Marys. Children and seniors pay a reduced rate for the ferry.

FACILITIES: Other than rest rooms and drinking water, there are no public facilities on the island. Privately owned Greyfield Inn offers overnight accommodations with meals included on the island. For additional information call (800) 717–0821 or (904) 261–6408 or check their Web site at www.greyfieldinn.com. Motels and restaurants are available near St. Marys. If you plan to spend the day on Cumberland Island, you should take your own lunch.

CAMPING: Sea Camp Beach (sixteen sites, two group camps) has rest rooms, showers, and drinking water. Reservations are necessary. Four primitive backcountry campgrounds require a permit. All have well water that should be boiled prior to drinking.

FISHING: Surf fishing yields red bass, spotted trout, and bluefish. Cumberland Sound offers croaker, drum, trout, and red bass. A Georgia fishing license is required.

FORT FREDERICA NATIONAL MONUMENT
Route 9, Box 286-C
St. Simons Island, GA 31522
(912) 638–3639
fofr_superintendent@nps.gov
www.nps.gov/fofr

Fort Frederica National Monument was authorized in 1936 to preserve the remains of an eighteenth-century British fort and town built during the Anglo-Spanish struggle for control of what is now the southeastern United States. The park is located in southeastern Georgia, 12 miles northeast of Brunswick on St. Simons Island via the Brunswick–St. Simons toll causeway.

The settlement of Frederica was established in 1736 as an English answer to Spanish operations in the New World. In addition to building a fort overlooking the inland waterway, Frederica's citizens also laid out a town that soon included permanent homes and shops. A regiment of 650 British soldiers, sent to protect the town, was able to turn back a Spanish invasion force in 1742. The disbanding of the regiment in 1749, combined with a major fire in 1758, spelled the end for Frederica.

The park is open daily from 8:00 A.M. to 5:00 P.M., and a visitor center is open daily from 9:00 A.M. to 5:00 P.M., containing museum exhibits and a twenty-five-minute film on the settlement. The remains of the town and fort are visible, and exhibits and audio messages are located throughout the site. During summer months, park rangers offer conducted tours, talks, and demonstrations. The grounds have many live oak trees covered with Spanish moss, making a leisurely walk through the town site a pleasant experience.

A detached unit of the park, the Bloody Marsh Battle Site (open daily from 9:00 A.M. to 4:00 P.M.) marks the general area where outnumbered British troops ambushed and defeated a Spanish column in 1742. This battle halted an attempt to attack Frederica and proved to be a turning point in the Spanish invasion of Georgia. The site is 6 miles south of Frederica and is open daily.

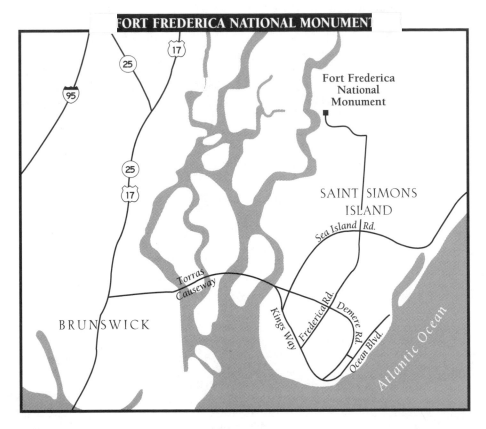

ENTRANCE FEE: $5.00 per vehicle or $3.00 per person; good for seven days.

FACILITIES: Food and lodging are available on St. Simons and in Brunswick and Jekyll. Modern rest rooms, water, and a soft-drink machine are in the park's visitor center.

CAMPING: No camping is permitted within the monument grounds. Jekyll Island State Park offers camping facilities 13 miles southeast of Brunswick via State Highway 50.

FISHING: Fishing is permitted within the monument grounds. Inquire at the visitor center for local regulations.

FORT PULASKI NATIONAL MONUMENT

Box 30757
Savannah, GA 31410-0757
(912) 786–5787
www.nps.gov/fopu

Fort Pulaski was proclaimed a national monument in 1924 to preserve a nineteenth-century fort that first demonstrated the ineffectiveness of old-style masonry fortifications when faced with rifled cannon. The 5,615-acre monument is located in southeastern Georgia, 17 miles east of Savannah via U.S. 80.

Construction on Fort Pulaski (named after Polish Count Casimir Pulaski, who was mortally wounded in Savannah during the American Revolution) began in 1829 as part of a coastal fortification system adopted after the War of 1812. On the eve of the Civil War, it was seized by several detachments of Georgia troops. Federal troops from Hilton Head Island were sent by ship to nearby Tybee Island, where they established artillery emplacements 2½ miles from Pulaski. Bullet-shaped shells fired by the experimental rifled cannon were able to penetrate Fort Pulaski's walls, thus forcing the garrison to surrender in April of 1862, after a thirty-hour bombardment.

The monument is open daily (except Christmas Day) from 8:30 A.M. to 5:30 P.M., with extended hours in the summer. A visitor center with exhibits and tour information is near the fort entrance. The fort contains various exhibits on soldier life and artillery in the Civil War. Nature trails are available for hiking, and a memorial to John Wesley, who landed on this island in 1736, is located just north of the fort.

ENTRANCE FEE: $2.00 per person.

FACILITIES: No food or lodging is available at the monument. Rest rooms and water are inside the fort and visitor center. A picnic area with tables, grills, rest rooms, and water is available on a first-come basis.

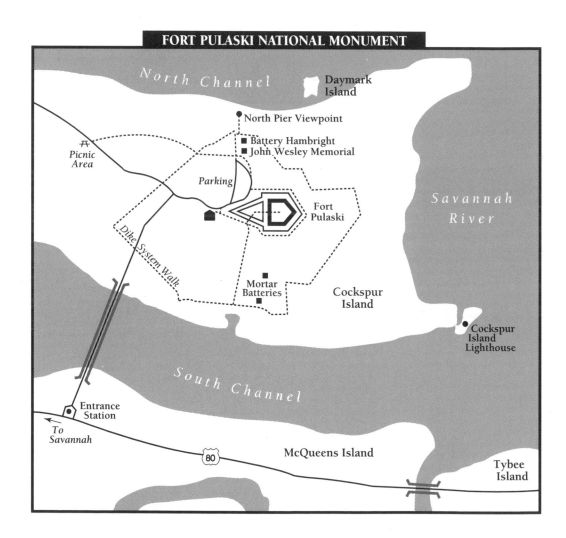

FORT PULASKI NATIONAL MONUMENT

North Channel

Daymark Island

North Pier Viewpoint

Battery Hambright
John Wesley Memorial

Picnic Area

Parking

Fort Pulaski

Savannah River

Dike System Walk

Mortar Batteries

Cockspur Island

Cockspur Island Lighthouse

South Channel

Entrance Station

To Savannah

80

McQueens Island

Tybee Island

CAMPING: No camping is permitted at the monument. Skidway Island State Park provides camping facilities a short distance southeast of Savannah.

FISHING: There is saltwater fishing from the shore of the island and a nearby pier. Boat ramp facilities are also available.

JIMMY CARTER NATIONAL HISTORIC SITE

300 North Bond Street
Plains, GA 31780-0392
(229) 824–4104
JICA_SITE_Supervisor@NPS.GOV
www.nps.gov/jica

Jimmy Carter National Historic Site was authorized in 1987 to preserve the sites and structures associated with the life and presidency of Jimmy Carter and to interpret the history and culture of the small rural town that gave the nation the thirty-ninth president of the United States. The historic site is located in southwest Georgia, 10 miles west of Americus on U.S. 280. Visitors interested in Civil War history should make a point to visit nearby Andersonville National Historic Site, 21 miles northeast of Plains.

More than any president in recent years, James Earl Carter, Jr., is closely identified with his hometown. Jimmy Carter was born in Plains, Georgia, on October 1, 1924. The eldest of four children, he grew up on a farm a short distance outside town. He graduated from Plains High School (closed in 1979) and attended Georgia Southwestern College (Americus, Georgia) and Georgia Institute of Technology before graduating from the U.S. Naval Academy in 1946. After his father's death, Carter resigned from the Navy and returned home to help run the family farm and the family seed and farm-supply store. He entered politics in 1963 as a state senator and was later elected governor of Georgia before being elected president of the United States in 1976. Carter was defeated in his 1980 presidential reelection bid by Ronald Reagan. The ex-president remains involved with the Carter Presidential Center in Atlanta and with several charitable organizations, including Habitat for Humanity, and he continues to spend a portion of his time in Plains. President Carter teaches Sunday School at Maranatha Baptist Church when he is in town. The public is welcome. The monthly schedule for this popular event can be obtained by calling the Jimmy Carter National Historic Site or the Maranatha Baptist Church (229–824–7896) or by checking their Web site at www.sowega/~alcrump/maranatha.

The park is open daily from 9:00 A.M. to 5:00 P.M. except for Thanksgiving, Christmas Day, and New Year's Day. The Plains High School, near the downtown area, serves as the historic site's visitor center and contains a museum, audiovisual presentations, and a book sales outlet. There are three ways to tour the park: park brochure contains a map and descriptions of the Carter sites; a driving tour booklet may be purchased that covers twenty-seven sites in and around Plains; and a self-driving audiotape tour may be rented or purchased—on the tape President and Mrs. Carter comment on their years growing up in Plains. The historic site consists of the railroad depot, Carter's 1976 campaign headquarters, Plains High School Visitor Center/Museum, Carter's boyhood farm, and the present Carter residence. Plains High School Visitor

Center/Museum, Carter's boyhood farm, and the railroad depot are currently open to the public. Check at the visitor center for the hours of operation for the depot and the farm.

ENTRANCE FEE: No charge.

FACILITIES: Limited food, lodging, and other public facilities are available in Plains. Full facilities are available in nearby Americus. Rest rooms and drinking water are in the visitor center, and there is a small picnic area on the grounds.

CAMPING: A small campground in the town offers RV spaces with full hookups. A private campground with hookups is a short distance east of town on U.S. 280. Also see the camping section under Andersonville National Historic Site (Georgia).

KENNESAW MOUNTAIN NATIONAL BATTLEFIELD PARK

905 Kennesaw Mountain Drive
Kennesaw, GA 30152
(770) 427–4686
www.nps.gov/kemo

Kennesaw Mountain Battlefield Park comprises 2,884 acres and was authorized in 1917 to commemorate the site of two major Civil War engagements in 1864 during Sherman's march toward Atlanta. The battlefield is located in northwestern Georgia, 3 miles north of Marietta, a short distance off U.S. 41 and Interstate 75 at exit 269.

In May of 1864, General William Sherman launched an army of nearly 100,000 soldiers toward the Confederate rail and manufacturing center of Atlanta. In his way were 70,000 Southern troops in the vicinity of Kennesaw Mountain. After an initial battle at Kolb's Farm, two unsuccessful Union attacks on June 27 resulted in an extremely heavy casualty toll. Sherman then decided to flank the Confederate position, which made the Southerners abandon Kennesaw Mountain to protect their supply line to Atlanta.

The visitor center contains exhibits and an eighteen-minute film. Additional wayside exhibits are located on the summit of Big Kennesaw Mountain, at Cheatham Hill, and at Kolb's Farm. At Kolb's Farm, the log house has been restored to its appearance during the Civil War but is not open to the public. A drive to the top of the mountain provides a panoramic view of the area. Hiking trails of 2, 5, 10, and 16 miles begin near the visitor center. The short trail is a self-guided history-and-nature trail.

ENTRANCE FEE: No charge.

FACILITIES: No lodging or food service is available in the park. Rest rooms and drinking water are in the visitor center. Restaurants, motels, and a grocery store are a few miles outside the park entrance.

CAMPING: No camping is permitted in the park. A private campground is a few miles outside the park entrance, and a number of U.S. Army Corps of Engineers campgrounds are nearby on Lake Allatoona. One especially nice unit is Clark Creek South (tables, grills, hot showers, fishing, no hookups) about 15 miles north on Interstate 75.

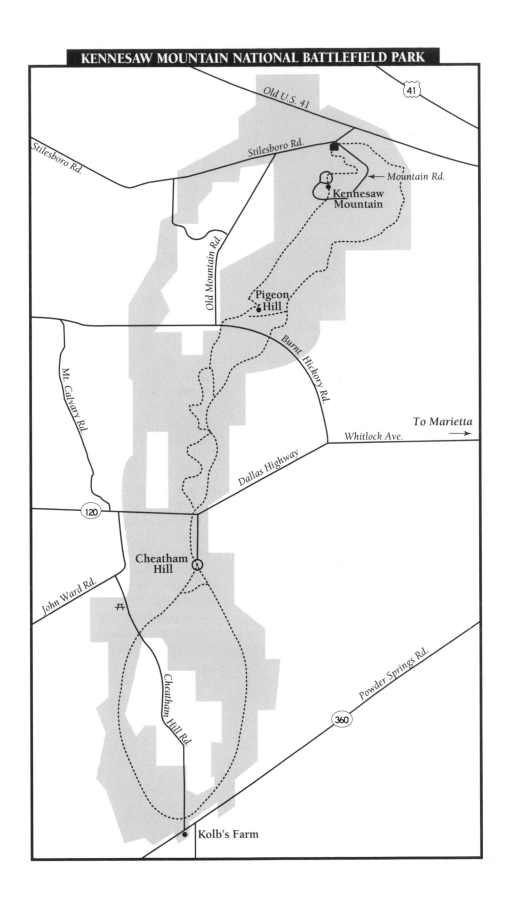

KENNESAW MOUNTAIN NATIONAL BATTLEFIELD PARK

41

Old U.S. 41

Stilesboro Rd.

Stilesboro Rd.

← Mountain Rd.

Kennesaw
Mountain

Old Mountain Rd.

Pigeon
Hill

Burnt Hickory Rd.

To Marietta →

Whitlock Ave.

Mt. Calvary Rd.

Dallas Highway

120

Cheatham
Hill

John Ward Rd.

Powder Springs Rd.

Cheatham Hill Rd.

360

Kolb's Farm

MARTIN LUTHER KING, JR., NATIONAL HISTORIC SITE

National Park Service
450 Auburn Avenue, N.E.
Atlanta, GA 30312-0526
(404) 331–3920
(404) 331–5190
www.nps.gov/malu

Martin Luther King, Jr., National Historic Site comprises thirty-nine acres and was established in 1980 to preserve a 2-block neighborhood containing the birthplace, church, and grave of famous civil rights activist Dr. Martin Luther King, Jr. The site and preservation district contain a total of ninety-two acres. The park is in downtown Atlanta, along Auburn Avenue just off Interstate 75/85.

Martin Luther King, Jr., was born on January 15, 1929, in Atlanta, Georgia. His father, Martin Luther King, Sr., was pastor of nearby Ebenezer Baptist Church. Martin entered Atlanta's Morehouse College at age fifteen and became an ordained Baptist minister in 1947, when he was only seventeen years old. After moving to Montgomery, Alabama, as pastor to a Baptist church, King began leading the local black community in the nonviolent struggle for civil rights. This leadership was to continue throughout the South and resulted in passage of the Civil Rights Act of 1964 and the Voting Rights Act of 1965. Dr. King was awarded the Nobel Peace Prize in 1964. In 1968, at age thirty-nine, Martin Luther King, Jr., was shot and killed in Memphis, Tennessee.

The historic site encompasses a 2-block area that includes Dr. King's home, church, and memorial grave site. The grave site is on property adjacent to Ebenezer Baptist Church, where Freedom Hall houses the Martin Luther King, Jr., Center for Non-Violent Social Change. Around the historic site, a preservation district includes residential and commercial sections of Sweet Auburn, the black community into which Dr. King was born and that had a significant impact on his life and on his struggle for civil rights. The visitor center at 450 Auburn Avenue is open from 9:00 A.M. to 5:00 P.M. daily (until 6:00 P.M. from Labor Day to Memorial Day) and has exhibits and a video presentation.

ENTRANCE FEE: No charge.

FACILITIES: Food and lodging are available nearby in downtown Atlanta.

MARTIN LUTHER KING, JR., NATIONAL HISTORIC SITE

Cornelia Street

Randolph Street

Auburn Ave.

Edgewood Ave.

Irwin Street

Charles L. Harper Home

Howell Street

Alexander Hamilton, Jr. Home

Bryant-Graves House

Martin Luther King, Jr. Birth Home

Double "Shogun" Row Houses

Fire Station No. 6

Our Lady of Lourdes Catholic Church and School

Boulevard

National Historic Site

Preservation District

The King Center

Watkins-Anderson Building

Fitzgerald St.

Parking

Grave Site

Ebenezer Baptist Church

Parking

Chamberlain Street

Jackson St.

John Wesley Dobbs Avenue

Visitor Center

Old Wheat Street

Auburn Ave.

Wheat Street Baptist Church

William Holmes Borders, Sr., Dr.

Hilliard Street

Prince Hall Masonic Building

Fort Street

75 85

Odd Fellows Building & Auditorium

Sweet Auburn Curb Market

Butler Street

Big Bethel African Methodist Episcopal Church

Herndon Building

Boaz St.

Pratt St.

Place

Royal Peacock Club

Butler Street YMCA

Coca-Cola Place

Butler St.

Ellis Street

John Wesley Dobbs Avenue

Atlanta Life Insurance Co. Building

Rucker Building

Atlanta Daily World Building

Piedmont Ave.

Auburn Ave.

APEX Museum

Edgewood Ave.

Auburn Avenue Research Library

Original Coca-Cola Bottling Building

Glimer St.

OCMULGEE NATIONAL MONUMENT

1207 Emery Highway
Macon, GA 31201-4399
(912) 752–8257
ocmu_interpretation@nps.gov
www.nps.gov/ocmu

Ocmulgee National Monument comprises 702 acres and was authorized in 1934 to preserve the remains of mounds and settlements that exhibit the evolution of Indian culture in the southern United States. The monument is located in central Georgia, on the eastern edge of the city of Macon. Exit Interstate 75 at Interstate 16 and take U.S. 80 east. A small detached area of the park located south of Macon is currently open to the public by permit only.

Ocmulgee National Monument has a rich history of Indian culture. Nomadic ice-age hunters camped on the site more than 12,000 years ago. From the hunters and gatherers who lived here for thousands of years, a transition to gardening and then farming began between 1000 and 500 B.C. In A.D. 900, a large town with an economy based on corn agriculture was constructed within the present boundaries of the park. These people built large temple mounds and earth lodges. After 200 years, the village declined. Around A.D. 1350, a palisaded village with two mounds was built in the nearby Ocmulgee River swamps. It continued to exist until after the Spaniard Hernando De Soto's expedition entered the middle-Georgia area in A.D. 1540. The Mound Builders' culture was altered forever by the coming of European colonists. The Mound Builders' descendants, the Muskogee (Creek) Indians, were removed to Oklahoma during the Trail of Tears period.

The monument is open daily (except Christmas Day and New Year's Day) from 9:00 A.M. to 5:00 P.M. The visitor center contains an archaeological museum, and park personnel are on duty to answer questions. A short movie, "Mysteries of the Mounds," is shown periodically each day. A ceremonial earthlodge, reconstructed on an original 1,000-year-old floor, is open on a self-guided basis. Ranger-programs are available by reservation. Mounds may be reached via a ½-mile-long paved road or walking trails. Opelofa Nature Trail winds along Walnut Creek, where swamp and forest ecology may be observed. The monument has more than 5 miles of walking trails.

ENTRANCE FEE: No charge.

FACILITIES: No food or lodging is available within the monument grounds. Most services can be found a short distance outside the entrance. Drinking water and modern rest rooms are located at the visitor center, and a picnic area with tables and shade is by the main parking area.

CAMPING: No camping is permitted in the park. Indian Springs State Park (via U.S. 23) and High Falls State Park (via Interstate 75) are each approximately 35 miles northwest of Macon and offer camping, fishing, and swimming. Another campground is at Tobesofkee Lake, about 18 miles from the monument.

FISHING: A small pond near the Opelofa Nature Trail contains bluegill and crappie; bass and bluegill may be found in Walnut Creek. A Georgia fishing license is required.

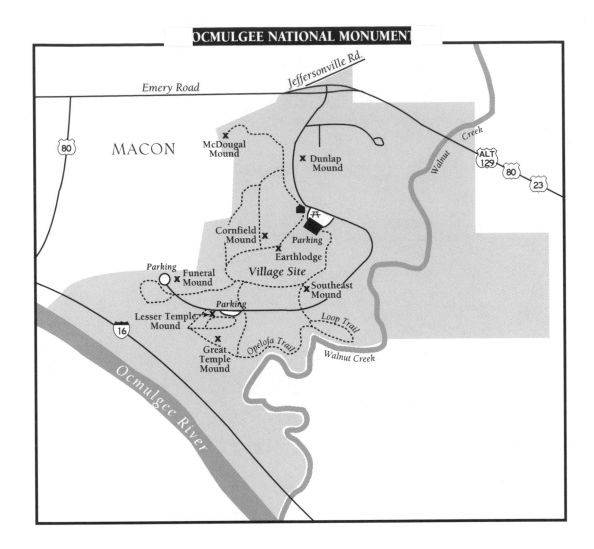

Emery Road

Jeffersonville Rd.

Walnut Creek

80

ALT 129

80

23

MACON

McDougal Mound

Dunlap Mound

Cornfield Mound

Parking

Earthlodge

Village Site

Parking Funeral Mound

Parking

Southeast Mound

Lesser Temple Mound

Loop Trail

16

Opelofa Trail

Great Temple Mound

Walnut Creek

Ocmulgee River

ILLINOIS

STATE TOURIST INFORMATION

(800) 226–6632
www.enjoyillinois.com

CHICAGO PORTAGE NATIONAL HISTORIC SITE

c/o Cook County Forest Preserve
536 North Harlem Avenue
River Forest, IL 60305
(800) 870–3666

Chicago Portage National Historic Site comprises ninety-one non-federal acres and was designated an affiliated area of the National Park Service in 1952 to help preserve a portage used by Native Americans and explorers as a link between the Great Lakes and the Mississippi River. The historic site is just west of the Chicago city limits, about ¼ mile south of U.S. 66 (Joliet Road) on Harlem Avenue.

The Chicago Portage was a short, low divide that served as an important route between the Great Lakes and the Mississippi River for generations of Indians and explorers. In 1673, Native Americans directed explorers Jolliet and Marquette up the Illinois and Des Plaines rivers to Portage Creek, where the travelers were required to portage their canoes to the south branch of the Chicago River. With completion of the Illinois and Michigan Canal in 1848, the Chicago River was connected with the Illinois River. The portage trail of these explorers, fur traders, and Native Americans that was a major factor in development of America's interior eventually became Route 66 and Joliet Road.

A monument and concourse area recognizing explorers Marquette and Jolliet and their Indian guides are just off Harlem Avenue at Chicago Portage Woods. Parking is available at the

Illinois and Michigan Canal National Heritage Corridor (opposite page)

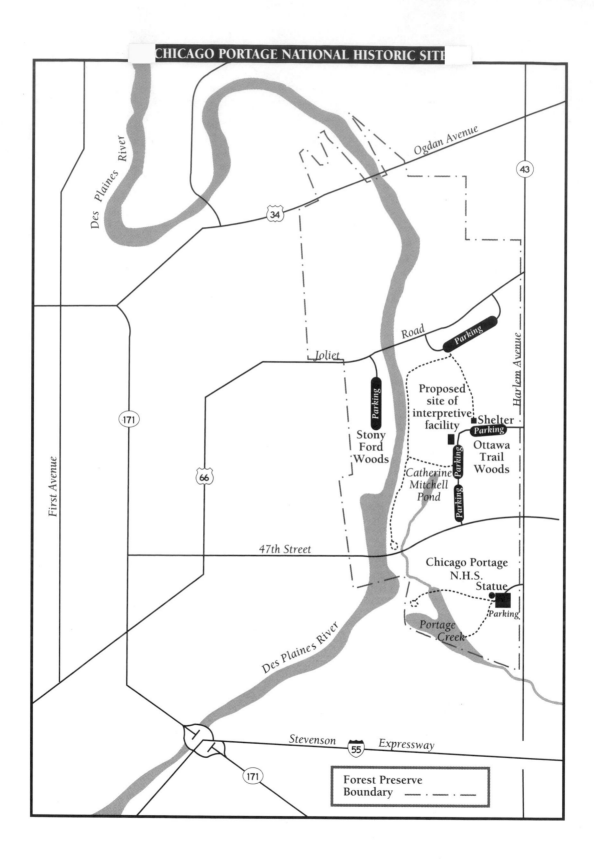

Des Plaines River

Ogdan Avenue

34

43

Road

Parking

Joliet

Parking

Proposed site of interpretive facility

Shelter

Parking

171

Stony Ford Woods

Ottawa Trail Woods

Harlem Avenue

First Avenue

66

Parking

Catherine Mitchell Pond

Parking

47th Street

Chicago Portage N.H.S. Statue

Parking

Portage Creek

Des Plaines River

Stevenson

55

Expressway

171

Forest Preserve
Boundary —·—·—

monument, where visitors can view a portion of Portage Creek. Ottawa Trail Woods, north of Forty-seventh Street, contains a ridge where visitors can walk beside the site of Laughton's Trading Post to Laughton's Ford. The Forest Preserve District in which the historic site is located offers recreational facilities including golf courses, bicycle trails, horseback riding trails, and nature centers.

ENTRANCE FEE: No charge.

FACILITIES: No food or lodging is available at the site, but both are located nearby. Picnic areas are north of Forty-seventh Street.

CAMPING: No camping is permitted.

FISHING: Fishing is available nearby at the Forest Preserve District. An Illinois fishing license is required.

ILLINOIS AND MICHIGAN CANAL NATIONAL HERITAGE CORRIDOR

15709 South Independence Boulevard
Lockport, IL 60441
(815) 740–2047
ilmi_administration@nps.gov
www.nps.gov/ilmi

Illinois and Michigan Canal National Heritage Corridor was authorized in 1984 to retain, enhance, and interpret the historic, natural, recreational, and economic resources of a land corridor that was instrumental in the opening of the West and the growth of Chicago. The corridor is located in northern Illinois along a narrow strip of land that begins in Chicago and follows the Des Plaines and Illinois rivers to the towns of La Salle and Peru.

Land comprising the Illinois and Michigan Canal National Heritage Corridor has been used for centuries as a link between the East Coast and mid-America. The movement of Native Americans along this strip of land was recorded in 1673 by French explorers Jolliet and Marquette when they returned north after exploring the Mississippi River. Although trade over the portage route had substantially increased by the late 1700s, construction of a canal to connect Lake Michigan with the Illinois River did not begin until 1836. Financial difficulties delayed the canal's opening until 1848.

The canal was made 6 feet deep, 60 feet wide at water level, and 36 feet wide at the bottom along a main route 96 miles long. Fifteen locks lifted or lowered boats through the canal. Completion of the canal caused commerce to and from Chicago to increase until the city surpassed St. Louis as the Midwest's hub of commerce and population. Other towns along the canal also prospered. By the mid-1800s, rail transportation had captured most of the passengers and, to the dismay of the canal boat operators, much of the freight traffic that previously would have been shipped on the canal.

The National Heritage Corridor offers a multitude of things to see and do. Visitors can stroll through several historic canal towns, visit museums, tour a large scientific research laboratory,

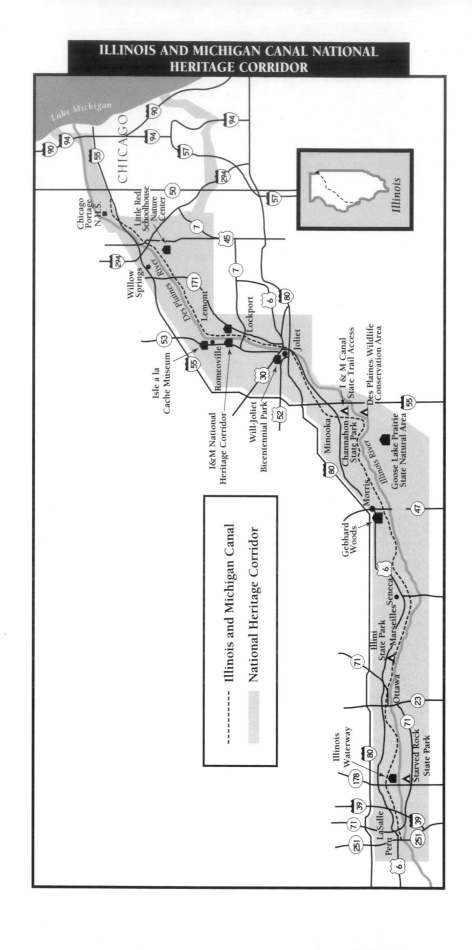

ILLINOIS AND MICHIGAN CANAL NATIONAL
HERITAGE CORRIDOR

Illinois

Lake Michigan

CHICAGO

Chicago Portage N.H.S.

Little Red Schoolhouse Nature Center

Willow Springs

Des Plaines River

Lemont

Lockport

Joliet

Isle a la Cache Museum

Romeoville

I&M National Heritage Corridor

Will-Joliet Bicentennial Park

I & M Canal State Trail Access

Des Plaines Wildlife Conservation Area

Minooka

Channahon State Park

Illinois River

Goose Lake Prairie State Natural Area

Morris

Gebhard Woods

Illini State Park

Marseilles

Seneca

Ottawa

Illinois Waterway

Starved Rock State Park

LaSalle

Peru

Illinois and Michigan Canal

National Heritage Corridor

walk a trail following the canal towpath, and visit a restored lock-tender's house. There are eight visitor centers within the corridor: Isle a la Cache Museum in Romeoville, I&M Canal Visitor Center in Lockport, Will County Historical Society Museum in Lockport, Will-Joliet Bicentennial Park in Joliet, Little Red Schoolhouse Nature Center in Willow Springs, Goose Lake Prairie State Natural Area in Morris, I&M Canal State Trail (Gebhard Woods Access) in Morris, and Illinois Waterway Visitor Center west of Ottawa.

ENTRANCE FEE: No charge. The Children's Farm admission fee is $3.50 per person. There is a $1.00 per person admission fee for the La Salle Historical Society Museum.

FACILITIES: Food and lodging are available all along the corridor.

CAMPING: Public camping is available at Starved Rock State Park (133 spaces, full hookups, showers) southeast of La Salle, Illini State Park (ninety-five spaces, flush toilets) near Marseilles, and Des Plaines Conservation Area (twenty-four spaces, pit toilets) south of Channahon. Two campgrounds for backpackers and bicyclists are on the Illinois and Michigan Canal State Trail in Morris and in Channahon.

LINCOLN HOME NATIONAL HISTORIC SITE

413 South Eighth Street
Springfield, IL 62701-1905
(217) 492–4241
lincolnhome@nps.gov
www.nps.gov/liho

This site, which contains approximately twelve acres, was established in 1972 to preserve the only home owned by Abraham Lincoln. The site is located between Seventh and Ninth Streets in downtown Springfield, Illinois. A parking lot (fee) for the site is on Seventh Street.

Although Abraham Lincoln was born in Kentucky and spent his youth in Indiana, he was married and lived most of his adult life in Springfield, Illinois. Beginning in 1834, he represented Sangamon County in the Illinois General Assembly, and in 1847 he began serving his one term in the U.S. Congress. In between, he was married in 1842 and bought his first and only home for $1,500 in 1844. He and his family lived there until his election to the presidency in 1860.

The house was built in 1839 and has been restored to its 1860s appearance. Although the Lincolns sold most of their household goods in 1861, the home has since been furnished with some of the furniture actually used by the family. The historic site includes 4 blocks surrounding the house, and the exteriors of neighboring homes and buildings are being restored to their 1860s appearances. Free tickets for a tour of the home are distributed daily at the visitor center on a first-come basis. Bus groups are required to make reservations through the Springfield Convention and Visitors Bureau (800–545–7300).

Within walking distance of the site are the Old State Capitol (free admission), where Lincoln delivered his "House Divided" speech; the Lincoln–Herndon Law Offices, where he practiced law; and the railway station where he delivered his farewell speech before leaving for Washington. Also in Springfield is the Lincoln Tomb in Oak Ridge Cemetery. Nearby is Lincoln's New Salem State Historic Site, where a reconstructed village marks the site of Lincoln's early years in

Illinois. A guide to historic attractions in Springfield is available in the visitor center.

ENTRANCE FEE: No charge.

FACILITIES: No food or lodging is available at the site, but all types of services are provided within walking distance. Drinking water and modern rest rooms are provided at the site.

CAMPING: No camping is permitted at the site. Lincoln's New Salem State Historic Site, 20 miles northwest of Springfield near Petersburg on Highway 97, offers tables, grills, flush toilets, and showers.

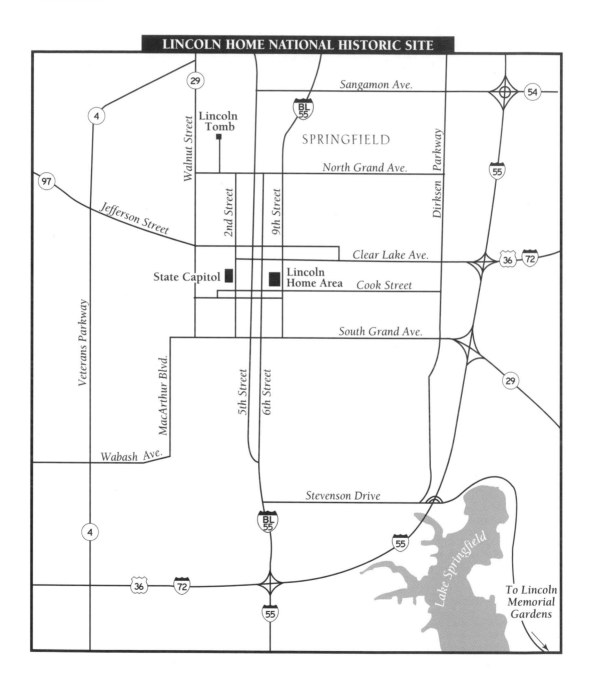

Lincoln Home National Historic Site, Springfield, Illinois

Clark Memorial, George Rogers Clark National Historical Park (photo by D. Latta)

INDIANA

STATE TOURIST INFORMATION
(800) 289–6646
www.indianatourism.com

GEORGE ROGERS CLARK NATIONAL HISTORICAL PARK

401 South Second Street
Vincennes, IN 47591-1001
(812) 882–1776
GERO_Ranger_Activities@nps.gov
www.nps.gov/gero

The twenty-six-acre George Rogers Clark National Historical Park was established in 1966. The park commemorates the capture of the British Fort Sackville by Colonel George Rogers Clark and his French-American army of 170 men. The victory occurred February 25, 1779. Today the Clark Memorial stands upon the former fort site in Vincennes, Indiana (approximately 53 miles south of Terre Haute). The park entrance is off Second Street, 4 blocks west of the downtown area.

During the spring and summer of 1778, George Rogers Clark and his meager Virginia army traveled down the Ohio River to attack the British posts north of that river. Capturing the villages of Kaskaskia and Cahokia along the Mississippi River, Clark subsequently led 170 men on a 180-mile mid-winter march. The eighteen-day trek across the flooded Illinois country brought them to their destination, the British Fort Sackville in Vincennes. After a siege of approximately thirty-eight hours, British commander, Lieutenant Governor Henry Hamilton, surrendered his fort. This victory, made possible with the aid of the local French Canadians, helped the United States secure the territory north of the Ohio River and east of the Mississippi River.

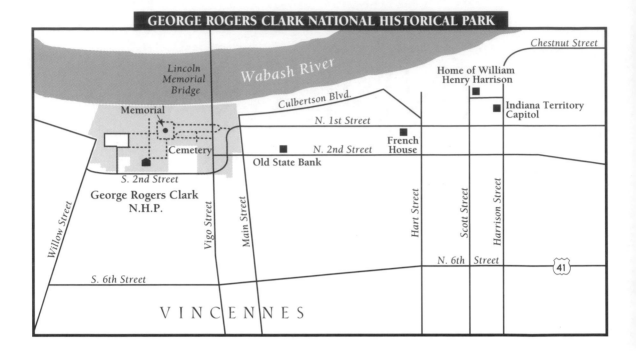

GEORGE ROGERS CLARK NATIONAL HISTORICAL PARK

During the early 1930s, a nearly 80-foot-high granite memorial was built upon the former fort site. The Clark Memorial was dedicated by President Franklin Roosevelt in 1936. The park also preserves approaches to the Abraham Lincoln Memorial Bridge and to the Buffalo Trace crossing of the Wabash River into Illinois.

Next to the grounds is St. Francis Xavier Catholic Church, which serves as a reminder of the city's early 1730s French Canadian roots. Approximately 12 blocks from the park are the Indiana Territory Capitol, the Elihu Stout Print Shop, and Grouseland, which was the home of territorial governor William Henry Harrison. Harrison became the territory's first governor in 1800 when Vincennes was chosen as the territorial capital. He later became the ninth president of the United States.

The park is open daily (except Thanksgiving, Christmas Day, and New Year's Day) from 9:00 A.M. to 5:00 P.M. Information, displays, and a twenty-three-minute video on the Clark Campaign are provided in the visitor center. The Spirit of Vincennes Rendezvous is an annual event held at the park on Saturday and Sunday of Memorial Day Weekend.

ENTRANCE FEE: $4.00 per family or $2.00 per person; visitors sixteen and under free.

FACILITIES: Rest rooms and drinking water are provided at the visitor center. Food and lodging are available nearby.

CAMPING: No camping is permitted in the park. Public camping is available at Ouabache Trails Park, 2 miles north of Vincennes along the Wabash River.

INDIANA DUNES NATIONAL LAKESHORE

1100 North Mineral Springs Road
Porter, IN 46304
(219) 926–7561
INDU_Interpretation@nps.gov
www.nps.gov/indu

Indiana Dunes was authorized by Congress in 1966. Today, it preserves over 15,000 acres of magnificent dunes, beaches, bogs, marshes, and prairie remnants. The park includes an 1830 restored homestead and a 1900s-era farm. The lakeshore is located in northwestern Indiana, approximately 40 miles southeast of Chicago via Interstate 80/94. It may be reached by the Chicago South Shore and South Bend Railroad.

In the Indiana Dunes area, visitors will stand on a flat bit of earth on which two things have been piled: sand and rocky glacial till. The piles of till, called moraines, tell the story of advancing glaciers that deposited this rocky earth in conveyor-belt fashion. The sand piles, called dunes, tell the story of a lake that shrank by stages after the glaciers disappeared. The glaciers pushed south, while the lake receded north.

The park's visitor center, located at U.S. 12 and Kemil Road in Porter County, Indiana, is open from 8:00 A.M. until 5:00 P.M. daily (8:00 A.M. to 6:00 P.M. in summer) except Thanksgiving, Christmas Day, and New Year's Day. The center offers information, an audiovisual program, nature walks, activity schedules, rest rooms, and a bookstore. A visitor center serving the Bailly Homestead and Chellberg Farm, on North Mineral Springs Road between Highways 12 and 20, is open daily during summer and during weekends through the fall.

Beaches with parking and bathrooms are at West Beach (showers), Kemil Road, Central Avenue, and Mt. Baldy. Hiking trails throughout the park provide access to historical structures, dunes, woods, beaches, prairie, marshes, and the Little Calumet River. The Bailly area contains the Joseph Bailly homestead, a historic cemetery, and the restored Chellberg farm.

ENTRANCE FEE: Only at West Beach from Memorial Day through Labor Day; $4.00 per vehicle or 50 cents per person.

FACILITIES: No food or lodging is provided by the park service. Vending machines are at West Beach. Lodging and restaurants are available in nearby communities.

CAMPING: Dunewood campground (fifty conventional sites, twenty-five walk-in sites) with flush toilets and showers is located at U.S. 12 and Broadway near Beverly Shores. A campground is also located in Indiana Dunes State Park, which is within the national lakeshore boundaries but is separately administered.

FISHING: Fishing is permitted within the national lakeshore. A current Indiana fishing license is required.

See the map on page 69.

Indiana Dunes National Lakeshore

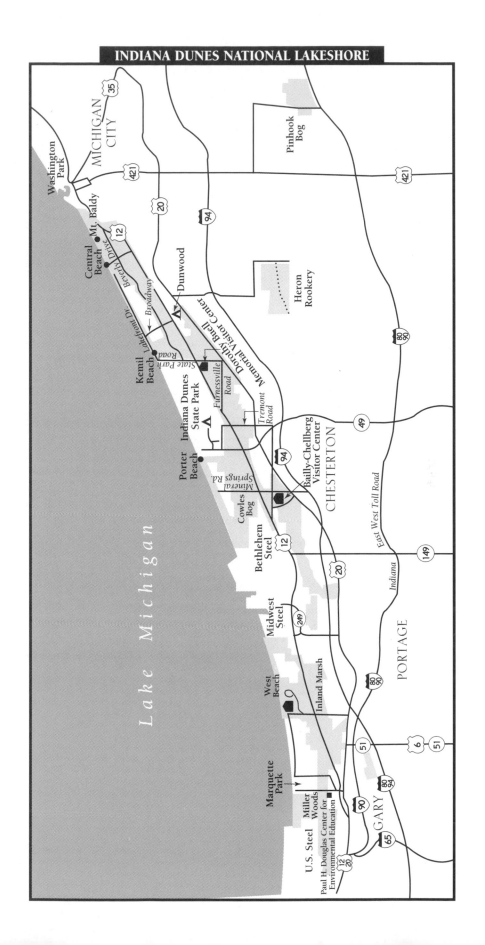

INDIANA DUNES NATIONAL LAKESHORE

Lake Michigan

MICHIGAN CITY

Washington Park

Mt. Baldy

Central Beach

Beverly Drive

Broadway

Lakefront Dr.

Kemil Beach

State Park Road

Dunwood

Indiana Dunes State Park

Porter Beach

Mineral Springs Rd.

Cowles Bog

Furnessville Road

Dorothy Buell Memorial Visitor Center

Tremont Road

Bailly-Chellberg Visitor Center

CHESTERTON

Bethlehem Steel

Midwest Steel

East West Toll Road

Indiana

PORTAGE

Inland Marsh

West Beach

Marquette Park

Miller Woods

U.S. Steel

Paul H. Douglas Center for Environmental Education

GARY

Pinhook Bog

Heron Rookery

35

421

20

94

421

80
90

49

94

12

20

249

149

80
90

51

6

51

80
94

90

65

12
20

LINCOLN BOYHOOD NATIONAL MEMORIAL

P.O. Box 1816
Lincoln City, IN 47552-1816
(812) 937–4541
LIBO_Superintendent@nps.gov
www.nps.gov/libo

Lincoln Boyhood National Memorial, comprising 200 wooded and landscaped acres, was authorized in 1962 to preserve the farm where Abraham Lincoln lived from 1816 to 1830. The memorial is in southern Indiana, 4 miles south of Dale on State Highway 162. Travelers on Interstate 64 can use exit 57, travel south on U.S. 231, and follow the signs to Lincoln Parks.

When Abraham Lincoln was seven years old, his family moved from Kentucky to Indiana and settled on 160 acres of wilderness land, where Abraham lived until he was twenty-one. This is where young Abraham helped his father, Thomas, clear the forest for a pioneer farm, and where his mother, Nancy, died when he was only nine. The growing youth split rails, plowed and planted, played, read, and learned to write. It was from here, in 1830, that Abraham Lincoln moved with his family to Illinois.

The memorial grounds are open daily year-round from dawn to dusk. The visitor center is open from 8:00 A.M. to 5:00 P.M. The memorial is closed Thanksgiving, Christmas, and New Year's Day. Rangers are on duty to orient visitors to the memorial's features, including the visitor center; the grave of Nancy Hanks Lincoln, Abraham's mother; and the Lincoln Living Historical Farm, a working pioneer farm where rangers dressed in period clothes present family living and farming activities daily from May through September. Most features of the park are wheelchair accessible. Admission is charged for individuals seventeen and older.

ENTRANCE FEE: $2.00 per person with a maximum of $4.00 per family; visitors sixteen and under free.

FACILITIES: No food or lodging is available in the park. Rest rooms and drinking fountains are in the visitor center.

CAMPING: Adjacent to Lincoln Boyhood National Memorial is the 1,747-acre Lincoln State Park, administered by the Indiana Department of Natural Resources. The state park offers camping, picnicking, hiking, swimming, boating, and fishing. Fees are collected for entering the state park and for camping.

KENTUCKY

STATE TOURIST INFORMATION
(800) 225–8747
Kentuckytourism.com

ABRAHAM LINCOLN BIRTHPLACE
NATIONAL HISTORIC SITE

2995 Lincoln Farm Road
Hodgenville, KY 42748-9707
(270) 358–3137
www.nps.gov/abli

This 116-acre park was established in 1916 to commemorate the site of Abraham Lincoln's birth. It is located in north-central Kentucky, 3 miles south of Hodgenville on U.S. 31E/Kentucky 61.

For $200, Thomas Lincoln bought the 300-acre Sinking Spring farm in 1808. Soon afterward, he moved his wife and one-year-old daughter into a one-room cabin where Abraham was born in February 1809. The Lincolns lived here about two-and-one-half years before a defective land title forced them to move 10 miles northeast to a farm on Knob Creek. For additional information on parks honoring Abraham Lincoln, see Lincoln Boyhood National Memorial (Indiana) and Lincoln Home National Historic Site (Illinois) in this book.

A visitor center, open daily except Thanksgiving, Christmas, and New Year's Days, contains an audio-visual program and exhibits depicting Abraham Lincoln's early life. Included is the original Bible of Thomas Lincoln. A short walk leads to the former site of a giant oak that served as a marker for early surveys and to Sinking Spring, which provided cool water for the Lincolns. A memorial building protects the log cabin that is the traditional birthplace. Hiking trails are located in the park.

ENTRANCE FEE: No charge.

FACILITIES: No food or lodging is available at the site, but both are provided in Hodgenville. Rest rooms and drinking water are at the visitor center. A picnic area is across U.S. 31E from the visitor center.

CAMPING: No camping is permitted in the park. A state park with camping facilities is northeast via U.S. 31E at Bardstown.

CUMBERLAND GAP NATIONAL HISTORICAL PARK

P.O. Box 1848
Middlesboro, KY 40965-1848
(606) 248–2817
www.nps.gov/cuga

Cumberland Gap National Historical Park, with more than 20,000 acres, was authorized in 1940 to memorialize the mountain pass on the Wilderness Road that served as a main entryway for settlers through the Alleghenies. The gap also was an important military objective in the Civil War. The park is located in southeastern Kentucky, with portions spilling over into Virginia and Tennessee. It can be reached by either U.S. 25E from Kentucky and Tennessee or U.S. 58 from Virginia.

From its discovery in 1750, Cumberland Gap proved to be a major focal point in early American history. The area was explored by Daniel Boone from 1769 until he helped mark the Wilderness Road in 1775. Soon after, settlers began to pour through the gap, setting the stage for Kentucky's statehood in 1792. The mountain pass was considered an important strategic location during the Civil War, and it changed hands a number of times.

The park's visitor center, near Middlesboro, Kentucky, is open daily (except Christmas Day) from 8:00 A.M. to 5:00 P.M. (8:00 A.M. to 6:00 P.M. in summer). Here visitors will find a museum, an orientation program, and an information desk. From this point, the 4-mile Pinnacle Road passes a small earthen Civil War fort on its way to a panoramic overlook and short-loop trail. Other interesting locations include Tri-State Peak, where a 2⅘-mile round-trip trail leads to the meeting point of three states. East on U.S. 58, Hensley Settlement is a restored mountain community accessible by hiking. It contains three restored farmsteads with houses, barns, fields, a schoolhouse, and cemetery. The park contains about 55 miles of trails.

ENTRANCE FEE: No charge.

FACILITIES: No food or lodging is available in the park, but both are in Cumberland Gap and Tazewell, Tennessee, and Middlesboro. Rest rooms and drinking water are in the visitor center.

CAMPING: Wilderness Road Campground (160 spaces, thirteen group sites) is open year-round and offers electricity, tables, grills, water, flush toilets, hot showers, and a dump station. Five backcountry campgrounds with primitive facilities are available by permit only.

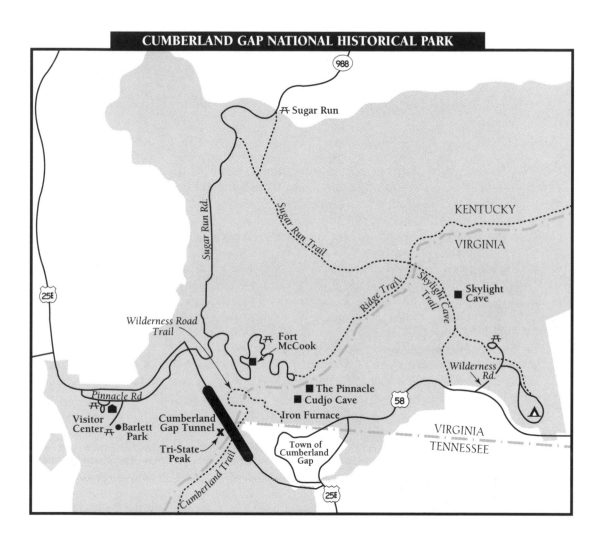

CUMBERLAND GAP NATIONAL HISTORICAL PARK

988

Sugar Run

KENTUCKY

VIRGINIA

Sugar Run Rd.

Sugar Run Trail

Skylight Cave Trail

Ridge Trail

Skylight Cave

25E

Wilderness Road Trail

Fort McCook

Wilderness Rd.

Pinnacle Rd

The Pinnacle
Cudjo Cave

58

Visitor Center

Barlett Park

Cumberland Gap Tunnel

Iron Furnace

VIRGINIA
TENNESSEE

Tri-State Peak

Town of Cumberland Gap

Cumberland Trail

25E

MAMMOTH CAVE NATIONAL PARK

P.O. Box 7
Mammoth Cave, KY 42259-0007
(270) 758–2328
maca_park_information@nps.gov
www.nps.gov/maca

This 53,000-acre park was established in 1941 to preserve the longest recorded cave system (more than 350 miles have been mapped) in the world, rugged hill-sides, beautiful rivers, and the surface landforms associated with caves. The park is located in central Kentucky, approximately 90 miles south of Louisville via Interstate 65.

For thousands of years, Mammoth Cave's passageways and chambers have fascinated people who lived nearby or who passed through the area. Trips through the caves offer access to deep pits, high domes, and formations such as stalactites, stalagmites, and gypsum crystals. Varying types of guided tours (fee charged) are offered year-round, with tickets available in the visitor center or in advance by reservation. One cave tour is handicapped-accessible. Wear comfortable shoes and a jacket (temperatures are mid-50s to low 60s) for these relatively strenuous walks. The center also contains an orientation film and a schedule of the various surface activities provided by park rangers. Tickets for an hour-and-ten-minute concessioner-operated cruise on the Green River also may be purchased here. The variety and frequency of cave tours and campfire programs are increased during the summer months. Cave tours sell out quickly during the summer, on holidays, and on weekends. Visitors are advised to reserve cave trips; call the National Park Reservation Service (800–967–2283).

A number of short walks and longer hiking trails are located throughout the park (some shown on map). Two surface walks (via boardwalks) with exhibits are handicap-accessible. A trail map is available at the visitor center.

ENTRANCE FEE: No charge. There is a charge for the cave tours, ranging from $3.50 (half hour, ¾ mile) to $35.00 (six hours, 5½ miles).

FACILITIES: Mammoth Cave Hotel, a motel-type lodge, and cottages are available year-round. Reservations are strongly recommended for summer months. Write: Mammoth Cave Hotel, P.O. Box 27, Mammoth Cave, KY 42259 (270–758–2225).

A dining room, coffee shop, craft center, and gift shop are located in the hotel. Laundry facility, post office, and groceries are available in a store near the campground. A service station also is located here.

CAMPING: An inviting, shaded campground (109 sites) near the visitor center is open March through November. It has flush toilets, picnic tables, and grills. A nearby store offers supplies and showers. At Houchin's Ferry a small campground (twelve sites, chemical toilets) is open year-round. Houchin's Ferry Campground is not suitable for large trailers or recreation vehicles. A group campground at Maple Springs is open March through November. It has flush toilets, picnic tables, and grills. Campground reservations can be made through the National Park Reservation System.

FISHING: Muskie, white perch, catfish, and bass live in Green and Nolin rivers. No license is required to fish at the park, but Kentucky regulations must be observed.

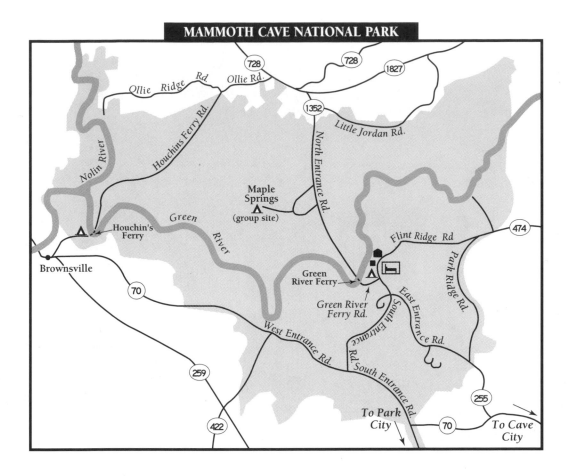

MAMMOTH CAVE NATIONAL PARK

728 728 1827

Ollie Ridge Rd. Ollie Rd.

1352

Little Jordan Rd.

Nolin River

Houchins Ferry Rd.

North Entrance Rd.

Maple
Springs
(group site)

Green
River

Houchin's
Ferry

Brownsville

70

Green
River Ferry

Green River
Ferry Rd.

Flint Ridge Rd

474

Park Ridge Rd.

East Entrance Rd.

South Entrance Rd.

West Entrance Rd.

259

422

255

To Park
City

70

To Cave
City

Roosevelt Cottage, Roosevelt Campobello International Park

MAINE

STATE TOURIST INFORMATION

(800) 533–9595
www.visitmaine.com

ACADIA NATIONAL PARK

P.O. Box 177
Bar Harbor, ME 04609-0177
(207) 288–3338
Acadia_information@nps.gov
www.nps.gov/acad

Acadia National Park comprises nearly 39,000 acres and was established as a national monument in 1916 (changed to Acadia National Park in 1929) to preserve a rugged coastal area of mountains, forests, and offshore islands. The park is located approximately two-thirds of the way up the Maine coast, 48 miles southeast of Bangor via U.S. 1A and State Highway 3.

Acadia National Park is divided into three parts: Mount Desert Island, on which the main section of the park is located, includes the town of Bar Harbor, fishing villages, and small resort communities; the second section, Schoodic Peninsula, is the only part of Acadia on the mainland; Isle au Haut, the third section, may be reached only by boat. Fare-free buses operate on seven routes that link hotels, inns, and private campgrounds with destinations in the park. Purchases of park entrance passes support the bus system.

On the way into the park, visitors should stop at the Hulls Cove Visitor Center (a short distance northwest of the town of Bar Harbor) to pick up a park map and schedule of activities. The center also offers a fifteen-minute film and pictures of the park. Most visitors in a hurry

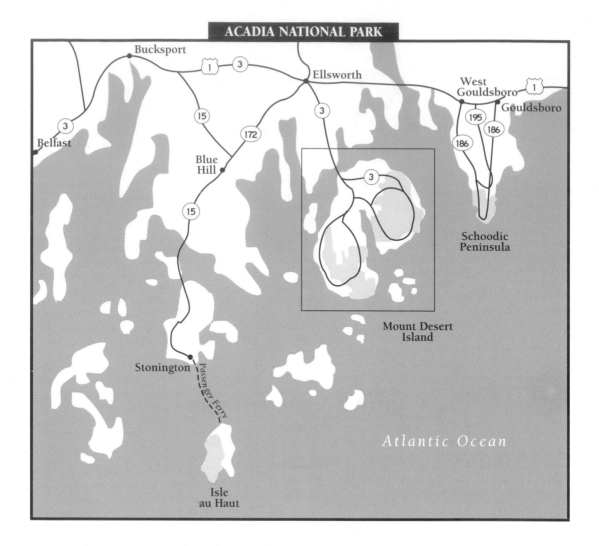

stop at the visitor center, drive the 20-mile scenic loop road, and travel up Cadillac Mountain Summit Road to the highest point on the East Coast. This point provides magnificent vistas of the surrounding coastline. For those able to spend more time, the park offers a historical museum on Little Cranberry Island (reached by ferry) and a museum, nature center, and wild-flower garden at Sieur de Monts Spring. Scheduled ranger-guided walks, hikes, boat trips, and amphitheater programs with descriptions and telephone numbers for making reservations are listed in the schedule of activities. Try one of these to better understand the park's environment, wildlife, and inhabitants. Swimming, with lifeguards on duty, can be found at Echo Lake and at Sand Beach. Numerous hiking trails lead throughout the park, and 45 miles of smooth broken-stone carriage roads circle Jordan Pond and Eagle Lake and wind around Sargent and Penobscot mountains. Ranger-guided walks of the tidal pools are particularly rewarding. Bicycles may be rented in Bar Harbor, Northeast Harbor, and Southwest Harbor. Carriage rides are available at Wildwood Stables near Seal Harbor.

Winter activities at Acadia National Park include cross-country skiing, ice fishing, and limited ice skating and ice boating. No downhill ski facilities are available.

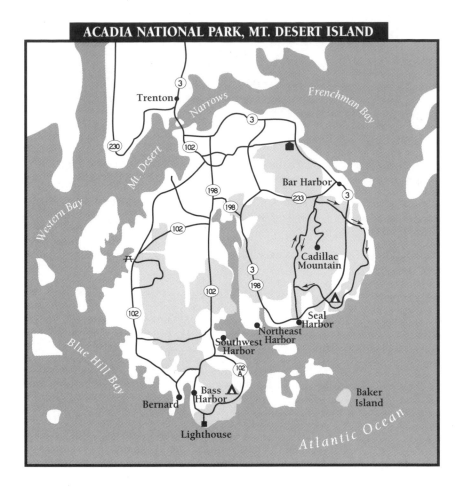

ACADIA NATIONAL PARK, MT. DESERT ISLAND

ENTRANCE FEE: $10.00 per vehicle or $5.00 per person; good for seven days.

FACILITIES: No lodging is available within the park, but hotels, motels, inns, and bed-and-breakfast establishments are located throughout the island; many of these are in the town of Bar Harbor. A concessioner offers meals and souvenirs at the south end of Jordan Pond and snacks at Cadillac Mountain and Thunder Hole.

CAMPING: Blackwoods (325 spaces) and Seawall (218 spaces of which 104 are walk-in-only at reduced cost). Campgrounds offer tables, grills, flush toilets, and dump stations. A private facility offering pay showers is near each of the campgrounds. Blackwoods accepts reservations and is the only campground open year-round. Blackwoods Campground is more centrally located, maybe a little nicer, and generally is filled first.

FISHING: Brook trout, lake trout, Atlantic salmon, pickerel, perch, and bass may be caught in the many lakes, with a Maine fishing license. Shore fishing (no license required) produces a variety of saltwater fish. Fishing is generally fair to good.

ROOSEVELT CAMPOBELLO INTERNATIONAL PARK

P.O. Box 129
Lubec, ME 04652
(506) 752–2922
info@fdr.net
www.fdr.net

Roosevelt Campobello International Park is a 2,800-acre park established in 1964 as a joint memorial by Canada and the United States, funded by both countries and administered by a joint United States–Canadian commission. The park includes the summer home of President Franklin D. Roosevelt. The park is located on Campobello Island in the Canadian province of New Brunswick and is reached via Franklin D. Roosevelt Memorial Bridge from Lubec, Maine.

In 1883 Franklin Roosevelt's father purchased four acres and a partially completed home on Campobello Island. The house was completed two years later, and subsequently the Roosevelt family spent most summers here. After Franklin and Eleanor were married, a cottage near the main home was purchased by Sara Roosevelt, the president's mother, in 1909, and later given to them. They and their children were also to spend summers on the island until Franklin was stricken with poliomyelitis here in 1921. Following this, he returned only three times, in 1933, 1936, and 1939.

The FDR cottage and reception center are open daily beginning on the Saturday prior to Memorial Day. The cottage remains open through Columbus Day and the reception center to the end of October. The grounds and natural area are open year-round. Visiting hours are from 9:00 A.M. to 5:00 P.M. eastern standard time. The Roosevelt cottage closes at 4:45. In the reception center, information is available and an interpretive display and short video tell the Roosevelt story and explain the significance of the park. A short walk from the reception center allows visitors to tour the Roosevelt cottage, which contains original furnishings and some personal belongings of the family. Tours of the home are self-guided, although guides are stationed throughout the cottage to provide information and answer questions.

Eight and a half miles of walking trails wander through the park's natural area, and three park drives have been developed for automobiles. A map and descriptions of the trails may be obtained at the reception center. Several park brochures are available for download through the park's Web site. Visitors may also want to stop just across the FDR Bridge at the New Brunswick information station to obtain maps and information on other sights on the island and in the province.

ENTRANCE FEE: No charge.

FACILITIES: The visitor center, first floor of the Roosevelt cottage, Eagle Hill Bog pathway, and Friar's Head lookout are all accessible to the disabled. Drinking water and modern rest rooms are in the reception center. Tourist facilities including restaurants, motels, and gift shops are available in the villages of Welshpool and Wilson's Beach on the island or at Lubec on the mainland.

CAMPING: No camping is permitted within the Roosevelt Campobello International Park, but only 2 miles away, Herring Cove Provincial Park provides camping facilities (eighty spaces) with tables, grills, flush toilets, showers, electrical hookups, and a dump station (506–752–7010). As is typical of provincial parks in New Brunswick, an enclosed picnic shelter has two wood-burning stoves complete with wood to burn. The provincial park accepts American money and will convert it to Canadian currency at the prevailing exchange rate.

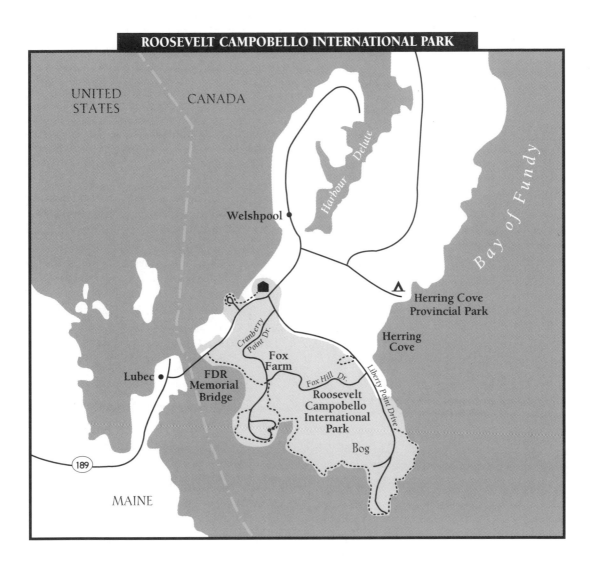

ROOSEVELT CAMPOBELLO INTERNATIONAL PARK

UNITED STATES

CANADA

Harbour Delute

Bay of Fundy

Welshpool

Herring Cove Provincial Park

Herring Cove

Cranberry Point Dr.

Fox Farm

Fox Hill Dr.

Liberty Point Drive

FDR Memorial Bridge

Lubec

Roosevelt Campobello International Park

Bog

189

MAINE

SAINT CROIX ISLAND INTERNATIONAL HISTORIC SITE

c/o Acadia National Park
P.O. Box 177
Bar Harbor, ME 04609-0177
(207) 288–3338
www.nps.gov/sacr

Saint Croix Island International Historic Site comprises thirty-five acres and was authorized in 1949 to commemorate the attempted French settlement here, which led to the founding of New France. The island is located off the mainland of eastern Maine, with the site entrance 8 miles south of Calais via U.S. 1. There is currently no ferry service to the island.

With a commission from a fur-trade monopoly to explore for minerals, settle the land, and spread Christianity, Lieutenant General Pierre Dugua, Sieur de Mons set sail from France for North America in 1604. After some exploration of the mainland, he sailed into the Bay of Fundy and up the St. Croix River in the early summer. De Mons found an island with a location that would provide control of the river and named it Saint Croix (above the island two long coves meet with the river to form a cross). The men set about constructing fortifications and shelters, and in August the two large ships returned to France, leaving seventy-nine men to spend the winter. The poorly prepared group fared badly, and by the time supply ships arrived the next June, thirty-five men were dead. After further exploration, a decision was made to move the settlement across the Bay of Fundy to Port Royal, near the present town of Annapolis Royal, Nova Scotia, and Saint Croix Island was abandoned.

With the exception of a Coast Guard navigation light, there are no federal facilities on the island. The park is administered by the superintendent of Acadia National Park. A reconstruction of the village founded after Saint Croix was abandoned can be seen at Port Royal National Historic Park in Nova Scotia.

ENTRANCE FEE: No charge.

FACILITIES: No facilities of any kind are on the island. Food service and lodging are available in Calais.

CAMPING: No camping is permitted within the historic site's grounds, which includes the entire island.

FISHING: Fishing is permitted. A Maine fishing license is not required for ocean fishing.

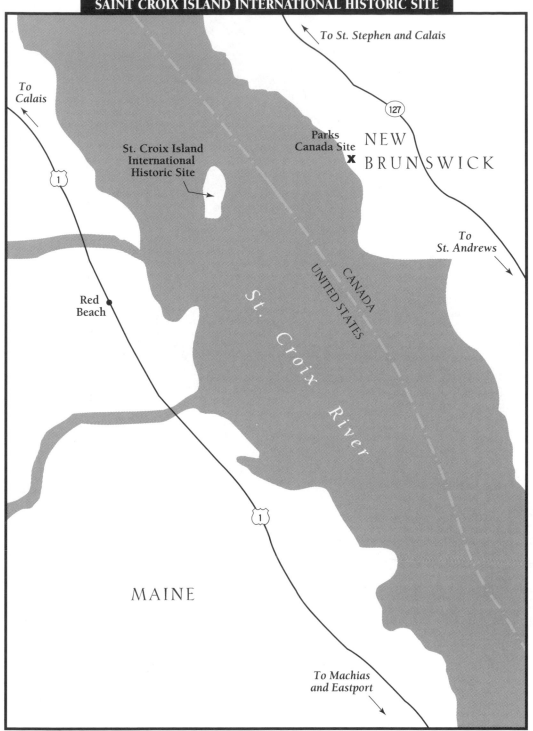

SAINT CROIX ISLAND INTERNATIONAL HISTORIC SITE

To St. Stephen and Calais

To Calais

127

Parks
Canada Site
X

NEW
BRUNSWICK

St. Croix Island
International
Historic Site

1

*To
St. Andrews*

CANADA
UNITED STATES

St. Croix River

Red
Beach

1

MAINE

*To Machias
and Eastport*

MARYLAND

STATE TOURIST INFORMATION
(800) 543–1036
www.mdisfun.org

ANTIETAM NATIONAL BATTLEFIELD
Box 158
Sharpsburg, MD 21782-0158
(301) 432–5124
www.nps.gov/anti

Antietam National Battlefield consists of 3,200 acres and was established in 1890 to commemorate the battlefield where General Robert E. Lee's first invasion of the North was ended in 1862. The battlefield is located in western Maryland, 12 miles south of Hagerstown via State Highway 65. It is approximately 70 miles northwest of Washington, D.C. It is also fifteen minutes south of Interstate 70 by way of exit 29.

During September of 1862, Robert E. Lee's 40,000 Confederate troops were being pursued by a Union force of 87,000 led by George B. McClellan. Lee's army took its position on the high ground to the west of Antietam Creek, and on September 17 the battle began. The bloodiest day in American military history left 12,410 Federals and 10,700 Confederates killed, wounded, captured, or missing. Although the battle, which took place over a 12-square-mile area, was tactically a draw, Lee's advance was halted, and President Lincoln was given the impetus to issue the Emancipation Proclamation.

"Chincoteague" Ponies, Assateague Island National Seashore (opposite page)

The visitor center, located north of Sharpsburg on Maryland Highway 65, is open daily 8:30 A.M. to 5:00 P.M. (8:00 A.M. to 6:00 P.M. in summer) except Thanksgiving, Christmas Day, and New Year's Day. Here visitors will find exhibits and two movies covering the battle and campaign. From this point, an 8½-mile self-guided tour highlights the main points of interest with wayside exhibits (*text numbers are keyed to the map*). The auto tour takes from forty-five minutes to one-and-a-half hours. Rental taped tours are available. Interpretive markers are at Turner's, Fox's, and Crampton's Gaps on South Mountain and at Shepherdstown Ford.

1. Dunker Church, a scene of repeated clashes, has been reconstructed.

2. North Woods, where General Hooker launched the initial attack but was stopped by Jackson's troops in the cornfield.

3. From East Woods, General Mansfield was fatally wounded as his corps attacked from the northeast.

4. Miller's twenty-five-acre cornfield changed hands several times in two-and-a-half hours.

5. In West Woods, Confederate troops cut down more than 2,200 Federals in twenty minutes.

125th Pennsylvania Monument behind Dunker Church, Antietam National Battlefield

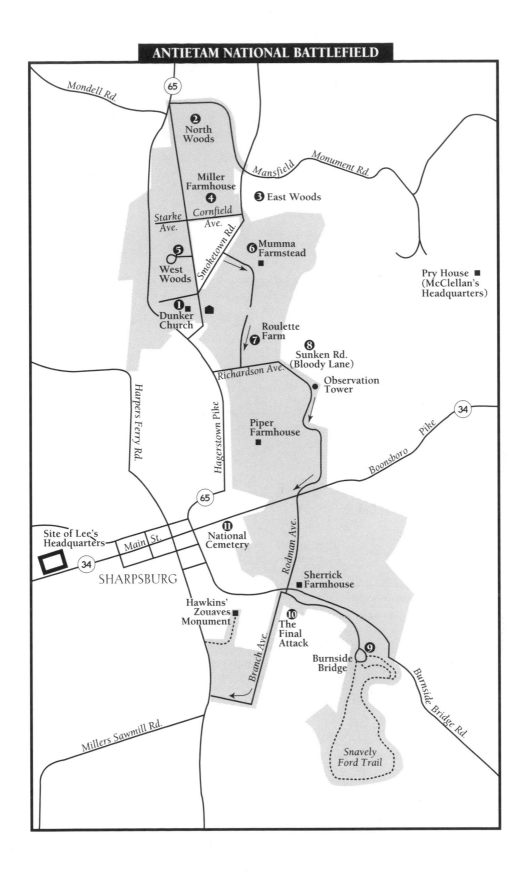

ANTIETAM NATIONAL BATTLEFIELD

Mondell Rd.

65

❷
North
Woods

Mansfield

Monument Rd.

Miller
Farmhouse
❹
Cornfield
Ave.

❸ East Woods

Starke
Ave.

Smoketown Rd.

❺

West
Woods

❻ Mumma
Farmstead

Pry House ■
(McClellan's
Headquarters)

❶ ■
Dunker
Church

Roulette
Farm
❼

❽
Sunken Rd.
(Bloody Lane)

Observation
Tower

Harpers Ferry Rd.

Hagerstown Pike

Richardson Ave.

Piper
Farmhouse ■

Boonsboro Pike

34

65

Site of Lee's
Headquarters

Main St.

❶❶
National
Cemetery

Rodman Ave.

34

SHARPSBURG

Sherrick
Farmhouse ■

Hawkins'
Zouaves ■
Monument

Branch Ave.

❶⓪
The
Final
Attack

❾

Burnside
Bridge

Burnside Bridge Rd.

Millers Sawmill Rd.

Snavely
Ford Trail

6. Mumma Farm, which was burned by Confederates to prevent use by Union sharp-shooters.

7. Roulette Farm, where Union troops crossed the fields on their way to meet Confederates posted in the Sunken Road.

8. Three hours of battle in Bloody Lane resulted in 5,000 casualties.

9. At Burnside Bridge, a few hundred Georgia riflemen held off four Union divisions for three hours.

10. Location of the final attack. After taking the bridge, Burnside's troops pressing toward Sharpsburg were stopped by Hill's Confederates arriving from Harpers Ferry.

11. Antietam National Cemetery contains the remains of 4,776 Federal troops.

ENTRANCE FEE: $4.00 per family or $2.00 per person; good for three days.

FACILITIES: Food and lodging are available nearby in Sharpsburg, a town of about 900 residents, and in Hagerstown, about 10 miles north of Sharpsburg. Water and rest rooms are in the visitor center.

CAMPING: Camping in the park is limited to organized groups, and reservations are required. A walk-in tent campground is located on the C&O Canal, 5 miles south on Harpers Ferry Road. Greenbrier State Park, 15 miles northeast via Highway 34 and alternates 40, 66, and 40, offers 200 sites with flush toilets, showers, laundry facilities, and a forty-two-acre lake for fishing, boating, and swimming.

FISHING: Fishing is permitted in Antietam Creek; a Maryland fishing license is required. Fishing is prohibited from Burnside Bridge.

ASSATEAGUE ISLAND NATIONAL SEASHORE
7206 National Seashore Lane
Berlin, MD 21811-9742
(410) 641–1441
www.nps.gov/asis

Assateague Island National Seashore was authorized as part of the National Park Service in 1965 to preserve nearly 50,000 acres of water area and sandy beach along a 37-mile barrier island. The park is located on the Atlantic coast of Maryland and Virginia. Visitor access to Assateague Island is at the extreme northern end near Ocean City, Maryland, or the extreme southern end near Chincoteague, Virginia. Between these two developed areas are 25 miles of roadless beach and marsh including a 12-mile strip of wild beach in Chincoteague National Wildlife Refuge that is accessible by foot only.

Assateague is a barrier island formed by sand rising from the ocean floor and shaped by wind and waves. The island's mild surf and moderate temperatures make this an ideal place for outdoor water-related activities, including swimming, fishing, canoeing, and beachcombing. The

ASSATEAGUE ISLAND NATIONAL SEASHORE

Ocean City

Berlin

Barrier Island
Visitor Center

Assateague
State Park
Entrance

National Seashore
Entrance

Atlantic
Ocean

Newark

Chincoteague
Bay

Snow Hill

MARYLAND
VIRGINIA

Girdletree

Stockton

Chincoteague
National
Wildlife
Refuge

Chincoteague
Island

Chincoteague

Wildlife Refuge
Visitor Center

NASA

Toms Cove
Visitor Center

Toms
Cove

island's most famous residents are ponies which, according to legend, came ashore 200 years ago from a wrecked Spanish galleon. Park historians, however, believe the horses were placed there by farmers to avoid taxation and fencing requirements on the mainland.

Assateague is one of the few remaining protected and undeveloped barrier islands on the East Coast. Assateague Island National Seashore preserves critical ocean, dune, forest, marsh, and coastal bay habitats for plant, animal, and marine life native to the mid-Atlantic coastal region.

The seashore's Barrier Island Visitor Center at the north end contains exhibits, publications, and information about the island. A paved road extends through Assateague State Park and into the national seashore, but only properly equipped over-sand vehicles are allowed on the 13-mile beach route that begins at the end of Bayside Drive. A permit is required. The shallow saltwater marshes in Chincoteague Bay provide excellent canoeing, and a canoe launch is at the end of Ferry Landing Road. Canoe rentals are available at the end of Bayside Drive near the picnic area. A protected beach and bathhouse are near the park entrance. Three ½-mile nature trails interpret three lesser known life zones of a barrier island: marsh, forest, and dunes.

At the park's south end, a 3-mile paved road leads through the national wildlife refuge to the beach. Beyond Toms Cove Beach, a 5-mile route is available to over-sand vehicles only (permit required). The Refuge Visitor Center provides information and literature on the wildlife refuge; a National Park Service visitor center is located on the shore of Toms Cove.

ENTRANCE FEE: $5.00 per vehicle or $2.00 per person; good for seven days.

FACILITIES: No lodging is available in the seashore area. During summer months, bathhouses, a concession shop, and food service are in Assateague State Park. Motels, restaurants, and stores are in the towns of Chincoteague, Virginia, and Ocean City, Maryland.

CAMPING: The only developed camping facilities are in the northern section. Assateague State Park (410–641–2120) has tables, hot showers, and flush toilets. Immediately south, the National Park Service operates the more primitive campgrounds of Bayside and Oceanside with tables, a sanitary station, portable toilets, and cold water. Two oceanside backpack campsites, four bayside canoe-in campsites, and a group camp are available. Write for specific information or call the campground office (410–641–3030).

FISHING: Surf fishing is permitted along most of the shoreline. No license is required. Clamming and crabbing are permitted throughout the bay behind Assateague Island.

CATOCTIN MOUNTAIN PARK

6602 Foxville Road
Thurmont, MD 21788-0158
(301) 663–9330
www.nps.gov/cato

Catoctin Mountain Park provides numerous outdoor recreational possibilities on nearly 5,800 acres of forested land along an eastern ridge of the Appalachian Mountains. The park is 65 miles northwest of Washington, D.C., with the main entrance on Maryland Highway 77, 3 miles west of Thurmont and U.S. 15.

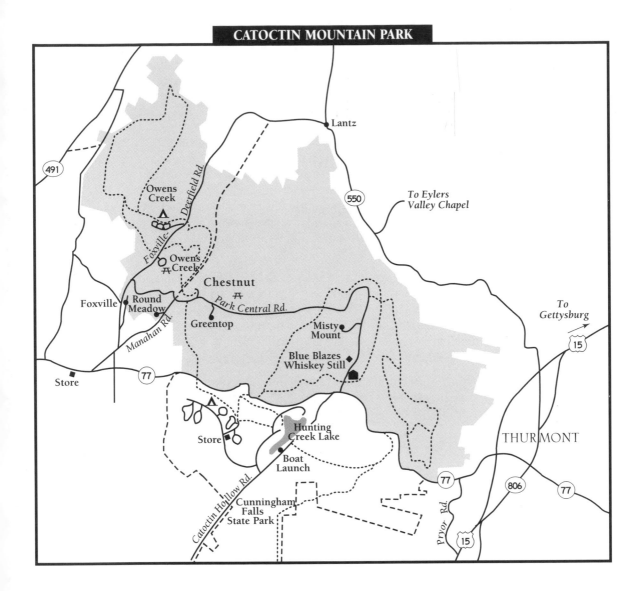

Settlers used the land and the mountain's natural resources for decades. Forests were cleared to obtain wood for making charcoal, trees were stripped of bark for tanning, sawmill industries were located along local streams, and the land was heavily farmed. After years of hard use, the land was no longer considered productive for industry. The land of Catoctin Mountain Park was purchased by the federal government in 1935 to demonstrate that non-productive land could be changed and made productive again. The Catoctin Recreational Demonstration Area was built and a park was born. In 1954 a portion of the land was transferred to Maryland and became Cunningham Falls State Park as part of the original Recreational Area agreement.

The park's visitor center, just off State Highway 77, provides information, a schedule of interpretive programs, and a small museum. The park contains picnic areas, a 6-mile horse trail, and 25 miles of foot trails. Hog Rock, Browns Farm Environmental Study Area, and Deerfield Nature trails are self-guided and nature-oriented; leaflets are available at the trailheads. Blue Blazes Whiskey Still, Charcoal, Sawmill, and Spicebush trails have descriptive signs along the way. During winter months, trails are used for cross-country skiing and snow-shoeing. Portions of park roads are also closed for winter recreation.

Many of the recreational activities mentioned are also available in Cunningham Falls State Park. In addition, the state park contains a man-made lake that provides opportunities for swimming, fishing, and boating. The park office in the William Houck area is open year-round.

ENTRANCE FEE: No charge.

FACILITIES: Rustic cabins are available for rent at Camp Misty Mount, about a mile from the visitor center. Modern rest rooms and showers are centrally located. For reservations call (301) 271–3140. Organized groups may rent Camp Greentop (140-person capacity) or Camp Round Meadow (120-person capacity). For additional information call (301) 663–9330. Seasonal picnic areas with rest rooms, tables, and fireplaces are at Owens Creek, Chestnut, Manor, and William Houck. Food can be obtained in the William Houck area of Cunningham Falls State Park during the summer.

CAMPING: Owens Creek Campground (fifty-one sites, 22-foot trailer limit) is heavily wooded and offers tables, grills, water, and modern rest rooms with showers from mid-April to mid-November on a first come–first served basis. Two campgrounds (148 sites) with similar facilities are in Cunningham State Park and may be reserved (888–432–2267). The state park campsites generally have less shade than those in Owens Creek. All the campgrounds are generally filled on weekends but have openings on week nights.

FISHING: Trout live in Big Hunting Creek (fly-fishing, catch-and-release only), and wild brook and brown trout are caught in Little Owens Creek. Additional fishing is available in the state park. A Maryland fishing license is required in either place.

CHESAPEAKE & OHIO CANAL NATIONAL HISTORICAL PARK

P.O. Box 4
Sharpsburg, MD 21782-0004
(301) 739–4200
www.nps.gov/choh

Chesapeake & Ohio Canal National Historical Park was established in 1971 to preserve a strip of land along the route of a historic 184.5-mile-long nineteenth-century canal. The canal follows the Potomac River between Washington, D.C., and Cumberland, Maryland.

Construction on the C&O Canal commenced in 1828 in an effort to provide economical water transportation between the industrialized East Coast and the resources of the Midwest. Designed to follow the Potomac and trans-Allegheny trade route to the Ohio River, the canal was used as each section was completed. The cost of building the completed 184.5 miles of canal was $11 million. It included seventy-four lift locks, eleven aqueducts, seven dams, a 3,117-foot tunnel, 165 culverts, and a variety of lock houses. The canal was never a financial success and was severely damaged by two major floods. The entire project became obsolete

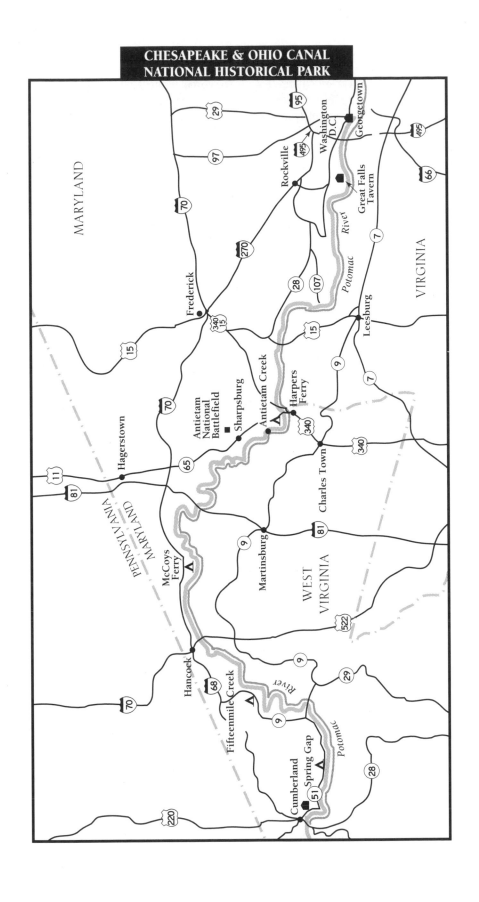

CHESAPEAKE & OHIO CANAL
NATIONAL HISTORICAL PARK

with the completion of the faster and less expensive Baltimore & Ohio Railroad, and by 1924 the C&O Canal had been abandoned.

One of the park's main visitor centers is at the Great Falls Tavern (301–767–3714). The center contains exhibits and information on conducted walks and other programs. Other Visitor Centers are located at Georgetown (202–653–5190), Brunswick, Williamsport, Hancock, and Cumberland. The canal towpath, which served as a walking surface for mules that pulled the boats, remains mostly unobstructed along the entire length of the canal. A detour is necessary between Dam 4 at mile 85.39 and McMahon's Mill at mile 88.10. Although it can become quite slippery during wet weather, the towpath generally makes a good path for hiking and bicycling. Boating is popular between Georgetown and Violettes Lock near Seneca, and canoes may be rented at Swains Lock and at Fletcher's Boat House.

ENTRANCE FEE: No charge with the exception of the Great Falls area; $4.00 per vehicle or $2.00 per person; good for three days.

FACILITIES: No food or lodging is available in the park. Camping supplies, ice, food, and soft drinks may be purchased at most stores along the various access roads.

CAMPING: Hiker-biker overnight campsites for tent camping are spaced approximately every 5 miles from Swains Lock (mile 16.6) to Stickpile Hill (mile 180.1). All have chemical toilets, picnic tables, grills, and water. Drive-in camping areas at McCoys Ferry, Antietam Creek, Fifteenmile Creek, Paw Paw Creek, and Spring Gap provide primitive facilities. The camping fee is $10 per night (drive-in only).

FISHING: Bass, sunfish, and a number of other species live in Big Pool near Fort Frederick, Little Pool at Hancock, and Battie Mixon Pond at Oldtown. Fishing is also permitted in the Potomac River. A Maryland fishing license is required.

CLARA BARTON NATIONAL HISTORIC SITE

5801 Oxford Road
Glen Echo, MD 20812-1201
(301) 492–6245
gwmp_clara_barton_nhs@nps.gov
www.nps.gov/clba

Clara Barton National Historic Site comprises about one acre and was established in 1975 to preserve the home of the founder of the American Red Cross. The house is located in Glen Echo, Maryland, a short distance northwest of the District of Columbia off MacArthur Boulevard via Massachusetts Avenue and Goldsboro Road or the Clara Barton Parkway.

Clara Barton first learned of the International Red Cross during a trip to Europe in 1869. After helping civilian victims of the Franco-Prussian War, she returned to the United States intent on expanding the organization to this country. Years of effort finally resulted in establishing the first chapter of the American Red Cross in 1881. As president of the American organization from its inception until 1904, Clara Barton was instrumental in having the American Red Cross engage in both peacetime and wartime aid.

The home was built in 1891 and given to Clara Barton by real estate developers who hoped to use her name and the name of the American Red Cross to promote their venture. The home was initially used as a Red Cross warehouse before being modified for living quarters and offices in 1897. Prior to acquisition by the National Park Service in 1975, the home passed through a number of owners. The house is shown by guided tour daily from 10:00 A.M. to 4:00 P.M. for thirty- to forty-minute guided tours that begin on the hour. It is closed Thanksgiving, Christmas Day, and New Year's Day.

ENTRANCE FEE: No charge.

FACILITIES: A small rest room is available in the house. A small picnic area is adjacent to the home. Concessions may be found next door in Glen Echo Park from May through September, and full services are available nearby in Glen Echo.

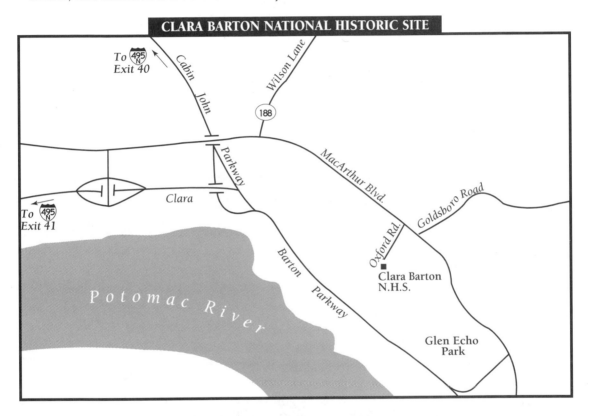

FORT McHENRY NATIONAL MONUMENT AND HISTORIC SHRINE

Baltimore, MD 21230-5393
(410) 962–4290
FOMC_Superintendent@nps.gov
www.nps.gov/fomc

Fort McHenry National Monument and Historic Shrine comprises forty-three acres and was authorized in 1925 to commemorate the site of a battle during the War of 1812 where Francis Scott Key was inspired to write "The Star Spangled

Banner." The fort is located 3 miles southeast of Baltimore's inner harbor via Light Street, Key Highway, Lawrence Street, and East Fort Avenue. It is also readily accessible from Interstate 95 (northbound or southbound), taking exit 55, Key Highway, Lawrence Street, and East Fort Avenue.

Fort McHenry was constructed in the 1790s to protect Baltimore against attack from either England or France, which were then engaged in a major war. In 1814, following Napoleon's defeat England was able to devote more effort to problems in the United States. After arriving in America, a British force attacked Washington. While negotiations for peace were being discussed, the British sailed up Chesapeake Bay to attack Baltimore. Anchored 2 miles below Fort McHenry, sixteen British warships bombarded the fort for twenty-five hours. At dawn on September 14, while the American flag was still waving over Fort McHenry, Francis Scott Key began writing the poem that was soon put to music and in 1931 became the national anthem of the United States.

Fort McHenry continued to serve a variety of roles following the War of 1812, although it never again came under attack. The fort served as a Union prison for Confederate soldiers and political prisoners during the Civil War. From 1917 until 1923 it was used as a U.S. Army hospital for World War I troops. Later, a portion of the current park served as a Coast Guard training facility.

Fort McHenry National Monument

The fort is open daily (except Christmas Day and New Year's Day) from 8:00 A.M. to 5:00 P.M. with extended summer hours. Before visiting, call the park to verify days and hours of operation. A visitor center near the star-shaped structure offers exhibits interpreting the fort's history and a sixteen-minute film. Guided activities are available during summer months. Wayside exhibits are located along the walk and audio stations can be found inside the fort buildings.

ENTRANCE FEE: $5.00 per person, visitors sixteen and under free; good for seven days.

FACILITIES: No food or lodging is available in the park. A concessioner sells souvenirs, postcards, and film; rest rooms and water are in the visitor center.

CAMPING: No camping is permitted on the monument grounds. The nearest public campsite is in Patapsco Valley State Park, west of Baltimore.

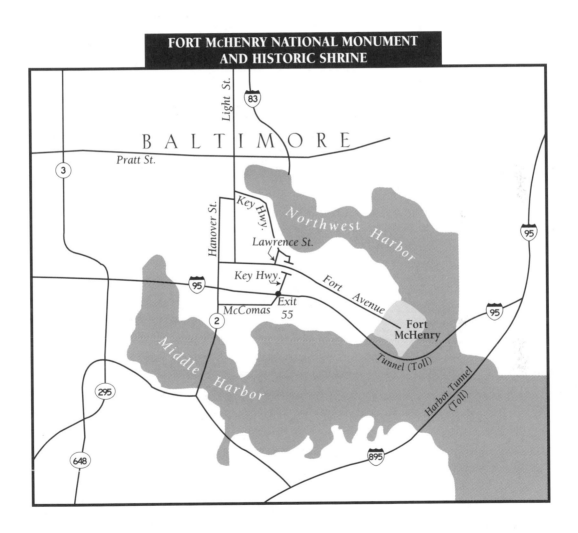

FORT WASHINGTON PARK

c/o National Capital Parks–East
1900 Anacostia Drive, S.E.
Washington, DC 20020-6722
(301) 763–4600
don_steiner@nps.gov
www.nps.gov/fowa

Fort Washington Park comprises 341 acres and preserves an outstanding example of an early-nineteenth-century coastal fortification. The park also includes recreational facilities. Fort Washington Park is located 8 miles south of the District of Columbia on the Maryland side of the Potomac River opposite Mount Vernon. It is reached from Interstate 495 (exit 3A South) by turning south onto Indian Head Highway (Highway 210) and then right onto Fort Washington Road. (See the map of the George Washington Memorial Parkway in the Virginia section for an approximate location.)

Construction of the first Fort Washington was completed in 1809 as part of America's effort to defend the ports and harbors of the new nation. In 1814 the fort was destroyed by American troops to prevent capture during the British invasion of the capital. Work on the present fort commenced almost immediately after the departure of British military forces, but because of delays and a greater feeling of security in the United States, it was not completed until 1824. The fort's masonry structure was later made obsolete by the introduction of rifled artillery. In the late 1890s, concrete gun batteries with breech-loading artillery were constructed on the military reservation around the original fort. The site was in use by the United States Army until the end of World War II. Fort Washington has the honor of being the only permanent fortification ever constructed to protect our nation's capital.

The park is open daily (except Christmas Day and New Year's Day) from 8:30 A.M. to dark. The fort and visitor center are open from 9:00 A.M. to 5:00 P.M. Fort Washington Park has hiking trails, a picnic area, tennis court, basketball court, and open park land for other recreational activities.

ENTRANCE FEE: $4.00 per vehicle or $2.00 per person; good for three days.

FACILITIES: No food service or lodging is available in the park. Picnic sites are available. Groceries may be purchased about 3 miles away.

CAMPING: No camping is permitted in the park. Cedarville State Park offers camping facilities 25 miles east near the town of Cedarville. The nearest National Park Service campground is at Greenbelt Park near Washington, D.C.

FISHING: Fishing off the banks of the Potomac River offers the possibility of catching carp and catfish. A Maryland fishing license is required.

GREENBELT PARK

6565 Greenbelt Road
Greenbelt, MD 20770-3207
(301) 344–3948
(301) 344–3944 (weekends)
www.nps.gov/gree

Greenbelt Park was made a part of the National Park Service in 1950 to preserve 1,175 acres of wooded land. It provides easily accessible camping facilities for Washington, D.C., visitors, and nature study and outdoor recreation to urban dwellers. The park is located 12 miles northeast of Washington, D.C., via the Baltimore–Washington Parkway. Exit at Greenbelt Road (Maryland Highway 193). From Interstate 495, use exit 23.

The Greenbelt Park area is in the process of recovering from 150 years of agricultural abuse. After clearing trees and depleting the land, farmers left the area in the early 1900s, and nature began healing its wounds. Now numerous varieties of plants and wildlife again have made their home here.

The park contains 12 miles of well-marked trails including Azalea (1⅕ miles), Blueberry (1⅕ miles), and Dogwood (1⅖ miles). A 6-mile loop trail, also used as a bridle trail, circles the western half of the park. Three developed picnic areas with tables, fireplaces, and rest rooms are in the park's northern section. Rest rooms and picnic areas are wheelchair-accessible.

Greenbelt Park provides a convenient place to camp for Washington, D.C., sightseers. Because downtown parking is generally limited, it is recommended that visitors either catch the Metro Bus at the stop located on Good Luck Road or drive to and park at either the College Park or Greenbelt Metro stations. Metro information is available at the campground.

ENTRANCE FEE: No charge.

FACILITIES: No lodging or food service is available in the park. Motels, restaurants, grocery stores, and service stations are nearby on Greenbelt Road and off Interstate 495 at exit 20.

CAMPING: A 174-site campground provides tables, grills, showers, a dump station, and flush toilets. Trailers are limited to 34 feet and a fourteen-day limit is imposed. The campground seldom fills. The camping fee is $13 per night (maximum fourteen days). For reservations call 1–800–365–CAMP.

See the map on page 100.

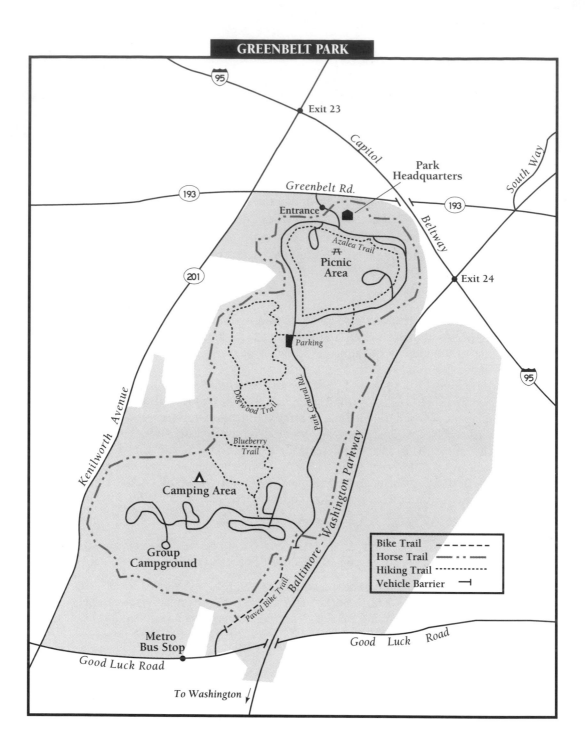

GREENBELT PARK

Bike Trail ----
Horse Trail —··—
Hiking Trail ········
Vehicle Barrier ⊢—

Exit 23

95

193

Capitol

South Way

Greenbelt Rd.

Park
Headquarters

Entrance

193

Beltway

Azalea Trail

**Picnic
Area**

Exit 24

201

Parking

Dogwood Trail

Park Central Rd.

Washington Parkway

*Blueberry
Trail*

Camping Area

Baltimore

**Group
Campground**

Paved Bike Trail

Kenilworth Avenue

**Metro
Bus Stop**

Good Luck Road

95

Good   Luck   Road

To Washington ↓

HAMPTON NATIONAL HISTORIC SITE

535 Hampton Lane
Towson, MD 21286-1397
(410) 823–1309
hamp_superintendent@nps.gov
www.nps.gov/hamp

Hampton National Historic Site comprises sixty-two acres and was designated a part of the National Park Service in 1948 to preserve a fine example of Georgian architecture. The park is located a short distance north of Baltimore. Take exit 27B (Dulaney Valley Road North) on Interstate 695 and turn east on Hampton Lane.

This sixty-two-acre national historic site near Baltimore preserves and interprets what was once a vast agricultural and commercial estate owned by the Charles Ridgely family for more than 150 years. A large workforce that included indentured servants and slaves supported the estate. The three-story mansion was the centerpiece of what once was an estate of 24,000 acres, including an iron foundry, farm, formal grounds, and gardens. Some twenty buildings and 40,000 artifacts survive. The mansion interior is decorated to reflect the late eighteenth

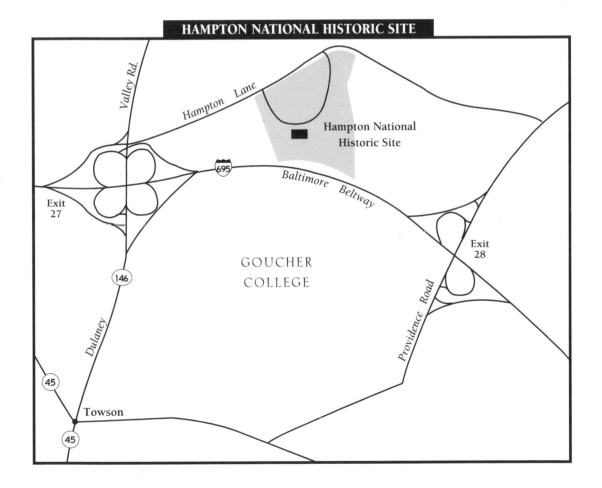

to late nineteenth century, and visitors may see many of the original Ridgely possessions.

The mansion is open for tours every day from 9:00 A.M. to 4:00 P.M. It is closed on Thanksgiving, Christmas Day, and New Year's Day. The formal gardens and grounds of Hampton, including many native and exotic specimen trees, contribute to the grandeur of the estate. Twenty-four outbuildings, including slave quarters and stables, may also be viewed.

ENTRANCE FEE: No charge. There is a $5.00 fee for a tour of the mansion.

FACILITIES: Lodging is not available at the site but can be obtained in nearby Towson. A gift shop, rest rooms, and drinking water are available.

CAMPING: No camping is permitted at the site. Patapsco State Park, near Interstate 695 on Baltimore's west side, offers camping facilities.

MONOCACY NATIONAL BATTLEFIELD
4801 Urbanna Pike
Frederick, MD 21704-7307
(301) 662–3515
Cathy_Beeler@nps.gov
www.nps.gov/mono

Monocacy National Battlefield was authorized in 1934 to commemorate the site of an 1864 Civil War battle in which Union forces, although defeated, delayed the Confederates long enough to mount a successful defense of Washington, D.C. The park is located in Maryland, 4 miles south of Frederick where Interstate 270 intersects the Monocacy River. The center of the battlefield may be reached by exiting off Interstate 70 to State Highway 355 south. From 270 take the Urbana exit.

With Grant's Federal forces stymied in their move toward Richmond and the other Union army in West Virginia, Robert E. Lee ordered Confederate General Jubal Early to march down the Shenandoah Valley and attack Washington. Near Frederick, a small Union force under the command of General Lew Wallace was able to delay the attack and provide time for reinforcements to arrive to Washington D.C., thus preventing the Confederates from taking the city.

Gambrill Mill Visitor Center, 3 miles south of Frederick on State Highway 355, offers an electric battle map and exhibits of artifacts. Self-guided auto tours of the battlefield and its five accessible monuments begin here. The visitor center is open daily 8:00 A.M. until 4:30 P.M. from April 1 to October 31 and until 5:30 on weekends, and Wednesday through Sunday the remainder of the year. Self-guided hiking trails are also within the park. Although the National Park Service is in the process of acquiring land within the park boundaries, some of the property currently remains under private ownership. Visitors to the battlefield should consider a walking tour of nearby Frederick. The county tourism council is at 19 East Church Street (301–663–8703).

ENTRANCE FEE: No charge.

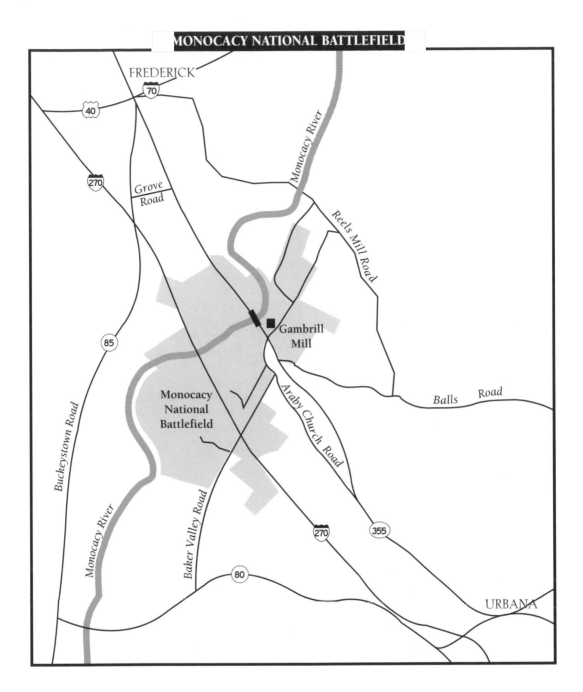

FREDERICK

Monocacy River

Grove Road

Reels Mill Road

Gambrill Mill

Monocacy National Battlefield

Balls Road

Buckeystown Road

Monocacy River

Araby Church Road

Baker Valley Road

URBANA

FACILITIES: Rest rooms and drinking water are available at the visitor center. Food and lodging are 2 miles north in the town of Frederick.

CAMPING: No camping is permitted in the battlefield. Nineteen miles north, Catoctin Mountain Park, a unit of the National Park Service, offers a nice campground with fifty-one heavily wooded sites with tables, grills, water, and modern rest rooms. Near Catoctin, Cunningham State Park offers 148 sites with showers.

PISCATAWAY PARK

c/o National Capital Parks–East
1900 Anacostia Drive, S.E.
Washington, DC 20020-6722
(301) 763–4600
www.nps.gov/pisc

Piscataway Park was authorized in 1961 and preserves more than 4,200 acres of scenic and historical land along the shoreline of the Potomac River across from Mount Vernon. The park is located 19 miles south of the District of Columbia via Indian Head Highway (Maryland Highway 210). Ten miles south of Interstate 495, turn right onto Bryan Point Road at the Accokeek traffic light. The park is 4 miles west on the Potomac River. Marshall Hall is accessible from Highway 210 onto Highway 223.

Piscataway Park, named for the Piscataway Indians who inhabited this area from the fourteenth to the eighteenth century, consists of cultivated fields, tidal swamps and marshes, and wood thickets. Foot access along the Potomac is available from the ends of Bryan Point and Wharf roads, where boat launching is also possible. At low tide, most of the shore is accessible for hiking. At the end of Bryan Point Road, National Colonial Farm, an agricultural-historical project of Accokeek Foundation, provides an exhibit and demonstration of agricultural methods, crops, and livestock of a modest tidewater farm of the mid-eighteenth century.

ENTRANCE FEE: No charge. The National Colonial Farm charges an admission of $5.00 per family, $2.00 for an adult, or 50 cents per child.

FACILITIES: Rest rooms and drinking water are available at the National Colonial Farm and Marshall Hall. Picnic facilities are in Saylor Memorial Grove.

CAMPING: No camping is permitted in the park.

FISHING: Fishing from the bank is permitted with a Maryland fishing license. Carp, catfish, and perch are possible catches. A fishing pier is available.

THOMAS STONE NATIONAL HISTORIC SITE

6655 Rose Hill Road
Port Tobacco, MD 20677-3400
(301) 934–6027
www.nps.gov/thst

Thomas Stone National Historic Site was authorized in 1978 to restore and preserve Haberdeventure, the Georgian mansion that was the home of Thomas Stone, a signer of the Declaration of Independence and a delegate to the Continental Congress. The site is in southern Maryland, about 35 miles south of

Washington, D.C., and 3 miles west of La Plata. It is 1 mile north of Maryland Highway 6 on the Rose Hill Road.

Thomas Stone was born in 1743 near Port Tobacco, Maryland. He completed his law education around 1765 and was elected to the Continental Congress in 1775. Although opposed to war, Stone voted for and signed the Declaration of Independence. He subsequently served three terms in the state Senate but declined his selection as a representative to the Constitutional Convention. Stone died October 5, 1787, after a lifetime of public service, and is buried alongside his wife, Margaret, on the Haberdeventure plantation.

Stone bought the plantation in 1770, two years after he married Margaret Brown. Many people believe that Stone purchased the 442-acre plantation with 400 pounds sterling from his wife's dowry. The tobacco plantation, which increased in size to over 1,000 acres by the time of Stone's death, was owned by the Stone family until 1936.

The site is open daily during the summer but is closed on Monday and Tuesday from Labor Day to Memorial Day. Guided mansion tours are given every hour on the hour from 10:00 A.M. to 4:00 P.M. The National Park Service plans to eventually restore the site to its 1900 appearance. Interpretation of the site centers on the life of Thomas Stone and on changes that have occurred at Haberdeventure.

ENTRANCE FEE: No charge.

FACILITIES: Rest rooms and drinking water are available at the site. Food and lodging are in La Plata, 3 miles east.

CAMPING: There are a limited number of campgrounds in the area. Information on camping is available at the visitor contact station.

Thomas Stone National Historic Site

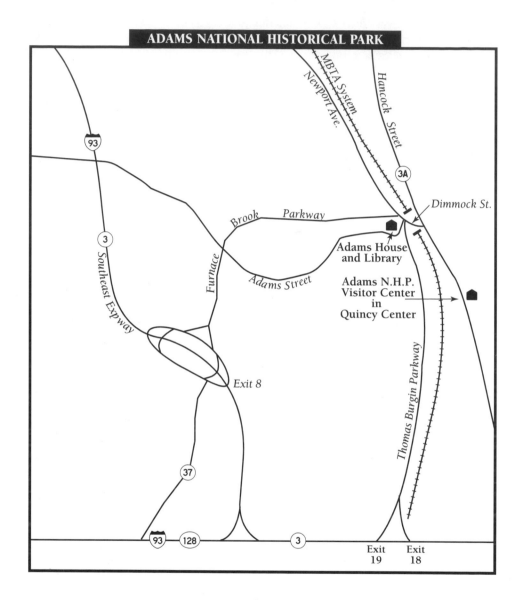

ADAMS NATIONAL HISTORICAL PARK

MBTA System

Newport Ave.

Hancock Street

93

3

3A

Brook Parkway

Dimmock St.

Adams House and Library

Adams N.H.P. Visitor Center in Quincy Center

Southeast Expway

Furnace

Adams Street

Thomas Burgin Parkway

Exit 8

37

93 128

3

Exit 19

Exit 18

MASSACHUSETTS

ADAMS NATIONAL HISTORICAL PARK

135 Adams Street
Quincy, MA 02169-1749
(617) 770–1175
ADAM_Visitor_Center@nps.gov
www.nps.gov/adam

Adams National Historical Park was designated as part of the National Park Service in 1946 to commemorate the distinguished men and women of the Adams family who dedicated their lives to the development and service of the United States. The thirteen-acre park comprises four units: the birthplaces of John Adams and John Quincy Adams; the "Old House," home to four generations of the Adams family; the United First Parish Church; and the park's visitor center, all located in Quincy, Massachusetts, 8 miles southeast of Boston. The visitor center is at 1250 Hancock Street in the Presidents Place Galleria.

The John Adams and the John Quincy Adams birthplaces are the oldest still-standing presidential birthplaces in the United States. In 1735, John Adams was born in the saltbox-style house located only 75 feet from where his son John Quincy Adams would be born in 1767. In the John Quincy Adams birthplace, young John and his bride Abigail started their family and the future president launched his career in politics and law. John Adams maintained his law office in the house and it was here that he, Samuel Adams, and James Bowdoin wrote the Massachusetts Constitution. This document, still in use, greatly influenced development of the United States Constitution.

The Old House, built in 1731 by a wealthy West Indian sugar planter, was to become the residence of four generations of the Adams family from 1787 to 1927. It was home to presidents John Adams and John Quincy Adams; first ladies Abigail and Louisa Catherine Adams; Civil War Minister to Great Britain Charles Francis Adams; and literary historians Henry and Brooks Adams. The Adams family's legacy of service to their nation is reflected as much by the 78,000 artifacts inside the Old House as by its historic landscape. Following a tour, visitors may stroll the Old House grounds, which include a historic orchard and an eighteenth-century-style formal garden containing thousands of annual and perennial flowers.

The United First Parish Church was constructed in 1828. This national landmark structure, designed by Alexander Parish, was partially financed through a generous land donation from John Adams. The crypt beneath the sanctuary of the church is the final resting place of presidents John Adams and John Quincy Adams, and first ladies Abigail and Louisa Catherine Adams.

Adams National Historical Park is open seven days a week from April 19 through November 10. The visitor center, located at 1250 Hancock Street, opens daily at 9:00 A.M. Guided tours of the site are offered approximately every hour until 3:00 P.M. Visitors must register for tours (fee charged) at the visitor center. The tour includes travel via a trolley to the historic homes. Tour space is limited and is filled on a first-come basis. Advance reservations (617–770–1175) are required for groups of eight or more.

ENTRANCE FEE: $2.00 per person, visitors sixteen and under free; good for seven days.

FACILITIES: No facilities are available at the site. Food and lodging are available in Quincy.

CAMPING: No camping is permitted at the site. Wompatuck State Park offers nice wooded campsites (400 sites) with tables, flush toilets, electrical hookups, and showers 11 miles southeast of the site in Hingham. Wompatuck State Park is reached via Highways 3, 3A, and 228. The park can be difficult to find but is seldom filled.

BLACKSTONE RIVER VALLEY NATIONAL HERITAGE CORRIDOR

1 Depot Square
Woonsocket, RI 02895
(401) 762–0440
blac_interpretation@nps.gov
www.nps.gov/blac

Blackstone River Valley National Heritage Corridor was established in 1986 to interpret the history and coordinate development along a 400,000-acre river valley that gave birth to the American Industrial Revolution. The corridor surrounds 46 miles of river and canals that run from Worcester, Massachusetts, to Providence, Rhode Island.

The American Industrial Revolution took seed and blossomed in the Blackstone River Valley of New England. The river initially attracted settlers in search of a source of food and drinking

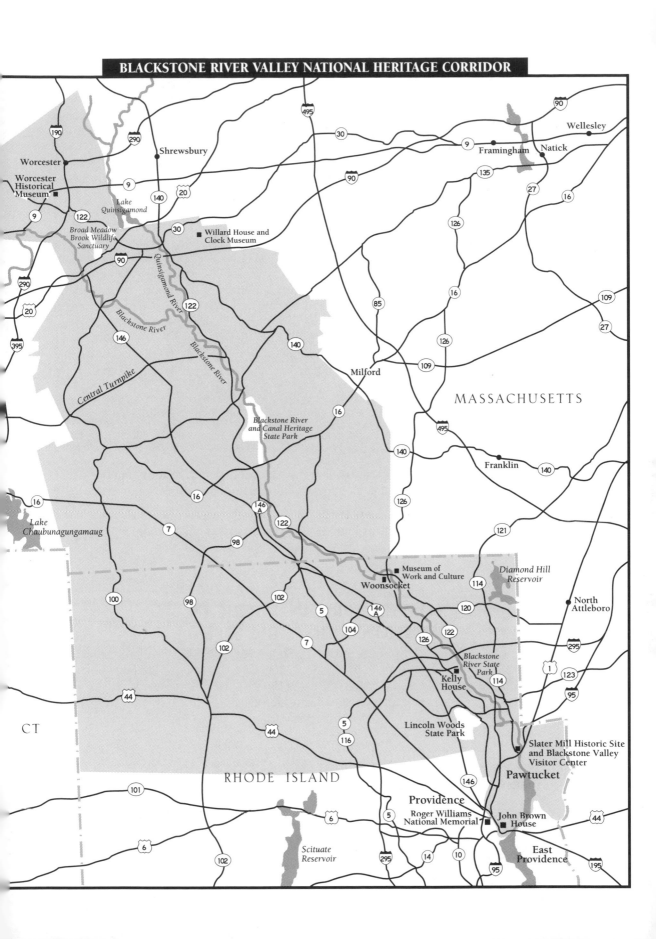

BLACKSTONE RIVER VALLEY NATIONAL HERITAGE CORRIDOR

Wellesley

Worcester

Worcester Historical Museum

Shrewsbury

Framingham

Natick

Lake Quinsigamond

Broad Meadow Brook Wildlife Sanctuary

Willard House and Clock Museum

Quinsigamond River

Blackstone River

Blackstone River

Central Turnpike

Milford

MASSACHUSETTS

Blackstone River and Canal Heritage State Park

Franklin

Lake Chaubunagungamaug

Museum of Work and Culture

Woonsocket

Diamond Hill Reservoir

North Attleboro

Blackstone River State Park

Kelly House

CT

Lincoln Woods State Park

Slater Mill Historic Site and Blackstone Valley Visitor Center

RHODE ISLAND

Pawtucket

Providence

Roger Williams National Memorial

John Brown House

Scituate Reservoir

East Providence

water. Later the river attracted craftsmen and industrialists who constructed diversionary dams to provide power for small machinery, textile mills, iron forges, and gristmills. Falls along the Blackstone prevented the river from being widely used for transportation until canals were constructed to circumvent these obstructions. Visitors can walk along sections of the canal and towpath in state parks in Lincoln, Rhode Island, and Uxbridge, Massachusetts. Railroads made water transportation along the canals obsolete by the mid-1800s.

The Blackstone River Valley continues to provide a link to its agricultural and industrial roots. Hilltop villages where settlers lived before the industrial development and mill villages that provided housing to the thousands of workers remain as a testament to the history of this valley. Farmlands characterized by open fields, stone walls, and orchards are uphill from the river.

No federal lands are within the heritage corridor. The National Park Service works with state and local governments and historic and environmental organizations to protect the valley's heritage and to plan for its future. The Blackstone Valley Visitor Center, located at 171 Main Street in Pawtucket, RI (401–724–2200), offers an introductory film about the valley and hundreds of brochures and guides to local sites, including a number of self-guided walking tours. Other information centers are at: Roger Williams National Memorial, 282 North Main Street, Providence, RI 02903 (401–521–7266); Museum of Work and Culture, 42 South Main Street, Woonsocket, RI 02895 (401–769–9675); River Bend Farm Visitor Center, Blackstone River and Canal Heritage State Park, 287 Oak Street, Uxbridge, MA (508–278–7604); Broad Meadow Brook Wildlife Sanctuary, Massachusetts Audubon, 414 Massasoit Road, Worcester, MA 01604 (508–753–6087).

ENTRANCE FEE: No charge.

FACILITIES: A wide variety of restaurants and accommodations are in the Blackstone River Valley.

CAMPING: Several private campgrounds are in the national heritage corridor. Camping facilities and directions can be obtained at an information center or chamber of commerce.

FISHING: Fishing is permitted in the Blackstone River, and the many other water ways in the corridor, with a valid Massachusetts or Rhode Island fishing license, depending on which side of the border you are on.

BOSTON AFRICAN-AMERICAN NATIONAL HISTORIC SITE

14 Beacon Street, Suite 506
Boston, MA 02108
(617) 742–5415
bernadette_williams@nps.gov
www.nps.gov/boaf

Boston African-American National Historic Site was established in 1980 to preserve and commemorate original buildings that housed the nineteenth-century free African-American community on Beacon Hill. The site is located in downtown Boston in the Beacon Hill area just north of Boston Common.

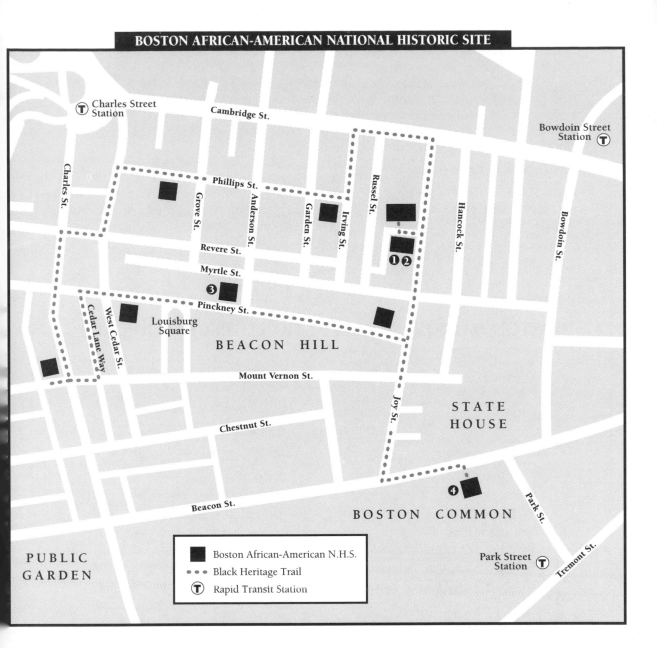

BOSTON AFRICAN-AMERICAN NATIONAL HISTORIC SITE

Charles Street Station

Cambridge St.

Bowdoin Street Station

Charles St.

Phillips St.

Grove St.

Anderson St.

Garden St.

Irving St.

Russel St.

Hancock St.

Bowdoin St.

Revere St.

Myrtle St.

❶❷

3

Pinckney St.

Cedar Lane Way

West Cedar St.

Louisburg Square

BEACON HILL

Mount Vernon St.

Joy St.

STATE HOUSE

Chestnut St.

Beacon St.

❹

BOSTON COMMON

Park St.

PUBLIC GARDEN

Park Street Station

Tremont St.

Boston African-American N.H.S.

Black Heritage Trail

Rapid Transit Station

The first Africans arrived in Boston in 1638 as slaves. Additional slaves continued to be brought to Boston, but at the same time, a significant free black population became a part of the city. By the late 1700s, a federal census listed no slaves in the entire state of Massachusetts.

Boston African-American National Historic Site comprises the area of the city where African-Americans pressed for civil rights, pursued the political process, and forced an end to school segregation and slavery. The site is best seen by following the Black Heritage Trail, which is identified by signs and winds through the Beacon Hill area. A fairly brisk walk along the trail requires about two hours and includes a couple of steep hills. Included on the walking tour are twelve private residences not open to the public, two public buildings, and the Robert Gould Shaw Memorial. Among the buildings are the African Meeting House (#1 on map), which is the oldest black church building still standing in the United States, the Abiel Smith School (#2 on map), built in

1834 by a white businessman for the education of black children, and the Phillips School (#3 on map), which is one of the city's first schools with an integrated student body. Guided tours of the Black Heritage Trail are offered by the park rangers Monday through Friday at 10:00 A.M. and 2:00 P.M. The tours last approximately two hours, cover 1⅗ miles, and begin at the Shaw Memorial (#4 on map) across from the gold-domed state house.

Brochures on the Black Heritage Trail may be obtained at 46 Joy Street or at the visitor center of Boston National Historical Park at 15 State Street. During summer months living-history programs and films on African-American history are presented.

ENTRANCE FEE: No charge.

FACILITIES: No food or lodging are provided by the National Park Service, but both are available nearby. Rest rooms and drinking water are at the African Meeting House and the Abiel Smith School.

CAMPING: No camping is available at the site. (See the camping section under Boston National Historical Park.)

BOSTON HARBOR ISLANDS NATIONAL RECREATION AREA

National Park Service
Office of the Project Manager
408 Atlantic Avenue
Boston, MA 02210-3350
(617) 223–8666
BOHA_information@nps.gov
www.bostonislands.com

The Boston Harbor Islands were added to the national park system in 1996. The thirty islands in Boston harbor range in size from less than one acre to more than 200 acres. The islands are within 2 to 4 miles of the mainland and 4 to 10 miles of the City of Boston. From downtown Boston, access is via a forty-minute ferry ride (call 617–223–8666 for schedules) from Long Wharf (Aquarium Station on the MBTA Blue Line). Ferry service is also available from Quincy, Hingham, and Hull on the South Shore. A free water shuttle offers frequent service from George's Island to several other islands.

The National Park Service is part of a thirteen-member partnership that manages the thirty islands comprising Boston Harbor Islands National Recreation Area. The islands offer activities such as beachcombing, hiking, swimming, picnicking, and birdwatching. Among the islands comprising the national recreation area are:

1. **Bumpkin Island** (thirty-five acres) has trails that lead to the remains of a stone farmhouse and children's hospital.

2. **Great Brewster Island** (twenty-three acres) has a path that leads to the summit of the northern bluff and several spur paths along the remains of WWII-era roads and paths.

3. **George's Island** (twenty-eight acres) houses Fort Warren, a National Historic Landmark,

consisting of a granite fort constructed between 1833 and 1869. Guided tours and special programs are offered from May through October.

4. **Grape Island** (fifty acres) is a wild island that serves as a haven for wildlife. Trails are available.

5. **Little Brewster Island** (four acres) is home to Boston Light, the oldest continually used light station in the U.S. Call (617) 223–8666 for information on scheduled tours. The program fee is $25–$29. Discounts are available for seniors, children, and groups.

6. **Lovell's Island** (sixty-two acres) offers dunes, a salt marsh, woods, and the remains of a fort. It includes picnic areas and a supervised swimming beach.

7. **Peddock's Island** (188 acres) has the remains of Fort Andrews, which was active from 1904 until the end of World War II. Hiking trails lead around a pond and salt marsh.

8. **Thompson Island** (157 acres) offers historic buildings, conference facilities, guided tours, hiking, and educational programs. Open to the public on Saturdays in the summer. Call (617) 223–8666 for information.

ENTRANCE FEE: No charge. There is a ferry fee: $8.00 adult, $7.00 senior, $6.00 ages four through twelve, three and under free.

FACILITIES: Visitors are advised to bring their own drinking water because none is available on the islands. George's Island has a concession stand.

CAMPING: Camping is available on Bumpkin Island, Grape Island, Lovell's Island, and Peddock's Island. Call (617) 223–8666 for information.

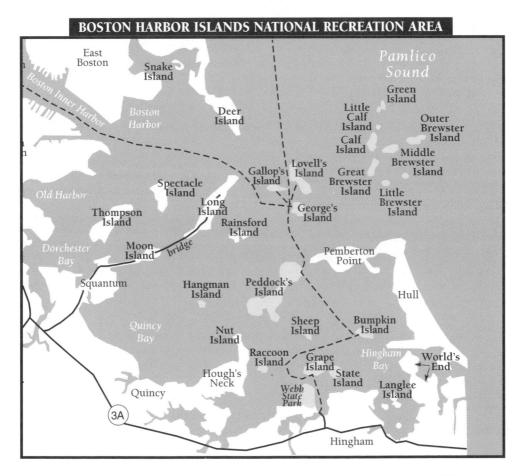

BOSTON HARBOR ISLANDS NATIONAL RECREATION AREA

BOSTON NATIONAL HISTORICAL PARK

Charlestown Navy Yard
Boston, MA 02129-4543
(617) 242–5642 and 242–5601
BOST_email@nps.gov
www.nps.gov/bost

Boston National Historical Park was established in 1974 to preserve a number of Boston's oldest and most important historic structures. Most, such as Faneuil Hall, have associations with the American Revolution. The park also includes the Charlestown Navy Yard, the location of the USS *Constitution* and the only American navy yard preserved as a historic site.

Although the original settlers of present-day Boston fled from England in an attempt to escape religious persecution, their descendants played an active role in the history of the British Empire. Great Britain emerged from the Seven Years' War in 1763 as the dominant power in North America. Starting in 1765, however, colonists began to openly resist the mother country's determined efforts to strictly control the colonies. John Hancock and Samuel Adams denounced oppressive British policies at town meetings in Faneuil Hall and the Old State House. In 1773 a town meeting in the Old South Meeting House resulted in a march to the waterfront, where cargoes of tea were dumped into the harbor. In 1775 lanterns were hung in the steeple of Old North Church to warn the Charlestown militia of the movement of British troops toward Concord, in case Paul Revere was unable to deliver the same message in person. Two months after the conflicts at Lexington and Concord, British troops landed near the present-day Charlestown Navy Yard and clashed with American soldiers from Charlestown in the Battle of Bunker Hill. In 1776, after the British had occupied Boston for twenty-one months, Washington's troops fortified Dorchester Heights with artillery, leading the enemy to abandon the city.

Boston National Historical Park is a group of federal, private, and municipal sites that have related themes. Many of the sites provide interpretive services such as exhibits and talks; some also have guided tours, concerts, encampments, historical demonstrations, audiovisual, and educational programs. A visitor's first stop should be the National Park Service Visitor Center at 15 State Street across from the Old State House. Here visitors will find park personnel to answer questions and a slide program on sites along the Freedom Trail. From mid-April through late November, rangers lead frequent one-and-one-half-hour walks along the downtown section of the trail. The Freedom Trail begins at Boston Common, winds through the historic district and the Charlestown Navy Yard, and ends in Charlestown at the Bunker Hill Monument. The Navy Yard is where the USS *Constitution* is berthed and another visitor center is located. Visitors may take guided tours of the *Constitution* and the USS *Cassin Young,* a World War II destroyer. The entire trail, which is marked by a red line on the sidewalk, is $2\frac{1}{2}$ miles long. Sixteen historic sites are along the route.

Unless you are staying in a downtown hotel, it is best to park outside the city and take the rapid-transit system into the downtown area. Limited parking is available at Charlestown Navy Yard. The Greater Boston Convention and Visitors Bureau maintains an information booth on Boston Common. The booth is near the Park Street exit of the T (rapid transit system). Freedom Trail maps are available at the information booth and at the visitor center.

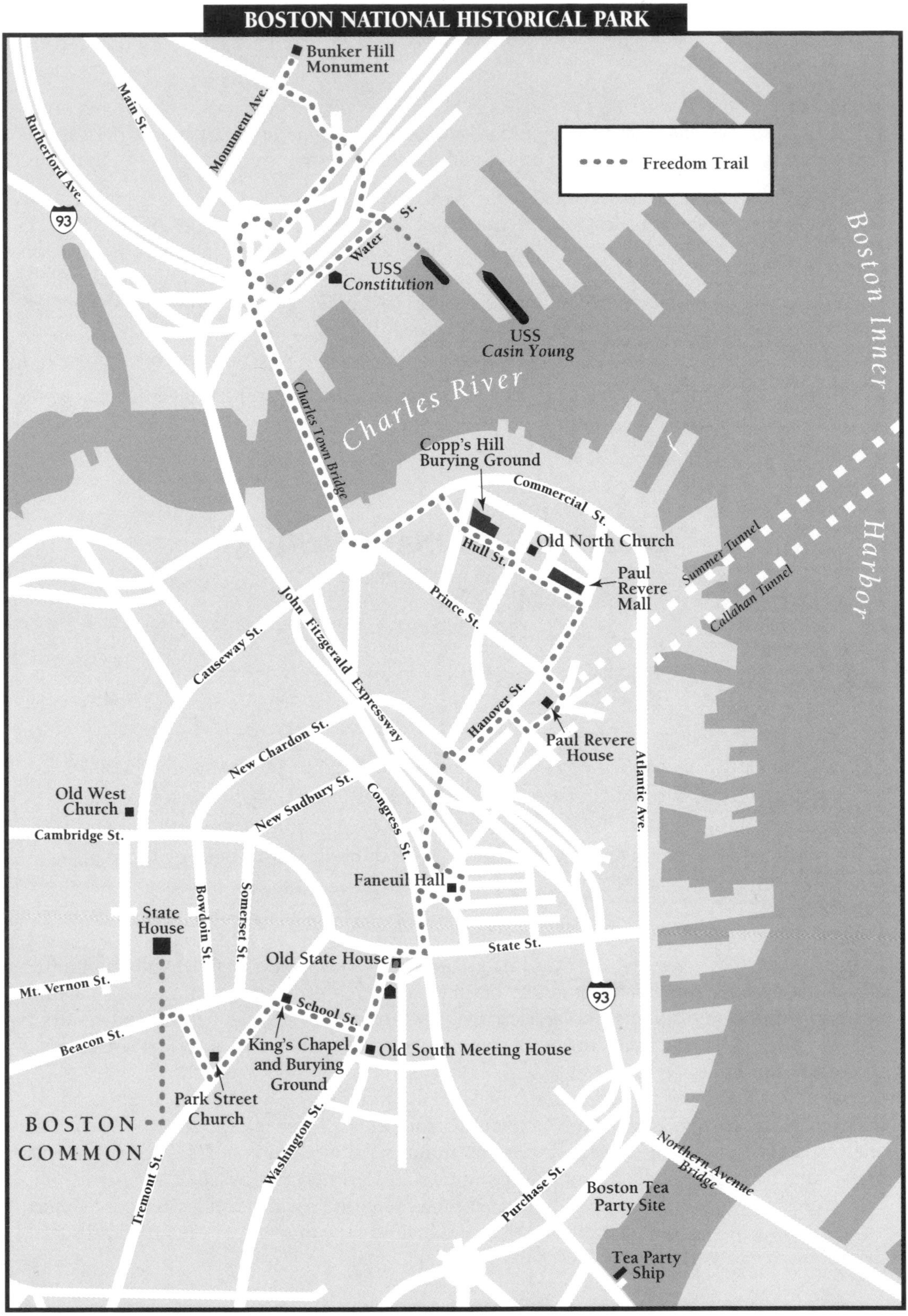

BOSTON NATIONAL HISTORICAL PARK

Bunker Hill Monument

Main St.

Monument Ave.

Rutherford Ave.

93

Water St.

USS *Constitution*

USS *Casin Young*

Charles Town Bridge

Freedom Trail

Charles River

Boston Inner Harbor

Copp's Hill Burying Ground

Commercial St.

Hull St.

Old North Church

Paul Revere Mall

Summer Tunnel

Callahan Tunnel

Prince St.

Causeway St.

John Fitzgerald Expressway

Hanover St.

Paul Revere House

Atlantic Ave.

New Chardon St.

Old West Church

New Sudbury St.

Congress St.

Cambridge St.

Faneuil Hall

Bowdoin St.

Somerset St.

State House

State St.

93

Old State House

Mt. Vernon St.

School St.

King's Chapel and Burying Ground

Old South Meeting House

Beacon St.

Washington St.

Park Street Church

BOSTON COMMON

Tremont St.

Purchase St.

Northern Avenue Bridge

Boston Tea Party Site

Tea Party Ship

ENTRANCE FEE: No charge at the sites run by the National Park Service. Other sites that do collect fees are the Old South Meeting House, Old State House, Paul Revere House, and the USS *Constitution* Museum.

FACILITIES: All visitor services are available along the route. A special treat is selecting something to eat among the great variety of food vendors in Faneuil Hall Marketplace. Rest rooms and drinking water are at the visitor center and the Charlestown Navy Yard.

CAMPING: No camping is permitted in the park areas. The nearest public camping for those wishing to visit downtown Boston is at Wompatuck State Park, south of the city in Hingham (617–749–7160). Here campers will find 400 shaded spaces with water, tables, grills, flush toilets, a dump station, and showers. Some sites have electricity. From Highway 3, take exit 15 and Highway 228 4½ miles north to Free Street. Turn right on Free Street and drive slightly less than a mile to the park. No reservations are accepted. Boston's rapid-transit system has a stop in Braintree, about 9 miles away from the park.

FISHING: Fishing is available at a number of spots in the city, including from the bridge crossing to the Charlestown Navy Yard.

CAPE COD NATIONAL SEASHORE

99 Marconi Site Road
Wellfleet, MA 02667-0250
(508) 349–3785
www.nps.gov/caco

Cape Cod National Seashore was authorized in 1961 to protect nearly 45,000 acres (27,000 acres of land area) of ocean beaches, dunes, woodlands, freshwater ponds, and marshes. The park is on the Cape Cod Peninsula in southeastern Massachusetts and is reached by auto via U.S. 6 or by air service or ferryboat from Boston to Provincetown.

On this peninsula, where the Pilgrims first glimpsed the New World, visitors will find numerous outdoor activities. Visitor centers in Eastham and Provincetown contain exhibits, audio-visual programs, and information services to help introduce the area's natural and historical features. The visitor centers are open from spring until early winter. Call ahead for seasonal closure dates and hours.

Self-guided trails are located at Beech Forest, Pilgrim Heights, Pamet Area, Great Island, the Marconi Station Site, Fort Hill, and Salt Pond Visitor Center. Three bike paths with bike rentals are nearby. Lifeguards are present during the summer for swimming at Coast Guard, Nauset Light, Marconi, Head of the Meadow, Race Point, and Herring Cove beaches. Over-sand vehicles require a permit and must use designated sand routes in Province Lands Area only. Guided walks, talks, and evening programs take place daily during summer and on a reduced schedule in spring and fall seasons.

Old North Church in Boston National Historic Park (opposite page)

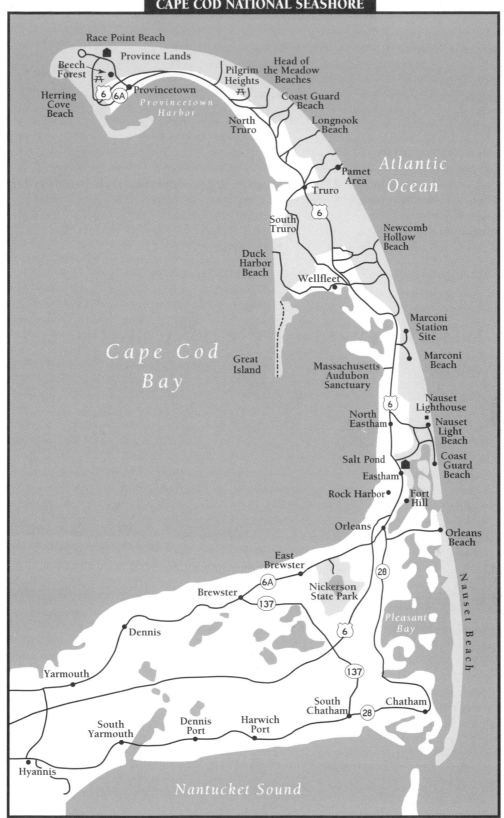

CAPE COD NATIONAL SEASHORE

Race Point Beach

Province Lands

Beech Forest

Pilgrim Heights

Head of the Meadow Beaches

Herring Cove Beach

Provincetown

6 6A

Provincetown Harbor

Coast Guard Beach

North Truro

Longnook Beach

Atlantic Ocean

Pamet Area

Truro

6

South Truro

Newcomb Hollow Beach

Duck Harbor Beach

Wellfleet

Cape Cod Bay

Great Island

Marconi Station Site

Marconi Beach

Massachusetts Audubon Sanctuary

6

Nauset Lighthouse

North Eastham

Nauset Light Beach

Salt Pond

Coast Guard Beach

Eastham

Rock Harbor

Fort Hill

Orleans

Orleans Beach

East Brewster

Nauset Beach

6A

28

Brewster

137

Nickerson State Park

Pleasant Bay

Dennis

6

Yarmouth

137

South Chatham

Chatham

South Yarmouth

Dennis Port

Harwich Port

28

Hyannis

Nantucket Sound

Nauset Lighthouse at Cape Cod National Seashore (opposite page)

ENTRANCE FEE: $7.00 per vehicle or $1.00 per person for beach access from late June to early September.

FACILITIES: No food or lodging is provided by the National Park Service, although a concessioner sells refreshments at Herring Cove Beach. Drinking water and modern rest rooms are located at both visitor centers and at the beaches. Motels, restaurants, groceries, and gas stations are in towns adjoining the park. Information and reservations for accommodations can be obtained by contacting the Cape Cod Chamber of Commerce, Hyannis, MA 02601 (508–362–3225).

CAMPING: No camping is provided by the National Park Service, although several private campgrounds are located in the area. The nearest public camping is at Nickerson State Park in Brewster. The campground has a dump station, water, flush toilets, and showers but no hookups. A limited number of reservations are accepted, and it fills up many months in advance of summer. Shawme Crowell State Forest, near Sandwich on Route 130, has the same facilities and fills up later in the day.

FISHING: Rainbow and brook trout and warm-water sport fish live in a number of freshwater ponds (license required). No license is required for surf fishing.

FREDERICK LAW OLMSTED NATIONAL HISTORIC SITE

99 Warren Street
Brookline, MA 02446
(617) 566–1689
FRLA_Superintendent@nps.gov
www.nps.gov/frla

Frederick Law Olmsted National Historic Site was authorized in 1979 to preserve and interpret the home and office of Olmsted, the great conservationist and founder of the profession of landscape architecture in America. The site is located 5 miles west of downtown Boston in the suburb of Brookline via Highway 9. Turn south off Highway 9 on Warren Street and drive to the intersection of Warren and Dudley. Parking is limited.

Frederick Law Olmsted (1822–1903) was born in Hartford, Connecticut, and began his career in landscape architecture with the design of New York's Central Park. It was the first of thousands of public and private landscapes throughout America attributed to the genius of Olmsted, his sons, and successors. In Brookline in 1883, Olmsted established a full-scale professional office that expanded and perpetuated his landscape design ideals, philosophy, and influence over the course of the next century. The Olmsted Archives is one of the most heavily researched museum collections in the National Park Service and contains design and planning documents detailing such treasured American landscapes as the U.S. Capitol Grounds, the White House, the Jefferson Memorial, the United States Military Academy at West Point, Great Smoky Mountains National Park, Niagara Falls Reservation, Yosemite Valley, and park systems in Boston, Chicago, Louisville, and Seattle.

Fairsted, the name given to the Olmsted home and office, serves as both a historic house museum and a center for the study and preservation of American landscapes. The scope and

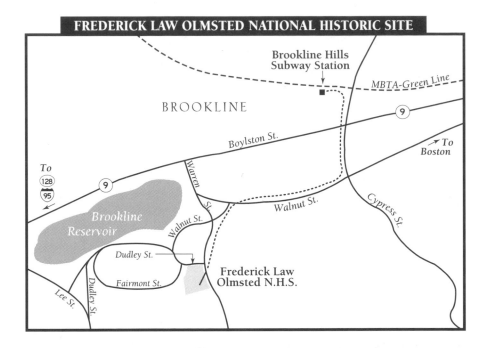

FREDERICK LAW OLMSTED NATIONAL HISTORIC SITE

Brookline Hills
Subway Station

MBTA-Green Line

BROOKLINE

Boylston St.

9

To
Boston

To
128
95

9

Warren St.

Walnut St.

Brookline
Reservoir

Walnut St.

Cypress St.

Dudley St.

Fairmont St.

Frederick Law
Olmsted N.H.S.

Lee St.

Dudley St.

Photographic archives in the historic Olmsted office, where photographs representing thousands of landscape design projects nationwide are stored. (Courtesy J. David Bohl)

magnitude of Olmsted's design work is presented to visitors through exhibits, films, and tours of the historic office and grounds. The Olmsted Archives assists researchers with documentation, while the Olmsted Center for Landscape Preservation shares technical expertise in historic landscape preservation and maintenance. Visitor hours are Friday, Saturday, and Sunday from 10:00 A.M. to 4:30 P.M. Groups and researchers are accommodated at other times by appointment.

ENTRANCE FEE: No charge.

FACILITIES: Full facilities are available in nearby Brookline.

CAMPING: No camping is permitted at the site. (See camping section under Boston National Historical Park.)

JOHN FITZGERALD KENNEDY NATIONAL HISTORIC SITE

83 Beals Street
Brookline, MA 02446-6010
(617) 566–7937
FRLA_Superintendent@nps.gov
www.nps.gov/jofi

John Fitzgerald Kennedy National Historic Site was authorized as part of the National Park Service in 1967 to preserve the house that was the birthplace and early boyhood home of the thirty-fifth president of the United States. The site is located a short distance west of Boston in the suburb of Brookline at 83 Beals Street. Limited street parking is available and the site is easily reached by public transportation.

This house was purchased by Joseph P. Kennedy in 1914 just prior to his marriage to Rose Fitzgerald. During their residence here, four of their children—Joseph Jr. (1915), John (1917), Rosemary (1918), and Kathleen (1920)—were born. In 1921, the house was sold to a friend, and the Kennedys moved to a larger home on the corner of Abbottsford and Naples Road (#1 on map). John F. Kennedy lived in this second house from age four to ten. The birthplace home was repurchased by the Kennedys in 1966, and the restoration and refurnishing to its 1917 appearance was supervised by Rose Kennedy.

The historic site is open Wednesday through Sunday (10:00 A.M. to 4:30 P.M.) from mid-April to mid-November. Park ranger–guided tours (fee charged) of the home are offered periodically throughout the day. Exhibits and a video presentation are available in the small visitor center. The site's interior is not wheelchair-accessible. In addition to this home and the second house purchased by Joseph P. Kennedy, the area also contains St. Aidan's Catholic Church, where the Kennedy children were baptized (#2 on map); Edward Devotion School, where John and Joseph, Jr., began their formal education (#4 on map); and the site of Dexter School, where the boys soon transferred (#3 on map). The historic house in front of the school building is open to the public on Tuesdays and Thursdays from 2:30 to 5:00 P.M. The house on Naples Road is privately owned, and the owner's privacy and property must be respected. Visitors are asked to view the home only from the sidewalk or from across the street. Neighborhood walking tours are offered by park rangers throughout the summer.

ENTRANCE FEE: No charge, but there is a $2.00 fee (visitors sixteen and under free) for entrance and a guided tour of the birthplace home.

FACILITIES: No facilities are available at the site, but food and lodging may be found nearby.

CAMPING: No camping is permitted at the site. (See the camping section under Boston National Historical Park.)

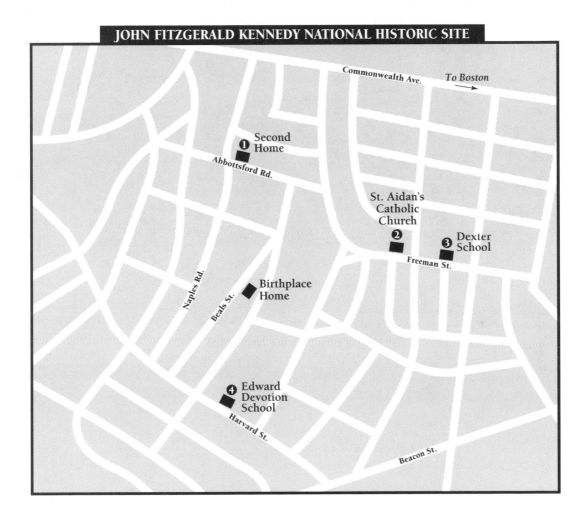

JOHN FITZGERALD KENNEDY NATIONAL HISTORIC SITE

John F. Kennedy National Historic Site—JFK's bedroom, which he shared with his brother.

LONGFELLOW NATIONAL HISTORIC SITE

105 Brattle Street
Cambridge, MA 02138-3407
(617) 876–4491
FRLA_Longfellow_NHS@nps.gov
www.nps.gov/long

Longfellow National Historic Site comprises two acres and was authorized in 1972 to preserve the home where poet Henry Wadsworth Longfellow lived from 1837 to 1882. The house is located at 105 Brattle Street in Cambridge, Massachusetts, a suburb of Boston.

Henry Wadsworth Longfellow was born in Portland, Maine, in 1807. In 1835, he accepted a position at Harvard after being graduated from Bowdoin College and studying in Europe for three years. The house into which he was to move two years later was built in 1759 for a wealthy Tory who fled prior to the Revolution. Later, during the siege of Boston, George Washington used the home as his headquarters. It was here that Longfellow wrote his most famous poetry, including *Evangeline, Hiawatha,* and *The Courtship of Miles Standish.*

The house is open for guided tours Wednesday through Sunday from mid-March to mid-December. The grounds are open all year. Visiting the site is sometimes a problem because of a lack of parking. There are several pay parking lots and garages in Harvard Square. Two handicapped-accessible parking spaces are on the site. Another solution is to park in Boston under the Boston Common and take the Red Line subway to Harvard Square. From here, a ⅗-mile walk up Brattle Street takes you past two colonial mansions. Returning to Harvard Square by way of Mason Street you pass the site of Washington Elm, under whose branches George Washington accepted command of the Continental Army.

An interesting side trip is a guided tour of Harvard University. The tours leave twice daily during summer months from an information center a short distance from the Harvard Square rapid-transit stop.

ENTRANCE FEE: No charge, but there is a $2.00 fee (visitors sixteen and under free) for entrance and a tour of the house.

FACILITIES: Drinking water and modern rest rooms are in the visitor center, and food and lodging can be found nearby. Harvard Square near the rapid-transit stop is filled with restaurants.

CAMPING: No camping is permitted on the site. (See the camping section under Boston National Historical Park.)

See the map on page 126.

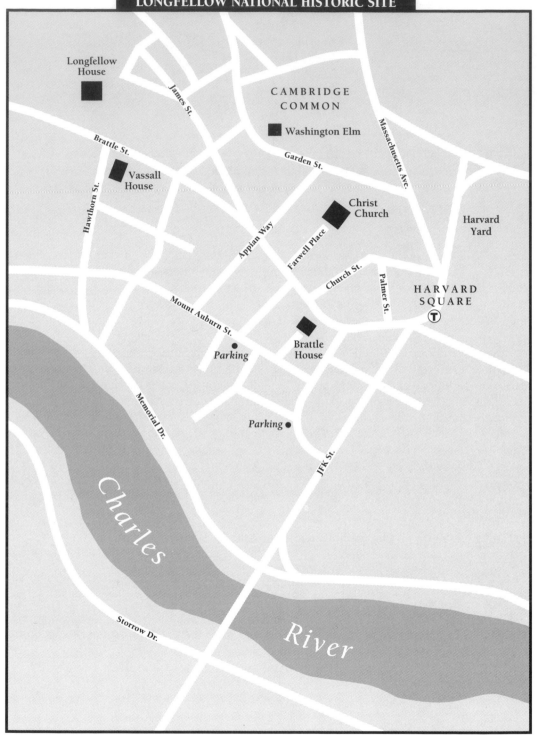

Longfellow
House

James St.

CAMBRIDGE
COMMON

Washington Elm

Massachusetts Ave.

Brattle St.

Garden St.

Vassall
House

Hawthorn St.

Christ
Church

Harvard
Yard

Appian Way

Farwell Place

Church St.

Palmer St.

HARVARD
SQUARE
Ⓣ

Mount Auburn St.

Parking

Brattle
House

Memorial Dr.

Parking

JFK St.

Charles

Storrow Dr.

River

LOWELL NATIONAL HISTORICAL PARK

67 Kirk Street
Lowell, MA 01852-1029
(978) 970–5000
(978) 970–5002 (TDD)
LOWE_Reservations@nps.gov
www.nps.gov/lowe

Lowell National Historical Park, with sites located throughout the city of Lowell, was authorized in 1978 to commemorate America's first planned industrial city. The park offers visitors a look at the country's past, including tours of a mill and a canal system. The historical park is in northeastern Massachusetts, approximately 30 miles northwest of Boston via U.S. 3. Take U.S. 3 or Interstate 495 to the Lowell connector. Exit the connector at Thorndike Street and follow the brown-and-white signs to Lowell National and State Parks visitor parking on Dutton Street.

The city of Lowell, America's first great industrial town, was named for Francis Cabot Lowell, who as a young man brought England's textile manufacturing technology to the United States. From a tiny rural hamlet, Lowell launched the United States into the industrial age by combining capital, labor, and technology to mass-produce cotton cloth. It is this past combined with the town's revival following decades of economic decline that is on display in the historical park.

The park's visitor center at the corner of Market and Dutton streets (246 Market Street) is open daily from 8:30 A.M. to 5:00 P.M. A large free-parking area is directly behind the visitor center. The center is in a restored mill complex on the site of one of the town's original textile facilities. Here, visitors can view exhibits and an outstanding twenty-minute multi-image video program that help to interpret the history of Lowell. Lowell National Historical Park includes historic cotton textile mills, worker housing, 5⅗ miles of canals, and industrial history exhibits. Among the latter is the Boott Cotton Mills Museum featuring a re-created weave room with ninety operating power looms and exhibits on the American Industrial Revolution. The park has numerous wayside exhibits located along the extensive network of canal walkways.

Visitors may make reservations at the visitor center for guided tours of the area. Among the tours offered are a mill and canal tour (two-and-one-half hours) by trolley, canal barge, and foot that includes a ride on the Pawtucket Canal and the Merrimack River; a waterpower tour (one-and-one-half hours) to the Guard Locks and Francis gate on the Pawtucket Canal; and Exploring Lowell tours to less frequently seen areas of the city. The mill and canal tour is given frequently and is probably the one to choose if time is limited. Another tour for visitors with limited time is the Pawtucket Canal tour.

Visitors may also take part in a variety of festivals, regattas, and markets taking place throughout the summer months. The Lowell Folk Festival, the largest free folk festival in the nation, takes place on the last full weekend in July. The Working People Exhibit is at 40 French Street. Visitors should plan on spending at least half a day and could easily take an entire day visiting the park facilities and taking two or more tours.

ENTRANCE FEE: No charge. There is a charge for the canal tours.

FACILITIES: In the vicinity of the visitor center there are a wide variety of ethnic, fast-food, and fine dining restaurants. Lodging may be found nearby. Drinking water and modern rest rooms are at the visitor center and the Boott Cotton Mills Museum.

CAMPING: No camping is permitted in the park. Harold Parker State Forest (134 sites) offers a campground with tables, grills, water, flush toilets, showers, swimming, and fishing. The forest is approximately 13 miles east of Lowell. From Highway 38, drive 7¾ miles north on Interstate 495 and 5½ miles southeast on Highway 114.

FISHING: Fishing for bass, perch, and catfish is available in the Merrimack River. A good location is directly below the Pawtucket Dam. Fishing is not permitted in the canals.

MINUTE MAN NATIONAL HISTORICAL PARK

174 Liberty Street
Concord, MA 01742-1705
(978) 369–6993
mima_info@nps.gov
www.nps.gov/mima

Minute Man National Historical Park comprises 967 acres and was designated a part of the National Park Service in 1959 to commemorate the scene of the fighting on April 19, 1775, that opened the American Revolution. The park is located northwest of Boston along Battle Road (State Highway 2A) between the towns of Lexington and Concord.

Upon hearing that colonists were stockpiling arms and ammunition in Concord, British Commander Thomas Gage sent 700 soldiers from Boston to confiscate the supplies. Patriots from Boston, including Paul Revere, heard of the plan and rode ahead to warn colonists along the way. After a short battle at Lexington Green the morning of April 19, British troops marched to Concord, where they destroyed military stores and engaged in additional fighting. As the British returned toward Boston, Americans took up positions along the route and continued to exchange fire. Later, the day's most extensive battle occurred as British forces moved out of Lexington. This action, combined with a great deal of inaccurate reporting, sparked the struggle that was to end in America's independence.

Minute Man Visitor Center is open daily from 9:00 A.M. to 5:00 P.M. (4:00 P.M. in winter). Here visitors will find interpretive exhibits, a twenty-five-minute multimedia theater presentation of "The Road to Revolution," and a park bookstore. The North Bridge Visitor Center, on Liberty Street in the town of Concord, provides interpretive exhibits, a slide show, park information, and a bookstore. The North Bridge Visitor Center is open from 9:00 A.M. to 5:00 P.M. (4:00 P.M. in winter). The best way to experience the park is to begin a tour at the Minute Man Visitor Center, take a walk along the Battle Road Trail, or attend an interpretive talk or demonstration. Other sites to visit within the park include: The Hartwell Tavern, an eighteenth-century tavern/living history center; and The Wayside: Home of Authors, once the home of Nathaniel Hawthorne, Louisa May Alcott, and Margaret Sidney (thirty-minute tour, fee charged).

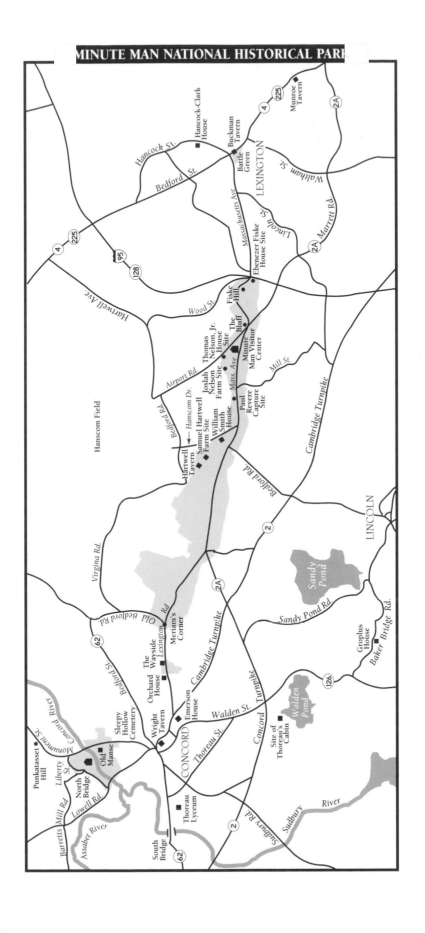

MINUTE MAN NATIONAL HISTORICAL PARK

Other interesting places include the Ralph Waldo Emerson Home (thirty-minute tour, fee); Concord Museum, with seventeen rooms of period furniture (fee charged); Old Manse, home of Emerson's grandfather (fee charged); and Walden Pond, path to site of Thoreau's cabin (parking fee). In Lexington, tours of Buckman Tavern, Munroe Tavern, and the Hancock-Clark House are sponsored by the Lexington Historical Society (fee charged). Visitors can easily spend from half a day to a full day touring the park and historic sites along the road.

ENTRANCE FEE: No charge. Wayside House tour is $4.00. (Other properties that charge fees are not operated by the National Park Service.)

FACILITIES: No food or lodging is available in the park, but both can be found nearby in Lexington or Concord. Rest rooms and water are provided at Minute Man Visitor Center and North Bridge Visitor Center as well as the Hartwell Tavern Historic Area.

CAMPING: No camping is permitted in the park. Harold Parker State Forest, 28 miles northeast of the historical park, provides 134 sites with water, tables, grills, flush toilets, showers, swimming, and fishing. From the Minute Man Visitor Center, drive ¾ mile east to Interstate 95, go 18½ miles north to U.S. 1, 1¾ miles north on 1 to Highway 114, and 6½ miles northwest on 114 to the park entrance.

NEW BEDFORD WHALING NATIONAL HISTORICAL PARK

33 William Street
New Bedford, MA 02740
(508) 996–4095
nebe_superintendent@nps.gov
www.nps.gov/nebe

New Bedford Whaling National Historical Park was authorized in 1996 to commemorate New Bedford's whaling heritage and its contribution to American history. The historical park comprises a 13-block area of New Bedford, a city of approximately 100,000, on the southeastern coast of Massachusetts; it is approximately 50 miles south of Boston via state highways 140 and 24.

New Bedford has been an American whaling center since the mid-1700s when small ships sought whales in order to collect whale blubber that was brought back to port and turned into lamp oil. Later in the 1700s, construction of larger ships allowed processing of whale blubber into oil while ships were at sea. By 1818, New Bedford had become the world center of whaling and some considered it to be one of the world's richest cities. Discovery of cheaper underground oil spelled the decline of the whaling industry and seamen living there were forced to find new employment.

This national historical park cooperates with existing organizations within a thirty-four-acre, 13-block area of New Bedford. These organizations include the New Bedford Whaling Museum, the Waterfront Historic Area League, the Schooner *Ernestina*, the city of New Bedford, and the Rotch-Jones-Duff House and Garden Museum. Information, brochures, and maps for self-guided walking tours are available from the visitor center at 33 William Street. Walking tours are offered daily during the summer months and on weekends during the rest of the year. Special programs are offered throughout the year. The visitor center is open from 9:00 A.M. to 4:00 P.M. daily except Thanksgiving, Christmas Day, and New Year's Day. A parking garage is 2 blocks away on Elm Street.

ENTRANCE FEE: No charge.

FACILITIES: Lodging and food service are in the immediate area. For information call the New Bedford Office of Tourism at (800) 508–5353. Rest rooms are in the park's visitor center.

CAMPING: Private campgrounds are in the New Bedford area. Horseneck Beach State Reservation (508–636–8816), 15 miles south of I–195 on Route 88, has one-hundred sites with flush toilets, showers, tables, grills, and a dump station.

SALEM MARITIME NATIONAL HISTORIC SITE

174 Derby Street
Salem, MA 01970-5186
(978) 740-1650
www.nps.gov/sama

This portion of the Salem waterfront was designated a national historic site in 1938 to preserve part of one of the famous port cities of early America. The nine-acre site is located on the northern Massachusetts coastline in the city of Salem. From Route 1A, turn east onto Derby Street.

Salem's maritime fame dated from the early 1700s when the town was known as home to the New World's most able sea captains. During the American Revolution, Salem's ships captured nearly 450 vessels, most of which were brought into port. Following the war, the city became a center for trade as its ships sailed to all corners of the earth in search of new markets for America's raw materials and products. Later, as ships increased in size and Americans moved westward, Salem's shallow harbor resulted in a diversion of trade to the deep-water ports of Boston and New York.

The historic site includes three wharves and a number of restored buildings clustered on the waterfront. Derby Wharf, the longest and oldest of the wharves, was built in 1762 and was once covered with fourteen warehouses. The Derby Wharf Trail leads to a small lighthouse built in 1871. Across from the wharves, the National Park Service has restored three homes, a warehouse, a scale house, a store, and the Custom House, which represented the U.S. government in issuing permits and collecting taxes.

The small Orientation Center is located on Central Wharf. The National Park Service offers guided tours and programs throughout summer months. The West India Goods Store is operated by Eastern National; goods in the store are sold to the public.

The city of Salem includes a number of tourist attractions in addition to the historic site. Among the museums and numerous restored homes are the House of the Seven Gables, the Salem Witch Museum, and the Peabody Essex Museum of Salem. The National Park Visitor Center on New Liberty and Essex streets in downtown Salem provides information on Salem and the Essex National Heritage Area, and a twenty-seven-minute film on the 400-year history of the area.

ENTRANCE FEE: No charge.

FACILITIES: No lodging or food service is available at the site, although both can be found nearby. Rest rooms and drinking water are behind the Central Wharf Orientation Center. There is no parking at the site. Visitors park in a facility across the street from the downtown visitor center.

CAMPING: No camping is permitted at the site. Approximately 10 miles northwest via Highway 114, Harold Parker State Forest offers camping (130 sites) with flush toilets, showers, boating, swimming, and fishing but no hookups. No reservations are accepted.

FISHING: Fishing is permitted along the wharf.

Custom House, Hawkes House, and Derby House, Salem Maritime National Historic Site

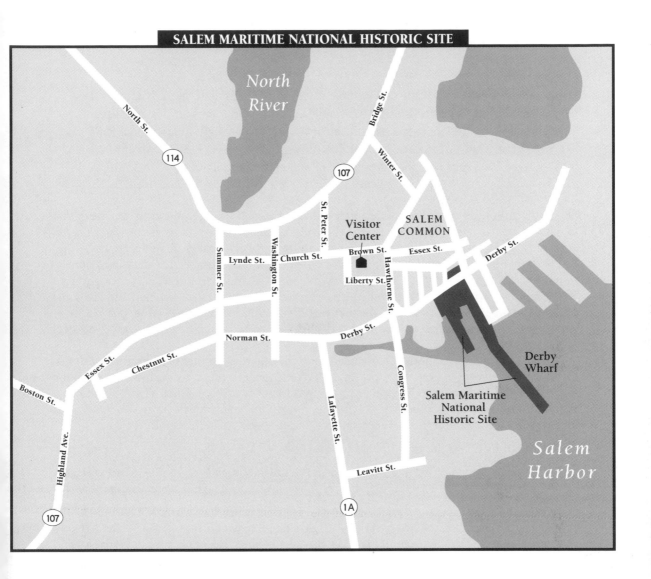

SALEM MARITIME NATIONAL HISTORIC SITE

North River

Bridge St.

North St.

114

Winter St.

107

St. Peter St.

Visitor Center

SALEM COMMON

Lynde St.

Washington St.

Church St.

Brown St.

Essex St.

Derby St.

Summer St.

Liberty St.

Hawthorne St.

Norman St.

Derby St.

Derby Wharf

Essex St.

Chestnut St.

Congress St.

Salem Maritime National Historic Site

Boston St.

Lafayette St.

Highland Ave.

Salem Harbor

107

Leavitt St.

1A

SAUGUS IRON WORKS NATIONAL HISTORIC SITE

244 Central Street
Saugus, MA 01906-2107
(781) 233–0050
www.nps.gov/sair

Saugus Iron Works National Historic Site comprises eight-and-one-half acres and was reconstructed to its mid-1600s appearance by the American Iron and Steel Institute in the 1950s. In 1969, the area was incorporated into the National Park Service. The site is located 10 miles northeast of Boston via U.S. 1. Exit at Main Street; the site is near the intersection of Main and Central Streets.

New England's need for manufactured items resulted in construction of North America's first integrated iron works at Saugus in 1646. The abundance of iron ore, streams for water power, and hardwood forests for buildings, machinery, and making charcoal prompted a group of English investors to import skilled workmen and raise capital for the project. The indirect process of producing liquid iron, which was poured into long bars and then forged into wrought iron, was used here. The works also included a rolling and slitting mill that flattened and slit some of the wrought-iron bars. Although the mill was eventually closed because of mismanagement and an inability to earn a profit, the iron works helped lay the foundation for the iron and steel industry in the United States.

Park personnel are stationed at a small entrance station to help answer visitor questions. Conducted walks begin here for a tour of the reconstructed furnace, forge, ironhouse, rolling mill, and Iron Works House. This latter building is the only original structure still standing. A brochure available at the visitor center helps visitors understand how iron was made and forged. A museum is near the entrance station. A nature trail is also available.

ENTRANCE FEE: No charge.

FACILITIES: No food or lodging is available at the site, although both can be found nearby. A drinking fountain and rest rooms are adjacent to the museum. There is a picnic area.

CAMPING: No camping is permitted at the site. Harold Parker State Forest (508–686–3391), approximately 13 miles northwest via U.S. 1 and State Highway 114, offers 130 shaded sites with flush toilets, showers, swimming, boating, and fishing. No hookups are available, and reservations are not accepted.

SPRINGFIELD ARMORY NATIONAL HISTORIC SITE

One Armory Square
Springfield, MA 01105-1299
(413) 734–8551
SPAR_Interpretation@nps.gov
www.nps.gov/spar

Springfield Armory National Historic Site was authorized in 1974 to preserve the history of the first National Armory. Armory technology and products profoundly affected the lives of soldiers and civilians alike. From Interstate 91 take Broad Street Exit (exit 4 northbound, exit 5 southbound) and follow the city's attractions sign system to the Armory. Free parking is available at museum.

The Arsenal at Springfield was established in 1777 to manufacture cartridges and gun carriages for the American Revolution. In 1794 President George Washington authorized the conversion of the arsenal to the first National Armory. For nearly 200 years the armory researched, developed, and manufactured military arms from the M1795 flintlock to the M-1 and M-14. Armory arms were essential in all major conflicts in U.S. history.

Visitors come from around the world to see the armory's last remaining operation, the museum. "Armory Industry" presents the story of important people and processes. Visitors become familiar with the "American System of Manufactures," and inventions such as the Blanchard Eccentric Lathe. The lathe and other armory inventions dramatically advanced the mass production of consumer products such as keys, shoes, baseball bats, and furniture. Important people include Women Ordnance Workers (WOWS) and inventors such as Erskine Allin, David Lyle, and John Garand. WOWS kept the armory operating and made improvements to the manufacturing process during World War II. The inventors developed the Trapdoor Springfield Rifle, Life Saving Gun, and the M-1 Rifle.

"Armory Arms" presents the story of U.S. shoulder arms, edged weapons, and pistols. Displayed are examples from our nation's largest collection of experimental and standard U.S. military arms and distinctive collections. Of special interest are Jefferson Davis's personal rifle, the collection of developmental M-1s from patent model to production model, a Texas Ranger Colt Walker, and the "Organ of Muskets" made famous by the Longfellow poem, *The Arsenal at Springfield.*

In addition, the site offers a self-guided walking tour, special exhibits, historical film, special events, and public or school programs.

ENTRANCE FEE: No charge.

FACILITIES: Open Tuesday through Sunday from 10:00 A.M. to 4:30 P.M. with the exception of Thanksgiving, Christmas Day, and New Year's Day. The buildings are wheelchair-accessible. Food and lodging are available nearby. Rest rooms and drinking water are in the museum.

CAMPING: No camping is allowed on-site. The nearest campground is at Granville State Forest, 20 miles west of Springfield on State Highway 57.

MICHIGAN

STATE TOURIST INFORMATION
(800) 543–2937
www.michigan.org

FATHER MARQUETTE NATIONAL MEMORIAL
720 Church Street
St. Ignace, MI 49781
(906) 643–9394

Father Marquette National Memorial, an affiliated fifty-two-acre area of the National Park Service, was authorized in 1975 to pay tribute to a French priest and explorer who contributed greatly to the settlement of this region of the country. The memorial is located in the southern tip of Michigan's Upper Peninsula, in Straits State Park, near the town of St. Ignace.

Jacques Marquette arrived in Quebec in 1666 as a newly ordained French priest. Over the next decade, he founded the towns of Sault Ste. Marie and St. Ignace, Michigan; discovered and helped map the upper stretches of the Mississippi River; and founded a mission at an Indian village in Illinois. In 1675, on the shore of Michigan's Lower Peninsula, Father Marquette died of disease at the age of thirty-seven.

The memorial is open 9:30 A.M. to 8:00 P.M. from mid-June to mid-September. The park comprises a memorial and an amphitheater.

ENTRANCE FEE: There is a state-park vehicle entrance fee.

FACILITIES: Food and lodging are available in St. Ignace. Rest rooms and drinking water are in the museum.

Pictured Rocks National Lakeshore (opposite page)

CAMPING: Developed campsites (275 sites) with flush toilets, showers, and electric hookups are available in Straits State Park.

ISLE ROYALE NATIONAL PARK

800 East Lakeshore Drive
Houghton, MI 49931-1895
(906) 482–0984
ISRO_Parkinfo@nps.gov
www.nps.gov/isro

Isle Royale National Park was legislated by Congress in 1931 to preserve a 571,790-acre roadless archipelago of pristine forests, lakes, and shores. The park, located in northwestern Lake Superior 16 miles from the Canadian mainland, is 45 miles long and 8½ miles wide. It is accessible only by boat or floatplane. Passenger ferries to the island are available at Houghton (National Park Service boat) or Copper Harbor, Michigan, and Grand Portage, Minnesota. A floatplane flies a regular schedule from Houghton. Reservations are required.

Isle Royale (named by French trappers) is the centerpiece of a park that is 77 percent under water. The island was created by volcanic lava flows and plate tetonics, then shaped by glaciers, wind, and water. Only 10,000 years ago the last glacier smoothed the island before pausing on its southwestern end. The interior portion of Isle Royale contains more than thirty lakes and is covered by hardwood and conifer trees. The shore areas and lake borders are generally mixed evergreen forests. More than 200 varieties of birds have been spotted here. Wildlife includes the beaver, moose, red fox, red squirrel, snowshoe hare, and timber wolf.

The island has been inhabited off and on for at least 4,500 years. Prehistoric Indians mined copper here beginning around 2500 B.C. and continued to do so until the time of European contact. Beginning in the 1840s, miners began to exploit the native copper, an industry that continued intermittently for fifty years. In the early 1900s the island was used as a vacation area; summer homes were built and a half dozen resorts were established.

The park is open to visitors April 16 to October 31, with full services offered mid-June to Labor Day. Rain is frequent, and evenings generally are cool. A variety of interpretive programs are available, including conducted walks and evening slide presentations. There are 165 miles of hiking trails in the park, including some that are self-guided. Boat tours and rental boats are available at Rock Harbor Lodge. A user fee is charged for visitors twelve and older. For current transportation schedules and rates, write the park superintendent.

ENTRANCE FEE: A $4.00 user fee is charged for visitors twelve and older.

FACILITIES: Rock Harbor Lodge has sixty motel-type units and twenty housekeeping cabins. Meals, campstore, and public showers also are available here. At Windigo, visitors will find a campstore selling snack food. For reservations and information, write Forever Resorts/N.P.C., Box 605, Houghton, MI 49931 (906–337–4993). In winter, write Forever Resorts/N.P.C., P.O. Box 27, Mammoth Cave, KY 42259 (270–773–2191).

ISLE ROYALE NATIONAL PARK

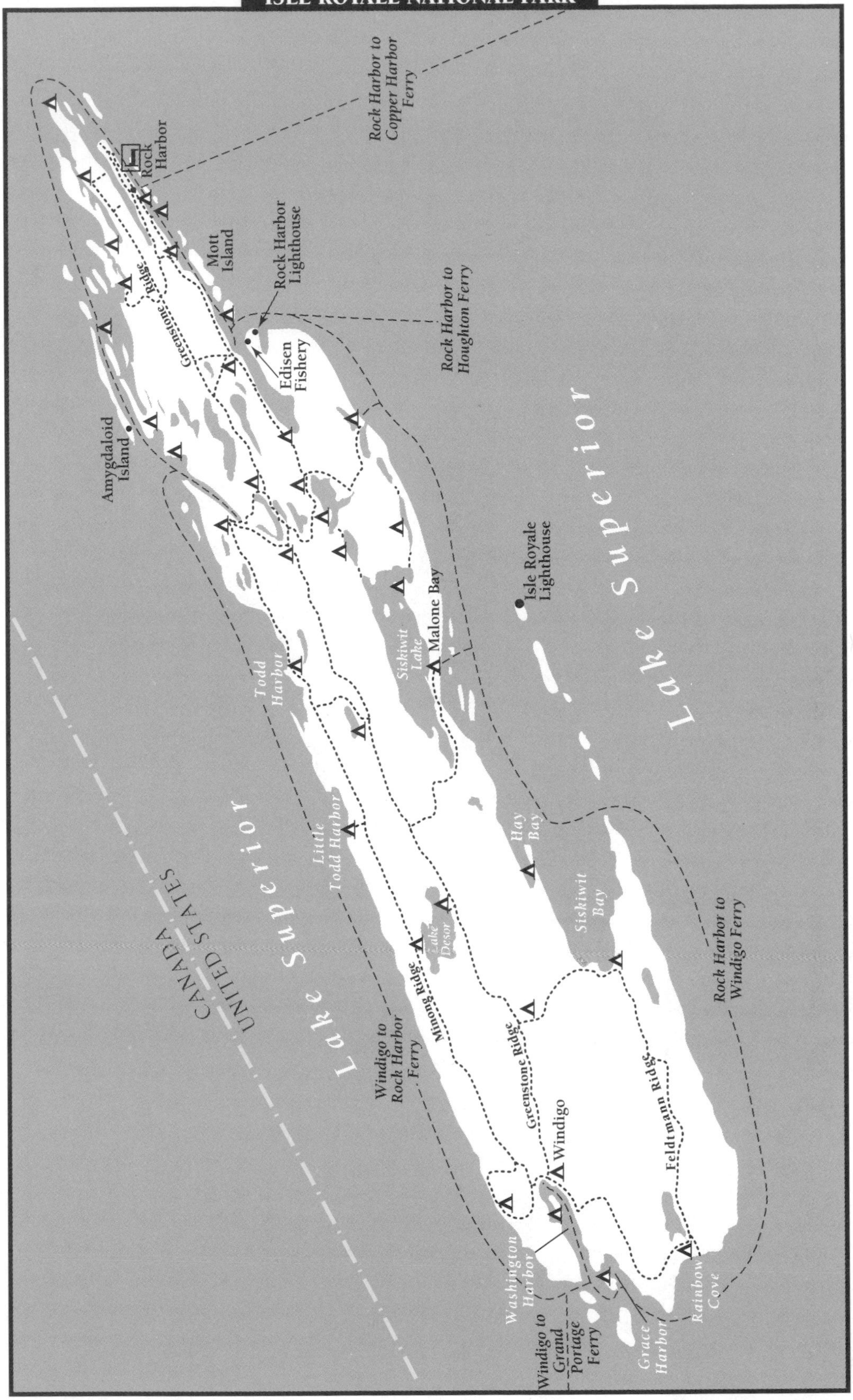

Rock Harbor to
Copper Harbor
Ferry

Rock Harbor

Mott
Island

Rock Harbor
Lighthouse

Rock Harbor to
Houghton Ferry

Edisen
Fishery

Greenstone Ridge

Amygdaloid
Island

Isle Royale
Lighthouse

L a k e   S u p e r i o r

Malone Bay

Siskiwit
Lake

Todd
Harbor

Little
Todd Harbor

Hay
Bay

L a k e   S u p e r i o r

Lake
Desor

Siskiwit
Bay

CANADA

UNITED STATES

Rock Harbor to
Windigo Ferry

Minong Ridge

Windigo to
Rock Harbor
Ferry

Greenstone Ridge

Windigo

Feldtmann Ridge

Washington
Harbor

Rainbow
Cove

Windigo to Grand
Portage Ferry

Grace
Harbor

CAMPING: Thirty-six campgrounds are on the island. Some have tables or grills, and only Rock Harbor and Washington Creek at Windigo have treated drinking water. A free camping registration permit is required and groups of seven to ten must make advance reservations.

FISHING: Northern pike inhabit twenty-eight inland lakes and Lake Superior, while lake trout are found in Lake Superior and Siskiwit Lake only. Other waters contain rainbow and brook trout, perch, walleye, and whitefish. A Michigan fishing license is required for Lake Superior waters but not for the island's inland lakes or streams. Michigan size and catch limits apply for all park waters; special rules apply to some species in the inland lakes—consult park information.

KEWEENAW NATIONAL HISTORICAL PARK

P.O. Box 471
Calumet, MI 49913-0471
(906) 337–3168
Kewe_Superintendent@nps.gov
www.nps.gov/kewe

Keeweenaw National Historical Park was established in 1992 to preserve and interpret the region's rich copper mining heritage. Two units, the Quincy and the Calumet, comprise about 1,700 acres of diverse landscape on the Keweenaw Peninsula of Michigan's Upper Peninsula.

The Keweenaw Peninsula that juts into Lake Superior is the only place in the world with commercially abundant quantities of pure native copper. It was here where America's first large-scale hard-rock industrial mining operations took place. The mines, with shafts that reached 9,000 feet deep, were critical to the development of the country.

This park is currently under development. Plans call for preservation assistance to private property owners. The National Park Service is also coordinating a series of cooperating sites that will provide interpretive and visitor services. The National Park Service offers limited ranger-guided walks and evening programs during summer months, with general visitor assistance provided by the Keweenaw Tourism Council offices in the towns of Houghton and Calumet. Call (800) 338–7982 for information. Historic Calumet is one of the focal points of the historical park, with a visitor center, museum, historic buildings, and a number of tours. Hiking and cross-country ski trails are at Fort Wilkins, Porcupine Mountains Wilderness, and McLain State Park.

Cooperating sites of Keweenaw National Historical Park include the following:

1. **A.E. Seaman Mineralogical Museum,** Michigan's official mineral museum, is located on the campus of Michigan Technological University in Houghton. Call for hours of operation, (906) 487–2572.

2. **Calumet Theatre** is one of the nation's first municipal theaters, enlarged in 1898 with a 1,200-seat opera house. Call (906) 337–2610.

Rock Harbor Lighthouse, Isle Royale National Park (photo by Bruce Weber) (opposite page)

3. **Copper Range Historical Museum,** in the village of South Range, tells the stories of the local mine workers. Call (906) 482–6125.

4. **Coppertown USA Museum** in Calumet operates out of a former Calumet & Hecla Mining Company pattern shop. Call (906) 337–4354.

5. **Delaware Copper Mine** is one of the oldest mines on the Keweenaw and offers daily tours. Call (906) 289–4688.

6. **Fort Wilkins State Park,** built in 1844, is a well-preserved example of a nineteenth-century military post. Just beyond Copper Harbor. Call (906) 289–4215.

7. **Hanka Homestead,** south of Chassell, preserves the largely unaltered small farm life of the 1900s. Call (906) 334–2601.

8. **Houghton County Historical Museum** is located in the former mill office of the Calumet & Hecla Mining Company and offers a glimpse into the daily life of a miner. Located in Lake Linden. Call (906) 296–4121.

9. **Keweenaw County Historical Museum,** in Eagle Harbor. Learn about shipping on Lake Superior and tour the lighthouse. Call (906) 289–4990.

10. **Keweenaw Heritage Center,** in the former Saint Anne's Church building in Calumet, will preserve and interpret area heritage. Currently under development. Call (906) 337–4579.

11. **Laurium Manor Inn** is a 13,000-square-foot, forty-five-room mansion built by a wealthy mining captain during the first decade of the twentieth century. Located in Laurium. Call (906) 337–2549 for reservations and tour information.

12. **McLain State Park** is located midway between Calumet and Hancock, at the north entry of the Keweenaw Waterway. Call (906) 482–0278.

13. **Old Victoria** is a well-preserved settlement of log houses built to accommodate the early settlers. Call (906) 886–2617.

14. **Porcupine Mountains Wilderness State Park** is Michigan's largest state park, containing numerous historic mining sites. Call (906) 885–5275.

15. **Quincy Mine Hoist & Underground Mine** interprets the story of the Quincy Mining Company and the largest steam hoist in the world. Call (906) 482–3101 for tour information.

16. **U.P. Firefighters Memorial Museum** is housed in the former Red Jacket (Calumet) Fire Station. Call (906) 337–4579.

ENTRANCE FEE: Fees are charged at the individual sites.

FACILITIES: Restaurants, motels, hotels, and grocery stores are located throughout the Keweenaw Peninsula.

CAMPING: McLain State Park, 7 miles west of Calumet via State Road 203, offers ninety sites with flush toilets, showers, tables, grills, and a dump station. Fort Wilkins State Park, 1 mile east of Copper Harbor on U.S. 41, has 165 sites with flush toilets, showers, tables, grills, and water. Private campgrounds are also available.

FISHING: Fishing opportunities are plentiful in this area. Both state parks offer fishing.

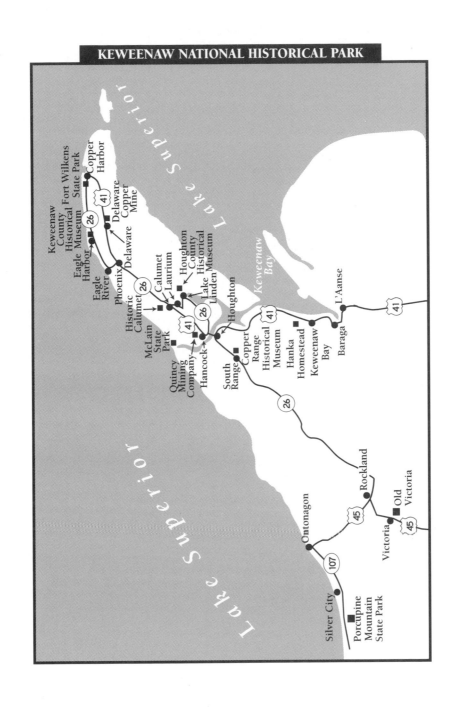

KEWEENAW NATIONAL HISTORICAL PARK

Lake Superior

Lake Superior

Keweenaw Bay

Copper Harbor

Fort Wilkens State Park

Keweenaw County Historical Museum

Eagle Museum

Delaware Copper Mine

41

26

Eagle Harbor

Eagle River

Phoenix

Delaware

Calumet

Laurium

Houghton County Historical Linden Museum

26

Historic Calumet

Lake Linden

McLain State Park

41

26

Houghton

L'Aanse

41

Quincy Mining Company

Hancock

41

Copper Range Historical Museum

Hanka Homestead

Keweenaw Bay

Baraga

South Range

Ontonagon

26

Rockland

45

Rockland

Victoria

Old Victoria

45

107

Victoria

Silver City

Porcupine Mountain State Park

PICTURED ROCKS NATIONAL LAKESHORE

P.O. Box 40
Munising, MI 49862-0040
(906) 387–3700
piro_information@nps.gov
www.nps.gov/piro

Pictured Rocks National Lakeshore, authorized in 1966, comprises more than 72,000 acres of multicolored cliffs, broad beaches, sand dunes, waterfalls, ponds, and forests. The park is located along a 40-mile stretch of Lake Superior's south shore. Michigan's Upper Peninsula, between the communities of Munising and Grand Marais.

The Pictured Rocks National Lakeshore offers a variety of sights. Along a 15-mile section at the western end of the park, multicolored sandstone cliffs rise as much as 200 feet above lake level. The Pictured Rocks cliffs are accessible by automobile at Miners Castle, by hiking along North Country Trail, and by boat from Lake Superior. Privately operated scenic cruises sail out of Munising from Memorial Day weekend to October 10. Twelvemile Beach lies east of the Pictured Rocks cliffs and offers a broad sand-and-pebble beach for sunbathing, beachcombing, and hiking. Lake Superior is generally too cold for all but the hardiest of swimmers. At the park's eastern terminus are the Grand Sable Banks, an exposed glacial deposit rising to 275 feet above the lake at a 35-degree angle. Perched atop the banks are the 85-foot-high Grand Sable Dunes.

Inland you will find a dense hardwood forest surrounding lakes, ponds, streams, waterfalls, and bogs. On the west side of the park, Munising Falls drops 50 feet over a sandstone bluff into a natural amphitheater. The Sable, Chapel, and Miners falls are popular sites to visit.

Lighthouse tours and campfire programs are conducted during the summer. Schedules are posted at ranger stations and camping areas. An interagency visitor center is operated jointly in Munising by the National Park Service and the U.S. Forest Service. It is open daily year-round; closed on Thanksgiving, Christmas Day, New Year's Day, and Sundays during winter months. The Munising Falls Interpretive Center, located near Munising on Sand Point Road, is unstaffed and open daily from mid-May to October. The Grand Sable Visitor Center, located just west of Grand Marais on County Road H-58, the Grand Marais Maritime Museum, and Miners Castle Information Station are open seasonally.

Popular winter activities include skiing on two groomed and tracked cross-country ski trail systems, snowshoeing, snowmobiling, ice fishing, and winter camping.

ENTRANCE FEE: No charge.

FACILITIES: Motels, restaurants, groceries, and camping supplies are available in Munising and Grand Marais.

CAMPING: Vehicle-accessible campgrounds are located at Hurricane River (twenty-two spaces), Little Beaver Lake (eight spaces), and Twelvemile Beach (thirty-seven spaces). Each campground has picnic tables, fire grills, tent pads, water, and vault toilets. Handicapped-accessible campsites are available at each of the campgrounds. Numerous other campgrounds are available in the nearby Hiawatha National Forest and Lake Superior State Forest.

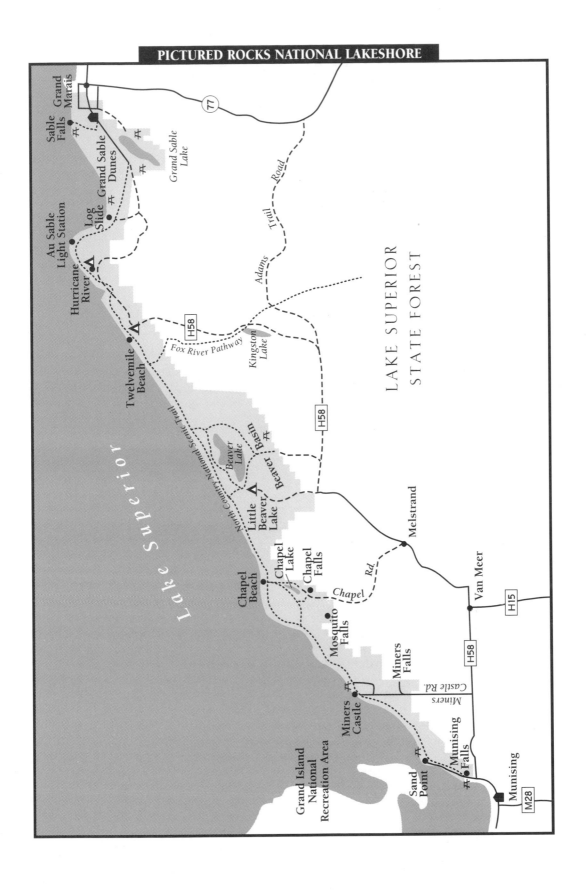

PICTURED ROCKS NATIONAL LAKESHORE

Backcountry camping also is popular along a 42-mile-long segment of the North Country National Scenic Trail. Campers are required to use the designated backcountry campgrounds, and a permit is required. A fee is charged for drive-in campsites and backcountry permits.

FISHING: Lake Superior offers lake trout, whitefish, and coho salmon, while inland lakes have sunfish, perch, bass, pike, and trout. Brook and rainbow trout are found in the streams and rivers. A Michigan fishing license is required.

SLEEPING BEAR DUNES NATIONAL LAKESHORE

9922 Front Street
Empire, MI 49630-9797
(231) 326–5134
SLBE_Interpretation@nps.gov
www.nps.gov/slbe

Sleeping Bear Dunes National Lakeshore, authorized in 1970, comprises more than 71,000 acres of beaches, sand dunes, forests, and lakes. The park is located west of Traverse City, along the northwestern shoreline of Michigan's lower peninsula.

Eleven thousand years ago, glacial ice began to melt, and the great quantities of rock, sand, and silt that it carried were deposited or washed away by meltwater to create the present-day landscape. The dunes of the Sleeping Bear Plateau formed as winds coming across Lake Michigan blew sand up the bluffs at the lake edge and across the plateau. The Valley of the Giants on South Manitou Island contains Atlantic white cedar trees that may be 500 years old.

The park visitor center, on Highway M-72 at the east edge of the village of Empire, is open daily except for winter holidays. Visitors will find exhibits, a schedule of programs including summer guided walks, maps, a slide program, and book sales. The Maritime Museum near Glen Haven is open in summer and features exhibits on Great Lakes maritime history housed in a restored Coast Guard station. Near Glen Haven, visitors can stop at the Dune Climb and clamber to the top of the Sleeping Bear Plateau. Also nearby is the Pierce Stocking Scenic Drive that offers outstanding views of the dunes, valleys, and Lake Michigan. Several small lakes in the park offer fishing and boating. Canoes may be rented for the Platte and Crystal Rivers. In season, passenger ferries originating at Leland carry campers and day visitors to North and South Manitou islands.

ENTRANCE FEE: $7.00 per vehicle; good for seven days.

FACILITIES: Handicapped-accessible rest rooms are at the Empire visitor center Maritime Museum and Dune Climb. Meals and lodging are available in Empire, Glen Arbor, Frankfort, and Traverse City.

CAMPING: On the mainland, D.H. Day Campground (eighty-eight sites) offers tables, grills, tent pads, vault toilets, water, and a sanitary dump station. The newly refurbished Platte River Campground (180 sites) offers tables, tent pads, grills, water, flush toilets, hot showers, and electrical hookups. There are also two primitive backcountry campgrounds. On South Mani-

SLEEPING BEAR DUNES NATIONAL LAKESHORE

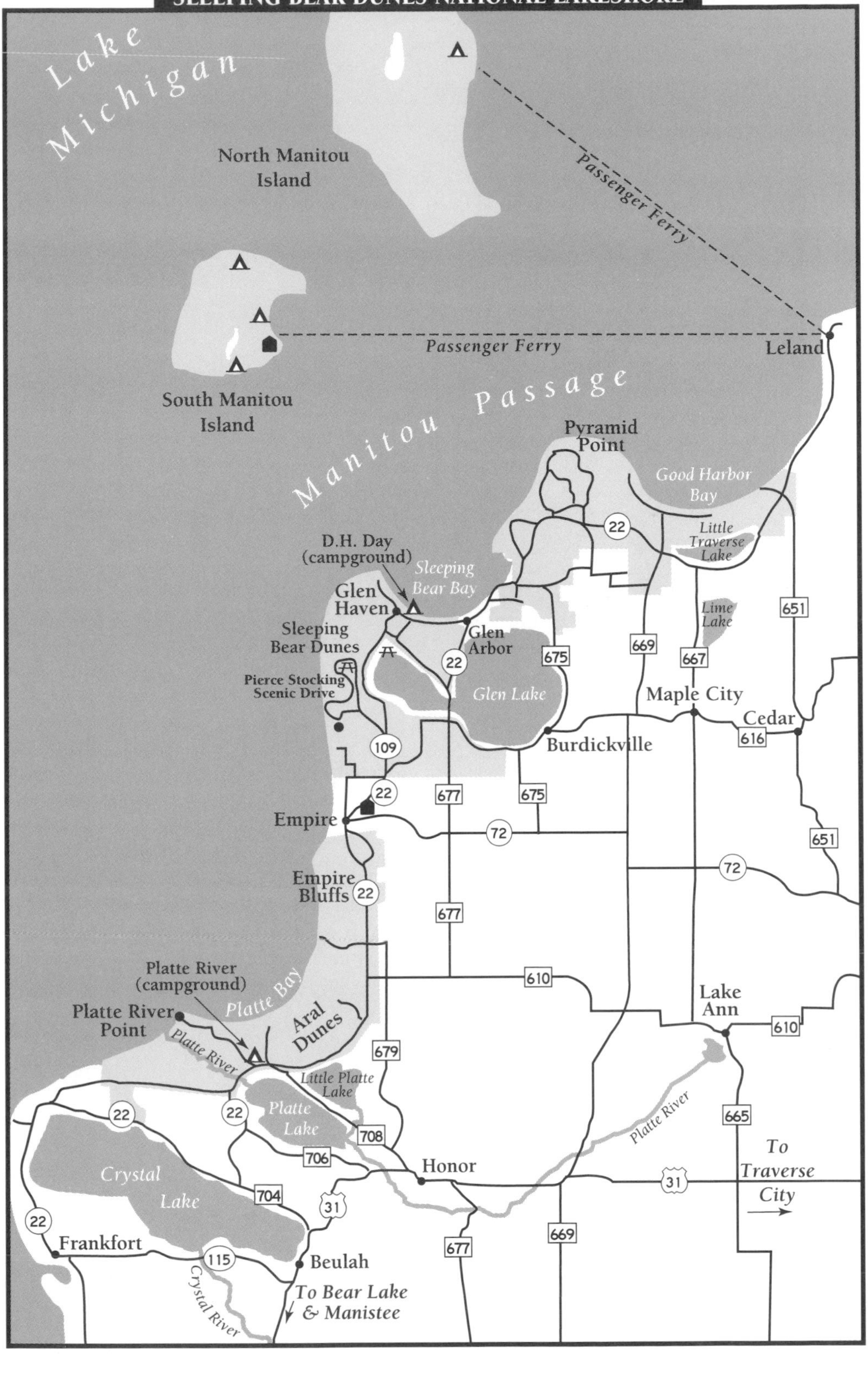

Lake Michigan

North Manitou Island

Passenger Ferry

South Manitou Island

Manitou Passage

Passenger Ferry

Leland

Pyramid Point

Good Harbor Bay

Little Traverse Lake

D.H. Day (campground)

Sleeping Bear Bay

Glen Haven

Glen Arbor

22

675

669

Lime Lake

651

Sleeping Bear Dunes

Pierce Stocking Scenic Drive

Glen Lake

Maple City

Cedar

616

109

Burdickville

675

651

22

677

72

Empire

Empire Bluffs

22

677

72

Platte River (campground)

610

Lake Ann

610

Platte River Point

Platte River

Platte Bay

Aral Dunes

679

Little Platte Lake

665

Platte River

To Traverse City →

22

22

Platte Lake

708

706

Honor

31

Crystal Lake

704

669

22

115

Frankfort

Beulah

677

To Bear Lake & Manistee

Crystal River

tou Islands are three primitive walk-in campgrounds, and North Manitou Island offers back-country camping.

FISHING: Fishing is good, with possibilities for bass, bluegill, trout, northern pike, and salmon. A Michigan fishing license is required.

See the map on page 147.

MISSISSIPPI

STATE TOURIST INFORMATION
(800) 927–6378
www.visitmississippi.org

BRICES CROSS ROADS NATIONAL BATTLEFIELD SITE
c/o Natchez Trace Parkway
2680 Natchez Trace Parkway
Tupelo, MS 38801-9718
(601) 680–4025
(800) 305–7417
www.nps.gov/brcr

Brices Cross Roads, situated on one acre, was established in 1929 to commemorate the site of a brilliant victory for Confederate forces during an 1864 Civil War battle. The park is located in northeastern Mississippi, 6 miles west of Baldwyn on State Highway 370. The hundred-plus Confederate soldiers who died during the battle are buried in the adjacent Bethany Church cemetery.

As Sherman's Union forces fought through northern Georgia, Confederate commanders decided to attack what they believed was the enemy's most vulnerable element—a single-track railroad acting as the Union supply line between Nashville and Chattanooga.

Beginning in Tupelo, Mississippi, the Confederate General Nathan Forrest set out on June 1, 1864, to strike at the Union line in middle Tennessee. Alerted to Forrest's objective, Sherman sent General Samuel Sturgis and 8,100 Union troops to head off the attack. Forrest withdrew to Tupelo and concentrated 3,500 troops along the railroad between Guntown, Baldwyn, and Booneville. The two forces met on the Baldwyn Road, approximately 1 mile east of Brices on June 10. During the daylong battle, Forrest's Confederate troops routed the opposition across the bridge over Tishomingo Creek and were able to capture most of the Union artillery and more than 1,500 Union troops. The engagement was considered a brilliant tactical victory for Forrest.

ENTRANCE FEE: No charge.

FACILITIES: No facilities or park personnel are at Brices, but visitors may view most of the area where the battle took place. Park folders are available at the site. A visitor center at Tupelo on the Natchez Trace Parkway serves as headquarters for this park.

CAMPING: No camping is permitted in the park, but J. P. Coleman State Park (east of Corinth) and Tombigbee and Trace state parks (near Tupelo) offer camping facilities.

GULF ISLANDS NATIONAL SEASHORE

Mississippi District
3500 Park Road
Ocean Springs, MS 39564-9709
(601) 875-9057
www.nps.gov/guis

Gulf Islands National Seashore, authorized in 1971, comprises nearly 96,000 acres in Mississippi and Florida. The seashore comprises both mainland units and offshore islands and keys with white-sand beaches, historic structures, and ruins. The Mississippi section consists of one mainland unit at Davis Bayou that is reached via Park Road off U.S. 90 and a series of islands accessible only by boat. The Florida section of the park is discussed in the Florida chapter of this book.

The site's white sand has been washed down streams and rivers from the north over a period of centuries. The islands are still evolving as they continue to build up on the western sides and erode on the eastern ends. One of the few stabilizing factors available is the protective covering of vegetation. The clean gulf waters and white sandy beaches plus old historic forts make Gulf Islands National Seashore one of the most heavily visited areas of the National Park Service. Although much of the visitation occurs during summer in swimming areas such as Langdon Beach on Santa Rosa Island in Florida and West Ship Island in Mississippi, miles of deserted beaches are open to exploration.

Beginning with the early 1500s, Europeans explored and maneuvered against each other along the northern Gulf Coast. Although long considered a possession by Spain, the French-Canadian explorer Pierre Le Moyne d'Iberville landed at Ship Island in 1699 to claim what would become the colony of French Louisiana. This included present-day Mississippi all the way to the Canadian border. In 1821 the United States purchased the last of West Florida, so that France and Spain were excluded from further development in the region. Beginning the next year and continuing through World War II, the United States developed and updated fortifications along the coast.

A visitor center is located at Davis Bayou on the mainland. Here visitors will find exhibits, an audiovisual presentation, and publications. Davis Bayou also has picnic shelters, a ball field, a self-guiding nature trail, campground, fishing pier, and boat ramps. There is no sandy swimming beach in this area. A concessioner-operated ferry boat offers daily passenger access to

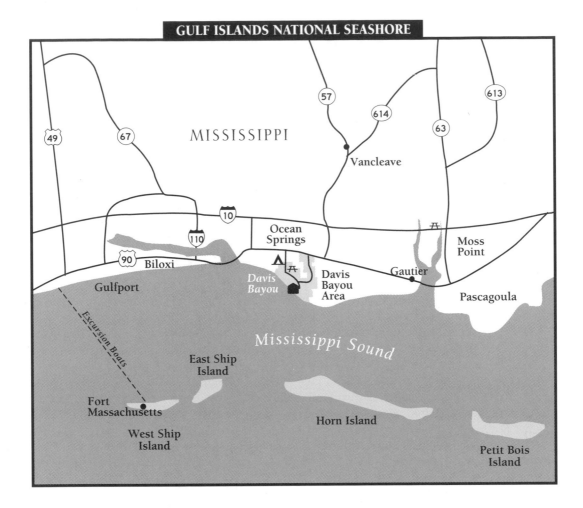

GULF ISLANDS NATIONAL SEASHORE

West Ship Island from Gulfport from the first Saturday in March to the last weekend in October. Write Pan Isles, Inc., P.O. Box 1467, Gulfport, MS 39502 (1–800–388–3290) or access their Web site (www.gcww.com/shipisland) for current information. Guided tours of Fort Massachusetts on West Ship Island are offered during summer months.

ENTRANCE FEE: $6.00 per vehicle or $3.00 per person; good for seven days.

FACILITIES: No lodging is available in the park. Limited food service is offered on tour boats and on West Ship Island. Rest rooms and drinking water are inside Fort Massachusetts on West Ship Island. West Ship Island also provides a bathhouse for swimmers using the beach area.

CAMPING: Davis Bayou offers camping (fifty-one spaces) with water, picnic pavilions, grills, tables, flush toilets, showers, hookups, and a dump station. No camping is allowed on West Ship Island. Primitive camping is permitted on East Ship, Horn, and Petit Bois Islands. These islands are accessible only by private boat or by a Park Service–licensed charter service. A free brochure, "Camping on a Wilderness Barrier Island," is available at the visitor center and by mail.

FISHING: Surf fishing—with possibilities for pompano, ling, mackerel, and sea trout—is permitted along the beach where there are no swimmers. A state fishing license is required for saltwater fishing in both Florida and Mississippi.

NATCHEZ NATIONAL HISTORICAL PARK

640 South Canal Street
Box E
Natchez, MS 39120
(601) 442–7047
www.nps.gov/natc

Natchez National Historical Park comprises nearly eighty-two acres and was authorized in 1988 to interpret the history of Natchez from its European settlement as a French trading post through the years before the Civil War when the city was a commercial, cultural, and social center of the South's cotton belt. The historical park's three units are within 4 miles of one another in the city of Natchez in southwestern Mississippi.

Natchez's location on a bend in the Mississippi River resulted in the city experiencing a rich and turbulent history. The French settled the area and established a trading post here in the early 1700s. It was successively occupied by the British, Spaniards, and Americans. The rich agricultural land of the lower Mississippi Valley and the strategic river location caused the city to become the center for the South's "King Cotton." To a large extent, the economic vitality of the cotton economy depended on the cheap labor supplied by slaves.

The historical park consists of three units, only one of which is fully operational. The visitor center, open daily from 8:00 A.M. to 5:00 P.M., is at 640 South Canal Street, near the site of the old fort.

Melrose Estate is the main operating unit of the historical park. This antebellum home was constructed in the late 1840s for a wealthy lawyer and cotton planter. The estate passed through several owners until the National Park Service purchased it in 1990. The site consists of the mansion, several outbuildings, a formal garden, carriage house, stable, cottage, and slavery exhibit. The grounds are open daily from 8:30 A.M. to 5:00 P.M. Guided tours of the mansion (fee charged) are conducted between 9:00 A.M. and 4:00 P.M.

The William Johnson House Complex at 210 State Street is in the process of restoration in late 2002. Johnson was a free African-American who chronicled life in antebellum Natchez. The home will include an exhibit on African-American history in Natchez. The upper floors will re-create the Johnson family living quarters and tell the story of his life.

Property comprising the site of Fort Rosalie, the French palisade built to protect the French trading post, is currently being purchased by the National Park Service.

ENTRANCE FEE: No charge. There is a $6.00 fee for a ranger-guided tour of the Melrose House.

FACILITIES: Rest rooms and drinking water are at park headquarters and at the Melrose Estate. Food and lodging are nearby. An RV dump station is also nearby.

CAMPING: No camping is permitted in the historical park. Natchez State Park, 13 miles northeast of town on U.S. 61, offers twenty-eight sites with water, flush toilets, tables, and grills.

FISHING: A large pond on the Melrose Estate may be fished from the banks only.

NATCHEZ TRACE PARKWAY

2680 Natchez Trace Parkway
Tupelo, MS 38801-9718
(601) 680–4025
(800) 305–7417
www.nps.gov/natr

Natchez Trace Parkway was established as part of the National Park Service in 1938. It contains over 49,000 acres along a route that generally follows the old Indian trace (trail) between Natchez, Mississippi and Nashville, Tennessee.

The Natchez Trace was originally no more than an Indian footpath connecting Natchez with the Choctaw villages near present-day Jackson and the Chickasaw villages in the northeastern portion of the state. After the American Revolution the trail was made into a crude road by traders who floated products down the Mississippi River and returned to Nashville along the path. After the United States created the Mississippi Territory with Natchez as its capital, money was appropriated to improve the road so that mail service could be extended into the area. From 1800 to 1820, the trace was the region's most heavily traveled road, but the later appearance of steamboats on the Mississippi caused it to diminish in importance.

The park's headquarters is located in Tupelo. Here, in the visitor center, a film explaining the trace's history is available. At various points along the parkway, visitors can find self-guided nature trails, exhibits, interpretive markers, and picnic tables. Some points of interest, with numbers keyed to those found on the map (in sequence from south to north), follow.

1. Old Trace exhibit shelter.
2. Emerald Mound (A.D. 1600) is the second largest ceremonial Indian mound in the United States.
3. Loess Bluff Nature Area displays a deep deposit of topsoil blown into the area during the ice age.
4. Restored Mount Locust Inn.
5. Bullen Creek Nature Trail wanders through a mixed hardwood-pine forest.
6. A section of the Old Natchez Trace is identified.
7. Copper ornaments and other artifacts were found in the hilltop graves of Mangum Site.
8. Grindstone Ford marked the beginning of wild territory to early-day travelers heading north.
9. Rocky Springs Site includes a campground, picnic area, nature trail to historic spring and town site, and a section of the Old Trace.
10. Ross Barnett Reservoir (not a part of the parkway) has picnicking, marina, and a boat landing.
11. Mississippi Crafts Center features demonstrations and sales of Mississippi crafts.
12. The Indian burial mounds were built more than 500 years ago.
13. Nature trail through Cypress Swamp.
14. Nature trail featuring native Southern plants.

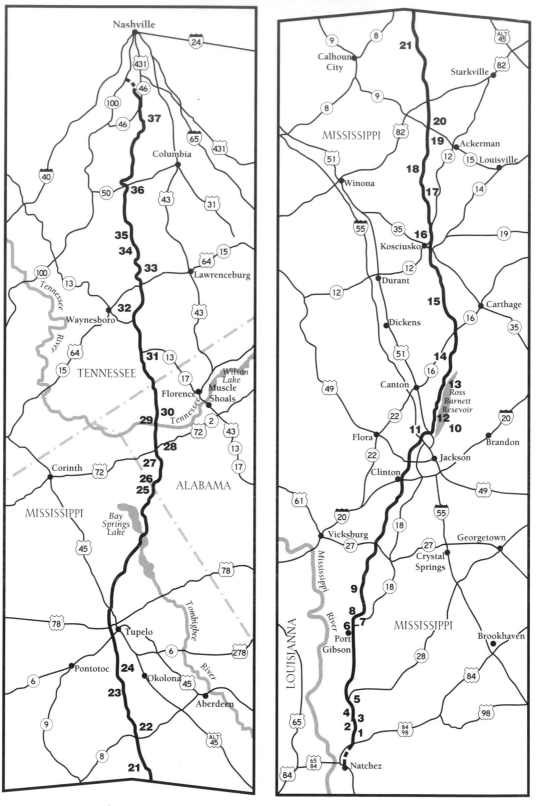

NATCHEZ TRACE PARKWAY

Northern Section

Nashville

24

431

46

100

46

37

65

431

Columbia

43

31

50

36

43

35

34

64

15

33

Lawrenceburg

40

100

13

Tennessee River

32

43

Waynesboro

64

31

13

15

TENNESSEE

17

Florence

Wilson Lake

Muscle Shoals

30

Tennessee

29

2

72

43

Corinth

72

28

13

27

17

26

25

ALABAMA

MISSISSIPPI

Bay Springs Lake

45

78

Tombigbee River

78

Tupelo

6

278

Pontotoc

24

6

Okolona

45

23

Aberdeen

9

22

8

ALT 45

21

Southern Section

9

8

21

ALT 45

Calhoun City

Starkville

82

8

9

MISSISSIPPI

82

20

19

Ackerman

51

12

15

Louisville

18

17

Winona

14

55

35

16

Kosciusko

19

12

Durant

15

Carthage

12

Dickens

16

35

51

14

49

16

13

Ross Barnett Resevoir

Canton

22

11

12

10

Flora

Jackson

20

Brandon

22

Clinton

49

61

18

55

20

Vicksburg

18

27

Georgetown

Mississippi River

27

Crystal Springs

9

8

18

Brookhaven

6

7

Port Gibson

28

MISSISSIPPI

84

LOUISIANNA

5

4

3

98

2

1

65

84

98

65

84

Natchez

84

15. Nature trail along an abandoned beaver dam (includes exhibit shelter).

16. Nature trail along a creek and up a hillside.

17. Nature trail through Cypress Swamp that is changing into a mixed hardwood forest.

18. Old Trace is visible as it winds through the woods.

19. Jeff Busby Site contains gas station, campground, picnic area, and nature trail.

20. Original Natchez Trace leads into woods along present roadway.

21. Section of original trace crosses parkway.

22. Bynum Mounds, a village site of prehistoric and historic Indians. Includes exhibit shelter (with recording) near still-visible burial mounds.

23. Davis Lake Forest Service Area has camping, picnicking, swimming, and boating.

24. Site of old Chickasaw village. Includes exhibit shelter and nature trail.

25. Trail to cave site.

26. Bear Creek Mound, an early Indian temple mound.

27. A steep ¼-mile trail leads to the highest point on the parkway in Alabama.

28. Exhibit shelter telling story of Chickasaw chief who owned an inn near this site.

29. Colbert Ferry has rest rooms, picnicking, bicycle camping, fishing, swimming, and boat-launching facilities.

30. Rock Creek Nature Trail follows a creek to a flowing spring.

31. Three sections of the Old Trace are visible.

32. Nature trail through forest, with identified plants.

33. A 2½-mile one-way loop drive over a section of the Old Natchez Trace.

34. Exhibit shelter illustrates mining.

35. Meriwether Lewis Site contains a campground, picnic area, hiking trail, and the grave of this famous explorer.

36. A tobacco farm and barn and Old Trace Drive are located here.

37. Gordon House, an 1818 home near the Duck River.

ENTRANCE FEE: No charge.

FACILITIES: There are no overnight facilities along the parkway, but motels and restaurants may be found in nearby towns. The only service station is at Jeff Busby. Drinking water and rest rooms are available at the visitor center, the campgrounds, and a number of picnic areas along the way.

CAMPING: Park Service campgrounds with tables, grills, water, and flush toilets are at Jeff Busby (eighteen sites, campstore), Meriwether Lewis (thirty-two sites), and Rocky Springs (twenty-two sites). All three are open year-round. Additional camping is available at Davis Lake and Tishomingo and Trace state parks. Numerous privately owned campgrounds are near the parkway.

FISHING: Fishing is available at various points along and near the parkway. Appropriate state licenses are required.

TUPELO NATIONAL BATTLEFIELD

c/o Natchez Trace Parkway
2680 Natchez Trace Parkway
Tupelo, MS 38801-9718
(601) 680–4025
(800) 305–7417
www.nps.gov/tupe

Tupelo National Battlefield, situated on one acre, was established in 1929 to commemorate the site of an important battle between Union forces and Confederate troops sent to cut General William Sherman's supply line. The park is located in northeastern Mississippi within the city limits of Tupelo. It is on Mississippi Route 6, 1 mile west of U.S. 45 and 1⅕ miles east of the Natchez Trace Parkway.

As General William Sherman battled through Georgia during the summer of 1864, one of his primary concerns was protection of the railroad bringing supplies from Louisville to his army. As a result, Grant assigned a large number of Union troops to the task of destroying a Confederate force that was trying to interrupt this supply line. On July 14, 1864, the two armies met in Harrisburg (now within the Tupelo city limits), and Confederate troops were badly mauled, sustaining heavy losses. Short of rations and ammunition, the Federals began their return to their base in La Grange, Tennessee, the following day. Although Union troops were unable to destroy the Confederate force, they did keep the railroad supply line from being damaged.

The park's visitor center is incorporated with the Tupelo visitor center of the Natchez Trace Parkway. Here visitors will find park interpreters to answer questions and provide information about the battle. Park folders are available at the battlefield.

ENTRANCE FEE: No charge.

FACILITIES: Both lodging and food service are available in the town of Tupelo.

CAMPING: No camping is permitted at the site. Tombigee State Park, approximately 10 miles from Tupelo, has twenty sites with tables, grills, water, flush toilets, and a dump station.

VICKSBURG NATIONAL MILITARY PARK

3201 Clay Street
Vicksburg, MS 39183-3495
(601) 636–0583
vick_interpretation@nps.gov
www.nps.gov/vick

The park, which contains 1,741 acres, was established in 1899 to preserve the site of a decisive Civil War battle that gave the Union control of the Mississippi River and split the Confederacy into two parts. The park is in western Mississippi in Vicksburg. Exit Interstate 20 at U.S. 80 (West Clay Street, exit 4-B).

From the outbreak of the Civil War, Union authorities realized that control of the Mississippi River would permit movement of troops and supplies into the Deep South. In addition, it would divide the Confederacy by isolating Arkansas, Texas, and most of Louisiana. By the late summer of 1862, Union forces had captured most of the Confederate strongholds along the river, leaving Vicksburg and Port Hudson as the only major obstacles to Union domination of the Mississippi.

Ulysses S. Grant and his Federal forces first attacked Vicksburg on May 8, 1863. Unable to capture the city in two assaults, Grant began a long siege using field guns, gunboats, and trench warfare. By the end of June, Confederate forces began to despair of relief. With munitions and food in short supply, they finally surrendered on July 4. The surrender at Port Hudson five days later gave the Union complete control of the river.

A visitor center, open daily from 8:00 A.M. to 5:00 P.M. except Christmas Day, contains exhibits and information to help interpret the park. From here, a 16-mile tour leads past many of the historic sites associated with the battle. Included are Shirley House, the only surviving wartime structure in the park; Vicksburg National Cemetery, where 17,000 Union soldiers are buried; and restored Federal approach trenches. Also included within the park is the USS *Cairo* Museum (601–636–2199). The museum displays artifacts recovered from the USS *Cairo*. Sailors' personal gear, cookware, and weaponry are among the many artifacts on display. The restored gunboat is open for visitors to walk aboard. The museum is open 8:30 A.M. to 5:00 P.M. November through March and 9:30 A.M. to 6:00 P.M. April through October.

ENTRANCE FEE: $4.00 per vehicle or $2.00 per person; good for seven days.

FACILITIES: No food and lodging are available in the park, but both are found nearby. Drinking water and rest rooms are provided in both the visitor center and *Cairo* Museum.

CAMPING: No camping is permitted in the park. The National Park Service operates the Rocky Springs Campground (twenty-two sites, tables, grills, flush toilets) on the Natchez Trace Parkway, 27 miles south of Vicksburg via Highway 27 and the Parkway.

See the map on page 158.

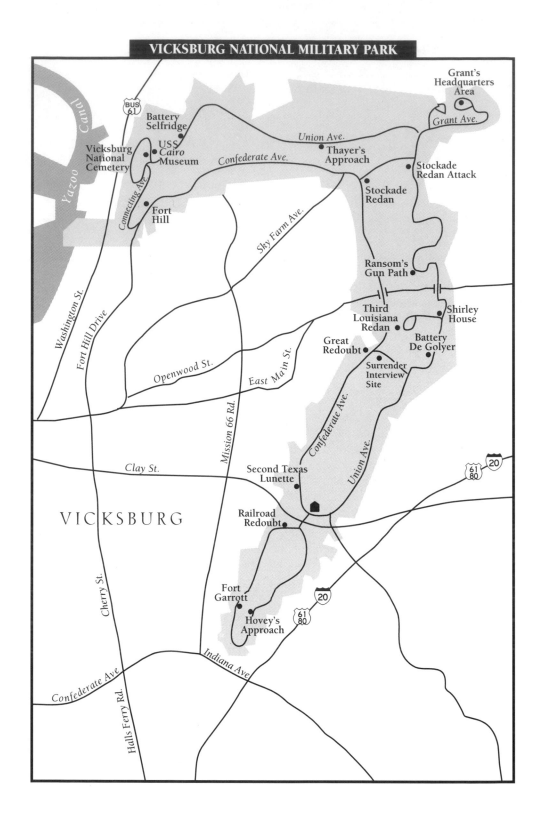

VICKSBURG NATIONAL MILITARY PARK

Grant's Headquarters Area

Grant Ave.

Yazoo Canal

BUS 61

Battery Selfridge

Vicksburg National Cemetery

USS Cairo Museum

Union Ave.

Thayer's Approach

Confederate Ave.

Stockade Redan Attack

Stockade Redan

Connecting Ave.

Fort Hill

Sky Farm Ave.

Ransom's Gun Path

Shirley House

Third Louisiana Redan

Battery De Golyer

Washington St.

Fort Hill Drive

Great Redoubt

Surrender Interview Site

Openwood St.

East Main St.

Confederate Ave.

Union Ave.

Mission 66 Rd.

Clay St.

Second Texas Lunette

61 80

61 20

VICKSBURG

Railroad Redoubt

Cherry St.

Fort Garrott

Hovey's Approach

20

61 80

Indiana Ave.

Confederate Ave.

Halls Ferry Rd.

NEW HAMPSHIRE

SAINT-GAUDENS NATIONAL HISTORIC SITE

Rural Route #3, Box 73
Cornish, NH 03745-9704
(603) 675–2175
saga@valley.net
www.sgnhs.org

Saint-Gaudens National Historic Site comprises 150 acres and was authorized in 1964 as a memorial to one of America's greatest sculptors, Augustus Saint-Gaudens. The site, containing his home, gardens, studio, and many original works, is located on the western New Hampshire border just off State Highway 12A and 2 miles north of the Cornish-Windsor covered bridge. From Interstate 89, take exit 20. From Interstate 91, use exit 8 if northbound or exit 9 if southbound.

Augustus Saint-Gaudens (1848–1907) was born in Dublin, Ireland, and at the age of six months, moved with his family to New York City. Upon completing an apprenticeship as a cameo cutter, he left America to study in Paris and Rome. Soon after his return, he received critical acclaim for his large sculptures and was widely regarded as the master of the portrait relief. His redesign of the $10 and $20 gold pieces in 1907 produced what many describe as the most beautiful coins minted in the United States. In 1885, Saint-Gaudens moved to this New Hampshire home that once served as an inn, and it was here that his most productive years were spent. The Cornish community eventually attracted many other artists, including poets, painters, playwrights, and musicians.

Saint-Gaudens' Home and Studio (Courtesy Saint-Gaudens National Historic Site)

The park is open daily until dusk from late May through October. Buildings are open from 9:00 A.M. to 4:30 P.M. daily. Ranger-led tours of the house and grounds are offered daily. Brochures for a self-guided tour of the gardens and studios are available. Saint-Gaudens' works in bronze, plaster, and marble are on display throughout the site. A 2½-mile trail that loops down to a pond in the Blow-Me-Down Natural Area and a ¼-mile Blow-Me-Down Ravine Trail are popular attractions.

In addition to changing exhibitions by contemporary painters and sculptors, the Saint-Gaudens Memorial Trustees sponsor a series of concerts at the site on Sunday afternoons from early July to late August. Visitors should make a point to drive a few miles south on Highway 12A to see the longest covered bridge in the United States, which crosses the Connecticut River to Windsor, Vermont.

ENTRANCE FEE: $4.00 per person; good for seven days.

FACILITIES: No food, lodging, or public telephone is available at the site. Rest rooms are near the parking area. (Note: There is no easy turnaround in the parking area for RVs towing vehicles.) Food can be found in Windsor, Vermont, 2 miles south.

CAMPING: No camping is permitted at the site. Vermont's Mt. Ascutney State Park, 5 miles southwest of Windsor and a short distance off U.S. 5, offers forty-nine sites with tables, grills, flush toilets, a dump station, and pay showers.

FISHING: Fishing is available in Blow-Me-Down Pond at the historic site as well as in the nearby Connecticut River.

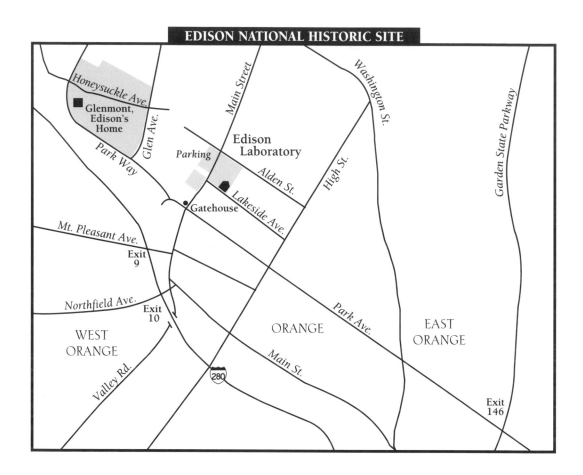

EDISON NATIONAL HISTORIC SITE

Honeysuckle Ave.

Glenmont,
Edison's
Home

Glen Ave.

Main Street

Washington St.

Garden State Parkway

Park Way

Parking

Edison
Laboratory

Alden St.

High St.

Lakeside Ave.

Gatehouse

Mt. Pleasant Ave.

Exit
9

Northfield Ave.

Exit
10

WEST
ORANGE

ORANGE

Park Ave.

EAST
ORANGE

Valley Rd.

280

Main St.

Exit
146

NEW JERSEY

STATE TOURIST INFORMATION
(800) 537–7397
www.visitnj.org

EDISON NATIONAL HISTORIC SITE

Main Street and Lakeside Avenue
West Orange, NJ 07052-5515
(973) 736–0550
FAX: (973) 736–8496
TDD: (973) 243–9122
edis_interpretation@nps.gov
www.nps.gov/edis/home.htm

Edison National Historic Site combines both Thomas Edison's West Orange laboratory and Glenmont, the Edison family estate, located about a mile away. The visitor center is located at the corner of Main Street and Lakeside Avenue in West Orange, New Jersey, 2 miles north of the Garden State Parkway and ½ mile east of Interstate 280. (On I–280; westbound drivers should take exit 10, but eastbound travelers should take exit 9.)

Born in Ohio in 1847, Thomas Alva Edison moved to the New York area to seek his fortune. Not only did he create 1,093 U.S. patents in his career—a record that still stands—but along the way he invented the modern research and development laboratory. He had three laboratories, all here in New Jersey: first in Newark in 1870; then in Menlo Park in 1876, where he developed the incandescent lightbulb; and finally his largest laboratory in West Orange in 1887, built one year after purchasing Glenmont. Here he improved the phonograph he had invented at Menlo Park and developed the motion picture camera, the alkaline storage battery, and many other inventions.

Today the National Park Service preserves the impressive Edison home, Glenmont, and six redbrick laboratory buildings that were used for Edison's experiments in the fields of chemistry, physics, and metallurgy. The home and laboratories are approximately 1 mile (fifteen minutes driving time) apart. The home and laboratories may be seen by guided tour. Here you will find exhibits illustrating Edison's experiments with phonographs, motion pictures, electricity, cement, and the storage battery. Please call the visitor center (extension 42) or visit the Web site for current hours. Visitors are advised to allocate approximately three hours for tours of the home, laboratories, and visitor center.

ENTRANCE FEE: $2.00 per person, visitors sixteen and under free; good for seven days.

FACILITIES: Food service and lodging can be found near the site.

MORRISTOWN NATIONAL HISTORICAL PARK
30 Washington Place
Morristown, NJ 07960
(973) 539–2085
clark_a_dixon_jr@nps.gov
www.nps.gov/morr

Morristown National Historical Park includes 1,699 acres and was authorized in 1933 to commemorate the site where the Continental Army under George Washington spent two winters during the American Revolution. The park is located in north-central New Jersey, in four separate sections in or near the town of Morristown.

In January 1777, George Washington moved the Continental Army into winter quarters at Morristown, where the easily defensible location saw his men through the winter in spite of a smallpox epidemic and shortages of food and clothing. As weather improved and the roads dried, the army left and did not return for two years. After wintering at Valley Forge the following year, Washington again selected Morristown in December 1779 as the location to spend the winter. The unusually severe weather and shortages during this second winter nearly destroyed the morale of both officers and enlisted men in what proved to be one of the Continental Army's severest trials. In spite of these hardships, Washington moved the troops to battle in the spring.

Washington's restored headquarters, the Ford Mansion, and the adjacent museum contain information and exhibits interpreting the army's stay in Morristown. The museum is open daily from 9:00 A.M. to 5:00 P.M. The Ford Mansion is shown only by daily guided tours at 10:00 and 11:00 A.M., 1:00, 2:00, 3:00, and 4:00 P.M. The Jockey Hollow Visitor Center and nearby Wick House that served as Major General St. Clair's headquarters are open from 9:00 A.M. to 5:00 P.M. and 9:30 A.M. to 4:30 P.M., respectively. A self-guided nature trail is in the encampment area. All buildings are closed on Thanksgiving, Christmas Day, and New Year's Day. At Fort Nonsense, soldiers fortified a ridge in May 1777, although no traces of the earthworks remain. Wayside exhibits at Fort Nonsense interpret the site.

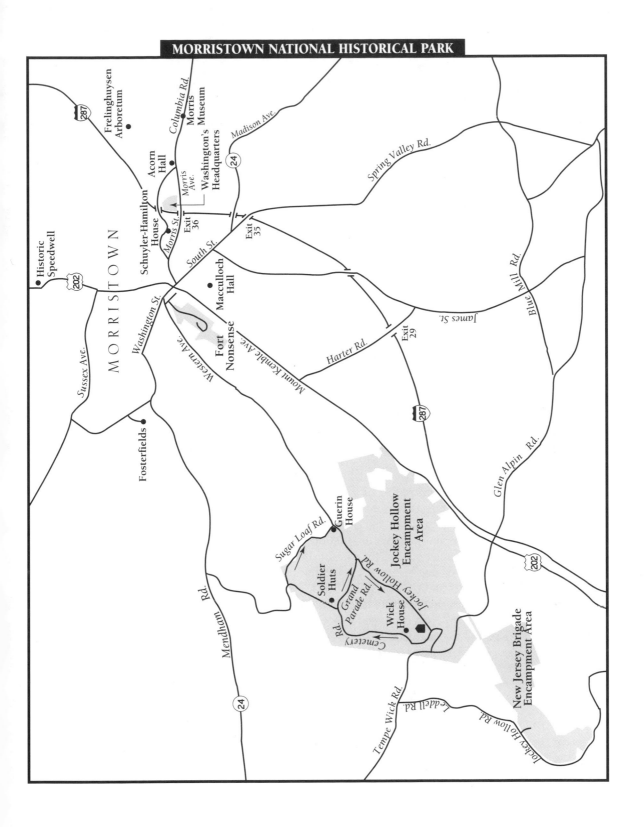

MORRISTOWN NATIONAL HISTORICAL PARK

Frelinghuysen Arboretum

287

Columbia Rd.

Morris Museum

Madison Ave.

24

Spring Valley Rd.

Acorn Hall

Washington's Headquarters

Morris Ave.

Schuyler-Hamilton House

MORRISTOWN

Morris St.

Exit 36

Exit 35

South St.

Historic Speedwell

202

Macculloch Hall

Blue Mill Rd.

James St.

Washington St.

Fort Nonsense

Western Ave.

Mount Kemble Ave.

Harter Rd.

Exit 29

Sussex Ave.

Fosterfields

287

Glen Alpin Rd.

Mendham Rd.

Sugar Loaf Rd.

Guerin House

Jockey Hollow Encampment Area

Soldier Huts

Grand Parade Rd.

Jockey Hollow Rd.

Wick House

202

Cemetery Rd.

24

New Jersey Brigade Encampment Area

Tempe Wick Rd.

Leddell Rd.

Jockey Hollow Rd.

ENTRANCE FEE: $4.00 per person; good for seven days.

FACILITIES: No food or lodging is available within park boundaries, although both can be found nearby. Rest rooms and drinking water are at the visitor center, museum, and the Ford Mansion.

CAMPING: No camping is permitted in the park. A public campground is approximately 20 miles northwest of Morristown National Historical Park at Allamachy Mountain State Park, 2 miles north of Hackettstown.

PINELANDS NATIONAL RESERVE

P.O. Box 7
New Lisbon, NJ 08064
(609) 894–7300
info@njpines.state.nj.us
www.state.nj.us/pinelands/

Pinelands National Reserve was authorized as an affiliated area of the National Park Service in 1978 to assist in shaping the future of the last vast forested area on the Atlantic coast between Boston and Richmond. The Pinelands National Reserve comprises 1.1 million acres (1,700 square miles) of forests, farms, and scenic towns. The reserve includes portions of seven southeastern New Jersey counties.

Congress created the Pinelands National Reserve so that governments at all levels could shape the future and balance protection of the area's natural resources with development in this mostly rural region of a heavily populated state. The Pinelands comprise slightly less than a quarter of New Jersey. Nearly 40 percent of the area is publicly owned. The reserve includes fifty-six municipalities and is home to 780,000 year-round residents.

Fifteen appointed members of the Pinelands Commission have produced a management plan in which an inner region of the reserve has been designated a preservation area. Long-time Pinelands villages and remains of historic towns dot this largely forested landscape where compatible agriculture, horticulture, and recreation uses are permitted. The preservation area is surrounded by a designated protection area in which orderly development is permitted as long as it maintains the character of the existing environment.

The Pinelands is home to 150 species of birds, about sixteen species of fish, and more than thirty species of mammals. The reserve contains approximately 580 native species and 270 introduced species of plants, including over 12,000 acres of dwarf pine and oak. An immense aquifer underlying the Pinelands is estimated to contain more than 17 trillion gallons of water.

FACILITIES: Food and lodging are available in small towns throughout Pinelands National Reserve. *Pinelands Guide,* a booklet describing recreational resources, historic sites, and nature centers, is available free from the Pinelands Commission at the New Lisbon address above.

CAMPING: Public and private campgrounds are scattered throughout the area. Bass River State Forest, Belleplain State Forest, Wharton State Forest, and Lebanon State Forest have campgrounds with hot showers. (Note: Camping fees are charged.)

NEW YORK

STATE TOURIST INFORMATION

(800) 225–5697

www.iloveny.com

ELEANOR ROOSEVELT NATIONAL HISTORIC SITE

4097 Albany Post Road

Hyde Park, NY 12538-1997

(845) 229–9422

www.nps.gov/elro

Eleanor Roosevelt National Historic Site was authorized in 1977 and comprises 180 acres including Val-Kill, Mrs. Roosevelt's home. The site contains fields, wetlands, a pond, and the cottage where Eleanor Roosevelt entertained friends and dignitaries during her long years of public service. The historic site is located in southeastern New York, approximately 6 miles north of Poughkeepsie on U.S. 9G, ½-mile north of the intersection of St. Andrews Road and Route 9G.

Eleanor Roosevelt was born in 1884 in New York City. In 1905, she was given in marriage to her distant cousin, Franklin D. Roosevelt, by her uncle, President Theodore Roosevelt. Following Franklin's polio attack in 1921, she became increasingly active in politics. By the time Franklin was first elected president in 1932, Eleanor was active in a number of causes and soon began touring the country on a variety of political missions.

Mrs. Roosevelt resided at Val-Kill after her husband's death in 1945. She was called to public service by President Harry S Truman. As chairman of the Human Rights Commission of the United Nations, she was largely responsible for the Universal Declaration of Human Rights, which was passed in 1948. This was followed by writing, lecturing, hosting a television talk show, participating in human rights organizations, and actively working in the

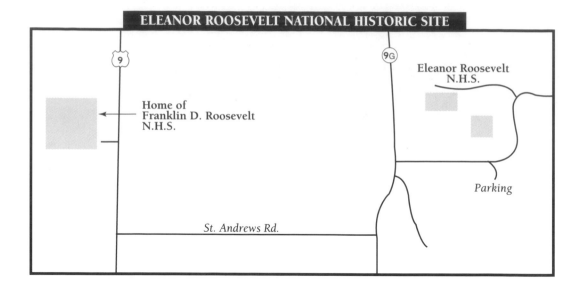

Democratic party. Eleanor Roosevelt died on November 7, 1962, and was buried in Hyde Park next to her husband.

Val-Kill grew out of an idea of Franklin D. Roosevelt's when he suggested in 1924 that Mrs. Roosevelt and two of her friends might like to build a cottage on the Val-Kill stream, a favorite picnic spot. A fieldstone cottage was built in 1925, and the following year a building was constructed to house a furniture factory. In 1929, a second factory building was added. When the business ceased to operate in 1936, the building was converted by Mrs. Roosevelt into a home of her own. For the next twenty-six years, Mrs. Roosevelt spent much of her time at Val-Kill, where she entertained people from all walks of life.

The site is open from 9:00 A.M. to 5:00 P.M. daily from May through October and Thursday to Monday from November through April. It is closed on Thanksgiving, Christmas, and New Year's Days. Tours are conducted every half-hour (last tour at 4:30) and include a film about Mrs. Roosevelt's career. A fee is charged for visitors seventeen and older. All groups of ten or more must make advance reservations (800–967–2283). Smaller groups or individuals may also make reservations.

ENTRANCE FEE: No charge for entrance to the grounds. There is a $5.00 user fee for a tour of the home; visitors sixteen and under are free.

FACILITIES: No food or lodging is available at the site, but both can be found in the town of Hyde Park.

CAMPING: See the camping section under Vanderbilt Mansion National Historic Site.

FIRE ISLAND NATIONAL SEASHORE

120 Laurel Street
Patchogue, NY 11772-3596
(631) 289–4810
fiis_interpretation@nps.gov
www.nps.gov/fiis

Fire Island National Seashore contains nearly 20,000 acres and was authorized in 1964 to preserve the natural features and recreational opportunities of a barrier island off the south shore of Long Island. The island can be reached by automobile via bridges from Bayshore and Shirley on each end of the park. Visitors must park at the Robert Moses State Park or Smith Point County Park lots and walk to Fire Island National Seashore; driving is not permitted. Visitors may also take ferries from Bayshore (631–665–5045), Sayville (631–589–8980), and Patchogue (631–475–1636) from May to November.

The barrier beach of Fire Island stretches 32 miles, with a width of from 200 yards to ½ mile. In addition to a wide beach on the Atlantic side, the island contains pines, patches of seaside plants, and hidden hardwood groves. The Sunken Forest at Sailors Haven is a 200-year-old forest full of holly, sassafras, tupelo, and shadblow providing a canopy with vines of catbrier and wild grape climbing from the forest floor. Fire Island is also a habitat for a wide variety of wildlife, including songbirds, deer, waterfowl, and foxes.

Visitor centers with information, exhibits, interpretive activities, and nature trails are at Sailors Haven, Watch Hill, and Smith Point. Lifeguards and park rangers work at Watch Hill and Sailors Haven during July and August. The first two locations also provide marinas, guarded swimming beaches, change rooms, and showers. A restaurant and a snack bar are available at Watch Hill, and a snack bar is available at Sailors Haven. The Fire Island Wilderness Visitor Center, formerly called Smith Point West, is the gateway to New York State's only federal wilderness area, which stretches 7 miles west to Watch Hill. Watch Hill is noted for its rich and beautiful salt marsh with an elevated boardwalk nature trail. The historic Fire Island Lighthouse at the western end of the National Seashore is open to the public. Call for dates and hours of operation (631–661–4876). The former Keepers' Quarters has been renovated as a visitor center with exhibits on the island's history. Park at Field 5 of the adjacent Robert Moses State Park and walk in (⅗ mile). There are no roads on the island except for the two entrance roads noted above.

The William Floyd Estate (631–399–2030) is a detached unit of the National Seashore located on Washington Avenue in Mastic Beach. This 275-year-old home of a signer of the Declaration of Independence is open seasonally for house tours. Call for dates and times.

ENTRANCE FEE: No charge.

FACILITIES: Food service and groceries are provided by concessioners at Sailors Haven and Watch Hill. Rest rooms are also at these two locations. Complete facilities—including hotels and restaurants—are available in neighboring communities on Fire Island. Lodging information can be obtained from the Fire Island Tourism Bureau (631–563–8448).

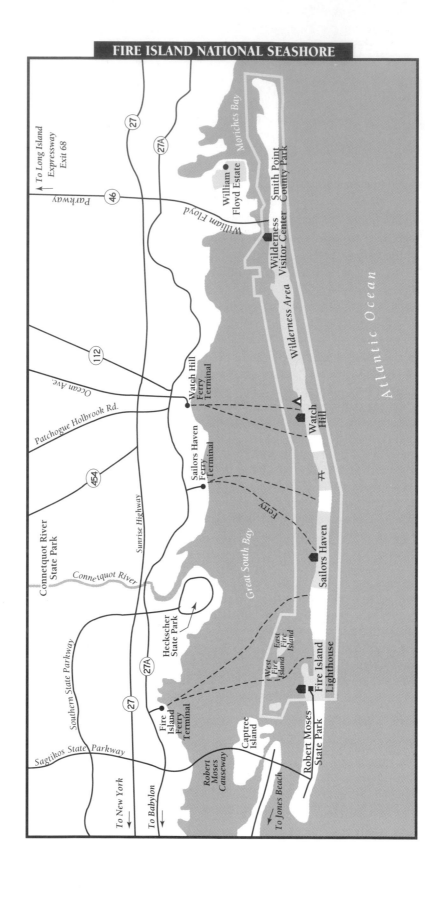

CAMPING: At Watch Hill (twenty-eight sites, two group camps) camping is available by reservation only from May 15 to October 15 (631–597–6633). No toilets or water are available during the remainder of the year. Access is by private boat or scheduled ferry only.

FISHING: Fishermen can fish in the surf for striped bass, bluefish, and weakfish. Great South Bay and Moriches Bay offer bluefish, blackfish, fluke, weakfish, kingfish, and winter flounder. Clamming and crabbing are also popular activities on the island.

FORT STANWIX NATIONAL MONUMENT

112 East Park Street
Rome, NY 13440-5816
(315) 336–2090
fost_interpretation@nps.gov
www.nps.gov/fost

Fort Stanwix National Monument comprises approximately sixteen acres. It was authorized in 1935 (acquisition was not completed until 1973) to preserve the site of an important stand by American forces during the Revolutionary War and the site where six American Indian treaties were negotiated that aided in the Westward expansion of the United States. The fort is located in central New York in the city of Rome. State Highways 26, 46, 49, 69, and 365 pass within sight of the monument.

Fort Stanwix was constructed by British forces in 1758 to protect an important portage between the Mohawk River and a water passage to Lake Ontario. After England conquered Canada in 1760, the post lost much of its importance until it was occupied by Americans in the summer of 1776 to protect against British invasion from the north. In 1777, a major siege against the fort was successfully repulsed. This marked the end of military actions against Stanwix, although the fort was garrisoned until 1781. Six British (later American) and American Indian treaties were negotiated and signed at the site. The first, in 1768, established a boundary line between the British colonial and American Indian lands. This boundary started at Fort Stanwix and went south and west to the confluence of the Tennessee and Ohio Rivers. The second, in 1784, ended the American Revolutionary War fought between the United States and the Iroquois Confederacy. The other four treaties were negotiated in 1788 and 1790 between the state of New York and the Oneida, Onondaga, and Cayuga nations. The nations ceded lands to the state of New York. These illegal treaties were later combined with the federal 1794 Treaty of Canadaigua and made legal.

The reconstructed fort is open from 9:00 A.M. to 5:00 P.M. daily April 1 through December 31 except Thanksgiving and Christmas Day. A city garage on James Street is available for visitor parking. Park personnel are stationed inside the entrance to provide directions to the visitor center, which contains exhibits and a movie. The fort also contains a small museum, and living-history programs take place throughout the day during summer months.

ENTRANCE FEE: $2.00 per person.

FACILITIES: No food or lodging is available in the park, but both are nearby in Rome. A Quality Inn is across the street from the fort. Drinking water and rest rooms are located inside the entrance.

CAMPING: No camping is permitted on the monument grounds. Delta Lake State Park (110 sites), 6½ miles northeast on State Highway 46, offers campsites with tables, grills, flush toilets, showers, and a swimming beach. A private campground with hookups is located off Route 365, 7 miles west of Rome.

GATEWAY NATIONAL RECREATION AREA

Floyd Bennett Field, Building 69
Brooklyn, NY 11234-7097
(718) 338–3338
www.nps.gov/gate

Gateway National Recreation Area contains over 26,000 acres and was established in 1972 to provide recreational activities for the millions of people living in the New York City metropolitan area. The park comprises four separate sections located in the New York City harbor area in both New York and New Jersey. All units are accessible by auto and by mass transit.

Gateway National Recreation Area is truly a gateway. Over the years, this land area surrounding New York harbor has formed a natural gateway for trade goods and millions of immigrants. The recreation area comprises four units. The Sandy Hook Unit in New Jersey and the Breezy Point District in New York are two arms of land that stretch across the water toward one another. The Staten Island Unit and Jamaica Bay District lie within the arms. The units and districts contain a variety of natural and historical items of interest to visitors, including beaches, dunes, bays, wooded uplands, a holly forest, a wildlife refuge, former airfields, forts, and the nation's oldest operating lighthouse. Facilities are available for numerous recreational activities.

Breezy Point District (718–318–4300): a fine ocean beach, Jacob Riis Park, with opportunities for swimming, surf fishing, bird watching, softball, baseball, football, paddleball, rugby, and handball. The unit also includes Fort Tilden. Rangers lead groups on guided walks, while craft shows and theatrical performances take place at Riis Park in spring and fall.

Jamaica Bay District (718–338–3799): the Jamaica Bay Wildlife Refuge (718–318–4340) provides a habitat for more than 300 species of birds and is open year-round. A bay provides fishing, while special programs take place at Canarsie Pier, Plumb Beach, Dead Horse Bay, Frank Charles Park, and Floyd Bennett Field. The latter was New York's first municipal airport and currently serves as park headquarters. Floyd Bennett Field has vintage aircraft to help interpret the field's aviation history. Environmental education programs, special cultural events, and overnight camping experiences attract thousands of schoolchildren annually.

Sandy Hook Unit (732–872–5911): the site of the oldest continually operating lighthouse in North America and a series of forts from colonial times, with the last fort still largely intact. Tours of the fort and a holly forest are offered daily. There are lectures and special events including lifesaving demonstrations during summer months and weekly tours and presentations in other seasons. It has one of the first stations of the U.S. Lifesaving Service, forerunner of the current U.S. Coast Guard. It includes 7 miles of sandy beaches.

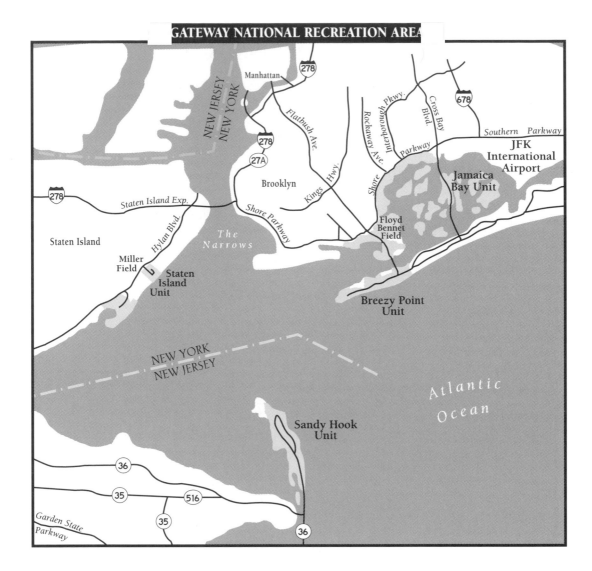

Staten Island Unit (718–354–4500): a hangar complex at Miller Field served seaplanes of the U.S. Air Service following World War I. Sports facilities and calm waters for fishing and swimming are at Great Kills Park. Guided walks and star watches are offered for the general public. Fort Wadsworth, a 200-year-old fort built to defend New York Harbor from attack, is open to the public. Tours relate the fort's batteries and its role in the military history of America.

ENTRANCE FEE: No charge. There is a fee for beach parking during the summer.

FACILITIES: Snack bars, food service, and vending machines are available throughout the four units on a seasonal basis. Marinas are located in the Staten Island and Jamaica Bay units. For additional information call the Gateway Public Affairs Office (718–338–3688).

CAMPING: Four primitive campsites in the Sandy Hook Unit are available by reservation only for organized youth groups.

FISHING: Fishing for flounder, fluke, striped bass, and bluefish is available at various locations around the park.

HOME OF FRANKLIN D. ROOSEVELT
NATIONAL HISTORIC SITE

4097 Albany Post Road
Hyde Park, NY 12538-1997
(845) 229–2501
www,nps.gov/hofr

Franklin D. Roosevelt's 290-acre homesite was designated a national historic site in 1944 to preserve the birthplace and lifetime residence of our thirty-second president. The home is located in southeastern New York, approximately 6 miles north of Poughkeepsie via U.S. 9.

Franklin D. Roosevelt, this country's thirty-second president, was born (January 30, 1882) and raised in this home that was originally a large farmhouse (built circa 1800). The home was purchased in 1867 by his father, James. Roosevelt's parents expanded and substantially altered the house. Although the family also owned a house on the Canadian island of Campobello (Roosevelt Campobello International Park in Maine is an affiliated area of the National Park Service) and generally spent the winters socializing in New York City, this house in Hyde Park, New York, was considered home. Following the death of his father in 1900, Roosevelt and his mother continued to live there. As governor of New York (1928–1932), Roosevelt came back to Hyde Park often, and three days after his death on April 12, 1945, he was buried here. Seventeen years later, Eleanor Roosevelt was buried beside her husband.

The hours of operation are 9:00 A.M. to 5:00 P.M. year-round. An admission fee is charged. Guided tours are given throughout the day, with the last tour beginning at 4:30. All groups of ten or more must make advance reservations. Smaller groups or individuals may also make reservations (800–967–2283). The site is closed Thanksgiving, Christmas Day, and New Year's Day. A leaflet providing additional information is available. Next to the site, the Roosevelt Library and Museum includes the president's study, his ship models, gifts, and exhibits about his life. The graves of Franklin and Eleanor are in a rose garden area between the house and library. Plan a full day to see the home, library, Vanderbilt Mansion, and Eleanor Roosevelt's Val-Kill retreat.

ENTRANCE FEE: There is no fee to enter the grounds. A $10 user fee is charged for a tour of the house and entrance to the musuem and library.

FACILITIES: No food or lodging is available at the site, but both may be found just outside the park. Rest rooms and drinking water are provided in a visitor facility in the stable/garage and in the library. The facility also contains a bookstore and Hudson Valley tourism information.

CAMPING: No camping is permitted at the site. Mills-Norrie State Park, 5 miles north on Highway 9, offers forty-five sites with flush toilets, showers, fishing, boating, and nature trails. The park's camping section is seldom filled, even on weekends (845–889–4646).

MARTIN VAN BUREN NATIONAL HISTORIC SITE

P.O. Box 545
Kinderhook, NY 12106-0545
(518) 758–9689
MAVA_Info@nps.gov
www.nps.gov/mava

Martin Van Buren National Historic Site in rural Columbia County was authorized in 1974 to preserve the home of the eighth president of the United States. The site is located in eastern New York, approximately 20 miles south of Albany via Highway 9. It is just southeast of the village of Kinderhook on Route 9H.

Martin Van Buren was born in Kinderhook in 1782. At age fourteen, he apprenticed in a local law office. Six years later, he decided to complete his apprenticeship in New York City under the supervision of an old friend, William Van Ness. Here he made important personal connections before returning to Kinderhook to practice law.

Following his marriage to Hannah Hoes in 1807, Van Buren and his wife moved to Hudson, New York, where he commenced an ambitious political career. Over the years he held positions as county surrogate, state senator, state attorney general, U.S. senator, governor of New York, secretary of state, vice-president, and, from 1837 to 1841, president of the United States. Van Buren was defeated for reelection in 1840, partially because of his opposition to the annexation of Texas.

Martin Van Buren purchased the Lindenwald estate in 1839 while serving as U.S. president. The home originally belonged to a local judge who had built it in 1797, and it is named after the linden trees growing on the estate. Numerous changes were made to the house by Van Buren during his twenty-one-year residence; he died at Lindenwald in 1862. The mansion has been restored by the National Park Service to its 1840–1862 appearance.

The site is open daily from 9:00 A.M. to 4:30 P.M., mid-May through October. From November 1 through December 5 the site is open Saturday and Sunday 9:00 A.M. to 4:30 P.M. The site is closed from December 6 to mid-May. Guided tours of the house and grounds and other interpretive programs are provided by rangers. Reservations are required for groups of ten or more. A fifteen-minute audio-slide presentation is given inside the visitor center. Van Buren's grave is in the Kinderhook Village Cemetery.

ENTRANCE FEE: $2.00 per person.

FACILITIES: Information about tours, fees, special events, food, and lodging can be obtained at the visitor center along Old Post Road, which is staffed by rangers. A bookstore and rest rooms are located in the visitor center.

CAMPING: No camping is permitted at the site. Lake Taghkanic State Park, approximately 15 miles southeast of Kinderhook via the Taconic State Parkway, offers campsites with tables, grills, flush toilets, swimming, and fishing. Many privately owned campgrounds are also in the vicinity.

PARK AREAS IN DOWNTOWN NEW YORK CITY

National Park Service, Manhattan Sites
26 Wall Street
New York, NY 10005-1907

1. **Castle Clinton National Monument** (southern tip of Manhattan Island in Battery Park; 212–344–7220; www.nps.gov/cacl): This structure, built from 1808 to 1811, was used for the military defense of New York harbor and New York City until 1821. Subsequently, it opened as Castle Garden, a promenade and entertainment center, and in 1855 became an immigrant landing depot through which more than eight million people entered the United States from 1855 to 1890. An exhibit and tours are available. It is open daily 8:30 A.M. to 5:00 P.M. except Christmas Day. There is no entrance fee.

2. **Ellis Island** (212–363–3200/3201): The immigration processing station for twelve million Americans from 1892 to 1924 is operated as part of the Statue of Liberty National Monument. The museum contains three stories of exhibits, displays, artifacts, and photos that explain the immigrants' trip across the ocean, processing at Ellis Island, and assimilation into the United States. A twenty-eight-minute film, "Island of Hope, Island of Tears," is shown continuously in two theaters. Ellis Island is open seven days a week except Christmas Day and is accessible by the Statue of Liberty Circle Line Ferry from Castle Clinton in Battery Park in Manhattan and Liberty State Park in Jersey City, New Jersey; boats leave 9:15 A.M. to 3:15 P.M. every thirty minutes. There is no entrance fee. The ferry that goes to Ellis Island and the Statue of Liberty costs $8.00 per person.

3. **Federal Hall National Memorial** (15 Pine Street; 212–825–6888; www.nps.gov/feha): This building, originally constructed as the Customs House of New York Port, is on the site of Federal Hall, the first capitol of the United States. It is also where the Second Continental Congress convened in 1785, where George Washington took the oath as first U.S. president on April 30, 1789, and where the Bill of Rights was adopted in 1789. The memorial contains a museum and provides a film and exhibits. Tours are available. It is open Monday through Friday 9:00 A.M. to 5:00 P.M. except federal holidays. There is no entrance fee.

4. **General Grant National Memorial** (Riverside Drive and 122nd Street; 212–666–1640; www.nps.gov/gegr): This granite structure, commonly known as Grant's Tomb, contains the tombs of Union Commander and U.S. President Ulysses S. Grant and his wife. An exhibit and tours are available. The memorial is open daily from 9:00 A.M. to 5:00 P.M.

5. **Hamilton Grange National Memorial** (287 Convent Avenue between West 141st Street and West 142nd Street; 212–283–5154; www.nps.gov/hagr): This was the home of Alexander Hamilton, first secretary of the treasury. It was named "The Grange" after Hamilton's grandfather's estate in Scotland. Visitors will find an interpretive exhibit and guided tours. The memorial is open Friday, Saturday, and Sunday from 9:00 A.M. to 5:00 P.M. There is no entrance fee.

6. **Statue of Liberty National Monument** (Liberty Island in New York Harbor; 212–363–3200/3201; www.nps.gov/stli): The famous 152-foot copper sculpture was given to the United States by France in 1886 in commemoration of the alliance between the two nations during the American Revolution. A museum in honor of the immigrants who came to America is located in an addition to the statue's pedestal. An elevator and stairway lead to the top of the pedestal. From here, a spiral stairway equivalent to twelve stories leads to the statue's crown. Both the statue and museum are open daily except Christmas Day. Boats from Castle Clinton in Battery Park and Liberty State Park run daily every thirty minutes

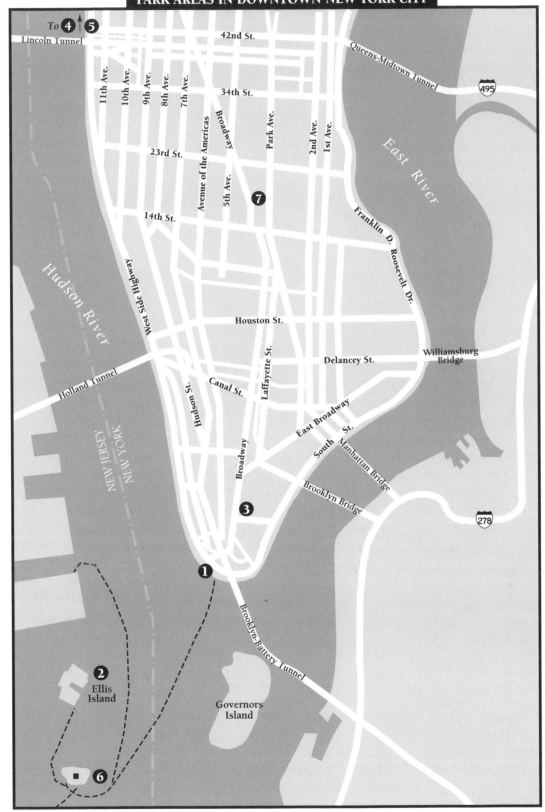

PARK AREAS IN DOWNTOWN NEW YORK CITY

To **4** ↑ **5**

Lincoln Tunnel

42nd St.

Queens-Midtown Tunnel

🛡 495

11th Ave.

10th Ave.

9th Ave.

8th Ave.

7th Ave.

34th St.

Broadway

Avenue of the Americas

5th Ave.

Park Ave.

2nd Ave.

1st Ave.

East River

23rd St.

7

14th St.

Franklin D. Roosevelt Dr.

Hudson River

West Side Highway

Houston St.

Laffayette St.

Delancey St.

Williamsburg Bridge

Holland Tunnel

Canal St.

Hudson St.

East Broadway

South St.

Manhattan Bridge

NEW JERSEY
NEW YORK

Broadway

Brooklyn Bridge

🛡 278

3

1

Brooklyn-Battery Tunnel

2

Ellis Island

Governors Island

■ **6**

from 9:15 A.M. to 3:15 P.M. daily. There is no entrance fee. The ferry that goes to the Statue of Liberty and to Ellis Island costs $8.00 per person.

7. **Theodore Roosevelt Birthplace National Historic Site** (28 East Twentieth Street; 212–260–1616; www.nps.gov/thrb): This four-story reconstructed Victorian brownstone home was the birthplace and boyhood home of our twenty-sixth president. The home has five rooms restored to their 1865 appearance and a museum that contains numerous items relating to Roosevelt's career. The historic site is open for guided tours from 9:00 A.M. to 5:00 P.M. Monday through Friday except federal holidays. A $2.00 entrance fee is charged.

SAGAMORE HILL NATIONAL HISTORIC SITE

20 Sagamore Hill Road
Oyster Bay, NY 11771-1807
(516) 922–4447
sahi_information@nps.gov
www.nps.gov/sahi

Sagamore Hill National Historic Site, established in 1963, was the home of the twenty-sixth President of the United States, Theodore Roosevelt (1858–1919). The site is located near the village of Oyster Bay on New York's Long Island. It is 35 miles from New York City and the Queens Midtown Tunnel. By car, take the Long Island Expressway (I–495) to exit 41 North (State Highway 106). Follow State Highway 106 north for 4 miles toward Oyster Bay, then go right on State Highway 25A for 2½ miles. Follow the brown historic site signs to Sagamore Hill. By rail from New York City's Pennsylvania Station (servicing Amtrak, NJ Transit, and the Long Island Railroad), take the Long Island Railroad Oyster Bay branch to Oyster Bay (3 miles away), or take the Port Jefferson branch to Syosset (6 miles away). Taxis meet all trains.

Theodore Roosevelt long loved the site of his Sagamore Hill home. In 1880 he graduated from Harvard, married, and purchased a hilltop farm field. In 1885 he finished the rambling twenty-three room Queen Anne–style house that was home for his wife and six children. It served as his summer White House from 1902 to 1908.

Sagamore Hill is furnished as it was in Roosevelt's lifetime, reflecting his incredibly wide interests as a hunter, conservationist, patron of the arts, author, farmer, and family man. Skirting the west and south sides of the house is the piazza and a hillside once used for political rallies. Nearby is the Old Orchard Museum, the former home of the president's son, Brigadier General Theodore Roosevelt, Jr. The museum contains exhibits on the lives of Theodore Roosevelt and his family.

The park's visitor center is open 9:00 A.M. to 4:30 P.M. daily except Thanksgiving, Christmas Day, and New Year's Day. The grounds are open from dawn to dusk. Access to the Roosevelt home is only by one of the forty-five-minute tours. With tickets sold at the visitor center, tours are limited to fourteen people and are offered every thirty minutes. The home is closed to tours Monday and Tuesday in the winter but is open daily May through October. Vis-

Sagamore Hill National Historic Site

itation is high in August and on weekends spring through fall. Tours often sell out in the early afternoons during these times.

ENTRANCE FEE: No charge for the grounds. There is a $5.00 fee (visitors sixteen and under free) for a guided tour of the home.

FACILITIES: Neither lodging nor food is available at the site. Rest rooms are located in the museum and near the parking lot. A small picnic area is located behind the visitor center.

Long Island Sound

Caumsett
State Park
Target Rock
N.W.R.

Bayville

Glen Cove

T. Roosevelt
Memorial Park

Sagamore Hill
National
Historic Site

Oyster Bay

Cold Spring
Harbor

T. Roosevelt
Gravesite and
Sanctuary

Huntington

Cove Road

A
25

110

Huntington
Station

Turnpike
Muttontown

E. Norwich

N. Hempstead

106

East Hills

107

25

Broad Hollow Rd.

Jericho Turnpike

Jericho

495

Long Island Expwy.

Exit 41

CAMPING: No camping is permitted at the site. Wildwood State Park (516–929–4314), located 60 miles farther east on Long Island, offers 322 sites with water, grills, flush toilets, cold showers, and a dump station. Reservations can be made by calling (800) 456–CAMP.

ST. PAUL'S CHURCH NATIONAL HISTORIC SITE

897 South Columbus Avenue
Mount Vernon, NY 10550-5018
(914) 667–4116
www.nps.gov./sapa

This affiliated area of the National Park Service was designated a national historic site in 1943 to memorialize and help preserve the eighteenth-century St. Paul's Church and its rich American history. The site is located just north of New York City in the town of Mount Vernon at 897 South Columbus Avenue.

The original St. Paul's parish was established in 1665, with the first recorded church completed in 1700. The present building was constructed during the period 1763–82. The church is best known as the site of the 1733 election whereby Quakers were denied the right to vote because of their religious convictions. During the Revolutionary War, St. Paul's was used as a barracks and hospital by Hessian troops. After the American Revolution, in 1787, it was used as Westchester County's courthouse. Aaron Burr practiced law here.

The site is open Monday through Friday year-round with the exception of holidays. Hours are 9:00 A.M. to 5:00 P.M. Free tours of the church, museum, grounds, and cemetery are available. Tours of the historic church tower are held Friday at 3:00 P.M. from April through October. Call for special programs. The Revolutionary War battle of Pell's Point is commemorated each year on the third Saturday of October from 10:00 A.M. to 4:00 P.M. There are occasional special weekend programs; call in advance for details (914–667–4116). Adjacent to the church, the museum is located in the former carriage shed–parish hall. Exhibits include artifacts, pictures, and maps relating to the history of St. Paul's and the American Revolution in this area.

ENTRANCE FEE: No charge.

FACILITIES: Most visitor services are available nearby.

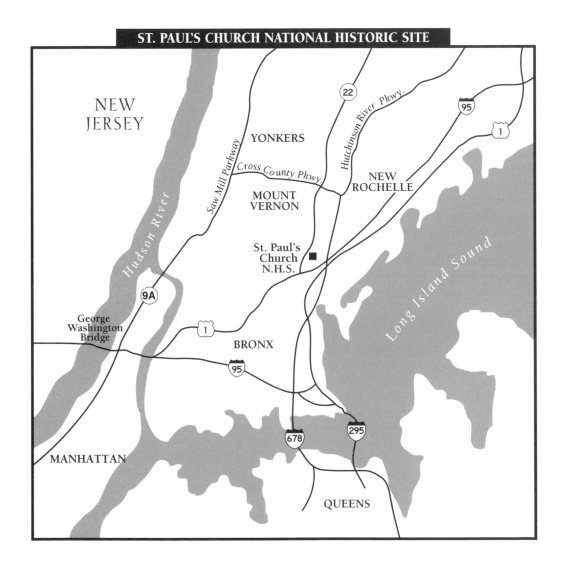

ST. PAUL'S CHURCH NATIONAL HISTORIC SITE

SARATOGA NATIONAL HISTORICAL PARK

648 Route 32
Stillwater, NY 12170-1604
(518) 664-9821
sara_info@nps.gov
www.nps.gov/sara

Saratoga National Historical Park comprises 3,400 acres and was authorized in 1938 to commemorate the site of an important American victory over the British in 1777. The Battle of Saratoga (Freeman's Farm) is considered the turning point of the American Revolution. The park is located in eastern New York, 30 miles north of Albany via Interstate 87 (exit 12).

In the summer of 1777, British forces under General John Burgoyne left Canada to invade the united colonies (states), which were seeking independence. The expedition started with approximately 9,000 men with an aim to advance down the Champlain Valley to the Hudson River, and from there to Albany. Once in possession of Albany, Burgoyne would open up communications with New York City and wait for further instructions.

At first Burgoyne succeeded, with Fort Ticonderoga falling and the Americans retreating, but the American forces under General Philip Schuyler delayed him by destroying roads and bridges. By the time Burgoyne reached the Freeman Farm on September 19, Schuyler had been replaced by General Horatio Gates, who fortified a strong position on Bemis Heights, 2 miles north of Stillwater.

There, at the Freeman Farm, part of the British forces, by then reduced to 7,500 men by deaths, desertions, and garrisoning of the supply line, met part of the 8,500-men American force on September 19. The fighting ended at nightfall, with British troops holding the field. The armies waited for two-and-one-half weeks before Burgoyne again attempted to pass the American lines on October 7. The second battle resulted in the loss of key positions on the British lines and forced Burgoyne to retreat to Saratoga (modern-day Schuylerville), where he surrendered on October 17, 1777. The victory at Saratoga is considered the turning point of the American Revolution and one of the world's most decisive battles.

The park's visitor center is open 9:00 A.M. to 5:00 P.M. daily except Thanksgiving, Christmas Day, and New Year's Day. It contains exhibits and a twenty-one-minute film. A 10.5-mile, self-guided auto-tour route begins near here; guide booklets and tour audiotapes are available in the visitor center. The tour road is open, weather permitting, from early April to mid-November. Extended hours are posted from June through August. The tour includes ten stops with historic markers, interpretive signs, trails, and the restored Neilson House, which is open, as staffing permits, in summer from 10:00 A.M. to 4:00 P.M. The Battlefield has several miles of hiking trails, including a 2-mile and a 4.2-mile loop. Trails are popular for cross-country skiing during the winter.

Two related sites are under park jurisdiction. From late June to Labor Day, guided tours are available through the restored country home of General Schuyler. The renovated Saratoga Monument, a 155-foot-tall stone spire erected for the centennial of the surrender, is undergoing continued renovations; call the park for details. The sites are located approximately 8 miles north of the battlefield in Schuylerville and can be reached by taking Route 4 or Route 32.

Directions and maps are available at the visitor center. The Schulyer House is open in summer from 10:00 A.M. to 4:00 P.M. Wednesday through Sunday.

ENTRANCE FEE: $4.00 per vehicle or $2.00 per person; good for seven days.

FACILITIES: No food or lodging is available in the park. Modern rest rooms and drinking water are in the visitor center. The visitor center and the battlefield tour stops are wheelchair-accessible.

CAMPING: No camping is permitted in the park. Moreau Lake State Park is a short distance north off Interstate 87 (exit 17). Moreau Lake offers tables, grills, water, flush toilets, swimming, and fishing (518–793–0511).

FISHING: No fishing opportunities are available in the park.

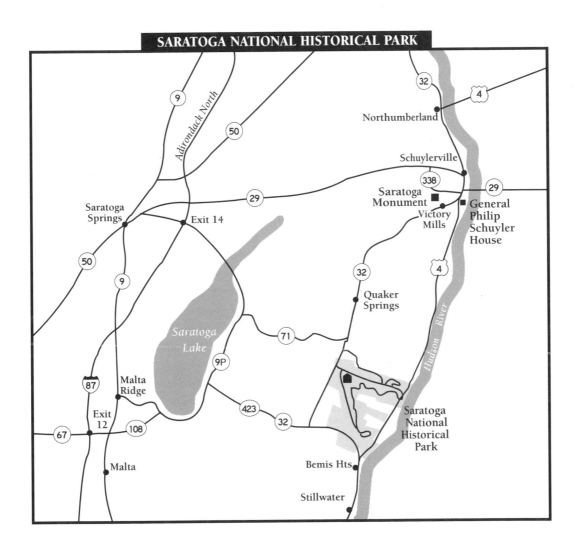

SARATOGA NATIONAL HISTORICAL PARK

THEODORE ROOSEVELT INAUGURAL NATIONAL HISTORIC SITE

641 Delaware Avenue
Buffalo, NY 14202-1079
(716) 884–0095
www.nps.gov/thri

Theodore Roosevelt Inaugural National Historic Site contains one acre and was authorized in 1966 to preserve the house where Theodore Roosevelt took the oath of office as president of the United States on September 14, 1901, following the assassination of President William McKinley. The home is located in western New York state in the city of Buffalo. In Buffalo, the site is at 641 Delaware Avenue, near North Street.

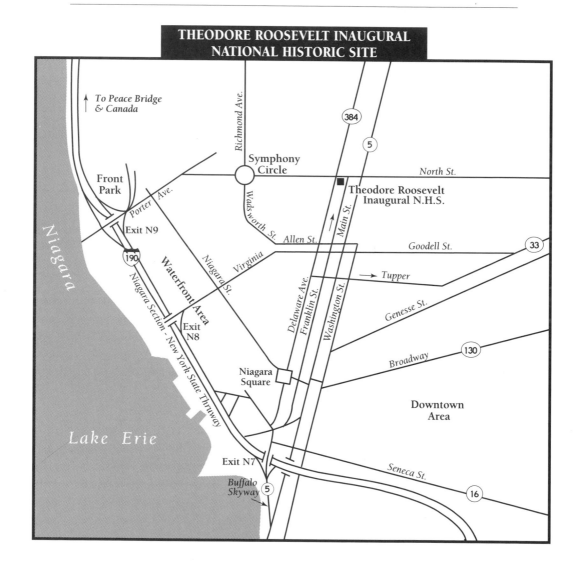

On September 6, 1901, while attending a reception at the Pan-American Exposition in Buffalo, New York, President William McKinley was shot by an anarchist. Vice President Theodore Roosevelt, on a speaking engagement in Vermont, was summoned to Buffalo following the shooting. He stayed 'at the Ansley Wilcox home until September 10 when it appeared that McKinley was out of danger. Roosevelt then joined his family for a vacation in New York's Adirondack Mountains. On September 13, McKinley's condition suddenly worsened and Roosevelt was notified to return to Buffalo as soon as possible. The vice president arrived in Buffalo on September 14 at 1:30 P.M., eleven hours after McKinley's death. Roosevelt took the oath of office in the Wilcox Library at 3:30 P.M. He wore borrowed clothing and no photographs were taken.

The restored house is open (fee charged) Monday through Friday from 9:00 A.M. to 5:00 P.M. and on Saturday and Sunday from noon until 5:00 P.M. The site offers an informational audiovisual presentation, several exhibit areas, and four restored period rooms that may be seen on a guided tour. The site is closed on major holidays. A parking lot is in the rear of the house and can be reached from Franklin Street (one-way north).

ENTRANCE FEE: No charge for the grounds. There is a charge for house tours: $3.00 adults, $2.00 seniors, $1.00 for visitors thriteen and under.

FACILITIES: No dining facilities are available at the site. Several restaurants and hotels are within walking distance of the site along Delaware Avenue.

CAMPING: No camping is permitted at the site. Darien Lake, Letchworth, Four Mile Creek, and Joseph Davis state parks all offer camping within a 30-mile radius of Buffalo. Campgrounds are also across the border in Canada.

VANDERBILT MANSION NATIONAL HISTORIC SITE

4097 Albany Post Road
Hyde Park, NY 12538-1997
(845) 229–7770
www.nps.gov/vama

Vanderbilt Mansion National Historic Site comprises 212 acres and was designated a part of the National Park Service in 1940 to preserve a lifestyle and era through one of the elegant mansions built around the turn of the twentieth century. The park is located in southeast New York, 6 miles north of Poughkeepsie via U.S. 9. It is just north of the village of Hyde Park on a bluff overlooking the Hudson River.

In 1895, this estate was purchased by Frederick Vanderbilt (one of four grandsons of Cornelius Vanderbilt) as a spring-fall cottage where he could pursue his interests in purebred livestock and horticulture. In 1896, a then-existing mansion was torn down, and construction commenced on the present fifty-four-room, $660,000 (excluding furnishings) structure. After the home's completion in 1899, the Vanderbilts lived here in the spring and fall and made the estate the scene of lavish parties that included the rich and famous.

Hours of operation are 9:00 A.M. to 5:00 P.M. daily year-round. The site is closed Thanksgiving, Christmas Day, and New Year's Day. Guided tours are given throughout the day, with the last tour beginning at 4:30. Groups of ten or more must make advance reservations (800–967–2283). Smaller groups or individuals may also make reservations.

The visitor center is located in the Pavilion, which served as housing when there was an overflow of guests and also as an occasional winter home. The mansion's interior and its furnishings are especially stunning. Signs explaining each room's use and furnishings are located at doorways in the mansion. Visitors should also walk a short distance to the large garden area. Volunteers, using donated funds, have completed several beds of flowers to match their 1938 grandeur.

ENTRANCE FEE: There is no fee to enter the grounds. There is an $8.00 user fee for the guided tour of the house.

FACILITIES: No food or lodging is available at the site, although both may be found a mile south in Hyde Park. Rest rooms and a drinking fountain are located in the visitor center. Cabins are available in Mills-Norrie State Park (see camping section).

CAMPING: No camping is permitted at the site. Mills-Norrie State Park, 3½ miles north on Highway 9, offers nice shaded sites with tables, flush toilets, hot showers, fishing, boating, a marina, and nature trails. The park's camping section is seldom filled, even on weekends (845–889–4646).

FISHING: Fishing is available at the site; a valid New York fishing license is required. The small creek, however, is not stocked, and most fish are smaller than the size allowed for removal.

Vanderbilt Mansion National Historic Site

WOMEN'S RIGHTS NATIONAL HISTORICAL PARK

136 Fall Street
Seneca Falls, NY 13148-1517
(315) 568–2991
www.nps.gov/wori

Women's Rights National Historical Park comprises nine acres and was authorized in 1980 to commemorate the beginning of the women's struggle for equal rights and the first Women's Rights Convention. The park includes the site of the 1848 Women's Rights Convention and the homes of several early women's rights activists. The historical park is in western New York, in the village of Seneca Falls, approximately midway between Rochester and Syracuse. The park is a fifteen-minute drive south of the New York thruway, exit 41 via Route 414 and Route 5/20.

The industrial revolution of the early 1800s had a significant impact on the women of the United States. Although asked to work and earn outside income, women were required to turn over incomes to their husbands, in addition to receiving lower wages for comparable work. Women also were not permitted to own property, enter a profession other than teaching, attend college, inherit their husbands' estates, or vote.

Nowhere did the change in women's lives become more apparent than in Seneca Falls, New York. Situated near the Great Western Turnpike, the Erie Canal, and a major railroad, the town was a major crossing point for a wide variety of individuals and ideas. In early July 1848, five courageous women met to discuss their difficulties in reconciling family and public responsibilities. This meeting led to the first Women's Rights Convention on July 19 and 20. This convention marked the formal beginning of the women's rights movement in the United States.

The park incorporates four historic buildings: the site of the convention and the homes of three individuals instrumental in the movement. The visitor center in downtown Seneca Falls (136 Fall Street) is open daily, 9:00 A.M. to 5:00 P.M., except November through February and federal holidays. Interpretive talks and guided tours (fee charged) of the restored Elizabeth Cady Stanton house are offered daily.

Other places of interest in Seneca Falls include the National Women's Hall of Fame at 76 Fall Street, the Seneca Falls Urban Heritage Area Visitor Center at 115 Fall Street, lower level, the Seneca Falls Historical Society Museum at 55 Cayuga Street, and the Seneca Museum of Waterways and Industry at 85 Fall Street. A number of interesting historic buildings remain in use near the park's visitor center.

ENTRANCE FEE: $2.00; visitors sixteen and under free. There is a $1.00 fee (sixteen and under free) for the Elizabeth Cady Stanton House tour.

FACILITIES: Food and lodging are available in Seneca Falls and Waterloo. Rest rooms and drinking water are in the visitor center.

CAMPING: Cayuga Lake State Park, located 4 miles east of Seneca Falls, offers 286 camping sites with tables, grills, flush toilets, a dump station, showers, fishing, boating, and swimming. Electric hookups are provided at thirty-six sites. From downtown Seneca Falls, drive 3 miles east on Bayard Street and 1 mile south on State Highway 89 (315–568–5163). The park is quite nice.

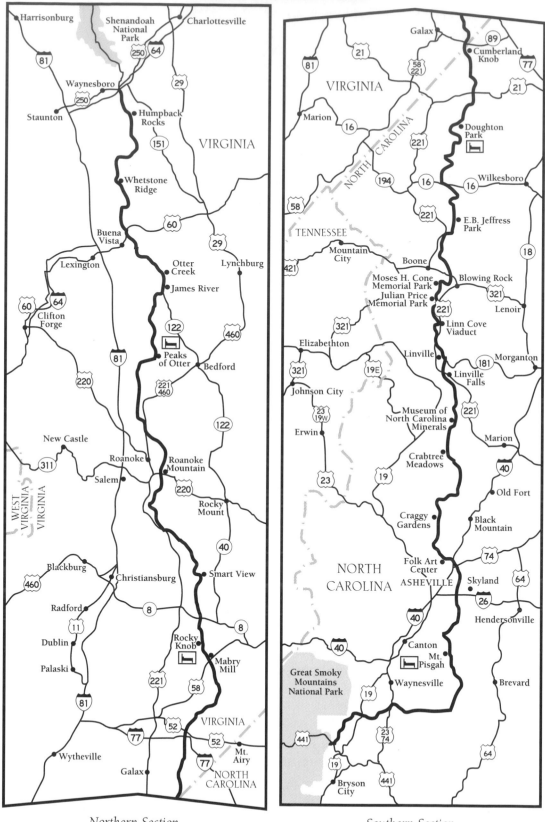

Northern Section

Northern Section

Southern Section

NORTH CAROLINA

STATE TOURIST INFORMATION
(800) 847–4862
www.visitnc.com

BLUE RIDGE PARKWAY
199 Hemphill Knob Road
Asheville, NC 28803
(828) 298–0398
Peter_Givens@nps.gov
www.nps.gov/blri

This first rural parkway comprises more than 81,000 acres along 470 miles of road that follow the crest of the Blue Ridge Mountains. The parkway, located in western North Carolina and Virginia, connects Shenandoah National Park and Great Smoky Mountains National Park.

The Blue Ridge Parkway is almost too good to be true. It provides quiet, leisurely (45 miles per hour maximum) travel on a road that is free of trucks, billboards, and commercial vehicles through a largely undeveloped stretch of the southern Appalachians. The complete drive without stops takes approximately sixteen hours. The scenery is beautiful, and the parkway is generally uncrowded except during fall-color season. Along the way, motorists will find trails, wayside exhibits, museums, picnic areas, craft centers, and campgrounds. A detailed map of the entire route may be obtained at any of twelve visitor centers and orientation facilities that are open May through October. Visitors also will find a schedule of guided walks, living-history programs, craft demonstrations, and evening talks that take place along the parkway. The Blue Ridge Parkway is the most visited of all the units of the National Park System.

Of particular interest is Mabry Mill, which contains a water-powered gristmill and black-smith shop along with other pioneer exhibits. For craft lovers, the Parkway Craft Center at the Moses H. Cone Memorial Park, the Northwest Trading Post, and the Folk Art Center near Asheville offer outstanding examples of local handicrafts. The 1,243-foot-long Linn Cove Viaduct, finished in 1987, was the last link in the completion of the parkway after fifty-two years of construction.

ENTRANCE FEE: No charge.

FACILITIES: Restaurants, gas stations, campgrounds, and picnic areas are located along the parkway and in nearby towns. Food, lodging, and gasoline are available at Peaks of Otter (540–586–1081), Doughton Park (336–372–4499), and Mount Pisgah (828–235–8228). Lodging only is at Rocky Knob (540–593–3503), and food only is at Otter Creek, Mabry Mill, and Crabtree Meadows.

CAMPING: Campgrounds with tables, grills, water, flush toilets, and dump stations are at Otter Creek (sixty-seven spaces), Roanoke Mountain (105 spaces), Julian Price Park (197 spaces), Linville Falls (seventy-five spaces), Crabtree Meadows (ninety-three spaces), Mt. Pisgah (140 spaces), Peaks of Otter (148 spaces), Rocky Knob (109 spaces), and Doughton Park (136 spaces). Campgrounds are open from May 1 to November 1. Winter camping (limited facilities) is available, depending on the weather, at one campground in each state.

FISHING: Streams contain brook, rainbow, and brown trout; some waters managed as native trout streams require reduced limits. Price Lake contains rainbow trout, and bass and bluegills are found in Bass Lake.

CAPE HATTERAS NATIONAL SEASHORE

Route 1, Box 675
Manteo, NC 27954-2708
(919) 473–2111
www.nps.gov/caha

Cape Hatteras National Seashore was authorized as part of the National Park Service in 1937 to protect 70 miles of beach land along Atlantic barrier islands. The seashore is located in eastern North Carolina and is reached from the north via U.S. 158, from the west by Highways 64 or 264, and from the south via ferries from Cedar Island or Swan Quarter.

Cape Hatteras National Seashore comprises a thin strip of beaches, marshes, woodlands, and dunes stretching across three barrier islands that provide shelter for North Carolina's mainland. This is an uncrowded and wild place where one can walk along the beach while observing the ever-present shore birds as they search for food. Glance out to sea where the Outer Banks, known as the "Graveyard of the Atlantic," serves as the resting place for more than 600 ship-wrecks.

From the time of the first English settlement in the New World on Roanoke Island in 1585 to the first successful flight of a powered airplane at Kill Devil Hill in 1903, this area along North Carolina's coast has a rich human history. Pirates roamed the ocean and inlets here along

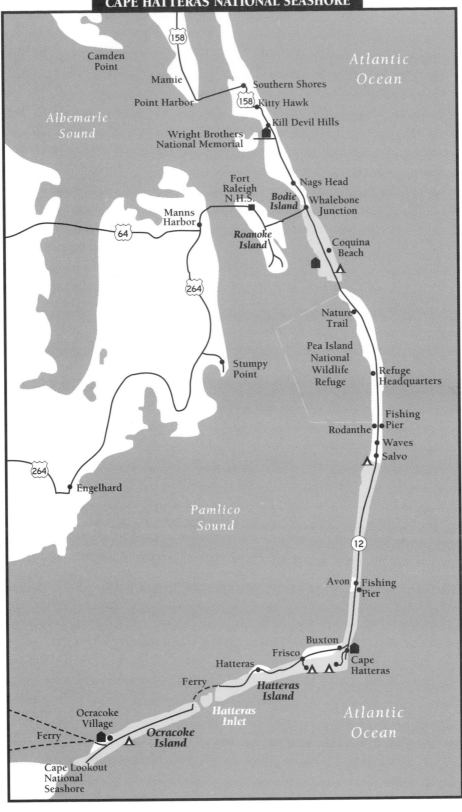

CAPE HATTERAS NATIONAL SEASHORE

Camden
Point

Mamie

Point Harbor

*Albemarle
Sound*

Southern Shores

158

Kitty Hawk

Kill Devil Hills

Wright Brothers
National Memorial

*Atlantic
Ocean*

Fort
Raleigh
N.H.S.

*Bodie
Island*

Nags Head

Whalebone
Junction

Manns
Harbor

64

*Roanoke
Island*

Coquina
Beach

264

Nature
Trail

Stumpy
Point

Pea Island
National
Wildlife
Refuge

Refuge
Headquarters

Fishing
Pier

Rodanthe

Waves

Salvo

264

Engelhard

*Pamlico
Sound*

12

Avon

Fishing
Pier

Buxton

Frisco

Hatteras

Cape
Hatteras

Ferry

*Hatteras
Island*

*Hatteras
Inlet*

Ocracoke
Village

Ferry

*Ocracoke
Island*

Cape Lookout
National
Seashore

*Atlantic
Ocean*

a cape made famous by its shipwrecks. At Coquina Beach, the remains of a four-masted schooner stranded in 1921 are accessible to visitors. The village of Ocracoke, at the south end of Ocracoke Island, retains its early charm.

A wide variety of recreational activities are available, including beachcombing, surfing, sailing, fishing, and nature study. The park's main visitor center at Cape Hatteras Light Station contains exhibits, and personnel are on duty to answer questions. All visitor centers, including the centers at Bodie Island and Ocracoke Island, are open year-round.

ENTRANCE FEE: No charge. There is a fee to climb Cape Hatteras Lighthouse: $3.00 for adults and $1.50 for visitors eleven and under.

FACILITIES: A number of concessioners operate fishing piers and sell tackle, bait, and beverages. A marina is located near Oregon Inlet.

CAMPING: Campgrounds with tables, grills, flush toilets, cold-water showers, and dump stations are at Cape Point (202 spaces), Frisco (127 spaces, no dump station), Ocracoke (136 spaces), and Oregon Inlet (120 spaces). Cape Point is open from Memorial Day through Columbus Day. The other three are open from mid-April to the first week in October. Reservations may be made for Ocracoke Campground (1–800–365–CAMP).

FISHING: A variety of saltwater fish are taken from the surf, the piers, and deep-sea chartered boats. These include channel bass, mullet, striped bass, bluefish, spot, marlin, sailfish, dolphin, and amberjack. A few freshwater ponds contain bass and bluegill.

CAPE LOOKOUT NATIONAL SEASHORE

131 Charles Street
Harkers Island, NC 28531-9702
(919) 728–2250
CALO_Information@nps.gov
www.nps.gov/calo

Cape Lookout National Seashore was authorized in 1966 to protect 56 miles of primitive barrier islands on the lower Outer Banks, including beaches, dunes, salt marshes, and the Cape Lookout Lighthouse. The seashore is located in eastern North Carolina, southwest of Cape Hatteras. There are no bridges to the islands. Passenger-only ferry service is available from Morehead City, Beaufort, and Harkers Island to the Cape Lookout Lighthouse area, and between Ocracoke and Portsmouth Village. Vehicle ferry service for four-wheel-drive vehicles or ATVs is available from Davis to Great Island Bay and from Atlantic to Long Point. There are no roads on the seashore.

The narrow ribbons of sand running from Ocracoke Inlet on the northeast to Beaufort Inlet on the southwest are continuously being changed by wind, waves, and currents. The islands are composed mostly of bare beaches and low dunes covered by scattered grasses, flat grasslands

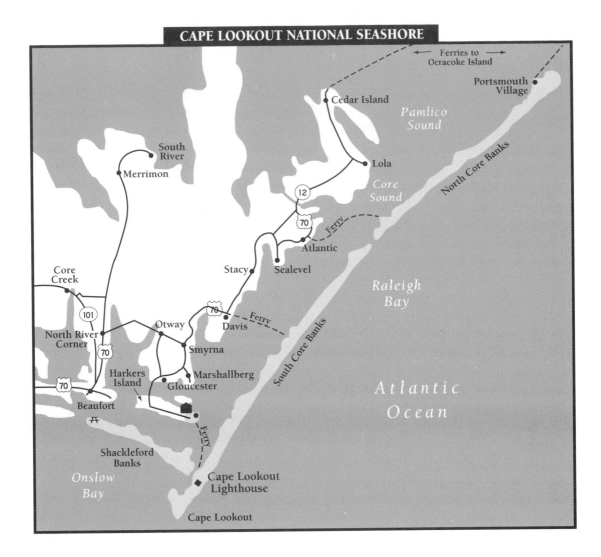

CAPE LOOKOUT NATIONAL SEASHORE

with dense vegetation, and large expanses of salt marshes on the west side. Mammals are relatively rare, but on Shackleford there is a population of horses formerly pastured in the area that became wild. Also on this island, visitors will find an extensive maritime forest.

The lighthouse built on Cape Lookout in 1859 is still in operation but closed to the public. The nearby Keeper's Quarters, which was built in 1873, is open seasonally as a visitor center. Portsmouth Village was established at the north end of the seashore in 1753. Originally a busy transshipment point for ship cargoes to the mainland, today it is a ghost village. Information on reaching Portsmouth Village or the Cape Lookout lighthouse may be obtained by writing or calling headquarters on Harkers Island or through its Web site: www.nps.gov/calo.

ENTRANCE FEE: No charge.

FACILITIES: There are two fishing camps on the islands that provide overnight accommodations—Morris Marina on North Core Banks and Willis Fish Camp on South Core Banks.

There is little shade, so proper clothing is a must, along with sunscreen and insect repellent. Water must be taken in, and any trash should be carried out.

CAMPING: Primitive camping is permitted, although there is no water, and toilet facilities are limited. No camping is permitted at Portsmouth Village or near the lighthouse.

FISHING: A variety of saltwater fish are taken from the surf, including channel bass, flounder, bluefish, spot, croaker, and sea trout.

CARL SANDBURG HOME NATIONAL HISTORIC SITE

1928 Little River Road
Flat Rock, NC 28731-9766
(828) 693–4178
www.nps.gov/carl

Carl Sandburg Home National Historic Site comprises 262 acres and was authorized in 1968 to preserve the farm home where this famous American author spent the last twenty-two years of his life. The park is located in western North Carolina, 26 miles south of Asheville via Interstate 26.

When Carl Sandburg and his family moved from Michigan to this farm (named "Connemara") in 1945, he had already produced much of his outstanding literary work, such as the two-volume *Abraham Lincoln: The Prairie Years* (1926), the four-volume *Abraham Lincoln: The War Years* (1940), and many volumes of poetry and children's books. He had also spent many years pursuing a career in journalism. While living here, he continued his writing, including his only novel, *Remembrance Rock* (1948), and an autobiography, *Always the Young Strangers* (1953). In 1967, Carl Sandburg died at age eighty-nine.

The site is open 9:00 A.M. to 5:00 P.M. daily except Christmas Day. An information station with films and literature is in the basement of the main house. Guided tours of the home (fee charged) begin here. Following the tour, visitors are invited to walk around the farm and visit the numerous buildings. Mrs. Sandburg raised prize-winning goats at the barn. Trails to Little Glassy Mountain (⅕ mile) and Big Glassy Mountain (1³⁄₁₀ miles) begin near the house. Readings are presented periodically throughout the day during summer months. Allow two to three hours for a visit.

ENTRANCE FEE: No charge for the grounds. There is a fee for the house tour: $3.00 for adults, visitors sixteen and under free.

FACILITIES: No food service or lodging is available. Restaurants and motels are in Hendersonville, 3 miles north.

CAMPING: No camping is permitted at the site. Camping is available in Pisgah National Forest. Pleasant Ridge County Park offers summer camping facilities across the South Carolina border on Highway 11.

FORT RALEIGH NATIONAL HISTORIC SITE

Route 1, Box 675
Manteo, NC 27954-2708
(919) 473–5772
www.nps.gov/fora

Fort Raleigh National Historic Site comprises 513 acres and was established in 1941 to commemorate the first attempted English settlement in North America. It was expanded in 1990 to include associated historical events. The park is located in eastern North Carolina, 3 miles north of Manteo via U.S. 64. (For a map of the vicinity, see Cape Hatteras National Seashore.)

In 1585, under the sponsorship and aid of Sir Walter Raleigh, a military venture was sent to establish an initial English settlement in a new colony called Virginia. After selecting the north end of Roanoke Island, the group built a fort and set out to explore the surrounding territory. Later, becoming short on food, the expedition set sail to England with Sir Francis Drake. By 1587, two additional groups totaling 115 men, women, and children had been dropped off at the earlier settlement. When English ships next returned in 1590, however, the colony had mysteriously disappeared.

The visitor center, open year-round, contains exhibits, excavated artifacts, and a film to help interpret the site. Visitors will also find the restored earthworks, which was part of the settlement site of 1585 and 1587. The Thomas Hariot Nature Trail begins near the fort. During summer months, a symphonic drama (fee charged) is produced in the Waterside Theatre. Adjacent to the site, the Elizabethan Garden (fee charged) is maintained by a private organization.

ENTRANCE FEE: No charge.

FACILITIES: Rest rooms and drinking water are available in the visitor center. Lodging and food service can be found in nearby communities.

CAMPING: No camping is permitted at the site. A private campground is located nearby, and a number of National Park Service campgrounds are available at Cape Hatteras National Seashore.

GUILFORD COURTHOUSE NATIONAL MILITARY PARK

2332 New Garden Road
Greensboro, NC 27410-2355
(336) 288–1776
GUCO_Administration@nps.gov
www.nps.gov/guco

Guilford Courthouse National Military Park comprises 224 acres and was established in 1917 to memorialize an important 1781 battle that opened the campaign that was to end the American Revolution. Guilford Courthouse is located in north-central North Carolina, 6 miles northwest of downtown Greensboro. Follow U.S. 220 northwest and turn east on New Garden Road. As you enter the park, turn right to the visitor center.

After England had resigned itself to losing its northern colonies and began concentrating forces in the South, British General Charles Cornwallis commenced a campaign that was designed to subdue North and South Carolina. After weeks of pursuing a force led by General Nathanael Greene, the latter's Continental troops took position at Guilford Courthouse and invited Cornwallis to attack. Although the bloody battle on March 15, 1781, resulted in Greene's withdrawing his troops, the British losses were severe; seven months later, the surrender of Cornwallis at Yorktown sealed the fate of England's ambitions in America.

The military park is open daily, except on Thanksgiving, Christmas, and New Year's Days, from 8:30 A.M. to 5:00 P.M. The visitor center offers modern exhibits, including artifacts of and information about the people and events of the American Revolution in the South and the battle of Guilford Courthouse. Also available in the visitor center are a new eleven-minute computer-animated tactical battle map and a movie, *Another Such Victory*. New outdoor exhibits tell the story of the battle and history of the park. Park personnel are on duty in the center to help visitors. A one-way auto road and bicycle trail begins at the visitor center. Exhibits are located at stops along the road.

ENTRANCE FEE: No charge.

FACILITIES: Food service and lodging are not available in the park but may be found nearby in Greensboro. Modern rest rooms and drinking water are in the visitor center.

CAMPING: No camping is permitted in the park. The city of Greensboro operates a nice campground south of town with tables, grills, flush toilets, and showers.

MOORES CREEK NATIONAL BATTLEFIELD

40 Patriots Hall Drive
Currie, NC 28435
(910) 283–5591
MOCR_Ranger_Activities@nps.gov
www.nps.gov/mocr

Moores Creek National Battlefield comprises eighty-seven acres and was established in 1926 to commemorate a 1776 battle between North Carolina patriots and loyalists. The battlefield is located in southeastern North Carolina, 20 miles northwest of Wilmington via U.S. 421 and State Highway 210. The battlefield can also be reached by taking State Highway 210 west from the Rocky Point exit off Interstate 40.

To reestablish strong British authority in the Carolinas, an army of 1,600 loyalists was recruited to march to the coast and join British troops. At Moores Creek on February 27, 1776, they were met by 1,000 patriots who not only halted the advance but also turned the loyalist retreat into a rout. The victory ended British authority in the colony and helped delay a full-scale invasion of the South. On April 12, 1776, North Carolina was the first colony to instruct its delegation to the Continental Congress to vote for independence.

The battlefield is open daily (except Christmas Day and New Year's Day) from 9:00 A.M. to 5:00 P.M. A visitor center contains an audiovisual program and exhibits interpreting the conflict. Included in the center are original weapons and a diorama. Conducted tours and self-guided walks begin here and lead past monuments and the patriot defense lines. Living-history programs are presented in the summer during various weekend afternoons.

ENTRANCE FEE: No charge.

FACILITIES: No lodging is available in the park. A soft-drink machine is at the visitor center. Rest rooms and drinking water are provided at the visitor center and at Patriots Hall.

CAMPING: No camping is permitted on the battlefield grounds. Carolina Beach State Park has camping facilities south of Wilmington on U.S. 421.

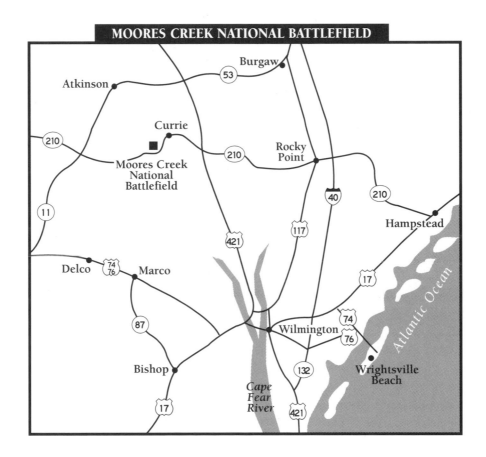

WRIGHT BROTHERS NATIONAL MEMORIAL

c/o Cape Hatteras National Seashore
Route 1, Box 675
Manteo, NC 27954-2708
(919) 473–2111
www.nps.gov/wrbr

Wright Brothers National Memorial comprises 431 acres and was authorized in 1927 to commemorate the site of the first sustained flight in a heavier-than-air machine. The flight was made here by Wilbur and Orville Wright on December 17, 1903. The park is located in eastern North Carolina, 50 miles southeast of Elizabeth City. It is approximately midway between Kitty Hawk and Nags Head on U.S. 158. (For an area map, see Cape Hatteras National Seashore.) The First Flight Airstrip, a 3,000-foot runway (VFR) with aircraft parking (limited to 24 hours per visit), is available for those wishing to arrive at the memorial by private aircraft.

Although the Wright brothers experimented at their home in Dayton, Ohio, they needed a location with relatively constant winds to test their aircraft designs. After checking weather bureau records, they decided upon the Kitty Hawk area. The brothers made more than 1,000 glider flights from the top of Kill Devil Hill in 1900, 1901, and 1902. Finally, on December 17, 1903, their motor-driven machine lifted off level sand and traveled 120 feet in twelve seconds. This was the first successful powered, man-carrying airplane flight in history. They made three more successful flights that day.

The visitor center contains exhibits and full-scale reproductions of the 1902 glider and the 1903 flying machine. The original motor-driven plane is in the Smithsonian Institution in Washington, D.C. A 60-foot granite memorial stands atop Kill Devil Hill, where many of the glider flights originated. Nearby are two reconstructed wooden buildings duplicating the Wrights' 1903 camp.

ENTRANCE FEE: $4.00 per vehicle or $2.00 per person; visitors sixteen and under free.

FACILITIES: Rest rooms and water are available in the visitor center. Lodging and food service can be found in nearby comunities.

CAMPING: No camping is permitted on the memorial grounds. A number of National Park Service campgrounds are located to the south in Cape Hatteras National Seashore.

OHIO

STATE TOURIST INFORMATION
(800) 282–5393
www.ohiotourism.com

CUYAHOGA VALLEY NATIONAL PARK

15610 Vaughn Road
Brecksville, OH 44141-3018
(216) 524–1497
cuva_canal_visitor_center@nps.gov
www.nps.gov/cuva
www.dayinthevalley.com

This 33,000-acre national park was established in 1975 to preserve the rural Cuyahoga River Valley, which links the two urban centers of Cleveland and Akron. The park is located in northeastern Ohio along a north–south strip paralleled on the west by Interstate 77 and on the east by State Highway 8.

Within a heavily populated urban area that was once the western boundary of the United States, Cuyahoga Valley offers a place to enjoy a wildflower walk, hike or bike along miles of trails, or hear a traditional music concert. The park's main visitor attraction is the Ohio & Erie Canal Towpath Trail, a 19-mile, multi-use trail extending the length of the park alongside remnants of the canal.

The Canal Visitor Center is at the north end of the park in a restored house next to the canal. Inside, visitors find information, exhibits, publications, and a museum of canal history. Park rangers and volunteers conduct canal lock demonstrations at the adjacent Lock 38 seasonally on weekends and holidays. The visitor center is located on Canal Road, south of Rockside Road in the village of Valley View, and is open daily from 8:00 A.M. to 5:00 P.M., except Thanksgiving, Christmas Day, and New Year's Day (216–524–1497).

Happy Days Visitor Center, located on State Route 303, offers information and a variety of activities. The rustic building was built by the Civilian Conservation Corps in the 1930s as a day camp for inner-city children. A network of trails leads from here through the Virginia Kendall unit of the park. The popular Cuyahoga Valley Lyceum Series of lectures, concerts, and dramatic presentations is presented at the visitor center each January through March. Visitor center hours are limited in off-season (330–650–4636).

A third facility, Hunt Farm Visitor Information Center, is in the south end of the park near the intersection of Bolanz and Riverview roads. The Hunt Farm property is typical of the small family farms that dotted the Cuyahoga Valley in the late nineteenth century. The building is open seasonally and houses exhibits about the area's agricultural history (330–650–4636).

The Boston Store is a renovated canal store that houses exhibits related to the boat-building history of the local towns of Boston and Peninsula. Exhibits include a full-size, partial replica of a canal boat and several interactive displays. The Boston Store is open weekends year-round and daily during summer. Hours vary.

There are a variety of other things to see and do in the park. The Stephen Frazee house is open seasonally, providing visitors a glimpse of life in Ohio's Western Reserve during the early period of settlement. Hale Farm and Village, a restored 1800s farm and village, is operated by the Western Reserve Historical Society. The Cuyahoga Valley Scenic Railroad runs the length of the park and beyond, with special excursions year-round. The Cleveland Orchestra spends its summers at Blossom Music Center. Summer stock is performed at Porthouse Theatre, which is owned and operated by Kent State University. Cleveland Metroparks and Metro Parks, serving Summit County, manage the Bike and Hike Trail, which extends from Bedford to Kent. A connector trail along Holzhauer Road provides access to the Towpath Trail. There are also golf courses, a water park, two ski resorts, and businesses that offer bicycle rentals and carriage rides.

ENTRANCE FEE: No charge.

FACILITIES: Food service is available nearby. Rest rooms, drinking water, and picnic facilities are located throughout the park area.

CAMPING: No camping facilities are provided within the park, but lodging is available nearby.

FISHING: Several ponds and fishing piers are located within the park; an Ohio fishing license is required.

DAYTON AVIATION HERITAGE NATIONAL HISTORICAL PARK

P.O. Box 9280
Wright Brothers Station
Dayton, OH 45409-9280
(937) 225–7705
DAAV_Interpretation@nps.gov
www.nps.gov/daav

Dayton Aviation Heritage National Historical Park was established in 1992 to preserve the area's aviation heritage and commemorate the legacies of Wilbur Wright, Orville Wright, and their friend, poet Paul Laurence Dunbar. The historical park

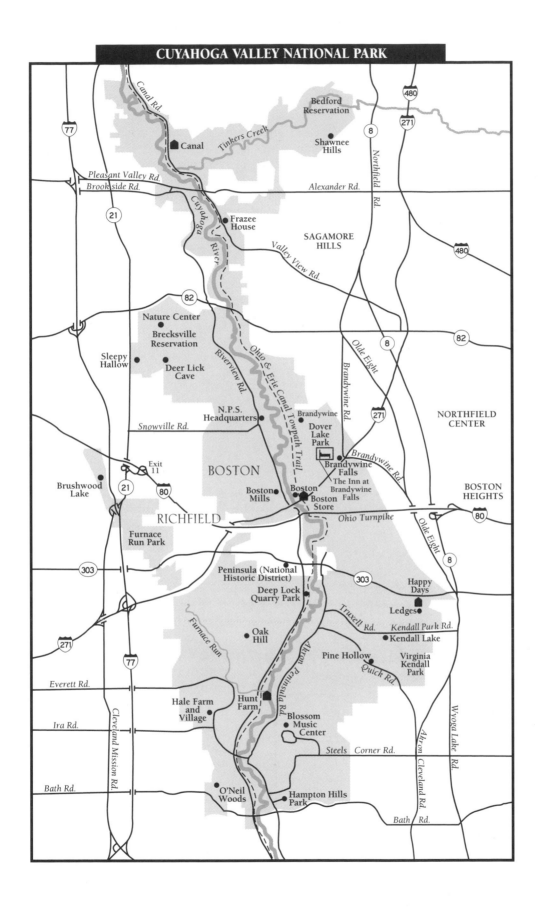

CUYAHOGA VALLEY NATIONAL PARK

Canal Rd.

77

Bedford Reservation

480

271

Canal

Tinkers Creek

Shawnee Hills

8

Pleasant Valley Rd.

Brookside Rd.

Alexander Rd.

Northfield Rd.

480

21

Cuyahoga River

Frazee House

SAGAMORE HILLS

Valley View Rd.

82

Nature Center

Brecksville Reservation

82

Sleepy Hallow

Deer Lick Cave

Riverview Rd.

Ohio & Erie Canal Towpath Trail

Olde Eight

Brandywine Rd.

8

271

NORTHFIELD CENTER

Snowville Rd.

N.P.S. Headquarters

Brandywine

BOSTON

Dover Lake Park

Brushwood Lake

Exit 11

21

80

Boston Mills

Boston

Brandywine Falls

The Inn at Brandywine Falls

BOSTON HEIGHTS

RICHFIELD

Boston Store

Ohio Turnpike

Olde Eight

80

Furnace Run Park

303

Peninsula (National Historic District)

Deep Lock Quarry Park

303

Happy Days

8

271

Oak Hill

Furnace Run

Ledges

Truxell Rd.

Kendall Park Rd.

Kendall Lake

Pine Hollow

Virginia Kendall Park

77

Quick Rd.

Everett Rd.

Akron Peninsula Rd.

Hale Farm and Village

Hunt Farm

Ira Rd.

Cleveland Mission Rd.

Blossom Music Center

Wyoga Lake Rd.

Steels Corner Rd.

Akron Cleveland Rd.

Bath Rd.

O'Neil Woods

Hampton Hills Park

Bath Rd.

is comprised of four separate units in and near the city of Dayton in southwestern Ohio.

Orville and Wilbur Wright, residents of Dayton, Ohio, were self-taught in engineering. Together they invented and flew the world's first human-controlled heavier-than-air powered flying machine in 1903. They later built and flew the world's first practical and controllable airplane. The Wrights were able to apply scientific methodology to the mechanical knowledge they honed, first in the printing business, and later in their now-famous bicycle shop. The brothers designed and constructed both the planes and the internal combustion engines that powered them. The Wrights later operated a flying school that trained over a hundred aviators.

The historical park is comprised of four units:

1. **The Wright Cycle Company building** and **Hoover Block** (22 South Williams Street): The last remaining building in Dayton occupied by the brothers' bicycle business. The Hoover Block served as one site of the Wright's printing business. This is the location for the National Park Service office.

2. **Paul Laurence Dunbar State Memorial** (219 North P. L. Dunbar Street): Home purchased by Wright friend Paul Dunbar for his mother. Dunbar, an African-American who achieved distinction as a writer of novels, plays, short stories, and poems, purchased the home in 1904. He died here in 1906. Fee charged.

3. **Wright Hall** (1000 Carillon Boulevard): The restored 1905 Wright Flyer III, the first practical aircraft capable of controlled flight, is on display at the Wright Brothers Aviation Center in Carillon Historical Park. Fee charged.

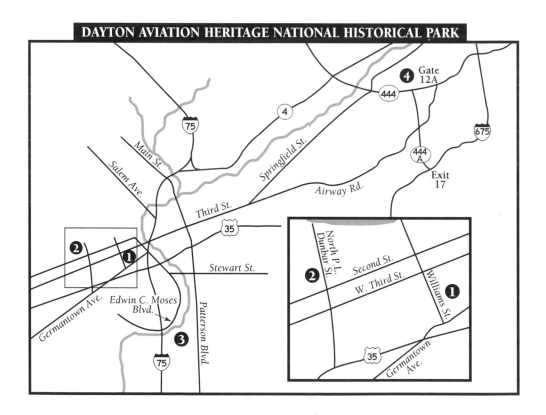

4. **Huffman Prairie Flying Field** (Wright-Patterson Air Force Base): The Wright brothers perfected the airplane here in 1904 and 1905. Later they had their training school there as well as their exhibition company. The U.S. Air Force Museum at Wright-Patterson Air Force Base is also a worthwhile stop.

ENTRANCE FEE: No charge for the Huffman Prairie Flying Field and the Wright Cycle Shop. Paul Laurence Dunbar State Memorial and Wright Hall each charge $3.00.

FACILITIES: Rest rooms and drinking water are in the National Park Service Office at 22 South Williams Street and Paul Laurence Dunbar State Memorial and Carillon Historical Park.

CAMPING: No camping is available in the historical park.

HOPEWELL CULTURE NATIONAL HISTORICAL PARK

16062 State Route 104
Chillicothe, OH 45601-8694
(740) 774-1126
HOCU_Superintendent@nps.gov
www.nps.gov/hocu

This site was established in 1923 as Mound City Group National Monument. Legislation in 1992 renamed the unit Hopewell Culture National Historical Park and expanded the park acreage to include three additional Hopewell sites. A visitor center is located at the Mound City Group, and limited facilities are available at the Hopewell Mound Group. The park is located in south central Ohio, and the visitor center is located 3 miles north of Chillicothe on State Route 104.

The Hopewell culture developed in southern and central Ohio between 200 B.C. and A.D. 500. The term "Hopewell" describes a broad network of political, economic, and spiritual beliefs and practices among different Native American groups over a large portion of eastern North America. The culture is characterized by the construction of geometric enclosures made of earthen walls and mounds of various shapes. The culture is also known for a network of contacts with other groups, stretching from central Canada to the Gulf of Mexico and from the Rocky Mountains to the Atlantic Ocean. This network brought materials such as cooper, shells, obsidian, and sharks' teeth to Ohio.

Visible remnants of the Hopewell culture are concentrated in the Scioto River valley, near present-day Chillicothe, Ohio. The most striking sites contain earthworks in the forms of circles, squares, and other geometric shapes. Mound City Group consists of a thirteen-acre rectangular earth enclosure with at least twenty-three mounds. The height of the earth walls is 3 to 4 feet, with a gateway on both the east and west sides. All of the mounds are dome-shaped except for one elliptical mound. Early explorers documented the largest mound as 90 feet in diameter and 17.5 feet high.

The Mound City Group visitor center is open daily from 9:00 A.M. to 5:00 P.M., with extended summer hours. The visitor center is closed Thanksgiving, Christmas, and New Year's Days. The visitor center contains a museum, an auditorium where an introductory video, *Legacy of the Mound Builders,* is shown, and a bookstore. It is also the starting point for a self-guided walk through the Mound City Group. Ranger-led walks and special programs are scheduled year-round. Check the park's Web site for the current schedule.

ENTRANCE FEE: $4.00 per vehicle or $2.00 per person; visitors sixteen and under free. There is no entrance fee from December through February.

FACILITIES: Park facilities are wheelchair-accessible. Rest rooms and water are available in the visitor center; food and lodging are available in Chillicothe.

CAMPING: No camping is permitted on the park grounds. Private campgrounds are available in Chillicothe and a number of state parks with camping facilities are within 30 miles of the park.

JAMES A. GARFIELD NATIONAL HISTORIC SITE

8095 Mentor Avenue
Mentor, OH 44060-5753
(440) 255–8722
jaga_interpretation@nps.gov
www.nps.gov/jaga

James A. Garfield National Historic Site preserves property associated with the twentieth President of the United States. Authorized in 1980, the 7.82-acre site includes the main house, from which the first successful front porch campaign was conducted; campaign office; visitor center; and outbuildings. The site is located in northeastern Ohio, east of Cleveland, in the city of Mentor.

Born November 19, 1831, in Orange Township (now Moreland Hills), Ohio, James A. Garfield was the last president to be born in a log cabin. From work as a tow boy on the Ohio and Erie Canal, Garfield went on to become a teacher, minister, college president, U.S. senator, U.S. representative, and twentieth president of the United States. On July 2, 1881, four months into his presidency, Garfield was shot by the disappointed office-seeker Charles Guiteau. Garfield succumbed to infection associated with his wounds on September 19, 1881.

Garfield purchased the run-down, one-and-one-half-story, nine-room house and 118 acres in 1876. The farm eventually grew to 158 acres. In 1880 he borrowed money to add eleven rooms to accommodate his large family. This addition included the front porch made famous during the 1880 presidential campaign. Reporters on site during the campaign named it "Lawnfield." In 1885 his widow added nine rooms, including the Memorial Library, which set the precedent for presidential libraries.

The site is owned by the National Park Service and operated by the Western Reserve Historical Society. Tours of the structure are available during normal operating hours. Group reservations are required. A fee is charged for the main house tour. The visitor center offers an eighteen-minute video and exhibits about Garfield's life. Hours for the main house and visitor center are Monday through Saturday from 10:00 A.M. to 5:00 P.M. and Sunday from noon to 5:00 P.M. It is closed most federal holidays. Visitors should call (440) 255–8722 or visit the Web site for up-to-date information.

ENTRANCE FEE: No charge for the grounds. There is a fee for the house tour: $6.00 adult, $5.00 seniors, $4.00 visitors six to eighteen, and visitors five and under free.

FACILITIES: Food, fuel, and lodging are available in Mentor.

CAMPING: No camping is available at the site. Punderson State Park, approximately 15 miles south of Mentor via SR 44, offers 201 sites with tables, grills, flush toilets, showers, and fishing (440–564–1195).

PERRY'S VICTORY AND INTERNATIONAL PEACE MEMORIAL

P.O. Box 549
Put-in-Bay, OH 43456-0549
(419) 285–2184
pevi_superintendent@nps.gov
www.nps.gov/pevi

Perry's Victory and International Peace Memorial comprises nearly twenty-six acres and was incorporated into the National Park Service in 1936. The Monument commemorates Commodore Oliver Hazard Perry's victory on Lake Erie in one of the most decisive naval battles of the War of 1812 and the resulting international peace between Canada and the United States. The park is located in northern Ohio on South Bass Island in western Lake Erie. In season, automobile and passenger ferries operate from Catawba Point and passenger-only ferries operate from Port Clinton. There is year-round air service to the island from the Port Clinton and Sandusky airports.

Early in the War of 1812, British ships controlled Lake Erie, an important lifeline for American troops and supplies in the Old Northwest. On September 10, 1813, this stranglehold was broken when nine vessels under the command of Commodore Oliver Hazard Perry won a decisive victory over six British warships under the command of Robert Heriott Barclay, about 10 miles northwest of South Bass Island. Since the end of the War of 1812, peaceful relations have existed between the United States and Canada. Canada and the U.S. share the world's longest undefended border, more than 4,000 miles, and the lessons of peace through negotiation and arbitration are still honored through the 1817 Rush-Bagot Agreement, one of the first disarmament treaties. It is still in effect today.

The park is best known for the granite memorial shaft built between 1912 and 1915 that rises 352 feet above its 45-foot-wide base. Visitors may ride an elevator from the second floor of the Memorial to an observation platform 317 feet above Lake Erie (fee charged). The memorial is open from mid-May to early October and is open by appointment during the rest of the year.

ENTRANCE FEE: $3.00 per person; visitors sixteen and under free.

FACILITIES: A full range of tourist facilities is available on the island in season. Full services are also available in mainland communities.

CAMPING: Camping is not available at the memorial. South Bass Island State park offers 130 sites with primitive camping on the island (no reservations; 419–285–2112). On the mainland, East Harbor State Park, northeast of Port Clinton, provides 570 sites with modern bathhouse facilities (no reservations; 419–734–5857).

FISHING: Fishing is available in Lake Erie from the memorial grounds; an Ohio fishing license is required. Catches include bass, catfish, crappie, pike, and walleye.

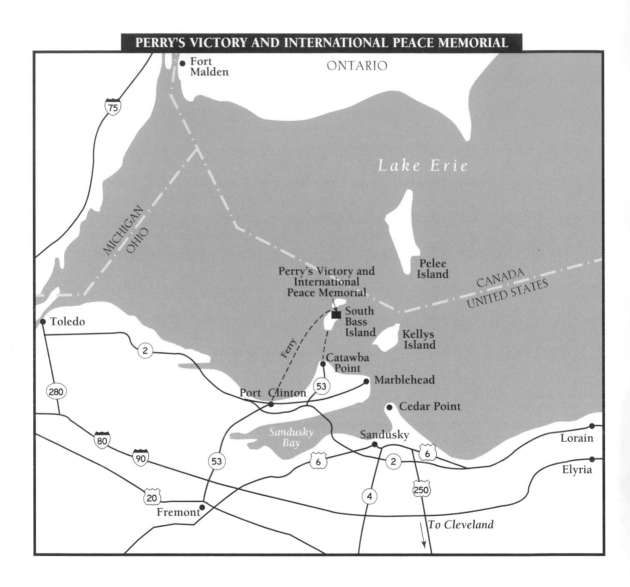

WILLIAM HOWARD TAFT NATIONAL HISTORIC SITE

2038 Auburn Avenue
Cincinnati, OH 45219-3025
(513) 684–3262
wiho_superintendent@nps.gov
www.nps.gov/wiho

William Howard Taft National Historic Site comprises three acres and was authorized in 1969 to preserve the birthplace and boyhood home of the only person to serve as both chief justice and president of the United States. The park is located at 2038 Auburn Avenue in the city of Cincinnati (see accompanying map).

This two-story brick home was purchased by William Howard Taft's father in 1851, and it was here that William Howard was born on September 15, 1857. After attending public schools in Cincinnati, he graduated second in his class at Yale and then returned to Ohio to earn a law

The parlor at the William Howard Taft home (Courtesy of William Howard Taft National Historic Site)

degree from Cincinnati Law School. Among Taft's many important positions were those of solicitor general of the United States, twenty-seventh president of the United States (1909–1913), professor of constitutional law at Yale, and chief justice of the United States (1921–1930). William Howard Taft died in Washington, D.C., on March 8, 1930, and was buried in Arlington National Cemetery.

Four restored rooms reflect the family life of the Tafts during the years 1857 to 1877. Museum exhibits emphasize the long and dedicated public career of William Howard Taft and the Taft family. Tours of the home begin at the Taft Education Center adjacent to the home. The education center houses both exhibits that reflect the extended Taft family's commitment to public service as well as traveling exhibits. The site is open from 10:00 A.M. to 4:00 P.M. seven days a week, except Thanksgiving, Christmas Day, and New Year's Day. An elevator is available in both facilities. Reservations are required for groups of ten or more.

ENTRANCE FEE: No charge.

FACILITIES: Drinking water and wheelchair-accessible rest rooms are available in both facilities.

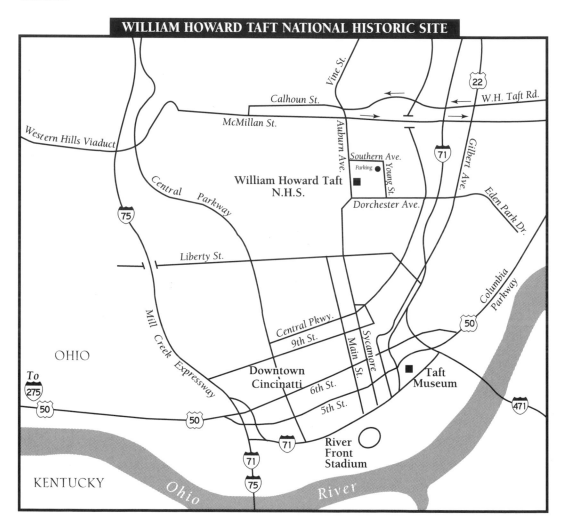

PENNSYLVANIA

STATE TOURIST INFORMATION
(800) 847–4872
www.experiencepa.com

ALLEGHENY PORTAGE RAILROAD
NATIONAL HISTORIC SITE

110 Federal Park Road
Gallitzin, PA 16641
(814) 886–6150
fone_superintendent@nps.gov
www.nps.gov/alpo

Allegheny Portage Railroad National Historic Site comprises 1,476 acres and was authorized in 1964 to commemorate the first railroad crossing of the Allegheny Mountains, which operated from 1834 to 1854. The park is located in central Pennsylvania, 12 miles west of Altoona via U.S. Highways 220 and 22. The visitor center can be reached from the Gallitzin Road exit off U.S. 22. (See the area map under Johnstown Flood National Memorial.)

Alarmed by the growth of New York City and Baltimore, the Pennsylvania legislature authorized funding for construction of a canal to the West in 1826. Crossing the Alleghenies presented the greatest problem, and a number of possibilities were considered. It was finally decided to build a portage railroad that would lift and lower cars from one level to another along a series of inclined planes. The 36-mile railroad consisted of five planes on each side of the mountain with a stationary steam engine providing power at the top of each plane. By 1854, the Pennsylvania Railroad was able to provide continuous rail service between the eastern seaboard and the Ohio Valley, thereby making the portage obsolete.

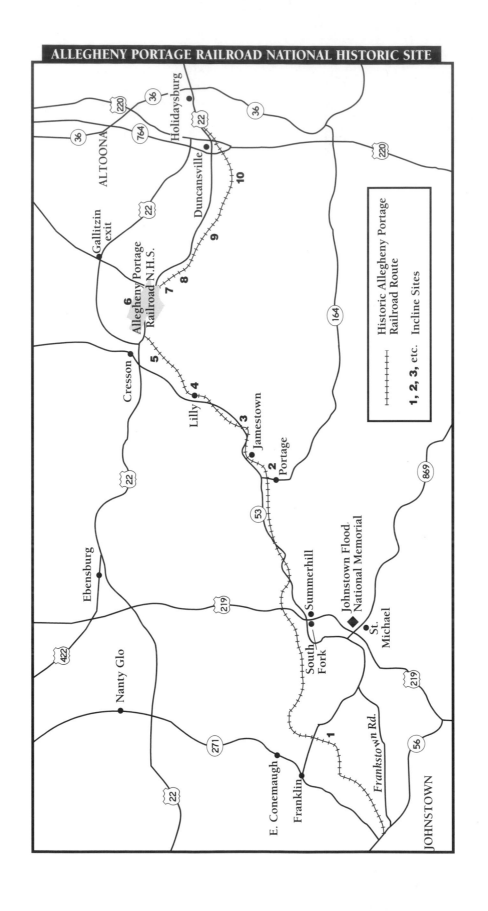

The Summit Level Visitor Center tells the story of the portage railroad through exhibits and a twenty-minute film. The visitor center is open daily (except Thanksgiving, Christmas Day, New Year's Day, Martin Luther King, Jr., Day, and Presidents' Day) from 9:00 A.M. to 5:00 P.M. (may be open to 6:00 P.M. during summer). Other park features include inclined planes 6, 8, 9, and 10, the historic Lemon House, Engine House #6 exhibit building, Skew Arch Bridge, the newly opened Staple Bend Tunnel, stone culverts, and stone railroad ties. A variety of interpretive programs are offered during the summer including guided walks, costumed demonstrations and Evenings on the Summit Programs, which are offered on Saturdays.

ENTRANCE FEE: $2.00 per person; visitors sixteen and under free.

FACILITIES: No food or lodging is available in the park, but there are rest rooms, grills, and picnic tables. Restaurants and lodging are in Cresson.

CAMPING: No camping is permitted at the site. Prince Gallitzin State Park, approximately 20 miles northwest of Altoona, provides camping facilities with tables, grills, flush toilets, showers, swimming, and fishing.

DELAWARE & LEHIGH
NATIONAL HERITAGE CORRIDOR

c/o DLNCNHC Commission
10 East Church Street, Room A-208
Bethlehem, PA 18018
(610) 861–9345
DELE3@fast.net
www.nps.gov/dele/

Delaware & Lehigh National Heritage Corridor was authorized in 1988 to conserve and interpret the valley's heritage and to enhance the region's quality of life. The National Heritage Corridor stretches for 160 miles in eastern Pennsylvania along the historic routes of the Delaware Canal and the Lehigh Navigation System.

The eastern Pennsylvania region encompassed by this National Heritage Corridor has witnessed an ongoing arrival of settlers, including the Lenape Indians, who built their villages where trails and waterways met. Later, European settlers, including William Penn's Quakers and the Moravians, who settled Bethlehem, used these same trails to journey to the region.

Poor roads hindered the region's development and resulted in a concentration of industry and settlements (many of which are still visible today) in areas with easy access to water. The need to transport goods and raw materials and to move large amounts of anthracite coal from the coal fields of Carbon County and the Wyoming Valley led to construction of the Lehigh Navigation System and the Delaware Canal. These waterways were built in stages between 1817 and 1832, with their most active period between the 1830s and the 1860s. The canals eventually succumbed to competition from railroads and highways, although the Delaware Canal and portions of the Lehigh Navigation System continued to operate until 1942. Today, the well-preserved Delaware Canal is the most intact watered towpath canal in the nation.

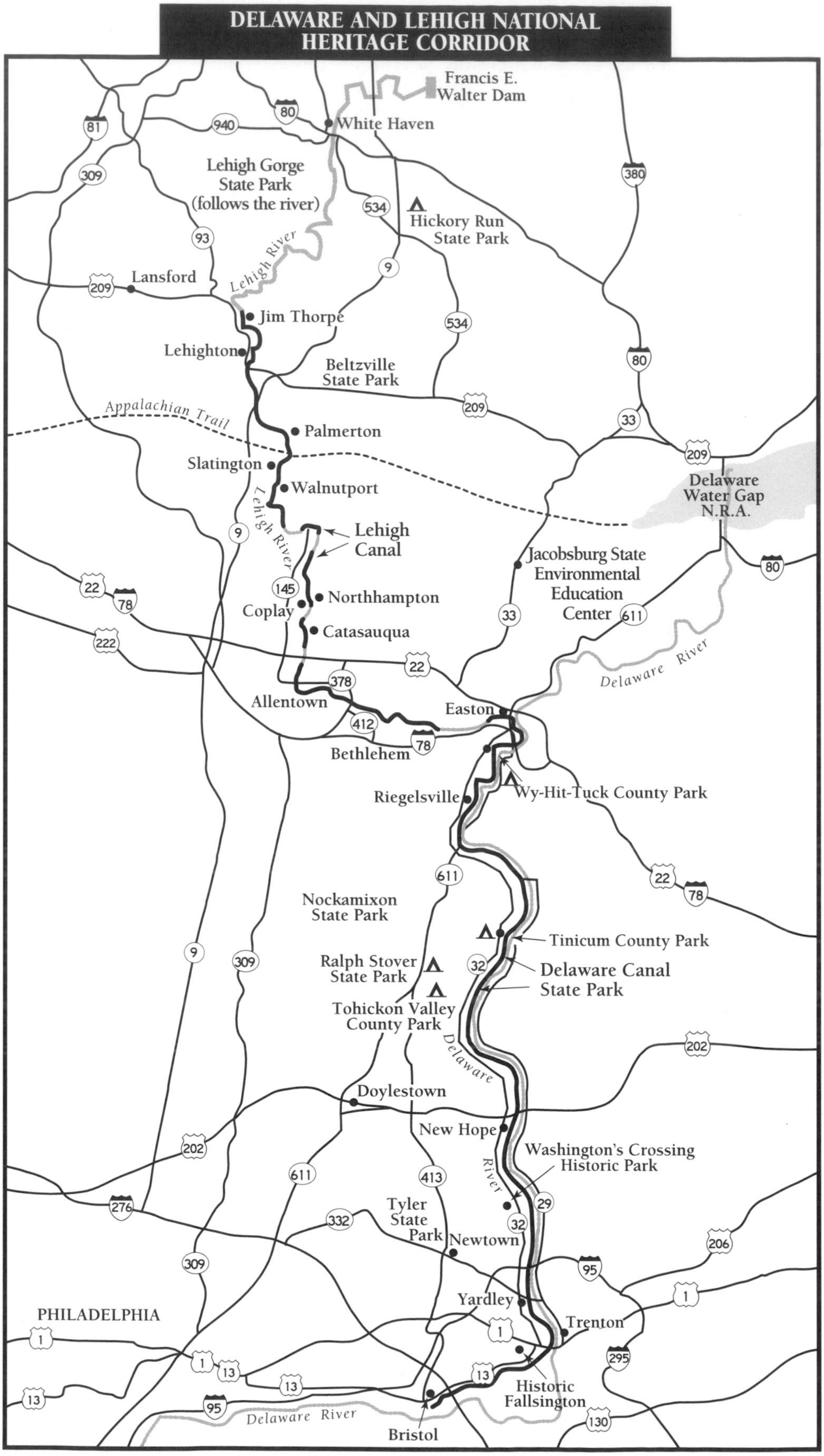

DELAWARE AND LEHIGH NATIONAL HERITAGE CORRIDOR
Francis E. Walter Dam
White Haven
Lehigh Gorge State Park (follows the river)
Hickory Run State Park
Lehigh River
Lansford
Jim Thorpe
Lehighton
Beltzville State Park
Appalachian Trail
Palmerton
Slatington
Walnutport
Lehigh River
Lehigh Canal
Northhampton
Coplay
Catasauqua
Allentown
Bethlehem
Easton
Delaware River
Delaware Water Gap N.R.A.
Jacobsburg State Environmental Education Center
Riegelsville
Wy-Hit-Tuck County Park
Nockamixon State Park
Ralph Stover State Park
Tohickon Valley County Park
Tinicum County Park
Delaware Canal State Park
Delaware River
Doylestown
New Hope
Washington's Crossing Historic Park
Tyler State Park
Newtown
Yardley
Trenton
Historic Fallsington
PHILADELPHIA
Bristol
Delaware River
81
940
80
309
380
534
93
9
209
534
80
209
33
209
9
22
78
145
33
611
80
222
22
378
412
78
611
22
78
9
309
32
202
202
611
413
29
32
276
332
206
309
95
1
1
295
1
13
13
13
13
95
130

The land encompassed by the National Heritage Corridor provides a wide variety of places, activities, and experiences for visitors. These include parks, trails, scenic landscapes, historic villages, historic structures, museums, and, of course, the waterways. Visitors may tour a restored Quaker village at Historic Fallsington, visit the site of Washington's crossing of the Delaware River, ride a mule-drawn canal boat at New Hope or Hugh Moore Park, and travel along the Lehigh Gorge on a steam train from Jim Thorpe's historic railroad station. Lehigh Gorge State Park, which extends along the river from the Francis Walter Dam (east of White Haven) to Jim Thorpe, offers 25 miles of Rail-to-Trail pathways for hiking, biking, and cross-country skiing. In addition, there are 60 miles of towpath along the Delaware Canal. Rafting is popular on both the Lehigh and Delaware rivers.

For information on sights and activities, write: Pocono Mountains Vacation Bureau-Carbon Office, P.O. Box 90, Jim Thorpe, PA 18229 (570–325–3673); Lehigh Valley Convention and Visitors Bureau, P.O. Box 20785, Lehigh Valley, PA 18002-0785 (800–747–0561); and Bucks County Conference and Visitors Bureau, P.O. Box 912, 152 Swamp Road, Doylestown, PA 18901 (800–836–2825).

ENTRANCE FEE: Each site, park, recreational activity, and event has its own fee.

FACILITIES: Food and lodging, including historic bed-and-breakfast facilities, are available throughout the corridor. The Weisel Youth Hostel is adjacent to Nockamixon State Park, and the Solly House Hostel is within Tyler State Park. Family cabins are available by reservation at Nockamixon and Ralph Stover State Parks. Visitor centers are located in Easton (Two Rivers Landing) and Jim Thorpe (Old Mauch Chunk Landing).

CAMPING: Camping is available at Hickory Run State Park, Mauch Chunk Lake Park, Tinicum County Park, and numerous private campgrounds. Wy-Hit-Tuk County Park on the Delaware Canal offers canoe camping.

FISHING: Rainbow, brook, and brown trout are in smaller streams. The Delaware and lower Lehigh offer shad, smallmouth bass, walleye, and muskellunge. Allentown's Little Lehigh and Bethlehem's Monacacy Creek offer good fishing. Lakes at Francis Walter Dam and at Beltzville and Nockamixon state parks are stocked. A Pennsylvania fishing license is required.

DELAWARE WATER GAP NATIONAL RECREATION AREA; MIDDLE DELAWARE NATIONAL SCENIC RIVER

Bushkill, PA 18324-9999
(570) 588–2451
dewa_interpretation@nps.gov
www.nps.gov/dewa

Delaware Water Gap National Recreation Area was authorized in 1965 to preserve 70,000 acres of relatively unspoiled land containing historical and natural features and provide numerous recreational opportunities. The park is located on both the Pennsylvania and New Jersey sides of the 40-mile-long Middle Delaware National Scenic River. The southern section of the park is intersected by Interstate 80.

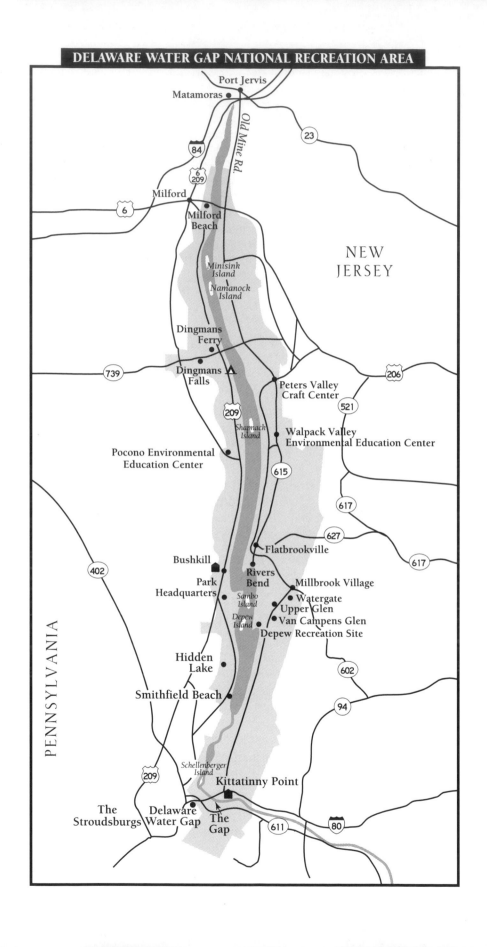

DELAWARE WATER GAP NATIONAL RECREATION AREA

Port Jervis

Matamoras

84

6
209

Milford

6

Milford
Beach

*Minisink
Island*

*Namanock
Island*

Dingmans
Ferry

739

Dingmans
Falls

209

Peters Valley
Craft Center

521

*Shapnack
Island*

Walpack Valley
Environmental Education Center

Pocono Environmental
Education Center

615

617

627

617

Flatbrookville

Bushkill

Rivers
Bend

Millbrook Village

Park
Headquarters

*Sambo
Island*

Watergate

Upper Glen

*Depew
Island*

Van Campens Glen

Depew Recreation Site

402

Hidden
Lake

602

Smithfield Beach

94

PENNSYLVANIA

NEW
JERSEY

Old Mine Rd.

23

206

*Schellenberger
Island*

209

Kittatinny Point

The
Stroudsburgs

Delaware
Water Gap

The
Gap

611

80

Delaware Water Gap and Middle Delaware National Scenic River lie between the Kittatinny Ridge of New Jersey and the Pocono Plateau of Pennsylvania in a region that was a resort haven for wealthy vacationers during the late nineteenth and early twentieth centuries. Although the large hotels are mostly gone, the natural beauty that attracted the well-to-do remains.

Just off the Interstate 80 bridge on the New Jersey side of the river, Kittatinny Point Visitor Center offers a picnic area, hiking trails, and a view of the gap.

While driving in Pennsylvania toward the park's northern end, additional points of interest are nature trails at Pocono Environmental Education Center (570–828–2319) and a boardwalk trail at Dingmans Falls. A visitor center is located in Bushkill.

At Millbrook Village in New Jersey, visitors can take an enjoyable walking tour of a re-created town of the late 1800s. Buildings include period homes, a blacksmith shop, general store, church, school, wagon shop, woodworker's shop, weaving and spinning house, cabin, and barn. Village grounds are open daily from 9:00 A.M. to 5:00 P.M. year-round. From April through October selected buildings are open to the public and crafts are demonstrated on weekends. A nineteenth-century folk-life festival is held on the first full weekend of October each year.

Peters Valley Craft Center is a community of artisans skilled in woodworking, fibers, blacksmithing, ceramics, fine metals, and photography. Selected studios are open to visitors in summer (973–948–5200).

A variety of natural and cultural interpretive programs are offered during the year. Contact the park for additional information.

ENTRANCE FEE: No charge. Some sites have a user fee, such as Smithfield Beach, Milford Beach, Bushkill Access, and Dingmans Ferry in Pennsylvania; and Watergate and Depew Recreation sites in New Jersey. It is $5.00 per vehicle weekdays, $7.00 per vehicle weekends and holidays, or $1.00 per person.

FACILITIES: No commercial food or lodging establishments are available in the park, but both can be found in nearby towns, such as Milford, Stroudsburg, and Delaware Water Gap. Picnic areas and rest rooms are located throughout the recreation area, while boat launching ramps are at Kittatinny Point, Poxono, Dingmans Ferry, Bushkill, Smithfield Beach, and Milford Beach.

CAMPING: Dingmans Campground, operated by a concessioner just south of Dingmans Ferry, offers more than one hundred sites with water, tables, fire rings, dump station, flush toilets, electricity, and pay showers. Reservations are accepted with a deposit. Write RD 1, Box 312, Dingmans Ferry, PA 18328 (570–828–2266). Other public campgrounds are located near the park on both the Pennsylvania and New Jersey sides of the river. Four miles north of Water Gap in New Jersey, Worthington State Forest has campsites with tables, grills, and pit toilets (908–841–9575). Near the park's north end on New Jersey Highway 23, High Point State Park offers campsites with tables, grills, and flush toilets. Numerous private campgrounds are located nearby. East of Peters Valley on U.S. 206, Stokes State Forest provides campsites.

FISHING: Within the park, catfish, carp, shad, smallmouth bass and walleye are the most important sport species in the Delaware River. During spring, American shad migrate up the river in great numbers. Pickerel, sunfish, and largemouth bass are in lakes and ponds. Ice fishing is popular during winter months.

EISENHOWER NATIONAL HISTORIC SITE

250 Eisenhower Farm Lane
Gettysburg, PA 17325-1080
(717) 338–9114
EISE_site_manager@nps.gov
www.nps.gov/eise

Eisenhower National Historic Site was authorized in 1969 and comprises 690 acres, including the farm and only home owned by General Dwight David Eisenhower and his wife, Mamie. The farm served as a retreat while Ike was president and became his retirement home in 1961. The park is located in south-central Pennsylvania, adjacent to Gettysburg National Military Park. Visitation to the site is only via the shuttle-bus service beginning at the Gettysburg Military Park visitor center.

Dwight Eisenhower first moved to Pennsylvania in 1918 when he assumed his first command at Camp Colt in Gettysburg. Following World War II, while Eisenhower was serving as president of Columbia University, he and Mamie purchased a 189-acre farm on the edge of the famous Civil War battlefield at Gettysburg. Although unable to move here permanently until 1961, following his two terms as thirty-fourth president of the United States, Eisenhower did use the home as a weekend retreat and as a temporary White House while recuperating from a 1955 heart attack.

The original farmhouse was found to be a brick structure supported by a much older wooden home. Mamie had a new house built around a portion of the early house. Landscaping and construction were completed in 1955. Eisenhower inherited a dairy operation when he bought the farm, which he changed in favor of raising purebred black Angus cattle and, later, developing feeder cattle for sale. After Ike died in 1969, Mamie continued to live here until her death in 1979.

The historic site offers self-guided and ranger-conducted tours of the farm. Visitors should obtain tickets for entrance to the site inside the National Park Service Visitor Center. Tickets purchased include both entrance and shuttle fees. The shuttle bus leaves the visitor center for the historic site. Near the shuttle-bus arrival point at the site, a reception center contains a bookstore as well as exhibits and a video of Eisenhower's life. At the main home, park rangers provide brochures and information for a tour of the home. Self-guided walking tours explore the grounds, the skeet range, and farm buildings. Eisenhower's farm equipment is on display in the show barn. Ranger-conducted talks and living-history programs are offered throughout the summer. The Junior Secret Service program provides children (ages seven to twelve) an opportunity to earn a Junior Secret Service badge and certificate.

ENTRANCE FEE: $5.25 adult, $3.25 for visitors thirteen through sixteen, $2.25 for visitors six through twelve, five and under free.

FACILITIES: Food and lodging are available in Gettysburg. Information about Gettysburg is available on their Web site at www.gettysburg.com. Rest rooms and water are at the reception center and at the Gettysburg visitor center where the shuttle buses leave.

CAMPING: See camping section under Gettysburg National Military Park.

EISENHOWER NATIONAL HISTORIC SITE AND GETTYSBURG NATIONAL MILITARY PARK

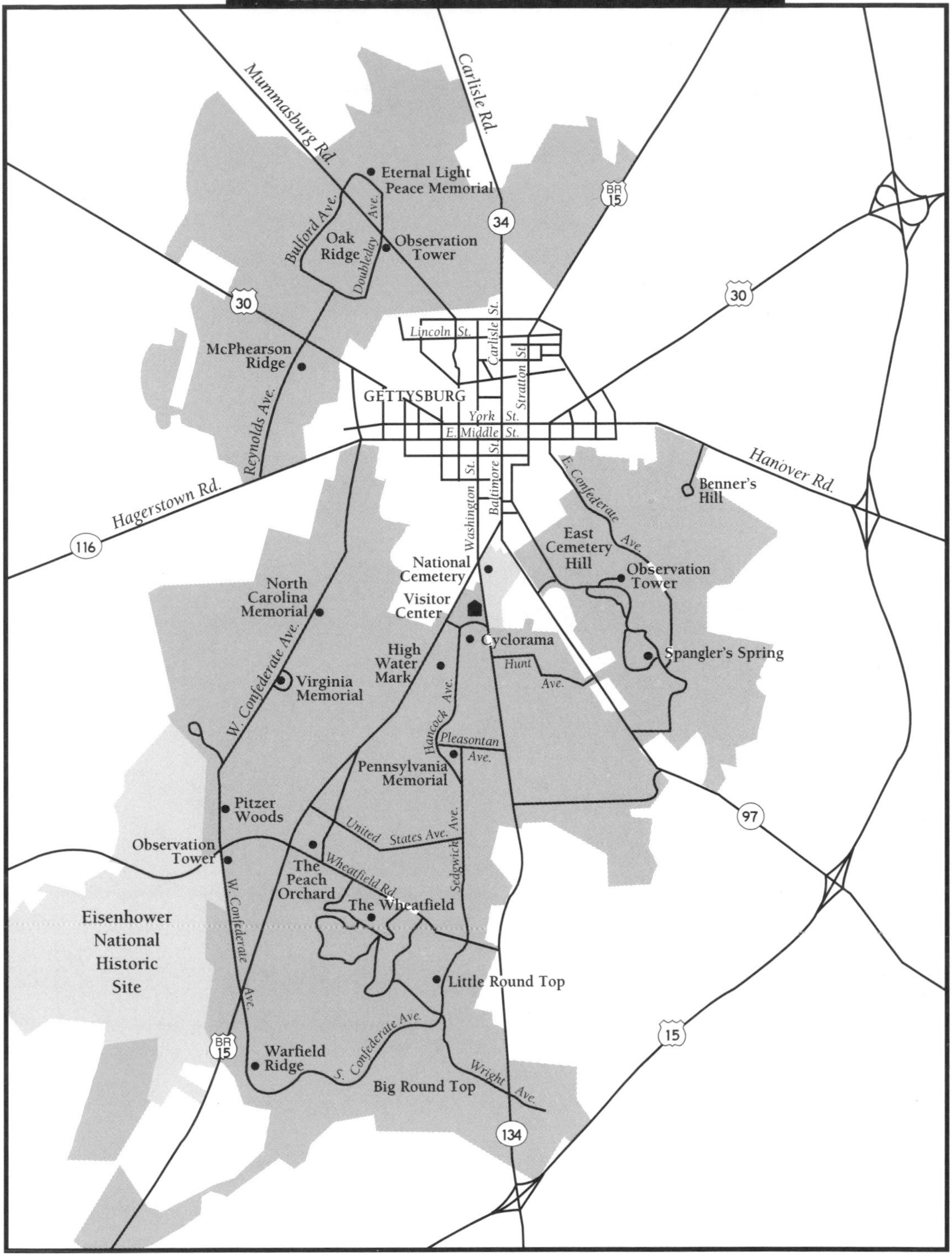

Mummasburg Rd.

Carlisle Rd.

Eternal Light Peace Memorial

Buford Ave.

Doubleday Ave.

Oak Ridge

Observation Tower

34

BR 15

30

30

McPhearson Ridge

Reynolds Ave.

Lincoln St.

Carlisle St.

Stratton St.

GETTYSBURG

York St.

E. Middle St.

Washington St.

Baltimore St.

Hanover Rd.

Hagerstown Rd.

116

Benner's Hill

E. Confederate Ave.

National Cemetery

Visitor Center

East Cemetery Hill

Observation Tower

North Carolina Memorial

W. Confederate Ave.

Cyclorama

Spangler's Spring

High Water Mark

Hunt Ave.

Virginia Memorial

Hancock Ave.

Pleasontan Ave.

Pennsylvania Memorial

Pitzer Woods

United States Ave.

Sedgwick Ave.

Observation Tower

Wheatfield Rd.

The Peach Orchard

The Wheatfield

W. Confederate Ave.

97

Eisenhower National Historic Site

Little Round Top

BR 15

Warfield Ridge

S. Confederate Ave.

Big Round Top

Wright Ave.

15

134

FORT NECESSITY NATIONAL BATTLEFIELD

1 Washington Way
Farmington, PA 15437-9514
(724) 329–5512
fone_superintendent@nps.gov
www.nps.gov/fone

Fort Necessity National Battlefield contains 900 acres and was established in 1931 to commemorate the site where, in 1754, Colonial troops commanded by Lieutenant Colonel George Washington were defeated in the opening battle of the French and Indian War. The park is located in southwestern Pennsylvania, 11 miles east of Uniontown via U.S. 40.

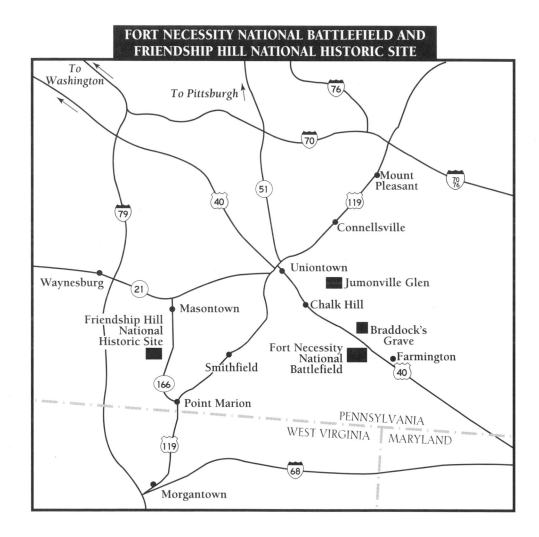

FORT NECESSITY NATIONAL BATTLEFIELD AND FRIENDSHIP HILL NATIONAL HISTORIC SITE

In April 1754 George Washington and a force of Virginians set out from Alexandria in an attempt to halt French expansion in North America. After defeating a small band of Frenchmen on Chestnut Ridge, Washington's troops built Fort Necessity and received reinforcements and additional supplies. On July 3, a force of 600 Frenchmen and 100 Indians attacked the fort, and by midnight Washington had surrendered; he and his troops were permitted to withdraw the following day. In 1755, another large British force under General Edward Braddock was again defeated by the French near present-day Pittsburgh. Braddock died during the retreat and was buried beneath the crude roadway.

A visitor center near the restored stockade is open daily from 9:00 A.M. to 5:00 P.M., except on Thanksgiving, Christmas Day, New Year's Day, Martin Luther King, Jr., Day, and Presidents' Day. The visitor center offers exhibits and a slide program to help interpret the battle. Also available are self-guided trails, seasonal living-history programs, and a picnic area. Nearby is Mount Washington Tavern, a restored stagecoach stop from the early 1800s that provided lodging and meals to travelers along the old National Road. The tavern is open for tours daily during summer months and on weekends during the winter. Guided tours are offered periodically throughout the year. The Braddock gravesite is open during daylight hours, year-round. Jumonville Glen, on nearby Chestnut Ridge, is open daily 10:00 A.M. to 5:00 P.M. from spring through autumn.

ENTRANCE FEE: $2.00 per person; good for seven days.

FACILITIES: No lodging or food service is available in the park, but both are in Uniontown. Rest rooms and water are in the visitor center.

CAMPING: No camping is permitted at the battlefield. A short distance northeast, Ohiopyle State Park offers camping with tables, grills, flush toilets, showers, fishing, and boating.

FRIENDSHIP HILL NATIONAL HISTORIC SITE

223 New Geneva Road
Point Marion, PA 15474
(724) 725–9190
fone_superintendent@nps.gov
www.nps.gov/frhi

Friendship Hill National Historic site comprises 661 acres and was authorized in 1978 to preserve a historic home on the Monongahela River that belonged to Albert Gallatin. Gallatin was secretary of the treasury under presidents Thomas Jefferson and James Madison from 1801 to 1814. The site is located in southwestern Pennsylvania, 3 miles north of Point Marion along Pennsylvania Route 166, about midway between Uniontown, Pennsylvania, and Morgantown, West Virginia.

Albert Gallatin first came to western Pennsylvania in the mid-1780s when the area was at the edge of the United States frontier. Gallatin was of the opinion that the Monongahela River would provide business opportunities as the areas to the west opened up and developed. In 1789, the brick house was begun. Nearly ten years later, a clapboard-sided, frame house was added. A large, square stone house, a second addition to the house, was built in 1823. Although Gallatin called Friendship Hill his home for more than forty years, he was frequently required to take extended periods of leave to serve his country in the fields of finance, politics, diplomacy, and scholarship. While serving as secretary of the treasury, Gallatin financed the Louisiana Purchase, reduced the national debt, and made internal improvements such as the National Road possible.

The park is open daily from 9:00 A.M. to 5:00 P.M., except on Thanksgiving, Christmas Day, New Year's Day, Martin Luther King, Jr., Day, and Presidents' Day. A visitor center contains exhibits as well as personnel to answer visitor questions. Guided tours of the house are offered every day during the summer season; brochures and compact disc players are available year-round for self-guided tours of the house. Ten miles of hiking trails are in the park. A twenty-minute loop trail passes the grave of Gallatin's first wife, Sophia, while a 3⅗-mile trail (two-and-a-half hours) follows the Monongahela River for nearly a mile, passing through a variety of meadows, woods, and streams.

ENTRANCE FEE: No charge.

FACILITIES: Rest rooms and drinking water are available at the historic site. Restaurants are in Point Marion, while both food and lodging are in Uniontown and Morgantown.

CAMPING: No camping is permitted in the park. Coopers Rock State Forest, 10 miles east of Morgantown, West Virginia, offers campsites with tables, grills, flush toilets, showers, and fishing.

FISHING: The Monongahela River fronts the site for 2 miles. Pennsylvania fishing and boating regulations apply.

See the map on page 218.

GETTYSBURG NATIONAL MILITARY PARK

97 Taneytown Road
Gettysburg, PA 17325-1080
(717) 334–1124
www.nps.gov/gett

This famous 5,900-acre park was established in 1895 to memorialize a great 1863 Civil War battle in which a Confederate invasion of the North was repulsed. The park surrounds the town of Gettysburg in south-central Pennsylvania, 36 miles southeast from Pennsylvania's capital city Harrisburg via U.S. 15. Eisenhower National Historic Site is adjacent to Gettysburg National Military Park and could be visited in conjunction with a tour of Gettysburg. (See separate write-up on the Eisenhower site in this section.)

Gettysburg National Military Park (opposite page)

Subsequent to being turned back at Antietam in August 1862, Confederate General Robert E. Lee reorganized his Army of Northern Virginia and, in the spring of 1863, began a second invasion of the North. After being followed by Union forces under the command of General George Gordon Meade, the two sides clashed at Gettysburg early on July 1. Following a three-day battle in which 51,000 men were killed, wounded, or missing, the two armies marched away. With the repulse of the Confederate Army, the Battle of Gettysburg was over. The Confederate Army that staggered back to Virginia was physically and spiritually exhausted. Never again would Lee attempt an offensive operation of such magnitude.

The Park may be seen in a number of different ways. The first stop should be the National Park Service Visitor Center, which contains a Civil War Museum with numerous exhibits, a schedule of ranger-conducted walks and programs (mid-June through September), free brochures and information, and an Electric Map orientation program (fee charged). The map helps interpret the Battle of Gettysburg before you venture out into the field. The visitor center offers several options for touring the battlefield: A free self-guided map of the 18-mile-long driving tour is available; individual visitors and bus groups may also hire a licensed guide for a two-hour conducted tour of the battlefield; and a self-guided taped tour can be purchased from the battlefield bookstore in the visitor center.

Adjacent to the visitor center, the Cyclorama Center offers a free twenty-minute-long film and presents the Cyclorama painting, a 356-by-26-foot original oil on canvas of Pickett's charge on the third day of the battle (fee charged).

For visitors interested in hiking, the High Water Mark Trail (¾ mile) begins at the Cyclorama and interprets the furious battle on July 3. The Soldier's National Cemetery Trail (1 mile) begins directly across from the visitor center and winds around the more than 6,000 veterans and their families that are buried here. Brochures for all these trails are available at the visitor center. Bicycles can be used on all park roads. An 8-mile-long bridle trail is also available for those with horses.

ENTRANCE FEE: No charge.

FACILITIES: No food service or lodging is provided by the National Park Service, but both are readily available nearby, including across the road from the visitor center. Information is available from the Gettysburg Convention and Visitors Bureau on their Web site at www.gettysburg.com. Rest rooms and water are provided at the visitor center, Cyclorama Center, and at various locations throughout the park.

CAMPING: No general camping is permitted in the park, although reservations may be made for organized youth group camping (April to October) by writing the superintendent. A number of private campgrounds are located near Gettysburg. Caledonia State Park, 15 miles west on U.S. 30, offers camping with tables, flush toilets, and showers. Corodus State Park, 20 miles east on highways 116 and 216, has similar facilities. The National Park Service operates Catoctin Mountain Park, 20 miles south of Gettysburg via U.S. 15 in Maryland. Catoctin is described in the Maryland chapter of this book.

See the map on page 217.

HOPEWELL FURNACE NATIONAL HISTORIC SITE

2 Mark Bird Lane
Elverson, PA 19520-9505
(610) 582–8773
hofu_superintendent@nps.gov
www.nps.gov/hofu

Hopewell Furnace National Historic Site was authorized in 1938 and comprises 848 acres, including an iron-making community that has been restored to its appearance in the 1820–40 period. The site is located in southeastern Pennsylvania, 5 miles south of Birdsboro via State Highway 345 or 10 miles northeast of the Morgantown interchange on the Pennsylvania Turnpike via State Highway 23 East and 345 North. Hopewell is 45 miles northwest of Philadelphia.

Hopewell Furnace National Historic Site

Hopewell Furnace was built on the headwaters of French Creek in 1771. Although England prohibited the manufacture of finished iron products by the colonists, the law was poorly enforced, and Hopewell began casting stove plates soon after its completion. Later, during the Revolutionary War, materials for armaments and ammunition were produced. The process used at Hopewell required iron ore, limestone (used as flux), and hardwood forests—(to produce fuel), all of which were abundant here. In 1883, after producing more than 65,000 stoves, Hopewell was closed because new iron-making technology made the charcoal process outdated.

The visitor center, open daily except some federal holidays, contains exhibits explaining the iron-making process and the furnace's history. A short slide program is also presented. From here, a self-guided tour through the restored community visits numerous buildings, including a charcoal house, furnace, water wheel, blacksmith shop, tenant houses, and ironmaster's mansion. Taped messages are at various locations along the trail, and park personnel provide limited living-history programs during the summer. Admission fee is charged year-round. Additional interpretive fees are charged during living-history programs.

ENTRANCE FEE: $4.00 per person, visitors sixteen and under free; good for seven days. For living-history programs and special events, an interpretive fee of $1.00 is added.

FACILITIES: No food or lodging is available at the site. Drinking water, a soft-drink machine, and modern rest rooms are at the visitor center. Meals and lodging are in Reading, Pottstown, and Morgantown.

CAMPING: No camping is permitted at the site. Adjacent to Hopewell Furnace, French Creek State Park (201 sites) has shaded spaces with tables, grills, water, flush toilets, and showers. Ten cabins are available for rent. Picnicking, swimming, nature trails, and boating (electric or non-powered only) are also available (610–582–9680).

FISHING: In the state park, Hopewell Lake has northern pike, largemouth bass, walleye, and panfish; Scotts Run Lake contains brook trout and rainbow trout.

INDEPENDENCE NATIONAL HISTORICAL PARK
313 Walnut Street
Philadelphia, PA 19106-2778
(215) 597–8974
(215) 597–1785 (TTY)
www.nps.gov/inde

Independence National Historical Park was established in 1956 and comprises nearly forty-five acres, including many of the famous sites and structures associated with the American Revolution. The park is located in downtown Philadelphia with a visitor center at the corner of Sixth and Market Streets. A parking garage is located underneath the visitor center, with access on Fifth and Sixth Streets. Four other areas affiliated with the National Park Service in Philadelphia are found on pages 227–229.

Independence National Historical Park (opposite page)

Independence National Historical Park, Philadelphia, the home of American statesman Benjamin Franklin and birthplace of the United States, is as full of history as any city in the country. From Carpenters' Hall, where the First Continental Congress met in 1774 to address a declaration of rights to the king of England, to the first federally chartered bank, a number of historical structures are available for visitation. Included among these are Independence Hall, where the Declaration of Independence was adopted and the U.S. Constitution was drafted; Congress Hall, where the U.S. Congress met from 1790 to 1800; Liberty Bell Pavilion, where the Liberty Bell is housed; Franklin Court, the site of Benjamin Franklin's home; the Second Bank of the United States (fee charged), with the park's portrait collection; Todd House, where Dolley Madison lived; Deshler-Morris House (fee charged), where President Washington held his cabinet meeting in 1793; and Christ Church, where patriots and loyalists worshiped.

The visitor center at Sixth and Market Streets provides a twenty-eight-minute film and a variety of books and maps to guide visitors through the park. The National Park Service recommends that visitors with approximately half a day's time available to tour the park see the visitor center, Carpenters' Hall, Independence Hall, the Liberty Bell Pavilion, and Franklin Court. Those wishing to visit most of the sites should plan on spending at least a whole day in the city. Independence Hall, the Liberty Bell Pavilion, and the visitor center are open daily from 9:00 A.M. to 5:00 P.M., with extended hours in summer. The hours of operation of other buildings in the park change seasonally. Current hours of operation are available by calling the visitor center at (215) 597–8974. Tickets (fee charged) for visitation to the Bishop White and the Todd houses are available at the visitor center.

A new visitor center is scheduled to open in late 2001. The Gateway Visitor Center will be located on Sixth Street between Market and Arch Streets. The new Liberty Bell Complex and the new National Constitution Center are currently under construction.

The National Park Service is required to maintain these historical buildings in their original condition, which may create some difficulty for handicapped visitors. Only the visitor center, the Liberty Bell Pavilion, and the Franklin Court Underground Museum are fully accessible to the handicapped. The first floors of Independence Hall, Congress Hall, and Old City Hall are accessible; Franklin Court and Declaration House have limited accessibility. The park brochure is available in large-print and braille versions, and assisted listening devices are available.

ENTRANCE FEE: A $2.00 fee is charged to tour the Bishop White and Todd houses, Second Bank of the U.S. Portrait Gallery, and the Deshler-Morris House.

FACILITIES: Food and lodging are available in downtown Philadelphia. Water and rest rooms are in the visitor center.

JOHNSTOWN FLOOD NATIONAL MEMORIAL

733 Lake Road
South Fork, PA 15956
(814) 495–4643
fone_superintendent@nps.gov
www.nps.gov/jofl

Johnstown Flood National Memorial comprises 164 acres and was authorized in 1964 to preserve the remains of the South Fork Dam, which collapsed in 1889 and caused the flooding of Johnstown with a loss of 2,209 lives. The park is located in southern Pennsylvania, 10 miles northeast of Johnstown near St. Michael on U.S. 219 and State Highway 869.

Heavy rains during May 30 and 31 of 1889 saturated the entire west-central section of Pennsylvania. The 30,000 residents of the Johnstown area were accustomed to spring floods and failed to heed warnings that the South Fork Dam was in danger of collapse. At approximately 3:10 P.M., the dam broke, and soon a 30- to 40-foot wall of water was traveling at up to 40 miles per hour down the narrow mountain valley. The result was the loss of 2,209 lives and $17 million in property damage; nearly everyone was left homeless.

A visitor center at the dam site, open daily (except Presidents' Day, Martin Luther King, Jr., Day, Veterans Day, Thanksgiving, Christmas Day, and New Year's Day) from 9:00 A.M. to 5:00 P.M. (to 6:00 P.M. during summer), will help interpret events leading up to the disaster. The visitor center features models, exhibits, and a thirty-five-minute motion picture. Nearby are interpretive trails and demonstrations. The South Fork Fishing and Hunting Club clubhouse and cottages, a retreat for the rich, were spared by the flood and may be seen in St. Michael, a small town at the edge of the old lake bed. Johnstown Flood Museum at 304 Washington Street in Johnstown provides a number of excellent exhibits interpreting the flood. The museum is not affiliated with the National Park Service.

ENTRANCE FEE: $2.00 per person; visitors sixteen and under free.

FACILITIES: No food or lodging is available at the memorial. Rest rooms and water are at the visitor center. A picnic area with tables and grills is nearby. Meals and lodging are available in Johnstown.

CAMPING: No camping is permitted at the memorial. (See camping section under Allegheny Portage Railroad National Historic Site.)

See the map on page 210.

PHILADELPHIA PARKS

In addition to Independence National Historical Park, which is discussed in detail under a separate heading in this section, the National Park Service has several interesting historic sites in the city of Philadelphia. Visitors stopping in the downtown area should make an attempt to take in these other sites to enrich their sense of the history of this charming city.

1. **Benjamin Franklin National Memorial** (Twentieth and Benjamin Franklin Parkway; 215–448–1200): Located in a large hall adjoining the Franklin Institute, the seated statue of Benjamin Franklin was dedicated as a tribute to America's foremost inventor-statesman. Exhibits are located around the rotunda, and guides are on hand near the entrance. There is no fee to visit the memorial, but a fee is charged to enter the Franklin Institute Museum.

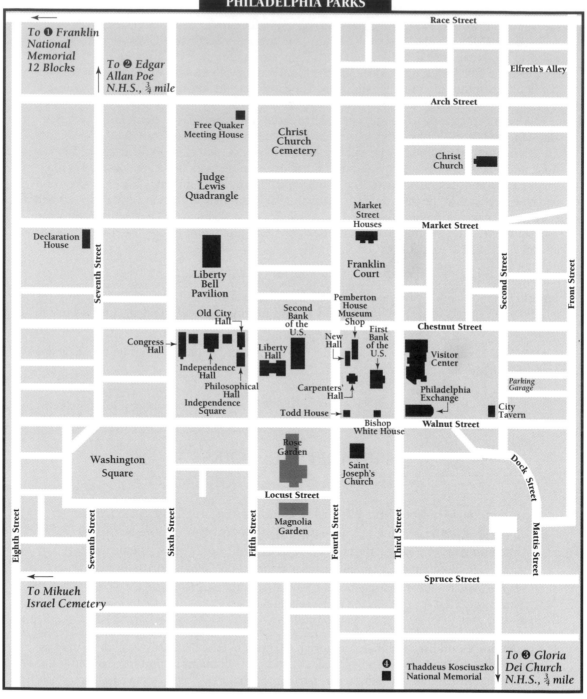

PHILADELPHIA PARKS

To ❶ Franklin
National
Memorial
12 Blocks

To ❷ Edgar
Allan Poe
N.H.S., ¾ mile

Race Street

Elfreth's Alley

Arch Street

Free Quaker
Meeting House

Christ
Church
Cemetery

Christ
Church

Judge
Lewis
Quadrangle

Market Street
Houses

Market Street

Declaration
House

Seventh Street

Liberty
Bell
Pavilion

Franklin
Court

Second Street

Front Street

Old City
Hall

Second
Bank
of the
U.S.

Pemberton
House
Museum
Shop

First
Bank
of the
U.S.

Chestnut Street

Congress
Hall

New
Hall

Visitor
Center

Parking
Garage

Independence
Hall

Liberty
Hall

Philosophical
Hall

Carpenters'
Hall

Philadelphia
Exchange

Independence
Square

Todd House

Bishop
White House

City
Tavern

Walnut Street

Washington
Square

Rose
Garden

Saint
Joseph's
Church

Dock Street

Eighth Street

Seventh Street

Sixth Street

Fifth Street

Locust Street

Magnolia
Garden

Fourth Street

Third Street

Mattis Street

To Mikueh
Israel Cemetery

Spruce Street

❹

Thaddeus Kosciuszko
National Memorial

To ❸ Gloria
Dei Church
N.H.S., ¾ mile

2. **Edgar Allan Poe National Historic Site** (532 North Seventh Street; 215–597–8780; www.nps.gov/edal): the only surviving Philadelphia home of this famous American author who spent six productive years in the city. Poe lived in this home from 1843 until 1844. Visitors may tour the home, where exhibits and an audiovisual program are available. There is no fee at this site.

3. **Gloria Dei (Old Swedes') Church National Historic Site** (Columbus Boulevard and Washington Avenue; 215–389–1513; www.nps.gov/glde): The present structure, constructed between 1699 and 1700, is on the site of an earlier log church built by Swedish settlers in 1677. This is the oldest surviving church in Pennsylvania and the second-oldest Swedish church in the United States. Gloria Dei contains numerous historic items and continues to serve an Episcopal parish. There is no fee at this site.

4. **Thaddeus Kosciuszko National Memorial** (301 Pine Street; 215–597–9618; www.nps.gov/thko): This park area was authorized in 1972 to preserve the home of a Polish military engineer who served with American forces during the Revolutionary War. Kosciuszko designed and constructed defense works, including those that were crucial to the American victory at Saratoga. Kosciuszko resided here during the winter of 1797–98. The outside and second floor of the building have been restored to their 1798 appearances. There is no fee at this site.

STEAMTOWN NATIONAL HISTORIC SITE

150 South Washington Avenue
Scranton, PA 18503-2018
(888) 693–9391
www.nps.gov/stea

Steamtown National Historic Site comprises fifty-two acres and was authorized in 1986 to restore and preserve a former major railroad yard and to interpret the story of early-twentieth-century steam railroading in America. The site is in the town of Scranton in northeastern Pennsylvania.

The Lackawanna & Western Railroad was chartered in 1849 to haul iron from furnaces in Scranton to market. The railroad began operating in 1851, then merged with the Cobb's Gap Railroad a few years later to form the Delaware, Lackawanna & Western Railroad. The line grew to include branches to New York City, Lake Erie, Lake Ontario, and the interiors of New York and eastern Pennsylvania. One of the line's selling points to passengers was that the railroad used cleaner-burning anthracite coal that produced much less soot than the coal burned by competing railroads. The DL&W remained busy hauling military freight and coal during World War II, but after the war much of this business dried up. In 1960, the railroad was forced to merge with the Erie Railroad.

The Delaware Lackawanna & Western facility includes the roundhouse, switchyard, steam locomotives, and passenger, freight, and work cars. Visitors can see the visitor center, theater, and history and technology museums. The history museum highlights the people and history

of U.S. railroading from the early 1800s to modern times. The technology museum highlights technological changes and advances through the years. Included in the technology museum is a working HO scale model railroad layout that represents DL&W's Scranton yard. There are frequent tours of the roundhouse, where locomotives receive routine maintenance, and of shops where crews restore rolling stock. Train rides are offered from late spring through November. Call ahead for time schedule, reservations, and rate information. The park is open daily from 9:00 A.M. to 5:00 P.M., except Thanksgiving, Christmas Day, and New Year's Day.

ENTRANCE FEE: No charge. There is a charge for the museum: $8.00 adult, $7.00 senior, $6.00 ages six through twelve, five and under free with a paying adult.

FACILITIES: Drinking water and rest rooms are at the site. Food and lodging are nearby. For local visitor information contact Northeast Pennsylvania Convention and Visitors Bureau (1–800–22–WELCOME).

UPPER DELAWARE SCENIC & RECREATIONAL RIVER

RR2, Box 2428
Beach Lake, PA 18405-9737
(570) 685–4871
upde_interpretation@nps.gov
www.nps.gov/upde

Upper Delaware Scenic & Recreational River was authorized in 1978 and includes a 73-mile stretch of a free-flowing river between Hancock and Sparrow Bush, New York. The river is located in northeastern Pennsylvania and southern New York, where it forms the border between the two states. New York Highway 97 follows the river for nearly its full length from Port Jervis to Hancock. Most land along the river is privately owned.

The Upper Delaware's initial residents relied on the river for transportation, which consisted primarily of canoes used by both frontiersmen and Indians. Larger boats eventually replaced canoes until, in the 1820s, coal was being shipped by boat from Pennsylvania to New York. Coal transportation involved use of a canal in conjunction with the river to connect Pennsylvania's anthracite coal mines to New York City. The canal started at Honesdale, Pennsylvania, where it followed the Lackawaxen River to the Delaware River. It then paralleled the Delaware to Port Jervis, where the canal cut cross-country to the Hudson River at Rondout. Initially, canal boats crossed the Delaware by means of rope ferry. This was updated in the late 1840s when a water aqueduct was built between Lackawaxen, Pennsylvania, and Minisink Ford, New York. During the 1850s, the canal transported a million tons of cargo annually.

The National Park Service's information center on Main Street in Narrowsburg, New York, is open weekends Memorial Day Weekend through the middle of October from 9:00 A.M. to 4:30 P.M. (845–252–3947). Here, visitors will find maps, publications, and exhibits. Kiosks or bulletin boards providing information, emergency first aid, and boating safety are located at boating access points at Skinners Falls, New York; Narrowsburg, New York; Ten Mile River,

Steamtown National Historic Site (opposite page)

New York; and Lackawaxen, Pennsylvania. One of the area's most interesting features is the Roebling Delaware Aqueduct at Minisink Ford. The aqueduct, the nation's oldest wire suspension bridge, was constructed by John Roebling, who later designed the Brooklyn Bridge. The aqueduct's purpose was to permit canal boats to cross over the Delaware River. Following abandonment of the canal in 1898, the aqueduct was purchased and converted to a bridge for trucks and cars. During the summer rangers are often stationed in the aqueduct's former tollhouse in Minisink Ford.

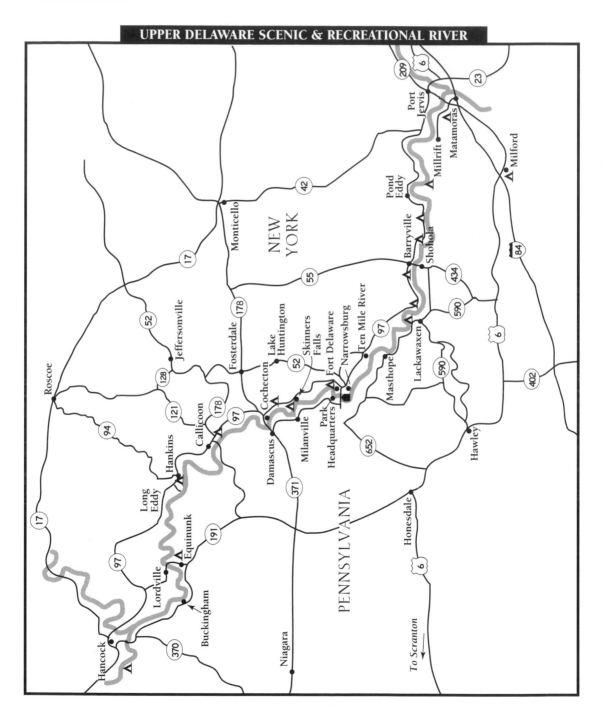

UPPER DELAWARE SCENIC & RECREATIONAL RIVER

The National Park Service operates the Zane Grey Museum in Lackawaxen. Zane Grey, the "Father of the Western Novel," resided in Lackawaxen for thirteen years beginning in 1905. While here, Grey first achieved success as a writer and established his place as one of America's most popular authors. *Riders of the Purple Sage,* written in Lackawaxen, is one of his most noted works. The museum is open Thursday through Sunday from 10:00 A.M. to 5:00 P.M., Memorial Day weekend through Labor Day weekend, and weekends only through the middle of October.

A major activity of visitors is to canoe the river. A number of firms offer boat rentals and the pickup and return of canoes and individuals at various points along the river. A directory of canoe liveries, boat rentals, and campgrounds is available by mail from headquarters, at various locations within the park, or on the Internet.

ENTRANCE FEE: No charge. The Zane Grey Museum charges $6.00 for adults, $1.00 for visitors ten through fifteen, nine and under free.

FACILITIES: Food and lodging are available in towns along the river. The Narrowsburg Information Center is wheelchair-accessible with rest rooms.

CAMPING: No camping is provided by the National Park Service. Private campgrounds are in various locations along the river.

FISHING: The river provides good fishing for brook, brown, and rainbow trout, smallmouth bass, and walleye. During May and June, American shad may spawn in deep pools. A fishing license from either New York or Pennsylvania is sufficient for boat fishing or fishing from either shore.

VALLEY FORGE NATIONAL HISTORICAL PARK

Valley Forge, PA 19482-0953
(610) 783–1077
www.nps.gov/vafo

Valley Forge National Historical Park comprises about 3,600 acres and was authorized in 1976 to commemorate the site of the 1777–78 winter encampment of George Washington and the Continental Army. This is considered the birthplace of the United States Army. The park's eastern entrance is approximately 18 miles northwest of Philadelphia via Interstate 76 (Schuylkill Expressway) and Route 422. When approaching from the Pennsylvania Turnpike, take exit 24 through the tollbooth and turn right on North Gulph Road.

On December 19, 1777, George Washington brought his ragged army of approximately 12,000 men to spend the winter at Valley Forge. The soldiers were short of food, supplies, and clothing, and many died in spite of the fact that no battles were fought here. Fortifications and log huts were built, Washington was able to establish a system of supply for his troops, and the army was rigorously drilled by General Frederick von Steuben. By the time spring had come, the Continental Army was well on its way to becoming a disciplined and skilled force that could take on the British Army and eventually win the War for Independence.

Valley Forge National Historical Park

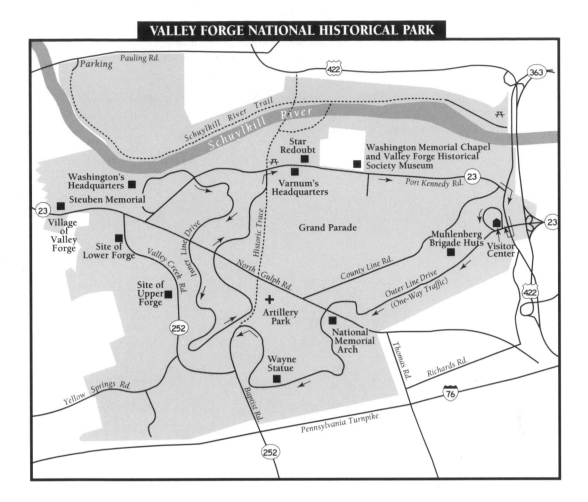

A very nice visitor center at the east entrance contains exhibits and personnel to help interpret this historic area. The visitor center bookstore offers a wide range of publications. Valley Forge is a fee area, and admission is charged (April through November) to enter Washington's Headquarters. A number of paved roads lead past extensive remains and reconstructions of major forts, lines of earthworks, reconstructed huts, monuments, and markers. Also of interest are Washington's Headquarters, the Grand Parade Ground where troops were drilled, and the National Memorial Arch. A paved trail for bicyclers, joggers, and walkers follows the tour route. Bus tours operate from the visitor center May through October, and tapes and tape players may be rented for use in private cars during those months. From November through April tapes may be purchased but no tape players are rented at the visitor center.

ENTRANCE FEE: $2.00 (April through November).

FACILITIES: No lodging is available in the park, but hotels and motels can be found nearby. Rest rooms are located at the visitor center and at other points in the park. Picnic areas are at Varnum's, Wayne's Woods, and Betzwood.

CAMPING: No camping is permitted in the park. Approximately 25 miles northwest via State Routes 23 and 345, French Creek State Park offers a nice campground. (For more information on this campground, see the camping section under Hopewell Furnace National Historic Site.) Other campground information is available at the visitor center.

FISHING: Catch and release fishing is permitted at Valley Forge National Historical Park in both the Valley Creek and the Schuylkill River. A Pennsylvania fishing license is required. For more information contact a park ranger.

PUERTO RICO

TOURIST INFORMATION
(800) 866–7827
www.prtourism.com

SAN JUAN NATIONAL HISTORIC SITE

Fort San Cristobal, Building 501, Norzagaray Street
Old San Juan, Puerto Rico 00901-2094
(787) 729–6777
saju_administration@nps.gov
www.nps.gov/saju

The world-famous castles and walls of Old San Juan, begun by the Spanish in the sixteenth century, are today protected by San Juan National Historic Site. Three and a half miles of walls and seventy-five acres of massive fortifications make up this World Heritage Site, which became part of the National Park Service in 1949. Forts El Morro and San Cristobal can be reached by auto by turning right on Calle Norzagaray at Plaza Colon off Avenida Munoz Rivera. From the international airport or Isla Verde tourist hotel zone, follow Highway 26 west. It merges into Highway 25 at the historic San Antonio Bridge. Look for signs marked SAN JUAN or VIEJO SAN JUAN along the road. Continue on Highway 25 past the Capitol building on your left; Fort San Cristobal covers the hillside to your right. Parking in the historic zone is extremely limited.

In Spanish Puerto Rico means "excellent harbor" and the sheltered deep-water anchorage found in San Juan Bay has been important to the history of this Caribbean island since Columbus discovered and named it in 1493. Spanish troops began to fortify this port city in the 1530s to protect its crucial shipping lanes to rich colonies in Mexico and Central America. To prevent the English, Dutch, and French from seizing Puerto Rico and using it as a base from which to attack Spanish shipping, fort building went on here for more than 350 years. Its peak came in the late 1700s, when the walls completely surrounding the city boasted more than 450 cannons.

After the wars of independence in Latin America in the early 1800s, there were no Spanish colonies left on the "Spanish Main," as the mainland of South and Central America was then called. Only the islands of Cuba and Puerto Rico remained loyal, remnants of a once vast domain. In 1898 a revolution in Cuba and the landing of American troops on Puerto Rico during the Spanish-American War ended the empire started 400 years earlier by Columbus.

The face of colonial Spain in the tropical Americas is still seen by walking among the historic homes, churches, and plazas of Old San Juan. The original fortified city is an area 7-by-7 blocks, ringed by battlements and bastions that connect the two giant fortresses: El Morro, on the western tip of the islet, which broods over the entrance to the harbor from the sea; and Castillo de San Cristobal, which towers over the northeast shoulder of the city near Plaza Colon. Information is available from rangers on duty at the entrances of both fortresses. Tours and a twelve-minute-long video in both English and Spanish are offered daily.

No parking is available at either El Morro or on nearby streets of the western sector of Old San Juan. San Cristobal has a small parking lot (seventeen cars) because of the steep hillside and huge eighteenth-century walls. Use the public parking at La Puntilla, Ballajá, and Covadonga and the free shuttle trams to move about the historic city. Built to a human scale, Old San Juan is best explored by walking; a hat and good walking shoes are a must.

ENTRANCE FEE: No charge for the grounds. There is a fee to enter the fort: $2.00 adult, $1.00 ages thirteen through seventeen and seniors, twelve and under free.

FACILITIES: No facilities are provided by the National Park Service. Food and lodging are available in Old San Juan.

RHODE ISLAND

STATE TOURIST INFORMATION

(800) 556–2484

www.visitrhodeisland.com

ROGER WILLIAMS NATIONAL MEMORIAL

282 North Main Street

Providence, RI 02903-1240

(401) 521–7266

rowi_interpretation@nps.gov

www.nps.gov/rowi

This four-and-one-half-acre park was established in 1965 to memorialize the founder of Rhode Island and pioneer of religious freedom. The memorial is located in downtown Providence, between North Main Street (one-way north) and Canal Street (one-way south) at the corner of Smith Street (Route 44). From Interstate 95, exit on Charles Street when traveling south or take the State Offices exit when driving north.

Roger Williams sailed from London in 1630 after becoming frustrated in England with the king's supremacy in church and spiritual matters. Equally unhappy in Massachusetts, Williams was banished from the Bay Colony for his beliefs; subsequently, in 1636, he founded with his small band of followers what is now the city of Providence. The new colony grew and prospered and was one of the first in the world to set forth in clear terms the principle that men should be permitted freedom of religious belief and that the state should govern "only in civil things." In 1676, most of Providence, including Williams's homestead, was destroyed in King Philip's War. In 1683, Roger Williams died and was buried in a simple ceremony.

A visitor center, housed in a renovated eighteenth-century structure, is open daily from 9:00 A.M. to 4:30 P.M. daily. Exhibits and a three-minute video offer a view of Roger Williams's life and the impact of religious freedom in this country. The center is closed on Thanksgiving, Christmas Day, and New Year's Day. Free parking is available in the memorial's lot on Canal Street. The Hahn Memorial on the grounds marks the site of the spring once used by the Williams family. Within walking distance of the memorial are a number of points of interest, including the Old State House and the first Baptist church in America.

ENTRANCE FEE: No charge.

FACILITIES: Rest rooms and water are available in the visitor center. Food service can be found near the memorial.

CAMPING: No camping is permitted at the memorial. Casimir Pulaski Memorial State Park, 20 miles northwest via U.S. 44, offers camping.

TOURO SYNAGOGUE NATIONAL HISTORIC SITE

85 Touro Street
Newport, RI 02840
(401) 847–4794
www.tourosynagogue.org

Touro Synagogue, the oldest synagogue in the United States, was designated an affiliated area of the National Park Service in 1946 to help preserve what many consider one of the most architecturally distinguished buildings of eighteenth-century America. The synagogue is in downtown Newport, Rhode Island. From Newport Bridge exit south on Farewell Street and merge left on Thames before turning east on Touro Street.

In a letter "To the Hebrew Congregation in Newport" in 1790, President George Washington eloquently defined the government's standard for religious freedom and civil liberties when he declared that the new nation would "give to bigotry no sanction, to persecution no assistance." Ground was broken for Touro Synagogue in 1759, and four years later the dedication was conducted by Rabbi Isaac Touro. The synagogue was designed by well-known colonial architect Peter Harrison and constructed with financial assistance from Jewish congregations in both the Old and New Worlds. With the new synagogue and cemetery land purchased in 1677 (1 block up from the synagogue), one of the earliest Jewish communities in what would soon become the United States could perform the three essential functions of Jewish communal life: worship, religious instruction of the children, and burial in sanctified ground.

Touro Synagogue is open daily for tours except Saturdays and Jewish holidays. Tours begin every half hour with the last tour one-half hour before closing. Hours are 10:00 A.M. to 5:00 P.M. from July 1 until Labor Day. From Labor Day through October 31 and May 1 to June 30, hours are 11:00 A.M. to 3:00 P.M. Sunday, and 1:00 to 3:00 P.M. Monday through Friday. Hours the remainder of the year are 11:00 A.M. to 3:00 P.M. Sunday, and 1:00 P.M. for one tour only Monday through Friday. Services are Friday at 6:00 P.M. (7:00 P.M. in summer) and Saturday morning at 8:45 A.M.

ENTRANCE FEE: No charge.

FACILITIES: No food or lodging is available at the site, but a major commercial area is located on Thames Street a few blocks away.

CAMPING: No camping is permitted at the site, and although private campgrounds are located in the Newport area, they are generally expensive.

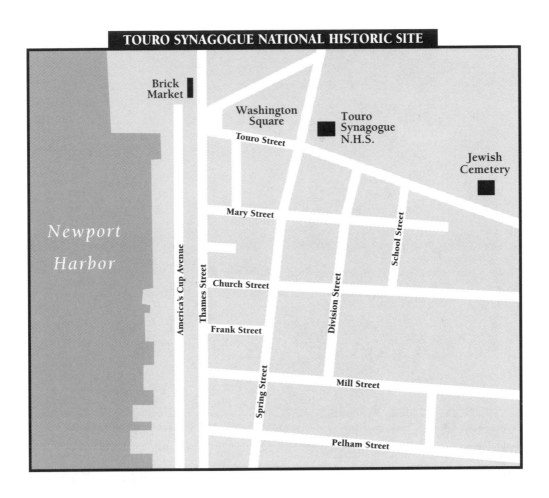

TOURO SYNAGOGUE NATIONAL HISTORIC SITE

Brick Market

Washington Square

Touro Synagogue N.H.S.

Jewish Cemetery

Touro Street

Mary Street

Newport Harbor

America's Cup Avenue

Thames Street

Church Street

School Street

Division Street

Frank Street

Spring Street

Mill Street

Pelham Street

U.S. Monument, Kings Mountain National Military Park

SOUTH CAROLINA

STATE TOURIST INFORMATION

(800) 872–3505

www.travelsc.com

CHARLES PINCKNEY NATIONAL HISTORIC SITE

c/o Fort Sumter National Monument

1214 Middle Street

Sullivans Island, SC 29482

(843) 881–5516

CHPI_Operations@nps.gov

www.nps.gov/chpi

Charles Pinckney National Historic Site comprises twenty-eight acres of a once-proud 715-acre plantation. It was authorized in 1988 to interpret the life of Charles Pinckney, a distinguished public servant in the early years of the nation and one of the principal framers of the Constitution. The site also preserves part of Pinckney's plantation, Snee Farm. The historic site is located 6 miles east of Charleston, South Carolina, within the city limits of Mt. Pleasant, South Carolina. It is approximately $\frac{1}{2}$ mile north of U.S. 17 on Long Point Road.

Charles Pinckney (1757–1824) was educated in Charleston and elected to the South Carolina legislature when he was twenty-two years old. He served as an officer in the American Revolution, and in 1787 he served as a delegate to the Constitution Convention in Philadelphia. He addressed the convention more than one hundred times and offered a draft of a new constitution. At least twenty-four points he proposed in that draft survived to become part of the U.S.

Constitution. He later served as a member of the state General Assembly, U.S. senator, minister (ambassador) to Spain, member of the U.S. House of Representatives, and served four terms as governor of South Carolina.

Charles Pinckney inherited Snee Farm from his father, who had purchased the plantation in 1754. The farm was originally part of a 1698 royal grant. A working plantation, rice, indigo, cotton, and vegetables were grown on Snee Farm for nearly 250 years. Today the visitor center is located in a rare example of a one-and-one-half-story, low-country cottage built in 1828 of cypress and pine. The site is open daily (except Christmas and New Year's Days) from 9:00 A.M. to 5:00 P.M.

ENTRANCE FEE: No charge.

FACILITIES: Full facilities including food and lodging are available near the historic site.

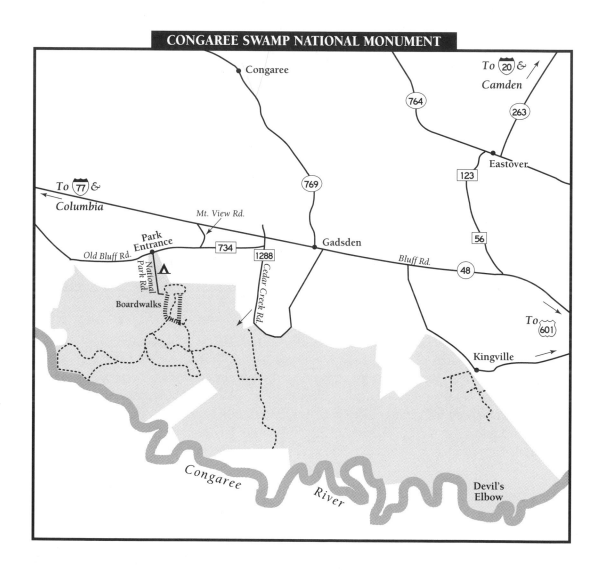

CONGAREE SWAMP NATIONAL MONUMENT

100 National Park Road
Hopkins, SC 29061
(803) 776–4396
COSW_information@nps.gov
www.nps.gov/cosw

Congaree Swamp National Monument, a designated wilderness area, preserves the largest intact tract of old-growth bottomland hardwood forest in the United States. The old-growth forest is among the tallest broad-leaved forests in the world. Congaree Swamp is in south-central South Carolina, about 20 miles southeast of Columbia. From Columbia, take SC 48 (Bluff Road) and follow the signs.

Congaree Swamp National Monument, a naturalist's paradise, is not truly a swamp. It is a forested floodplain with state and national champion-size trees in a river-bottom environment once common in the southeastern United States. It is also a birder's delight. The forest supports unusually high densities of migrating and breeding neotropical birds. Twenty miles of hiking trails range in length from 1 to almost 11 miles. A 2½-mile boardwalk loop trail is available for walking and is wheelchair-accessible. A 1¼-mile boardwalk is usually above water even during flooding conditions. Visitors should check at the ranger station for program schedules. Cedar Creek provides an 18-mile canoe trail through the swamp.

A visitor center with interpretive displays is located inside the monument entrance. Visitors may pick up information here. The center is open daily from 8:30 A.M. to 5:00 P.M. except Christmas Day. Long pants, long-sleeved shirts, sneakers or boots, maps, compass, first aid kit, and insect repellent are recommended.

ENTRANCE FEE: No charge.

FACILITIES: No food or lodging is available in the monument, but both are found in Columbia.

CAMPING: Primitive camping is allowed in the monument by permit only. There is no fee. Open fires are prohibited except in the primitive group campsite. Poinsett State Park (east of the monument on Highway 261) and Sesquicentennial State Park (northwest of the monument on U.S. 1) have campgrounds with tables, grills, water, flush toilets, showers, electrical hookups, swimming, and fishing. Both state parks are located on South Carolina state highway maps. Directions are available at the visitor center.

FISHING: Fishing includes catches of bass, bream, and catfish. A South Carolina fishing license is required. Federal regulations prohibit the use of minnows, fish eggs, or amphibians as bait.

COWPENS NATIONAL BATTLEFIELD

P.O. Box 308
Chesnee, SC 29323-0308
(864) 461–2828
COWP_superintendent@nps.gov
www.nps.gov/cowp

Cowpens National Battlefield comprises 842 acres and was established as a national battlefield site in 1929 to commemorate a decisive victory by American forces in the Revolutionary War. The battlefield is located on U.S. 11, 10 miles northwest of Gaffney and 2 miles east of Chesnee, South Carolina.

To protect British outposts in the Carolinas from the American army, Lord Cornwallis sent Lieutenant Colonel Banastre Tarleton after an American detachment led by Brigadier General Daniel

COWPENS NATIONAL BATTLEFIELD

To Cliffside, N.C.

To Chesnee

Cherokee Foothills Scenic Hwy.

x = Exhibit

End one-way

U.S. Memorial Monument

Parking

Thicketty Mountain Viewpoint

Parking

11

110

Washington Light Infantry Monument 1856

Green River Road

Parking

Robert Scruggs House

To Gaffney

Cowpens Battlefield Scenic Hwy.

Begin one-way

Shelter

Richard Scruggs Chimney

To Town of Cowpens

Morgan. On January 17, 1781, a successful stand by Morgan's troops at the Cowpens resulted in a rout of the British forces and an important American patriot victory. During the one-hour battle, the British incurred losses approaching 80 percent of their forces (110 dead, more than 200 wounded, and more than 500 captured). American losses were much lighter, with only twelve dead and sixty wounded.

The park's visitor center, ½ mile inside the entrance, contains museum exhibits, an excellent slide presentation, and a battlefield map display. The only charge is for admission to the presentation, *Daybreak at the Cowpens,* which is shown on the hour. A self-guided trail (1¼ miles, forty-five minutes) to battlefield sites begins behind the visitor center. The trail is level with gentle grades and has benches. A cassette describing the battle may be rented or purchased to take along on the walk. A one-way, 3-mile auto-tour road circles the battlefield. The park is open daily from 9:00 A.M. until 5:00 P.M. except Thanksgiving, Christmas Day, and New Year's Day. The tour road and picnic facility close at 4:30 P.M.

ENTRANCE FEE: No charge. There is a fee to see *Daybreak at the Cowpens.*

FACILITIES: Food and lodging can be found in Gaffney and Spartanburg. A picnic area with water, toilets, tables, and a group shelter is at the far end of the park's auto-tour road. Water, rest rooms, and a soft-drink machine are in the visitor center.

CAMPING: No camping is permitted at the park. A state park with camping facilities is adjacent to Kings Mountain National Military Park, 30 miles east of Cowpens. A privately owned campground is 12 miles from the park.

FORT SUMTER NATIONAL MONUMENT

1214 Middle Street
Sullivan's Island, SC 29482
(843) 727–4739
FOSU_Ranger_activities@nps.gov
www.nps.gov/fosu

This 189-acre monument was authorized in 1948 to memorialize the site of the first engagement of the Civil War. The park also includes Fort Moultrie, the scene of a Patriot victory in 1776. Fort Sumter is located in Charleston Harbor and can be reached only by boat. Tour boats leave from the Monument's visitor education center in downtown Charlestown at Liberty Square.

Construction of five-sided Fort Sumter commenced in 1829 as one part of a series of coastal fortifications. The fort, designed for 135 guns, was nearly complete in time for the Confederate shelling, which began at 4:30 A.M. on April 12, 1861. On April 14, following the surrender of the fort, Federal troops were allowed to evacuate. For the next four years, Fort Sumter remained a Confederate stronghold. The fort was abandoned in February 1865 with the approach of Sherman's army.

Fort Sumter is open daily from 10:00 A.M. to 5:30 P.M. from April 1 to Labor Day and shorter periods the rest of the year (closed Christmas and New Year's Days). Park personnel are on duty, and a museum is located inside the fort. Brochures are available for a self-guided tour. Across

Charleston Harbor, Fort Moultrie is the site of a fortification that saw service from the Revolutionary War to World War II. This restored fort is open for self-guided tours from 9:00 A.M. to 5:00 P.M. This fort is also closed on Christmas and New Year's Days. A visitor center providing audiovisual presentations is located at Liberty Square, near the intersection of Concord and Calhoun Streets.

ENTRANCE FEE: No charge.

FACILITIES: No food or lodging is available in the monument, but both can be found nearby.

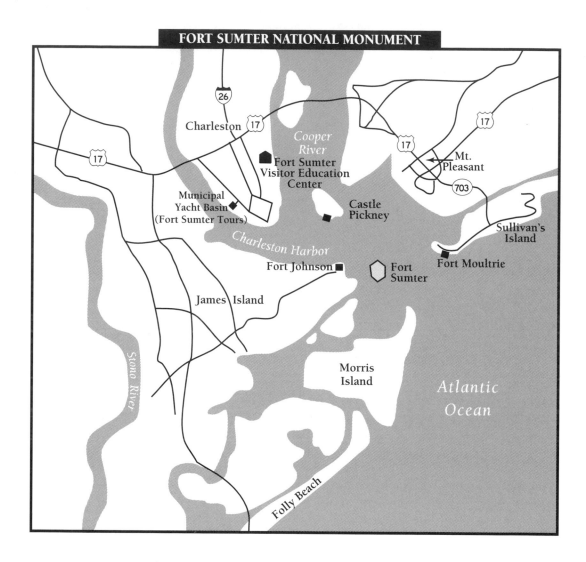

HISTORIC CAMDEN REVOLUTIONARY WAR SITE

222 Broad Street
Camden, SC 29020
(803) 432–9841
hiscamden@camden.net
www.Historic-Camden.net

Historic Camden Revolutionary War Site comprises ninety-eight acres and was authorized as an affiliated area of the National Park Service in 1982 to assist in restoration and interpretation of this colonial village, established in the mid-1730s. Historic Camden Revolutionary War Site is in central South Carolina, about 30 miles northeast of Columbia via either Interstate 20 or U.S. 1.

Fredricksburg Township (the original name of the Camden area) was laid out during the winter of 1731–32 as a result of instructions from King George II to locate a township "on the River Watery." By the time the current name was adopted in 1768 in honor of Lord Camden, a British Parliament champion of colonial rights, the settlement had become an inland center of population and trade.

Camden was occupied by British troops following the fall of Charleston in 1780. British General Cornwallis established military posts at several interior locations in the state, including Camden. The British fortified the town with a stockade wall and six small forts around the perimeter. Although the British successfully defended the town against American forces, heavy losses caused the British to evacuate, burning the fortifications as they left.

Historic Camden Revolutionary War Site includes seven buildings and period structures that have been reconstructed or moved to this location. The Cunningham House (circa 1840) at the end of the parking lot serves as tour headquarters. Adjacent to the museum center, the original town site offers archaeological findings and reconstructions. This includes a partial reconstruction of the town wall, the reconstructed foundation of the powder magazine, and the reconstructed home of Camden's founder, commandeered by Cornwallis as British headquarters. Historic Camden Revolutionary War Site is open daily except major holidays. Guided tours (fee charged) are offered Tuesday through Friday at 10:30 A.M., 1:30 P.M., and 3:00 P.M.; Saturday from 10:30 A.M. to 4:00 P.M.; and Sunday from 1:30 to 4:00 P.M. Free self-guided tours are available daily (except as noted above) from 10:00 A.M. to 5:00 P.M. A museum shop is open daily except Monday from 10:00 A.M. to 5:00 P.M.

ENTRANCE FEE: No charge.

FACILITIES: Food and lodging are available in Camden.

CAMPING: No camping is permitted at Historic Camden Revolutionary War Site. Sesquicentennial State Park between Camden and Columbia on U.S. 1 offers full camping facilities including hookups. Lee State Park, east of Bishopville, offers similar facilities. Lake Wateree State Park, northwest of Camden, offers seventy-two sites with water and electrical hookups.

KINGS MOUNTAIN NATIONAL MILITARY PARK

2625 Park Road
Blacksburg, SC 29702
(864) 936–7921
chris_revels@nps.gov
www.nps.gov/kimo

Kings Mountain National Military Park contains nearly 4,000 acres and was established in 1931 to commemorate the site where American frontiersmen defeated a British force on October 7, 1780, at a critical point during the American Revolution. The park is located in north-central South Carolina—close to the state line—between Spartanburg, South Carolina, and Charlotte, North Carolina, via Interstate 85.

Five years after the beginning of the American Revolution, England turned its attention toward conquering the South. As part of this effort, Major Patrick Ferguson was charged by General Cornwallis with building the Loyalists into a strong Carolina militia. After recruiting several thousand Carolinians, Ferguson headed north with an ultimate objective of carrying the war into Virginia. However, on October 7, he and more than 1,000 men were attacked and defeated while camped on Kings Mountain. The American victory delayed Cornwallis' plan and permitted the Continental Army to organize a new offensive in the South.

The park's beautiful visitor center contains historical exhibits and a film to help interpret the battle. From here, a paved 1½-mile self-guided battlefield trail (forty-five minutes to one hour with some steep grades) leads around the battlefield ridge and to the military park's chief features. A variety of monuments and interpretive signs are scattered along the trail.

ENTRANCE FEE: No charge.

FACILITIES: No food or lodging is available in the park, but both can be found in the towns of Gaffney, York, and Spartanburg, South Carolina, and Kings Mountain, North Carolina. Rest rooms and water are in the visitor center.

CAMPING: Only primitive backpack camping is permitted in the park. South Carolina's Kings Mountain State Park is adjacent to the military park and offers a campground with tables, water, flush toilets, showers, a dump station, laundry, store, and swimming (803–222–3209).

FISHING: Fishing is not available in the military park. Fishing access is in adjacent Kings Mountain State Park.

NINETY SIX NATIONAL HISTORIC SITE

P.O. Box 496
Ninety Six, SC 29666-0496
(864) 543–4068
nisi_interpretation@nps.gov
www.nps.gov/nisi

Ninety Six National Historic Site comprises 989 acres and was authorized in 1976 to memorialize the site of an important colonial trading village and Revolutionary War stronghold held briefly by the British. The historic site is located in western South Carolina, 9 miles east of Greenwood and 2 miles south of the town of Ninety Six on State Highway 248.

The first store at Ninety Six, named because it lay an estimated 96 miles down a major trail from an important Cherokee village, was opened about 1752. A fort built near the trading post withstood two Indian attacks before the Cherokees made peace in 1761. Soon, the area began to grow, and in 1769, Ninety Six was established as the seat of a judicial district. After the English seized control of South Carolina in 1780, Ninety Six became a major military post and recruiting depot and was occupied by British or Loyalist forces. An earthen star-shaped fort constructed by the Loyalists was the object of a major siege by Patriots under the command of Nathanael Greene in 1781. Although the fort was never captured by the Patriots, the Loyalists eventually withdrew to Charleston.

The site is open 8:00 A.M. to 5:00 P.M. daily except Thanksgiving, Christmas Day, and New Year's Day. A visitor center contains museum exhibits to help interpret the history of Ninety Six. A mile-long (one hour) interpretive trail takes visitors by the earthen fort abandoned by the British, reconstructed earthwork embankments of the old fortifications, and through the town site of old Ninety Six. The hike provides a nice leisurely walk, and numerous interpretive signs are along the way. Benches are located in shaded areas along the trail.

ENTRANCE FEE: No charge.

FACILITIES: A soft-drink machine and rest rooms are at the administration building, and drinking water is in the visitor center. Food and lodging are in the town of Greenwood and the town of Ninety Six.

CAMPING: No camping is permitted in the park. Nine miles north of the historic site on Lake Greenwood (north on 248, right on 34, left on 702), Greenwood State Recreation Area (864–543–3535) offers 125 sites with tables, water, flush toilets, showers, electrical hookups, swimming, and fishing. Many of the sites are on the water, and a boat ramp is available.

FISHING: Fishing is available on a seasonal basis at the site. A South Carolina fishing license is required.

Andrew Johnson National Historic Site

TENNESSEE

STATE TOURIST INFORMATION
(800) 836–6200
www.tnvacation.com

ANDREW JOHNSON NATIONAL HISTORIC SITE
P.O. Box 1088
Greeneville, TN 37744-1088
(423) 638–3551
www.nps.gov/anjo

Andrew Johnson National Historic Site, which comprises seventeen acres, was authorized in 1935 to preserve the home, tailor shop, and burial site of the seventeenth president of the United States. The site is located in northeastern Tennessee in the town of Greeneville, 29 miles southwest of Johnson City via U.S. 11E.

In 1826, when he was seventeen years old, Andrew Johnson and his family moved to Greeneville, where he soon established himself as a successful tailor. After his first venture into politics in 1829, he progressed to five terms as a U.S. representative, governor of Tennessee, and a U.S. senator. An opponent of secession, he became military governor of Tennessee during the Civil War and ran as Lincoln's vice president in 1864. Upon Lincoln's assassination in April 1865, he began a stormy career as United States president.

During Andrew Johnson's term in the White House, his political views and Reconstruction policies differed from that of the powerful Radical Republicans in Congress. The Radicals vigorously challenged President Johnson's policies and eventually led Congress in instituting its own Civil War Reconstruction Program in 1867. Additional problems resulted

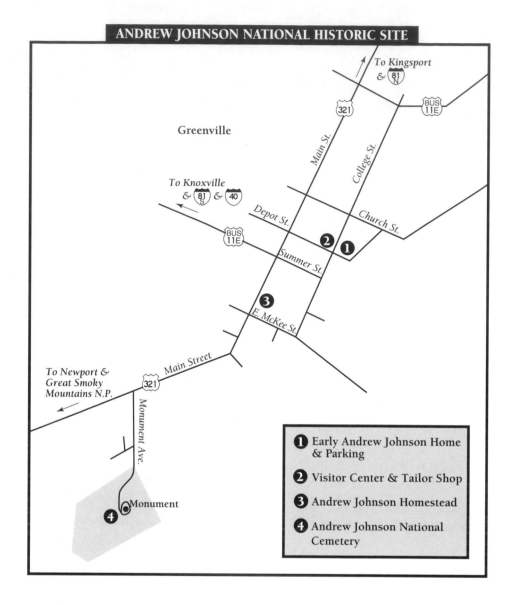

ANDREW JOHNSON NATIONAL HISTORIC SITE

To Kingsport
& 81

321

BUS 11E

Greenville

Main St.

College St.

To Knoxville
& 81 S & 40

Depot St.

Church St.

BUS 11E

❷ ❶

Summer St.

❸

E. McKee St.

To Newport &
Great Smoky
Mountains N.P.

321

Main Street

Monument Ave.

❹ ◉Monument

❶ **Early Andrew Johnson Home & Parking**

❷ **Visitor Center & Tailor Shop**

❸ **Andrew Johnson Homestead**

❹ **Andrew Johnson National Cemetery**

in Johnson's being impeached by the House, with only a single vote keeping him from being judged guilty and removed from office by the Senate. After serving as president, Johnson returned to Greeneville. He was elected to the U.S. Senate in 1875 and died six months later, on July 31, 1875.

The historic site is open daily except Thanksgiving, Christmas Day, and New Year's Day from 9:00 A.M. to 5:00 P.M. The visitor center houses a museum, bookstore, theater, and Johnson's tailor shop at the corner of Depot and College streets. Across the street is the early home in which Johnson lived from the 1830s until 1851. In 1851 Johnson purchased and moved into the Homestead located on Main Street. The Homestead, restored to its 1869–75 appearance, is fully furnished with many Johnson family belongings. The Homestead is open to visitors by guided tour only. Tickets for the guided tour (fee charged) are available at the visitor center only. Andrew Johnson is buried in the Andrew Johnson National Cemetery, located 1 block south of West Main Street at the end of Monument Avenue.

ENTRANCE FEE: No charge for the grounds. The tour of President Johnson's homestead is $2.00 for adults ages eighteen through sixty-one; others are free. Tickets for the tour are available only at the visitor center.

FACILITIES: Food and lodging are available in the town of Greeneville. Picnics are not allowed on park property.

CAMPING: No camping is permitted in the park. National Forest Service campgrounds are located southeast of Greeneville.

BIG SOUTH FORK NATIONAL RIVER
AND RECREATION AREA

4564 Leatherwood Road
Oneida, TN 37841-9544
(931) 879–3625
BISO_Information@nps.gov
www.nps.gov/biso

Big South Fork National River and Recreation Area, which will eventually encompass over 123,000 acres, was authorized in 1974 to preserve an area of the Cumberland Plateau that contains scenic gorges and valleys with a wide range of unique natural and historical features. The park is located in northeastern Tennessee and southeastern Kentucky, with main access via Leatherwood Ford Road, Tennessee 297, connecting Oneida and Jamestown, Tennessee. U.S. 27 follows the park's eastern border.

Big South Fork National River and Recreation Area is an effort by the federal government to protect the Big South Fork River and its major tributaries as natural and free-flowing streams while developing the adjacent plateau area for its full recreational potential. The area now contains lush vegetation where homesteads, mines, logging camps, and roads once dotted the landscape. Flowing through the center of the area is the Big South Fork of the Cumberland River, which is fed by the Clear Fork and New rivers. Immediately adjacent to the Big South Fork is Historic Rugby, a restored 1880s settlement originally built for sons of British gentry; the Daniel Boone National Forest; and Pickett State Park.

One of the major recreational activities in the Big South Fork is to float the river, where visitors find everything from a tame, slow-moving stream to bubbling, churning rapids. Hiking, mountain biking, and horseback riding, also popular recreational activities, offer access to the heart of the recreation area, where one may find scenic overlooks, huge sandstone arches, chimney rocks, abundant wildlife, or peaceful solitude. For those driving, Devil's Jump or Yahoo Falls in Kentucky and East Rim or Honey Creek in Tennessee each provide access to gorge overlooks. Leatherwood Ford provides convenient river access.

A visitor center at the Bandy Creek Campground in Tennessee, offering exhibits and information, is open daily from 8:00 A.M. to 4:30 P.M. The Kentucky visitor center, located just off U.S. 27 on Highway 92, offers exhibits and information and is open daily between May and October from 9:30 A.M. to 5:30 P.M. The Blue Heron Mining Community 9 miles west of

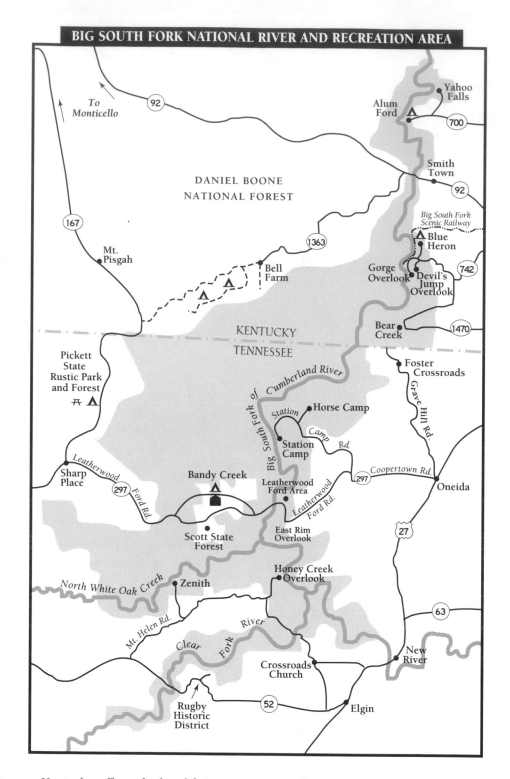

BIG SOUTH FORK NATIONAL RIVER AND RECREATION AREA

To Monticello

92

DANIEL BOONE
NATIONAL FOREST

167

Mt.
Pisgah

1363

Bell
Farm

Yahoo
Falls

Alum
Ford

700

Smith
Town

92

Big South Fork
Scenic Railway

Blue
Heron

Gorge
Overlook

Devil's
Jump
Overlook

742

KENTUCKY
TENNESSEE

Bear
Creek

1470

Foster
Crossroads

Pickett
State
Rustic Park
and Forest

Big South Fork of Cumberland River

Grave Hill Rd.

Horse Camp

Station

Station
Camp

Camp Rd.

Coopertown Rd.

Oneida

Sharp
Place

Leatherwood

297

Ford Rd.

Bandy Creek

Leatherwood
Ford Area

297

Leatherwood
Ford Rd.

East Rim
Overlook

27

Scott State
Forest

North White Oak Creek

Zenith

Honey Creek
Overlook

63

Mt. Helen Rd.

Clear Fork River

Crossroads
Church

New
River

Rugby
Historic
District

52

Elgin

Stearns, Kentucky, offers a look at life in a company coal-mining town. Access to Blue Heron is by car or via the Big South Fork Scenic Railway (about forty minutes one way by train) that operates between mid-April and October. Call (606) 376–5330 for information and schedule. Brandy Creek Stables (931–980–4013) is adjacent to Brandy Creek Campground.

ENTRANCE FEE: No charge. There is a boat-launch fee of $3.00 at Alum Ford Boat Ramp.

FACILITIES: Rustic lodging including water, bunk beds, toilets, and kitchens, are available at Charit Creek Lodge, a park concessioner. Charit Creek is accessible by foot or horseback. Reservations are recommended. Write Charit Creek Lodge, 250 Lonesome Valley Road, Sevierville, TN 37862 (423–429–5704). Groceries, food, and lodging are available in surrounding towns. Hospitals are in Oneida and Jamestown.

CAMPING: The Bandy Creek Campground (180 sites), located off Highway 297 in Tennessee, provides water and electrical hookups, tables, grills, hot showers, flush toilets, and a swimming pool. Reservations are available from April 1 to October 31 (800–365–2267). The Blue Heron Campground (forty-nine sites), located off Highway 741 in Kentucky, provides water and electrical hookups, tables, grills, hot showers, flush toilets, and a dump station. Reservations are available from April 1 to October 31 (800–365–2267). Station Camp (Tennessee) and Bear Creek (Kentucky) Equestrian Camp each offer campsites with water and electrical hookups, horse stalls, and access to rest rooms and shower facilities. Concessioners operate both campgrounds (423–569–3321). Pickett State Park also offers camping facilities. Backcountry camping is permitted throughout the park.

FISHING/HUNTING: Fishing and hunting are permitted in accordance with state and federal regulations throughout most of the recreation area. An appropriate state license is required. Hunting and fishing licenses may be purchased in surrounding towns.

FORT DONELSON NATIONAL BATTLEFIELD

P.O. Box 434
Dover, TN 37058-0434
(931) 232–5706
FODO_Administration@nps.gov
www.nps.gov/fodo

Fort Donelson National Battlefield comprises 551 acres and was established in 1928 to commemorate the site of the first major victory for the Union in the Civil War. The victory gave an obscure brigadier general—Ulysses Grant—the acclaim he needed to become one of the most important forces in the war. The story involved both army and naval action in the struggle to control the Confederate-built earthworks on the Cumberland River. The park protected the remains of Fort Donelson proper, the water batteries that repulsed the Union fleet, and almost 3 miles of rifle pits. Today, the park includes the building where the surrender took place and several hundred acres of land where the troops maneuvered. The park is located in northern Tennessee, on the west side of the town of Dover, on U.S. 79.

After months of attempting to break through Confederate defense lines, Union forces captured Fort Henry and moved on to Fort Donelson in February 1862. Confederate guns were able to drive off Union gunboats on the Cumberland River, but superior Union forces under the command of Ulysses Grant surrounded the fort and forced the surrender of nearly 13,000 Confederate troops on February 16. The victory opened the heartland of the South to Federal invasion.

The park visitor center is normally open from 8:00 A.M. to 4:30 P.M. It offers information, a ten-minute slide program, a museum, and an interpretive leaflet for a 6-mile self-guided auto tour of the fort and the battlefield.

Within the fort walls there are reproductions of soldiers' cabins. Artillery pieces representative of the Confederate armament are positioned along the rifle pits and exhibited at the lower river battery. The exterior of the Dover Hotel where General Simon Buncker surrendered to General U.S. Grant has been restored. Fort Donelson National Cemetery adjoins the park and is under National Park Service administration. The grounds close at sundown.

ENTRANCE FEE: No charge.

FACILITIES: Food and lodging are available in Dover. Rest rooms and water are in the visitor center.

CAMPING: No camping is permitted in the park. The Tennessee Valley Authority's Land Between the Lakes offers full camping facilities, including electric and water hookups, showers, and a dump station at Piney Campground, 9 miles west of Fort Donelson on Highway 79. Paris Landing State Park provides similar facilities 4 miles farther west.

FISHING: Fishing is permitted in the Cumberland River with a valid Tennessee fishing license. Catches include bass, catfish, and crappie.

GREAT SMOKY MOUNTAINS NATIONAL PARK

107 Park Headquarters Road
Gatlinburg, TN 37738-4102
(865) 436–1200
GRSM_Smokies_Information@nps.gov
www.nps.gov/grsm

Great Smoky Mountains National Park was established in 1934 to preserve more than 520,000 acres of unspoiled forests on the loftiest range east of South Dakota's Black Hills. The park is located along the Tennessee–North Carolina border, with main access via Newfound Gap Road, which bisects the park and connects Gatlinburg, Tennessee, and Cherokee, North Carolina.

Although the Great Smoky Mountains (named for the smokelike haze that is often present in this area) usually reach their peak of beauty around the middle of October, they offer outstanding scenery and outdoor activities year-round. More than 800 miles of horse and foot trails wind through the park, and paved roads provide access to some of the more popular locations. At Cades Cove, an 11-mile-loop road leads past nineteenth-century homesteads and small frame churches, where early mountain people lived. Newfound Gap Road winds through the high mountains and provides access to a side road that climbs to the highest elevation at 6,643 feet on Clingmans Dome and goes to within ½ mile of an observation tower. The walk to the tower is very steep but well worth the effort, because the vistas of the park from the tower are outstanding.

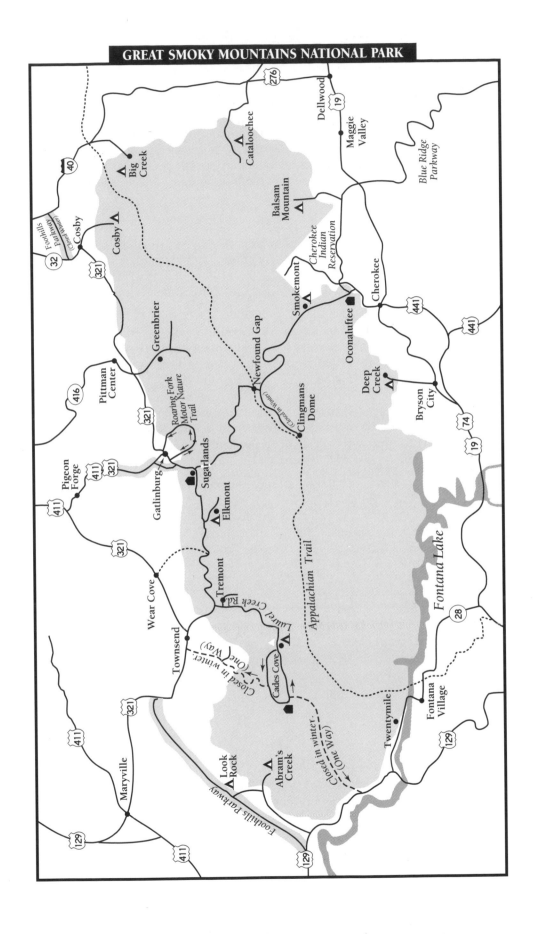

276

Dellwood

19

Maggie Valley

Blue Ridge Parkway

Cataloochee

Big Creek

40

Balsam Mountain

Cosby

Foothills Parkway (Closed Winter)

32

321

Cherokee Indian Reservation

Cherokee

441

Greenbrier

Smokemont

Newfound Gap

Oconaluftee

441

Pittman Center

416

Roaring Fork Motor Nature Trail

Clingmans Dome (Closed in Winter)

Deep Creek

Bryson City

74

19

Sugarlands

Pigeon Forge

411

321

Gatlinburg

Elkmont

Appalachian Trail

Fontana Lake

321

Wear Cove

Tremont

Laurel Creek Rd.

28

Townsend

Closed in winter (One Way)

Cades Cove

321

411

Twentymile

Fontana Village

Maryville

Look Rock

Abram's Creek

Closed in winter (One Way)

129

Foothills Parkway

129

411

129

Self-guided trails are scattered throughout the area, and park interpreters present talks and conduct walks during summer months. Activity schedules are available at visitor centers, ranger stations, and campgrounds.

When entering from Cherokee, North Carolina, stop at the Oconaluftee Visitor Center for exhibits and the Mountain Farm Museum. Nearby is an operating water-powered mill (opened seasonally) for grinding corn. From the Gatlinburg, Tennessee entrance, Sugarlands Visitor Center has exhibits, an orientation film, and park information. In Cades Cove, near Townsend, Tennessee, stop at the visitor center located at the historic Cable Mill area halfway around the loop road.

ENTRANCE FEE: No charge.

FACILITIES: Le Conte Lodge, which can be reached only via an all-day hike, offers several cabins from late March to mid-November. For reservations (which are necessary), write Le Conte Lodge, Gatlinburg, TN 37738 (865–429–5704). A campground store is at Cades Cove. Saddle horses may be rented at the stables in Cades Cove, Smokemont, McCarter's, Smoky Mountain, and Deep Creek.

CAMPING: Developed campgrounds with cold running water, fire grills, tables, flush toilets (no showers), and sanitary stations are at Balsam Mountain (forty-six sites, no dump station), Cosby (175 sites, three group camps), Deep Creek (122 sites, three group camps), Cades Cove (161 sites, four group camps), Elkmont (220 sites, four group camps), Smokemont (140 sites, three group camps), Abrams Creek (sixteen sites), Big Creek (twelve sites), Look Rock (sixty-eight sites), and Cataloochee (twenty-seven sites, three group camps).

There is a camping limit of seven days between May 15 and November 1. Reservations are required from May 15 through October 31 at Cades Cove, Elkmont, and Smokemont. For reservations, call 1–800–365–CAMP or through the Internet at reservations.nps.gov.

FISHING: Smallmouth and rock bass and brook, brown, and rainbow trout inhabit the 730 miles of fishing streams in the park. Bass live at lower elevations. Fishing regulations require a 7-inch minimum size and set a daily limit of five fish, except for rock bass, which has no size limit and a twenty-per-day possession limit. The brook trout is a protected species and possession is prohibited. A Tennessee or North Carolina fishing license is required to fish all open waters within the park.

OBED WILD AND SCENIC RIVER

P.O. Box 429
Wartburg, TN 37887-0429
(423) 346–6294
OBRI_Superintendent@nps.gov
www.nps.gov/obed

Obed Wild and Scenic River, which comprises 5,057 acres, was authorized in 1976 to preserve one of the most rugged and scenic river systems in the Southeast. The river is located in eastern Tennessee, with major access via Interstate 40.

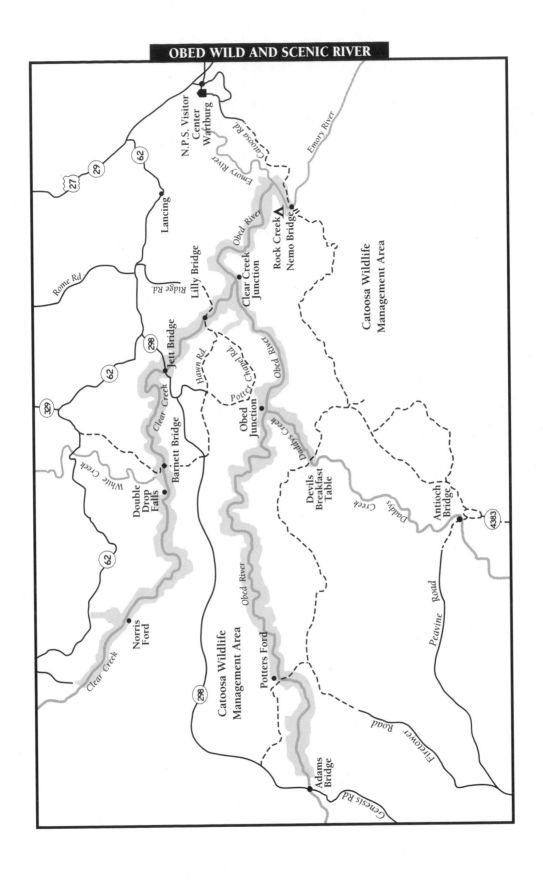

OBED WILD AND SCENIC RIVER

N.P.S. Visitor Center
Wartburg

Emory River

Catoosa Rd.

Lancing

27 29 62

Rome Rd.

Obed River

Clear Creek Junction

Rock Creek
Nemo Bridge

Catoosa Wildlife
Management Area

Ridge Rd.

Lilly Bridge

298

62

329

Jett Bridge

Hawn Rd.

Pottery Chapel Rd.

Obed River

Obed
Junction

Daddys Creek

Barnett Bridge

White Creek

Double
Drop
Falls

Devils
Breakfast
Table

Daddys Creek

Antioch
Bridge

4383

62

Norris
Ford

Clear Creek

Obed River

Catoosa Wildlife
Management Area

298

Potters Ford

Peavine Road

Firetower Road

Adams
Bridge

Genesis Rd.

The primary attraction of this park is the clean, clear waters of the Obed River and its principal tributaries, Clear Creek and Daddy's Creek. The area is rich in plant life and provides a habitat for forty-one identified species of mammals and 138 species of birds. The 45-mile section of the Obed system offers recreational activities in the form of white-water canoeing, kayaking, rafting, tubing, hiking, rock climbing, and nature study. The whitewater runs in the Obed system are generally Class III–IV, with long rapids and ledges, undercut rocks, and isolated conditions. Only experienced and expert boaters should run the whitewater. The Obed system is not for beginners or even intermediate-level boaters. There are a limited number of access points to the rivers. A free park brochure includes a map of the area.

The Obed's stream system has cut 400-foot gorges in the area's sandstone. These gorges cut through a variety of soil environments that produce vastly different vegetation, including blooming plants and hardwood trees. Float trips are best during the rainy season, from December through April, when the rivers are full. A visitor center is located in Wartburg, Tennessee.

ENTRANCE FEE: No charge.

FACILITIES: There are currently no federal facilities within the authorized park area. The area's major town, Wartburg, offers most visitor facilities.

CAMPING: No developed campgrounds are within the park boundaries, but primitive camping is available at Rock Creek Campground at Nemo. A developed campground is available at Cumberland Mountain State Park, 8 miles south of Crossville. Primitive camping is also available at Frozenhead State Natural Area, 2 miles from Wartburg near State Highway 62.

FISHING: These rivers support populations of smallmouth, rock, and largemouth bass, catfish, bluegill, and carp. A Tennessee fishing license is required.

SHILOH NATIONAL MILITARY PARK

1055 Pittsburg Landing Road
Shiloh, TN 38376-9704
(901) 689–5275/5696
shil_interpretation@nps.gov
www.nps.gov/shil

Shiloh, which comprises 3,972 acres, was established in 1894 to commemorate the site of a bitter 1862 Civil War battle. The park is located in southern Tennessee, 110 miles east of Memphis. The battlefield is 22 miles north of Corinth, Mississippi, via Mississippi 2 and Tennessee 22.

After the capture of Confederate garrisons at Fort Henry and Fort Donelson (February 1862), Tennessee, General Ulysses S. Grant ascended the Tennessee River in mid-March with a 50,000-man Union army transported on a vast flotilla of steamboats. Grant disembarked at Pittsburg Landing and established a base to support further operations against two important trunk railroads—the Memphis & Charleston and Mobile & Ohio. These Southern railroads intersected at Corinth, Mississippi, 22 miles southwest of Pittsburg Landing. Grant was directed to wait for General Don Carlos Buell, commander of the army of the Ohio, whose

Obed Wild and Scenic River (opposite page)

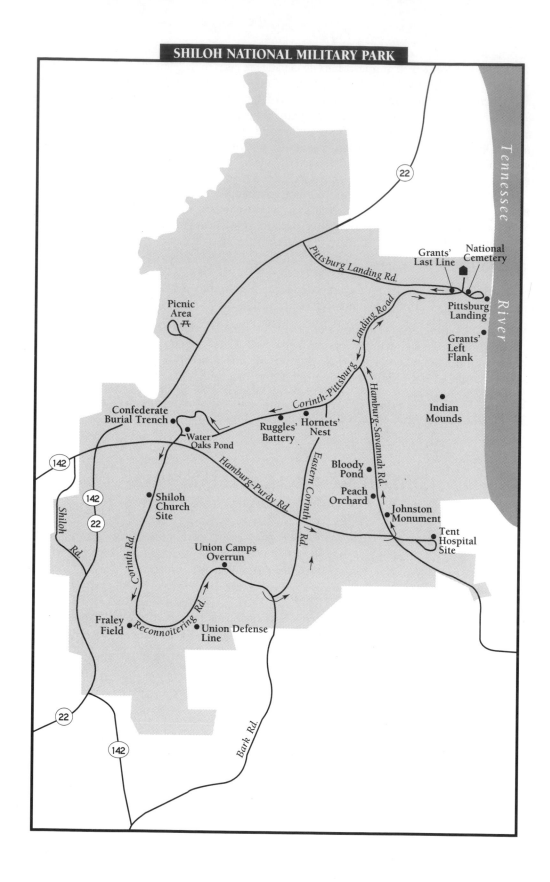

SHILOH NATIONAL MILITARY PARK

Tennessee River

22

Pittsburg Landing Rd.

Grants' Last Line

National Cemetery

Pittsburg Landing

Grants' Left Flank

Landing Road

Picnic Area

Indian Mounds

Corinth-Pittsburg

Confederate Burial Trench

Ruggles' Battery

Hornets' Nest

Hamburg-Savannah Rd.

Water Oaks Pond

142

Hamburg-Purdy Rd.

Bloody Pond

142

Eastern Corinth Rd.

Peach Orchard

22

Shiloh Rd.

Shiloh Church Site

Johnston Monument

Tent Hospital Site

Corinth Rd.

Union Camps Overrun

Reconnoitering Rd.

22

Fraley Field

Union Defense Line

142

Bark Rd.

troops were marching overland from Nashville to join the army of the Tennessee at Pittsburg Landing. When Buell arrived, the advance on Corinth would continue

Meanwhile, having concentrated western Confederate forces around Corinth, General Albert Sidney Johnston launched a surprise offensive (April 6) against Grant before Buell arrived. In a savage day of fighting, General Johnston was killed by a stray bullet, while his 44,000-man Confederate army drove the Union forces back nearly 2 miles before darkness delayed further combat. That night Buell reinforced Grant. With nearly 23,000 fresh troops, the combined Union armies counterattacked on April 7. The weakened Southern army, now commanded by General P. G. T. Beauregard, grudgingly contested the Union advance until evening, then retreated to Corinth. There was no Union pursuit. The awful carnage of "bloody" Shiloh resulted in a combined total of 23,746 Union and Confederate soldiers killed, wounded, or missing. Within two months the victorious Union forces captured both Corinth and Memphis.

The park visitor center at Pittsburg Landing is open daily except Christmas Day. Visitors can view artifacts, exhibits, and a twenty-five-minute film, as well as obtain a brochure for a self-guided tour. Over 600 monuments and iron troop markers, and 217 Civil War cannons mark the battlefield. Shiloh Indian Mounds National Historic Landmark, a forty-five-acre prehistoric mound and village site, is located on bluffs near the river. The bodies of nearly 4,000 American soldiers, representing military service in seven wars, are buried within a ten-acre National Cemetery and several Confederate mass graves. An entrance fee is required for all visitors over sixteen years of age. Other nearby attractions are: the Savannah Tennessee River Museum (901–925–2364), Pickwick Landing Lock & Dam; and in Corinth, the Civil War Interpretive Center (601–287–9501), Northeast Mississippi Museum (601–287–3120), and Corinth National Cemetery.

ENTRANCE FEE: $4.00 per vehicle or $2.00 per person.

FACILITIES: Rest rooms and drinking water are at the visitor center. A picnic area is 1 mile south of the main park entrance via Tennessee 22. Eastern National Bookstore, stocked with interpretive materials, provides vending machines with soft drinks and snacks. Meals and lodging are available in Savannah (12 miles), Adamsville (10 miles), Selmer (17 miles), Counce/Pickwick (15 miles), and Corinth (25 miles).

CAMPING: No camping is permitted in the park. Pickwick Landing State Park, 15 miles southeast, offers full camping facilities, including a swimming pool (901–689–3135, extension 337). A Tennessee Valley Authority campground is located across Pickwick Dam (901–925–4346). Big Hill Pond State Park, 27 miles to the west, also provides camping facilities (901–645–7968).

STONES RIVER NATIONAL BATTLEFIELD

3501 Old Nashville Highway
Murfreesboro, TN 37129-3094
(615) 893–9501
STRI_Information@nps.gov
www.nps.gov/stri

Stones River, which comprises about 570 acres, was established in 1927 to memorialize a fierce 1862–63 Civil War battle that ended with 23,000 casualties and both sides claiming victory. The park is located in central Tennessee, 28 miles southeast of Nashville in the northwest corner of the town of Murfreesboro.

After capturing Forts Henry and Donelson and occupying Nashville, 43,000 Union troops set out in late 1862 to sweep a force of 38,000 Confederates from the Murfreesboro area. The battle resulted in a combined total of 23,000 casualties but ended inconclusively. Within days the Confederates retreated 40 miles to Tullahoma, Tennessee, and Union forces occupied Murfreesboro. In early 1863, Union troops constructed Fortress Rosecrans, one of the largest earthen forts of the Civil War, from which they supplied the army in its drive to Chattanooga.

The park is open daily (except Christmas Day) from 8:00 A.M. to 5:00 P.M. A visitor center near the entrance has a museum, an audiovisual program, and folders for a self-guided tour through the battlefield. Stops are identified by numbered markers, and short trails and exhibits help to interpret the events that occurred at each site. A trail and exhibits interpret the remains of Fortress Rosecrans, located at Old Fort Park. One of the interior fortifications, Redoubt Brannan is located on West College Street. Only 3,000 feet of the original 14,000 feet of earthworks remain. Interpretive programs including ranger walks and talks are offered daily from May through October and occasionally during the rest of the year. Living-history programs are offered during some summer and fall weekends and during the anniversary of the battle.

ENTRANCE FEE: No charge.

FACILITIES: Food and lodging are not available in the park, but nearly all facilities can be found in nearby Murfreesboro. Rest rooms and drinking water are in the visitor center.

CAMPING: No camping is permitted in the park. Several state parks with camping facilities are within 30 miles.

See the map on page 267.

STONES RIVER NATIONAL BATTLEFIELD

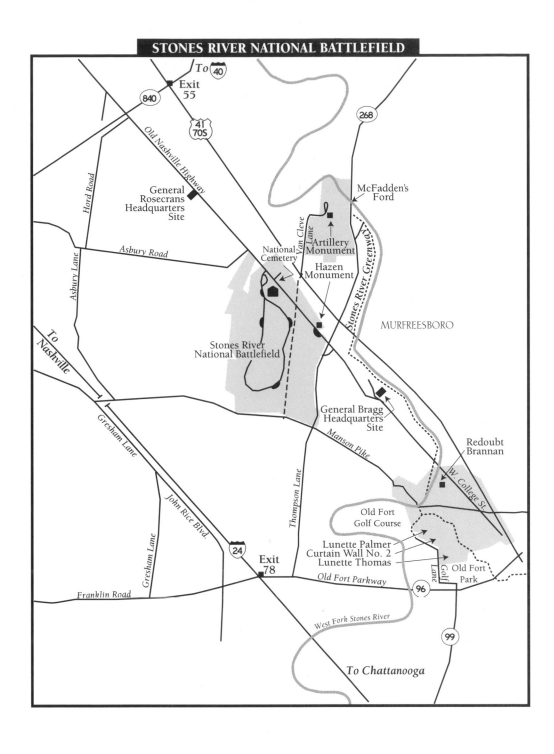

VERMONT

MARSH-BILLINGS-ROCKEFELLER NATIONAL HISTORICAL PARK

P.O. Box 178
Woodstock, VT 05091
(802) 457–3368
MABI_Superintendent@nps.gov
www.nps.gov/mabi

Marsh-Billings-Rockefeller National Historical Park focuses on conservation history and the evolving nature of land stewardship in America. Opened in June 1998, Vermont's first National Park Service area preserves and interprets the historic Marsh-Billings-Rockefeller property. The national historic park is in east-central Vermont, off Route 12 in the small town of Woodstock.

The historical park is named for George Perkins Marsh, one of the nation's first global environmental thinkers, who grew up on the property; for Frederick Billings, an early conservationist who established a progressive dairy farm and professionally managed forest on the former Marsh farm; and for Frederick Billings's granddaughter, Mary French Rockefeller, and her husband, conservationist Laurance S. Rockefeller, who sustained Billings's mindful practices in forestry and farming on the property over the latter half of the twentieth century. In 1983 they established Billings Farm & Museum to continue the farm's working dairy and to interpret rural Vermont life and agricultural history. The Billings Farm & Museum is operated as a private non-profit educational institution by the Woodstock Foundation.

Marsh-Billings-Rockefeller National Historical Park was created in 1992, when the Rockefellers donated the estate's residential and forest lands to the people of the United States. Today the park interprets the history of conservation, and park personnel provide tours of the Marsh-Billings-Rockefeller mansion and the surrounding 550-acre forest. The mansion contains an extensive art collection, including American landscape paintings by such renowned artists as Thomas Cole, Albert Bierstandt, John Frederick Kensett, and Asher B. Durand. This collection illustrates the influence of art and artists on the developing conservation movement in the mid- to late 1800s and changing popular perceptions of the environment. The adjoining forest has been actively managed for wood products, public recreation, aesthetics, education, and ecological values for more than a century, making it one of the oldest planned and continuously managed woodlands in America.

Working in partnership, Marsh-Billings-Rockefeller National Historical Park and the Billings Farm & Museum present historic and contemporary examples of conservation stewardship and explain the lives and contributions of George Perkins Marsh, Frederick Billings, and Billing's descendants, Mary F. and Laurance S. Rockefeller.

The national historical park and the Billings Farm & Museum are open daily from late spring to fall from 10:00 A.M. to 5:00 P.M. Guided tours and programs are offered at both sites during the summer months. Special programs are available on some weekends throughout the year. Twenty miles of carriage roads and trails provide free access to the 550-acre forest on Mount Tom and are open year-round. In the winter the carriage roads are groomed for cross-country skiing and snowshoeing. Contact the Ski Touring Center in Woodstock (802–457–6674) for more information.

ENTRANCE FEE: No charge. The fee for the Mansion and Garden Tour is $6.00 for adults and $3.00 for visitors age fifteen and under. A separate fee is charged for the Billings Farm and Museum: $8.00 adult, $7.00 senior, $6.00 for ages thirteen through seventeen, $4.00 for ages five through twelve, and $1.00 for ages three to four.

FACILITIES: Water and rest rooms are at the Carriage Barn visitor center. Lodging and food services are available in the village of Woodstock.

CAMPING: Silver Lake State Park, northwest of Woodstock on State Route 12, offers forty-three sites with flush toilets, showers, tables, grills, and a dump station.

FISHING: No fishing is available at the historical park. Nearby Silver Lake State Park offers fishing and boat rental.

VIRGINIA

APPOMATTOX COURT HOUSE
NATIONAL HISTORICAL PARK

P.O. Box 218
Appomattox, VA 24522-0218
(804) 352–8987
www.nps.gov/apco

Appomattox Court House National Historical Park comprises approximately 1,700 acres and was authorized by act of Congress August 13, 1935, as Appomattox Court House National Monument. Its designation was changed to a national historical park in 1954. The park commemorates and preserves the site where Robert E. Lee surrendered to Ulysses S. Grant on April 9, 1865. The site is located in south-central Virginia, 20 miles east of Lynchburg. It is on State Highway 24, 3 miles northeast of the town of Appomattox.

After having his escape blocked by Federal troops, General Robert E. Lee decided to surrender his tired and starving Army of Northern Virginia at Appomattox Court House. On April 9, 1865, General Lee and General Grant met in the home of Wilmer McLean and agreed upon terms. On April 12, the Confederates surrendered their rifles and began the journey home.

   The park's main attractions are in the village of Appomattox Court House, which has been largely restored to its 1865 appearance. A visitor center located in the reconstructed courthouse building provides an information desk, exhibits, and an illustrated slide program. Other buildings open to the public include McLean House, where the surrender took place; Meeks

General Store; Woodson Law Office; Clover Hill Tavern, built in 1819 and the village's oldest structure; and the county jail. All except the McLean House, which is reconstructed, have been restored to their appearance during the period of the surrender. West of the village is a Confederate cemetery, while northeast is the site of Lee's headquarters. A 5-mile-long hiking trail connects all of the park's sites, and living-history interpretations are given periodically during the summer.

ENTRANCE FEE: From Memorial Day to Labor Day, $4.00 per person, with a maximum of $10 per vehicle, visitors sixteen and under free. The other months the fee is $2.00, with a maximum of $5.00 per vehicle.

FACILITIES: No lodging or food service is available in the park. Rest rooms with access for the handicapped are located in the old Clover Hill Tavern servants' quarters. Motels, restaurants, and stores are in the town of Appomattox, 3 miles southwest.

CAMPING: No camping is permitted in the park. Holliday Lake State Park is 12½ miles northeast via State Highways 24, 626, 640, and 692. Turn left on Highway 24 leaving the historical park and then right on 626 and follow the signs. Here, campers will find sixty-one sites (no hookups), flush toilets, showers, a dump station, and a 150-acre lake offering boat rentals, swimming, and fishing. Several miles of trails are available for hikers (804–248–6308).

FISHING: While fishing is permitted (state fishing license required) in the Appomattox River, which flows through the historical park, catches are minimal. Better fishing is available at Holliday Lake, which is stocked with bass, bluegill, and crappie.

ARLINGTON HOUSE, THE ROBERT E. LEE MEMORIAL

c/o George Washington Memorial Parkway
Turkey Run Park
McLean, VA 22101-0001
(703) 557–0613
www.nps.gov/arho

This twenty-eight-acre park was authorized in 1925 to preserve the antebellum home of the Custis and Lee families. The house is located in northeastern Virginia, across the Arlington Memorial Bridge from Washington, D.C. It may be reached by walking from the Arlington Cemetery Visitors Center or by taking the concessioner-operated tourmobiles.

Arlington House was constructed over a fifteen-year period beginning in 1802 by George Washington Parke Custis, the adopted son of George Washington. He planned the house as a collection point for Washington heirlooms and entertained many distinguished people here. In 1831, Custis's only surviving child, Mary, married Robert E. Lee in this house, which was eventually left to her at her father's death. Although the Lees enjoyed the house, they found it necessary to abandon Arlington soon after the beginning of the Civil War. The property was confiscated by the Federal government in 1862 and two years later became the site for a national cemetery.

The house is open for self-guided tours from 9:30 A.M. to 4:30 P.M. Park guides are on duty, and a free leaflet explaining the history of each room is available at the entrance. In Arlington National Cemetery surrounding the house, visitors may wish to walk to President John F. Kennedy's gravesite and the Tomb of the Unknown Soldier.

ENTRANCE FEE: No charge.

FACILITIES: No snack bars, restaurants, or lodging are at the site or in Arlington National Cemetery.

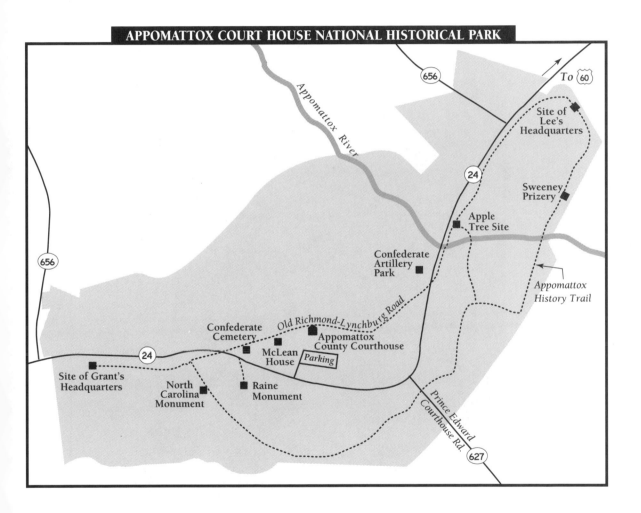

APPOMATTOX COURT HOUSE NATIONAL HISTORICAL PARK

BOOKER T. WASHINGTON NATIONAL MONUMENT

12130 BTW Highway
Hardy, VA 24101-9688
(540) 721–2094
bowa_interpretation@nps.gov
www.nps.gov/bowa

Booker T. Washington National Monument comprises 224 acres and was authorized in 1956 to preserve the birthplace and early childhood home of this famous black leader and educator. The park is located in southern Virginia, 30 miles southeast of Roanoke via State Highways 220 and 122.

On this small plantation, Booker T. Washington was born into slavery on April 5, 1856. After being declared free nine years later, he left with his mother, brother, and sister for West Vir-

Booker T. Washington

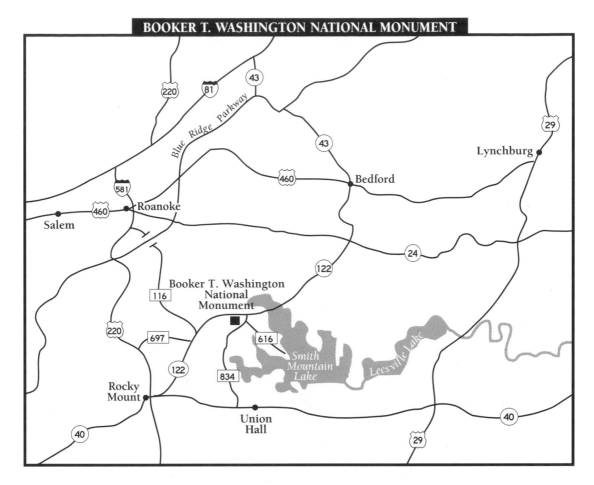

BOOKER T. WASHINGTON NATIONAL MONUMENT

ginia. Booker later graduated from Hampton Institute, a school for ex-slaves, and in 1881, established Tuskegee Institute in Tuskegee, Alabama. From an initial enrollment of thirty and a beginning salary budget of $2,000, Washington led the school through a period of growth that resulted in a campus of 1,500 students with a $2 million endowment. The respected educator and leader died on November 14, 1915.

The park's visitor center and grounds are open daily from 9:00 A.M. to 5:00 P.M., except Thanksgiving, Christmas Day, and New Year's Day. Visitor center exhibits focus on the life and legacy of Booker T. Washington. The monument is a nineteenth-century tobacco farm, and although none of the original buildings are still standing, several have been reconstructed to help visitors visualize what life was like when Booker T. Washington lived here. A ¼-mile-long self-guided trail leads through a farm complete with crops and farm animals. Park rangers give daily tours. The Jack-O-Lantern Branch Trail is a 1½-mile meandering walk through park fields and forests. A trail map and guide are available at the visitor center.

ENTRANCE FEE: No charge.

FACILITIES: No food service or lodging is available. Rest rooms and drinking water are in the visitor center. A shaded picnic area with tables only is on the park grounds. Meals and lodging are in Bedford, Roanoke, Smith Mountain Lake, and Rocky Mount.

CAMPING: No camping is permitted on the monument grounds. Roanoke Mountain Campground on the Blue Ridge Parkway is 19 miles northwest of the monument via Highways 122 and 116. This campground, operated by the National Park Service, provides tables, grills, water, and flush toilets but no hookups. Private campgrounds are closer; directions are available from personnel at the monument.

COLONIAL NATIONAL HISTORICAL PARK

P.O. Box 210
Yorktown, VA 23690-0210
(757) 898–2401
www.nps.gov/colo

Colonial National Monument was authorized in 1930 (redesignated a National Historical Park in 1936) to preserve a variety of historical areas within its 9,316 acres. Included are the following: Jamestown, the site of the first permanent English settlement in America; Yorktown Battlefield, scene of the last major battle of the Revolutionary War; and the Colonial Parkway, a 23-mile scenic parkway that connects them and passes by the city of Williamsburg.

Jamestown Glasshouse at Colonial National Historical Park

York River

U.S. Naval Supply Center Cheatham Annex

Colonial Parkway

U.S. Naval Weapons Station

17

17

Yorktown

Site of Washington's Headquarters

Newport News Park

143

64

238

Exit 247

60

Exit 243

Busch Gardens Amusement Park

Exit 242

Williamsburg

143

64

Exit 238

199

James River

To Richmond

132

5
31

31

60

Colonial Williamsburg

Colonial Parkway

The Thorofare

Jamestown

Sandy Bay

To Green Spring

5

614

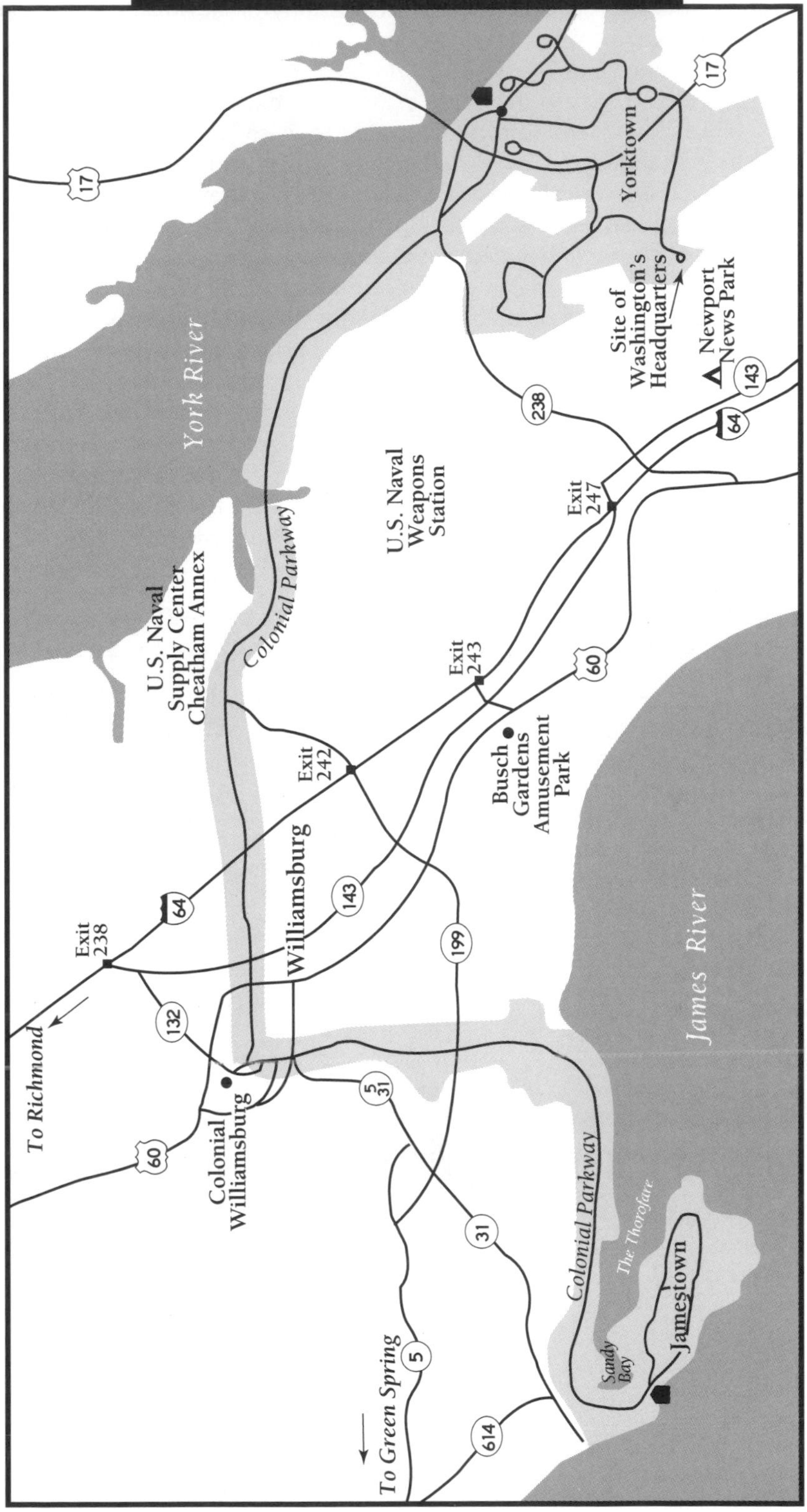

Colonial National Historical Park tells the story of our country's early history. Founded in 1607, Jamestown was the first successful English colony in North America. Although it did not become a very large town, Jamestown did serve as the principal town and seat of government of Virginia for ninety-two years.

A tour of Jamestown begins at the visitor center, which contains exhibits and a theater program to help explain the town's history. A walking tour leads through ruins of the old town site, although the Old Church Tower is the only seventeenth-century structure remaining above ground. An archaeological excavation currently underway is uncovering the remains of the original James Fort. Three- and 5-mile loop roads provide access to the rest of the island. Near the entrance, at the reconstructed glasshouse, costumed craftsmen demonstrate the art of glass blowing. An admission is charged for entrance to Jamestown. Part of the Jamestown site is owned and administered by the Association for the Preservation of Virginia Antiquities.

At the other end of the Colonial Parkway is the Yorktown Battlefield, scene of the 1781 military siege that proved to be the culminating battle of the American Revolution. A visitor center provides exhibits and a theater program on the battle that produced the surrender of 8,000 British troops to an allied American and French force under the command of General George Washington. A self-guided auto tour (audiotapes available in the visitor center) begins at the center and circles points of interest on the battlefield. The Moore House, where negotiations for the surrender took place, is open for tours daily during the summer and on weekends during spring and fall. Admission is charged for Yorktown Battlefield areas.

ENTRANCE FEE: Jamestown—$5.00 per person; Yorktown—$4.00 per person; both sites—$7.00 per person, with visitors sixteen and under free; good for seven days.

FACILITIES: Antiques and handicrafts are sold by concessioners in Yorktown. A cafe is located near Jamestown at Jamestown Settlement. Food and lodging are available at Williamsburg and Yorktown. Rest rooms are in both visitor centers, and a picnic area is in Yorktown. Marinas are located at Jamestown on the James River and at Gloucester Point on the York River. Boats may not be launched from the Colonial Parkway nor from Jamestown Island.

CAMPING: No camping is permitted in the park, but private campgrounds are located in the area. A city park in Newport News provides campsites with tables, grills, water, showers, electrical hookups, and laundry facilities. The campground is off Route 143 near the intersection of Fort Eustis and Jefferson Avenue (757–887–5381).

FISHING: Fishing is available at various locations along the Colonial Parkway. A valid Virginia fishing license is required.

FREDERICKSBURG AND SPOTSYLVANIA COUNTY BATTLEFIELDS MEMORIAL NATIONAL MILITARY PARK

120 Chatham Lane
Fredericksburg, VA 22405-2508
(540) 371–0802
frsp_info@nps.gov
www.nps.gov/frsp

This 8,500-acre park was established in 1927 to preserve portions of four major Civil War battlefields: Fredericksburg, Chancellorsville, Wilderness, and Spotsylvania Court House. The widely scattered park is located in northeastern Virginia, in seven units in the city of Fredericksburg and four surrounding counties.

After Lee's army was stopped at Antietam in September 1862, Union forces were again ready to move southward. The next two battles—Fredericksburg in December of 1862 and Chancellorsville in May of 1863—ended in Confederate victories, resulting in a change of Union command. After another unsuccessful push by Robert E. Lee into the North was halted at Gettysburg, Union forces again marched south, where they were to engage the Confederates at the Wilderness and Spotsylvania Court House. Unable to break through Lee's front, Ulysses S. Grant sidestepped southeast toward Richmond, where more bloody fighting would eventually result in Confederate surrender.

The military park consists of four battlefields and several historic buildings. The main visitor center, on U.S. 1 (Business) in Fredericksburg, contains exhibits and information about the park. Nearby, Fredericksburg National Cemetery contains the remains of more than 15,000 Federal soldiers who died in the Civil War. A second visitor center is at the Chancellorsville Battlefield. Both centers contain schedules of various programs that are available throughout the park. Handicapped visitors are encouraged to use Chancellorsville Visitor

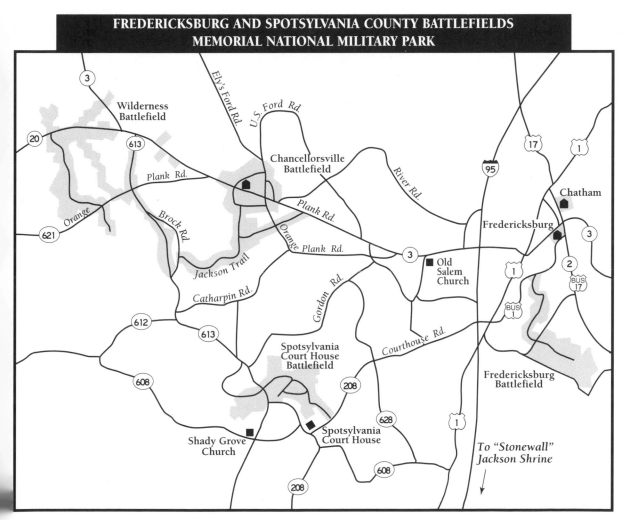

FREDERICKSBURG AND SPOTSYLVANIA COUNTY BATTLEFIELDS MEMORIAL NATIONAL MILITARY PARK

Center, which is fully accessible, while the Fredericksburg Visitor Center is only partially accessible.

"Stonewall" Jackson Shrine, located south on Interstate 95 and east on Highway 606, preserves the scene of the famous Confederate's death on May 10, 1863. Chatham, an eighteenth-century mansion used extensively by Union forces during the war, is open daily. Old Salem Church provided the focal point for a bloody battle during the Chancellorsville campaign. Interpretive hiking trails are available at each of the four battlefields.

ENTRANCE FEE: $4.00 per person; good for seven days.

FACILITIES: No food or lodging is provided by the National Park Service. Rest rooms are in each visitor center, and picnic facilities are at each of the four battlefields and at Chatham and the "Stonewall" Jackson Shrine.

CAMPING: No camping is permitted in the park. Prince William Forest Park, 23 miles north of Fredericksburg on Interstate 95, offers 120 sites with tables, grills, water, and flush toilets.

GEORGE WASHINGTON BIRTHPLACE NATIONAL MONUMENT

1732 Popes Creek Road
Washington's Birthplace, VA 22443
(804) 224–1732
www.nps.gov/gewa

George Washington Birthplace National Monument comprises 550 acres of some of the most beautiful pristine land in the National Park System. The monument was established in 1930 to preserve the birthsite of the first U.S. president, as part of the bicentennial celebration of Washington's birth in 1932. Located 38 miles east of Fredericksburg via State Highways 3 and 204 and bounded by the Potomac River and Popes Creek, the park is one of the most serene spots one can visit.

George Washington is remembered as the "Father of Our Country." During the revolution he turned undisciplined militia into the victorious army at Yorktown. Under his guidance the Constitutional Convention forged a people's government that has lasted more than two hundred years. With a keen sense of history, he carried out his presidency with the full knowledge that he was establishing the model subsequent presidents would follow. And, most remarkably of all, he willingly gave up power.

This extraordinary man was born on his father's Pope Creek tobacco plantation on February 22, 1732. He spent his formative years on three of his father's plantations, learning the culture of the Virginia aristocracy, experiencing the community of master, servants, and slaves, and absorbing the legacy of three generations of Washingtons preceding him in America.

A Memorial House stands near the site of the original Washington home, which burned in 1779. The re-created plantation captures the life in which George came of age. Here, in these sublime surroundings, one can sense the character and spirit of this great man.

The park is open 9:00 A.M. to 5:00 P.M. daily except Thanksgiving, Christmas, and New Year's Days. At the visitor center are a fourteen-minute film, rest room facilities, an exhibit of

Washington family history, and artifacts. Other park facilities include the historic birthplace homesite, the colonial farm area, burial grounds, nature trail, picnic area, and beach (no swimming allowed). Regularly scheduled guided tours with park rangers are available. A leisurely visit will take one to two hours.

ENTRANCE FEE: $2.00 per person; visitors sixteen and under free; good for seven days.

FACILITIES: No food or lodging is available at the monument. Both are in Fredericksburg, Montross, and Colonial Beach. Rest rooms, a gift shop, vending machines, and drinking water are at the visitor center. Rest rooms and drinking water are also in a beautiful picnic area.

CAMPING: No camping is permitted in the park. Westmoreland State Park offers a shaded campground with tables, grills, water, flush toilets, showers, fishing, swimming (both river and a large pool), and boating. The park is approximately 6 miles southeast of the monument on Highway 3 (804–493–8821).

FISHING: Fishing is permitted from the picnic area (designated area only) or in the Potomac River within the park. A Virginia fishing license is required.

GEORGE WASHINGTON MEMORIAL PARKWAY
Turkey Run Park
McLean, VA 22101-0001
(703) 289–2500
gwmp_superintendent@nps.gov
www.nps.gov/gwmp

The parkway links many landmarks in the life of George Washington. It is primarily located in northeastern Virginia, where it connects Great Falls with Mount Vernon along the Potomac River. A smaller section on the Maryland side connects Great Falls with Chain Bridge.

At the same time that George Washington Memorial Parkway preserves scenery along the Potomac River, it connects a number of areas important in the life of America's first president. At the parkway's southern terminus, Washington's home of Mount Vernon is now managed by a nonprofit association that opens the house for daily tours from 9:00 A.M. to 5:00 P.M. March through September and from 9:00 A.M. to 4:00 P.M. October through February (703–780–2000). Driving north, the parkway passes through Alexandria, Washington's hometown, and Washington, D.C., the nation's capital, which he founded. At the parkway's northern end, Great Falls Park (703–285–2965) contains the ruins of engineer George Washington's Patowmack Canal.

Additional places of interest along the parkway include Fort Hunt, where batteries guarded the approach to Washington in the late 1800s; Dyke Marsh, which contains a variety of aquatic plants and birds; Jones Point Lighthouse, where a small beacon warned of sandbars from 1836 to 1925; Theodore Roosevelt Island, an eighty-eight-acre wooded island sanctuary in the Potomac River commemorating the twenty-sixth president of the United States (see separate writeup under District of Columbia); Fort Marcy, a Civil War earthwork defense fort; the Clara Barton House, the thirty-eight-room home of the founder of the American Red Cross and, for eight years, the headquarters of that organization (see separate write-up under Maryland); and Glen Echo Park, an arts and cultural center with a 1921 Dentzel carousel. These

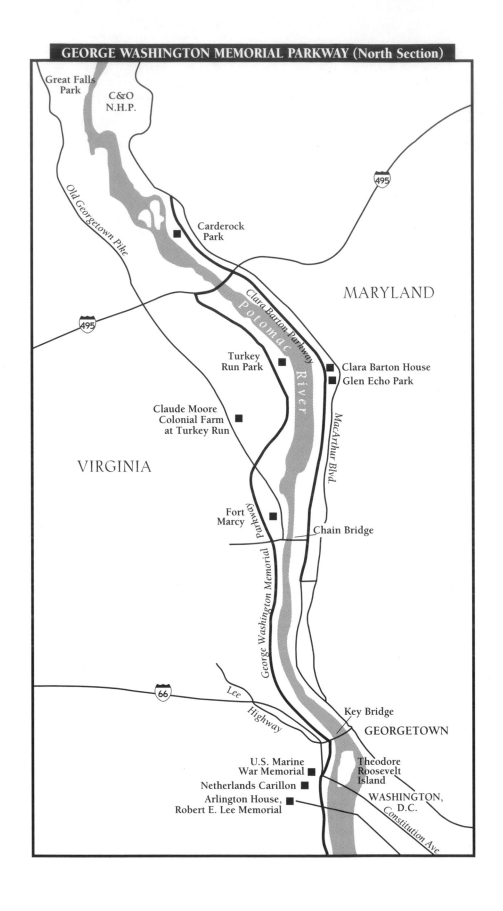

GEORGE WASHINGTON MEMORIAL PARKWAY (North Section)

Great Falls Park

C&O N.H.P.

Old Georgetown Pike

Carderock Park

495

495

MARYLAND

Clara Barton Parkway

Potomac River

Turkey Run Park

Clara Barton House
Glen Echo Park

Claude Moore Colonial Farm at Turkey Run

MacArthur Blvd.

VIRGINIA

Fort Marcy

Chain Bridge

George Washington Memorial Parkway

66

Lee Highway

Key Bridge

GEORGETOWN

U.S. Marine War Memorial

Netherlands Carillon

Arlington House, Robert E. Lee Memorial

Theodore Roosevelt Island

WASHINGTON, D.C.

Constitution Ave

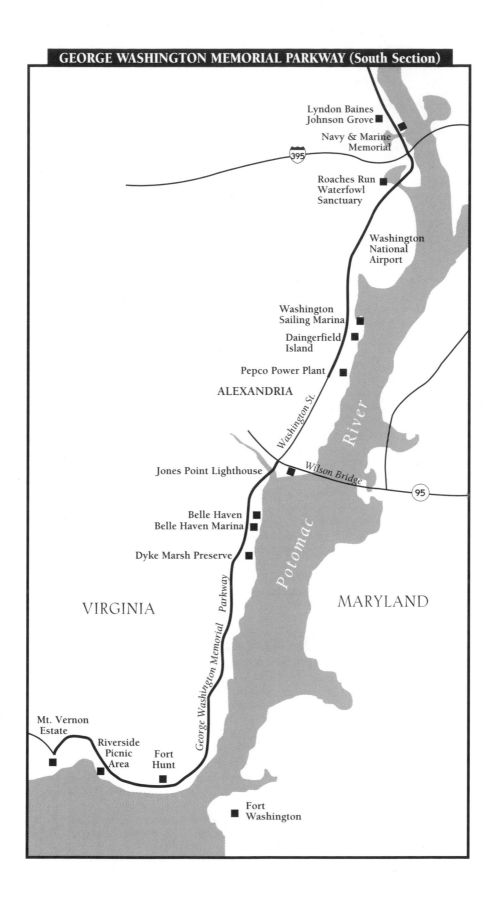

Lyndon Baines
Johnson Grove

Navy & Marine
Memorial

395

Roaches Run
Waterfowl
Sanctuary

Washington
National
Airport

Washington
Sailing Marina

Daingerfield
Island

Pepco Power Plant

ALEXANDRIA

Washington St.

River

Jones Point Lighthouse

Wilson Bridge

95

Belle Haven
Belle Haven Marina

Potomac

Dyke Marsh Preserve

VIRGINIA

MARYLAND

George Washington Memorial Parkway

Mt. Vernon
Estate

Riverside
Picnic
Area

Fort
Hunt

Fort
Washington

are but a few of the places of interest along the George Washington Memorial Parkway.

ENTRANCE FEE: No charge.

FACILITIES: No lodging is provided by the National Park Service, although both are available nearby. The Mount Vernon Inn near the Mount Vernon entrance gate serves breakfast, lunch, and dinner. The Potowmack Landing Restaurant at Dangerfield Island and the snack bar at Columbia Island Marina offer food services to visitors. Public rest rooms are available at Belle Haven, Columbia Island Marina, Fort Hunt, Theodore Roosevelt Island, and Turkey Run Park.

CAMPING: No camping is provided by the National Park Service, but public campgrounds are in the area. (See the camping section under Greenbelt Park, Maryland.)

FISHING: Fishing from the bank is permitted unless otherwise posted. The waters of the Potomac accessed from the parkway are under the jurisdiction of Maryland, Virginia, and the District of Columbia. A valid fishing license from the appropriate state or the District is required. Bass, carp, catfish, and perch are possible catches.

See maps on the previous two pages.

GREEN SPRINGS NATIONAL HISTORIC LANDMARK DISTRICT

c/o Shenandoah National Park
22591 Spotswood Trail
Elkton, VA 22827
(540) 999–3500
www.nps.gov/grsp

Green Springs National Historic Landmark District is an area of approximately 14,000 acres. In 1977, the secretary of the interior accepted preservation easements of nearly half the district's area. The historic district, which contains a wide variety of architectural styles, is located in central Virginia, in Louisa County.

Green Springs National Historic Landmark District is an area where early American architecture is concentrated with examples of fine rural manor houses and related buildings in a pristine landscape. The district was declared a Virginia Historic Landmark and nominated to the National Register of Historic Places in 1973. One year later, the district was declared a National Historic Landmark. The Green Springs area is cooperatively managed by the National Park Service, the Commonwealth of Virginia, and landowners and community organizations.

Buildings in the district range from farmhouses to large plantations. Thirty-five buildings constructed from the early to mid-1700s to the early 1900s are considered to be architecturally significant. All thirty-five structures are privately owned, and none are open to the public.

ENTRANCE FEE: No charge.

FACILITIES: Food and lodging are available in a number of communities around the Green Springs area, including Gordonsville, Louisa, and Zion Crossroads.

CAMPING: Private campgrounds are near Gordonsville and Louisa.

MAGGIE L. WALKER NATIONAL HISTORIC SITE

c/o Richmond National Battlefield Park
3215 East Broad Street
Richmond, VA 23223-7517
(804) 771–2017
malw_interpretation@nps.gov
www.nps.gov/malw

Maggie L. Walker National Historic Site comprises approximately 1¼ acres and was authorized in 1978 to commemorate the life and achievements of the first woman founder and president of a chartered bank, Maggie Lena Walker (1867–1934). This African-American woman earned unusual success in finance and business through self-determination and leadership, building success within the African-American community locally and nationally. The site is in Richmond at 110½ East Leigh Street in Jackson Ward, a National Historic Landmark District.

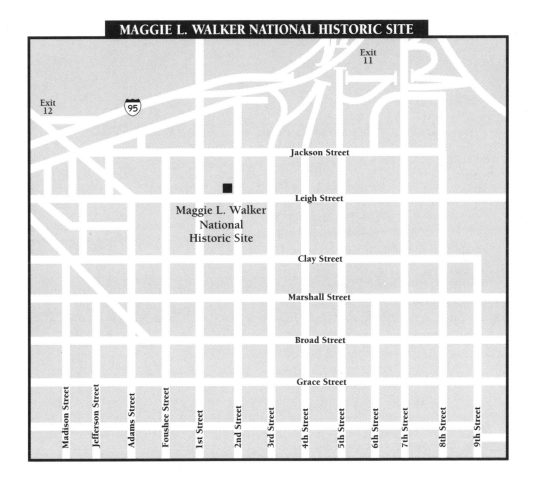

Maggie Lena Walker began her professional career as a schoolteacher, but she achieved her extraordinary mark on society with the Independent Order of St. Luke, a fraternal organization that provided financial aid to its members in sickness and a proper burial at death. She joined the society at age fourteen. In 1899, at age thirty-three, Walker assumed leadership of the Order and reoriented its management to be financially sound and profitable. Walker, in association with the Order, established a newspaper, a department store, and a bank where depositors were urged to "save their nickels and watch them turn into dollars." The bank opened in 1903 as the St. Luke Penny Savings Bank, with Walker as president. It continues in operation today as the Consolidated Bank and Trust Company. Walker's stewardship of the bank and the Order, and her lifelong commitment to uplift the African-American community, provided a great legacy.

The site at 110½ East Leigh Street was Maggie Lena Walker's residence from 1904 until her death in 1934 and remained in the Walker family until acquisition by the National Park Service. Walker and four generations of her family shared this Victorian-era structure, which she expanded to accommodate her needs. The house contains many items belonging to the Walker family and has been restored to its 1930 appearance.

The historic site is open Monday through Saturday 9:00 A.M. to 5:00 P.M., except Thanksgiving, Christmas Day, and New Year's Day. Reservations for groups of five or more are required. Admission is free. A visitor center is located at 600 North Second Street, ½ block from the Walker home. This facility contains a film, bookstore, and museum exhibits.

ENTRANCE FEE: No charge.

FACILITIES: Rest rooms are available. Food and lodging can be found in Richmond.

CAMPING: See the camping section under Richmond National Battlefield Park (Virginia).

MANASSAS NATIONAL BATTLEFIELD PARK

6511 Sudley Road
Manassas, VA 20109
(703) 361–1339
(703) 361–7075 (TDD)
mana_superintendent@nps.gov
www.nps.gov/mana

Manassas National Battlefield Park comprises 5,100 acres and was designated in 1940 to commemorate the site of two important Civil War battles. The battlefield is located in northern Virginia, 26 miles southwest of Washington, D.C., via U.S. 29 or Interstate 66. The visitor center is on State Highway 234 (Sudley Road), ½ mile north of the interchange with Interstate 66 (exit 47-B).

The first battle of Manassas (also known as Bull Run), on July 21, 1861, was the initial major confrontation between opposing armies in the Civil War. This clash of approximately 34,000 naive and inexperienced men on each side resulted in a Confederate victory, as the Union army was routed, and retreated back to Washington. Both sides suffered the death of innocence, as the battle made it evident that the war would be long and bloody. Thirteen months later, on

August 28–30, 1862, a second and much larger battle between veteran armies at Manassas proved equally disastrous to Union forces. The confederate victory resulted in the opportunity for the first invasion of the north, repulsed at Antietam in Maryland.

The park visitor center, housing a museum and audiovisual orientation program, is open daily except Thanksgiving and Christmas Day from 8:30 A.M. to 5:00 P.M. (to 6:00 P.M. mid-June through Labor Day). The park maintains an extensive trail system for hiking and horseback riding. A 1-mile-long self-guided walking tour of Henry Hill, site of the first battle, begins at the visitor center. A 5-mile loop trail from Henry Hill to the Stone Bridge and Matthews Hill also covers areas associated with first Manassas battle. Short (½-mile to 1-mile) trails focus on the combat at the Brawner Farm, Unfinished Railroad, and Deep Cut tour stops of the second Manassas battlefield. Maps are available at the visitor center. The visitor center at Stuart's Hill has a small exhibit area, rest rooms, and park information. It is open daily from mid-June through Labor Day.

ENTRANCE FEE: $2.00 per person; good for three days.

FACILITIES: Rest rooms and drinking water are at the visitor center. The park maintains a picnic area but no food service or lodging is available in the park. Restaurants and lodging are situated nearby on State Highway 234 in Manassas.

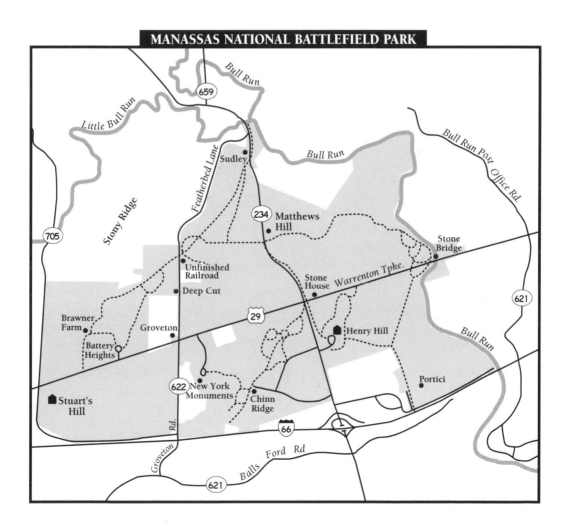

MANASSAS NATIONAL BATTLEFIELD PARK

CAMPING: No camping is permitted on the battlefield. Bull Run Regional Park, approximately 2 miles southeast of the visitor center, offers camping (150 sites) with tables, grills, water, showers, flush toilets, and electric hookups.

FISHING: Angling for bass, catfish, and other species in Bull Run is permitted; a Virginia fishing license is required.

PETERSBURG NATIONAL BATTLEFIELD

1539 Hickory Hill Road
Petersburg, VA 23803-4721
(804) 732–3531
PETE_Interpretation@nps.gov
www.nps.gov/pete

Petersburg National Battlefield comprises 2,700 acres and was established as a national military park in 1926 (name changed to a national battlefield in 1962) to commemorate the site of a ten-month Civil War campaign in which the Union army attempted to seize the railroad center supplying Richmond and Lee's army. The main unit of the battlefield is located in southeastern Virginia, just east of the city of Petersburg via State Highway 36. Also included in the battlefield are outlying forts southwest of the city, the City Point Unit in the city of Hopewell, Virginia, and the Five Forks Unit in Dinwiddie County.

After failing to capture Richmond by direct attack, Ulysses S. Grant and the Union army decided to move farther south and attempt to cut off Robert E. Lee's railroad supply lines. Early assaults against the Confederate line failed, and Grant was forced to settle down to a siege that was to last nearly ten months and result in 70,000 American casualties.

During the lengthy campaign at Petersburg, Grant selected City Point, a strategic location at the junction of two rivers within easy water communication of Fort Monroe and Washington, D.C., as his headquarters. This location became the logistical and communication center for the Union forces until Grant disbanded the headquarters and moved closer to the front for the final campaign of the war. Lee had placed a large Confederate force at Five Forks under the command of General George Pickett, but the force was put out of action by Union troops who were then able to cut off the last rail supply line into Petersburg. On the night of April 2, 1865, Lee evacuated Petersburg and moved toward Appomattox, where his final surrender was to occur a week later.

The visitor center contains exhibits, a seventeen-minute map presentation that is conducted every half hour, and a schedule of programs taking place throughout the park in summer months. Programs include cannon firings, mortar demonstrations, and reenactments of camp life. Visitors may also obtain maps for a self-guided driving tour of the battlefield. A number of the tour's stops provide short interpretive walking trails. An audiotape for the driving tour is available for purchase.

ENTRANCE FEE: June–August, $5.00 per person with a maximum of $10.00 per vehicle. September–May, $3.00 per person with a maximum of $5.00 per vehicle.

FACILITIES: No food service or lodging is available in the park, but both can be found nearby. Rest rooms and drinking water are in the visitor center.

CAMPING: No camping is permitted on the battlefield grounds. Campsites are available in Pocahontas State Forest and Park, northwest of Petersburg via Interstate 95 and State Highway 10.

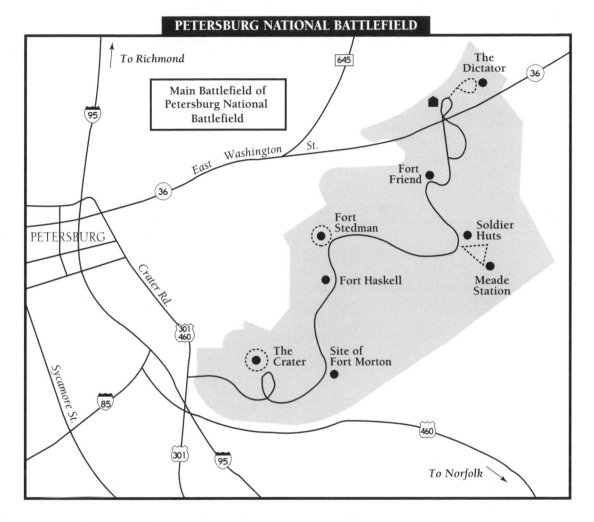

PRINCE WILLIAM FOREST PARK

18100 Park Headquarters Road
Triangle, VA 22172-0209
(703) 221–7181
www.nps.gov/prwi

A sanctuary for native plants and animals in rapidly urbanizing northern Virginia, Prince William Forest Park protects more than 17,000 acres of Piedmont forest in the Quantico Creek watershed and is the largest national park area within the Washington, D.C., metropolitan area. Rustic cabins built by the Civilian

Conservation Corps are now listed on the National Register of Historic Places and are used by group and family campers. The park provides a place to hike, picnic, camp, and fish, with 37 miles of trails, several lakes, and two picnic areas. The park entrance is about 35 miles south of Washington, D.C., via Interstate 95, ¼ mile off exit 150 to state road 619 West.

Prince William Forest Park is primarily used as a recreational retreat from the urban Washington area. This land was temporarily ruined following extensive tree cutting and farming by early pioneers so that, by the late 1800s, most of the farms had been abandoned. The result is an extensively forested watershed.

Numerous activities are available to park visitors. Bicycle riding is permitted on all roads (including fire roads), and 37 miles of trails and fire roads are accessible to hikers. Major trails are marked, and self-guided trails, exhibits, conducted walks, and talks are available at various areas of the park. Information may be obtained at the park visitor center.

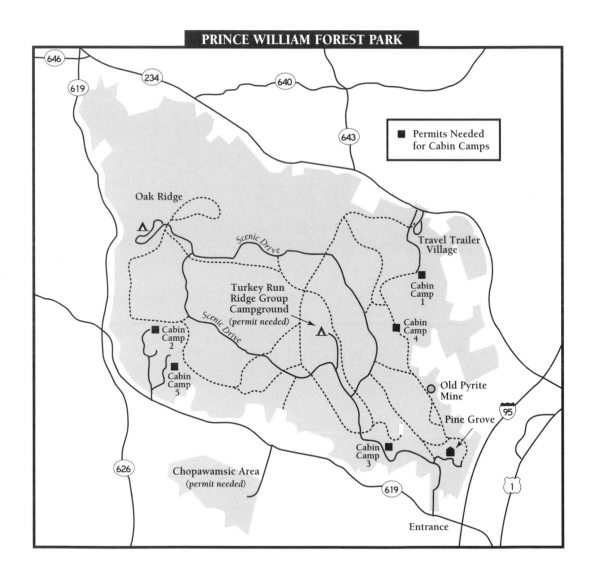

FACILITIES: Individual family cabins and group cabins are available April through October. Organized groups may rent Cabin Camp 5 year-round. For reservations call 703–221–5843. The cabins are grouped together in camps with each camp having a central kitchen-dining hall and a washhouse. No food service is available in the park. Rest rooms are located at both picnic areas, Turkey Run Environmental Center (TREC), and Oak Ridge Campground.

ENTRANCE FEE: $4.00 per vehicle or $2.00 per person; good for three days.

CAMPING: Oak Ridge (seventy-nine spaces), the major campground, is 6 miles from the park entrance. It is open year-round (two-week limit per year) and provides flush toilets, tables, water, and paved parking slips. The Travel Trailer Village (seventy-six spaces) is a concessioner-operated campground with hookups, showers, and a laundry, located off Virginia Highway 234 North. For information, write Prince William Travel Trailer Village, 16058 Dumfries Road, Dumfries, VA 22026 (703–221–2474). For organized groups, Turkey Run Ridge group camping area is open all year by reservation only and has tables, grills, and flush toilets. Chopawamsic Backcountry Campground is primitive, and permits are required. More information may be obtained by writing or calling the park (703–221–7181) from 8:30 A.M. to 5:00 P.M.

FISHING: Native fishes such as bass, bluegill, perch, pickerel, and catfish are available in several park lakes and ponds. A Virginia fishing license and artificial bait are required.

RED HILL PATRICK HENRY NATIONAL MEMORIAL

1250 Red Hill Road
Brookneal, VA 24528
(804) 376-2044
www.redhill.org

Red Hill Patrick Henry National Memorial comprises 233 acres and was authorized by Congress in 1986 to honor the life of this famous Virginia legislator, revolutionary patriot, and orator who made Red Hill his last home. Red Hill is also Patrick Henry's burial place. The memorial is in south central Virginia, 28 miles south of Appomattox and 35 miles southeast of Lynchburg via U.S. Highway 501.

Patrick Henry was born at Studley in Hanover County, Virginia, on May 29, 1736. He was the "Voice of the Revolution" and in 1775 gave the celebrated speech of the Second Virginia Convention at St. John's Church in Richmond, stating in regard to the troubles with Great Britain, "I know not what course others may take, but as for me, give me liberty or give me death." After a stint as commander-in-chief of the Virginia forces, he was elected the first governor of the state in 1776, an office he held five times. Henry assured the individual freedoms of Americans by being a principal proponent of the Bill of Rights. Despite his years of public service, in and out of office, and a busy law practice, he managed to father seventeen children. Beginning in 1794 Henry made his home at Red Hill, which he called "the garden spot of Virginia." In 1799 Henry died and was buried at Red Hill.

Red Hill is an eighteenth-century plantation that contains Patrick Henry's original law office and reconstructed home, kitchen, smoke house, cook's cabin, stables, cemetery, and the national champion Osage orange tree. The main house was destroyed by fire in 1919 and has been reconstructed on its original foundation. The visitor center contains a museum that houses the largest collection of Patrick Henry memorabilia in the world, including the famous painting of *Patrick Henry Before the Virginia House of Burgesses* by Peter Rothermel, a fifteen-minute video, and a gift shop. Red Hill is open daily from 9:00 A.M. to 5:00 P.M. (4:00 P.M. from November through March). A fee is charged to tour this site. The memorial is closed on Thanksgiving, Christmas Day, and New Year's Day.

ENTRANCE FEE: No charge.

FACILITIES: Rest rooms, drinking water, and soft drinks are available at the visitor center. A picnic area is located on the grounds. Food and lodging are available in Brookneal.

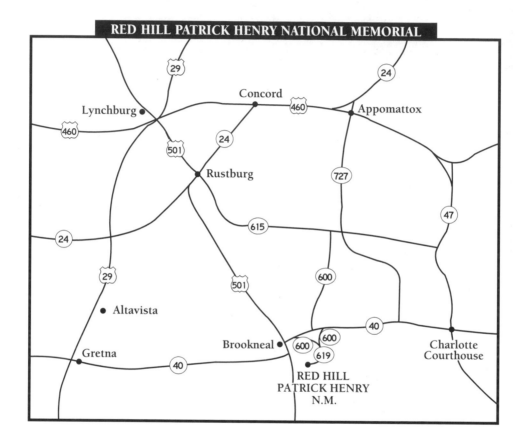

RICHMOND NATIONAL BATTLEFIELD PARK
3215 East Broad Street
Richmond, VA 23223-7517
(804) 226–1981
www.nps.gov/rich

Richmond National Battlefield Park was authorized in 1936 to commemorate the battlefields around the Confederate capital of Richmond. The park's 769 acres are in and around the city of Richmond, Virginia, as eleven separate sites in three counties.

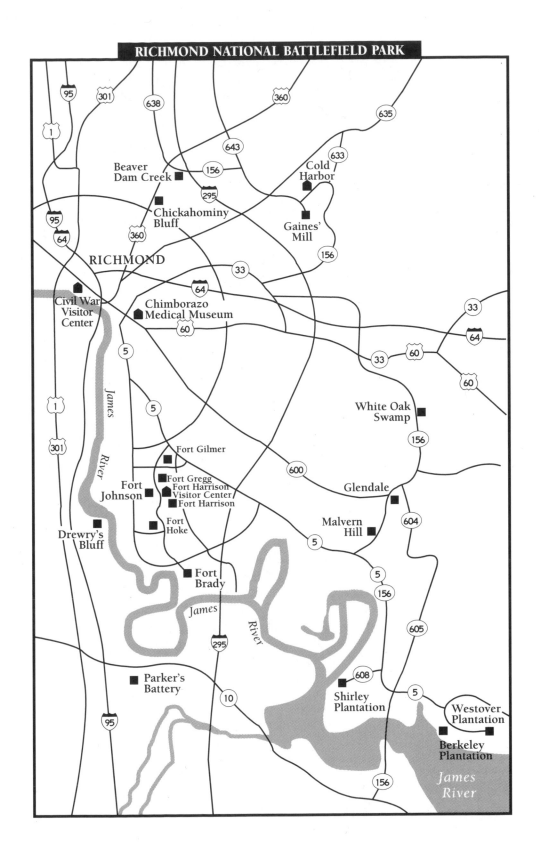

RICHMOND NATIONAL BATTLEFIELD PARK

95
301
638
360
635
1
643
633
156
Beaver
Dam Creek
Cold
Harbor
295
95
64
Chickahominy
Bluff
360
Gaines'
Mill
156
RICHMOND
33
64
Civil War
Visitor
Center
Chimborazo
Medical Museum
60
33
60
5
33
60
James
River
1
5
White Oak
Swamp
301
156
5
Fort Gilmer
600
Glendale
Fort Gregg
Fort Harrison
Visitor Center
Fort Harrison
Fort
Johnson
604
Drewry's
Bluff
Fort
Hoke
Malvern
Hill
5
Fort
Brady
5
James
156
River
605
James
295
River
608
Parker's
Battery
Shirley
Plantation
5
10
Westover
Plantation
95
Berkeley
Plantation
156
James
River

The city of Richmond served as a political, medical, manufacturing, and supply center for the South; it also was an important symbol of the Confederacy. For these reasons, Union forces launched repeated major drives toward the city and the Confederate army that was defending it. Two of the drives, the Seven Days Campaign in 1862 and Ulysses S. Grant's campaign of 1864, are particularly significant. Richmond withstood all attacks until Grant's successful siege of Petersburg forced Robert E. Lee's army to retreat from Richmond on April 2, 1865. The city fell the next day, and the final collapse of the Confederacy soon followed.

The park's new Civil War Visitor Center at Tredegar Iron Works is located at 470 Tredegar Street on the Canal Walk in Richmond. The visitor center offers exhibits, audiovisual programs, and a brochure with a map that outlines a self-guided battlefields tour. Visitors will also find a schedule of living-history programs and special events during the summer. Smaller welcome stations with exhibits are located at the Chimborazo Medical Museum, the Glendale Cemetery Lodge, Cold Harbor and Fort Harrison; Fort Harrison and Glendale are only staffed seasonally. Hiking trails are at Gaines' Mill, Fort Harrison, Fort Brady, Cold Harbor, Malvern Hill, and Drewry's Bluff. Interpretive facilities with audio stations and/or signs are at each park site.

ENTRANCE FEE: No charge.

FACILITIES: No food service or lodging is provided in park areas, although both are available nearby. Rest rooms and water are in each of the visitor centers. Picnic facilities exist at Tredegar and Fort Harrison and in the vicinity of Cold Harbor.

CAMPING: No camping is permitted in the park. Pocahontas State Park and Forest, a short distance southwest of Richmond via highways 10 and 655, provides camping with tables, grills, water, flush toilets, a dump station, swimming, and fishing.

SHENANDOAH NATIONAL PARK

3655 U.S. 211E
Luray, VA 22835-9036
(540) 999–3500
www.nps.gov/shen

Shenandoah National Park was established in 1935 and comprises 196,000 acres along a 70-mile stretch of the Blue Ridge Mountains. The drive along the ridge of mountains provides visitors with splendid vistas of the Shenandoah Valley and the Piedmont. The park is located in northern Virginia, with the northern entrance approximately 60 miles southwest of Washington, D.C.

Shenandoah National Park lies astride the Blue Ridge Mountains, which form the eastern boundary of the Appalachian Range. To the west, the Shenandoah River flows northeastward between the Blue Ridge and Allegheny mountains. To the east is the rolling Piedmont country.

Main access to the park's features is along 105-mile Skyline Drive, which winds along the crest of the range. Numerous pullouts are provided for viewing the spectacular scenery. Visitor centers with exhibits, audiovisual programs, and maps are at Dickey Ridge near the north entrance and at Big Meadows, 51 miles south. The Dickey Ridge Visitor Center is usually open daily 9:00 A.M. to 5:00 P.M. from spring through November. The Byrd Visitor Center at Big Meadows is usually open daily 9:00 A.M. to 5:00 P.M. from spring through November. At these

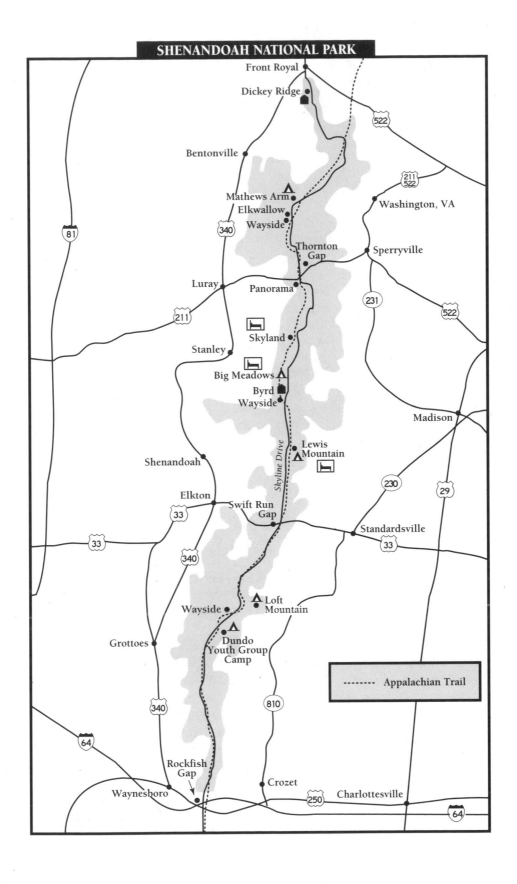

SHENANDOAH NATIONAL PARK

Front Royal

Dickey Ridge

Bentonville

Mathews Arm

Elkwallow
Wayside

Thornton
Gap

Washington, VA

Sperryville

Luray

Panorama

Skyland

Stanley

Big Meadows

Byrd
Wayside

Madison

Lewis
Mountain

Shenandoah

Elkton

Swift Run
Gap

Standardsville

Wayside

Loft
Mountain

Grottoes

Dundo
Youth Group
Camp

Skyline Drive

- - - - Appalachian Trail

Rockfish
Gap

Crozet

Charlottesville

Waynesboro

centers, at Loft Mountain Information center 79½ miles south, and at the entrance stations, visitors may obtain a visitor guide (listing activities and services) and a guide map to features along Skyline Drive. Over 500 miles of trails, including 101 miles of the Appalachian Trail, are in the park. Ranger programs, including hikes, and evening talks, are provided at several locations during summer months and less frequently during spring and fall.

ENTRANCE FEE: $10.00 per vehicle or $5.00 per person; good for seven days.

FACILITIES: Food service is available at Elkwallow, Panorama, Skyland, Big Meadows, and Loft Mountain. There are seven picnic areas in the park. Service stations and camper-supply stores are at various points along the drive. Overnight accommodations are at Big Meadows, Lewis Mountain, and Skyland. For information or reservations, write ARAMARK Parks and Resorts, P.O. Box 727, Luray, VA 22835 (540–743–5108 or 800–999–4714).

CAMPING: Campgrounds with tables, grills, flush toilets, and water are at Mathews Arm (179 sites, tables, grills, flush toilets, and dump station), Big Meadows (217 sites, dump station, coin showers, coin laundry, and camp store), Lewis Mountain (thirty-two sites, flush toilets, coin shower, coin laundry and camp store), Loft Mountain (219 sites, dump station, flush toilets, coin laundry, coin showers, and store), and Dundo Youth Group Camp (seven group sites, pit toilets, water; reservations required). All but Big Meadows are open from May to October. Big Meadows usually opens earlier, closes in late fall, and is on a reservation system (800–365–2267). Although Big Meadows is generally the first to be filled, it is also the most noisy and crowded. Many people prefer the campground at Loft Mountain.

FISHING: Angling is limited to trout fishing with single hook artificial lure in the more than 100 miles of streams contained in the park. The Commonwealth of Virginia regulations apply. Most streams are catch and release. A Virginia fishing license is required.

WOLF TRAP FARM PARK FOR THE PERFORMING ARTS

1551 Trap Road
Vienna, VA 22182-1643
(703) 255–1800
(703) 255–9432 (TDD)
(703) 255–1860 (Ticket Information)
www.nps.gov/wotr

This 130-acre park was authorized in 1966 to establish the first national park for the performing arts. For information on coming attractions and tickets, check the Wolf Trap Foundation's Web site (www.wolftrap.org) or call (703) 255–1860. The park is located in Vienna, Virginia, approximately 15 miles (thirty minutes) west of Washington, D.C. From Route 495 (the Washington Beltway) take exit 45 (the Dulles Toll Road westbound) and follow it to the Wolf Trap exit.

Wolf Trap Farm Park was created through Mrs. Catherine Filene Shouse's gift of farmland and funds for construction of a performing arts center. Wolf Trap is a joint venture between the United States government and the private, nonprofit Wolf Trap Foundation. Wolf Trap Farm

Park is administered and managed by the National Park Service, which also has technical and operational responsibilities for the Filene Center. The Wolf Trap Foundation is responsible by cooperative agreement for selecting and funding Filene Center programming, providing publicity and promotion of the Filene Center, and operating the box office. A full range of artistic performances is offered during the summer months. Free lectures, which may include in-depth discussions and/or demonstrations, are part of the performance previews.

The National Park Service operates an interpretive program during the summer in the rustic Theatre-in-the-Woods. Programs for children of all ages are offered during July and August and include puppet shows, dance, mime, and instrumentalists. For information about these activities, call (703) 255–1827.

ENTRANCE FEE: No charge for entrance to the grounds. Prices for the performances vary.

FACILITIES: A nonprofit gift shop is open during Filene Center performances. A dining pavilion offers food service beginning two hours prior to each performance. Snack bars are also available. Picnicking is permitted in the park, but sites are first come, first served.

VIRGIN ISLANDS

TOURIST INFORMATION
(800) 372–8784
www.usvi.net

BUCK ISLAND REEF NATIONAL MONUMENT
2100 Church Street, Lot #100
Christiansted, St. Croix, U.S. Virgin Islands 00820-4611
340–773–1460
CHRI_Superintendent@nps.gov
www.nps.gov/buis

Buck Island Reef National Monument comprises more than 19,000 acres of submerged lands and 174 acres of tropical dry forest island. The island is surrounded by the only example of a continuous elkhorn coral barrier reef in U.S. waters. Created in 1961 and expanded by presidential proclamation in 2001, the monument was established to preserve one of the finest marine gardens in the Caribbean. The monument is home to many threatened and endangered animals and plants. It is located 1½ miles off the north shore of St. Croix and may be reached by boat from Christainsted and Green Cay Marina.

Beginning in the 1750s Buck Island was leased to lumbermen. After the extensive lumber cutting of the 1700s, the island was used as a pasturage. Overgrazing by goats ended in the 1940s. It will take centuries for the island to return to its natural state of tropical vegetation. While the island itself is impressive (rising from sea level to 300 feet), it is the water surrounding the island that contains the major attractions.

An elkhorn coral barrier reef wraps around the eastern two-thirds of the island, creating a quiet lagoon where snorkelers, beginner and expert, can safely explore the reef. Hundreds of species of reef fish swim through the massive branches of coral, which rise to the surface from a depth of 30 feet. The turquoise water teems with marine life, including trumpet fishes, sea urchins, sharks, sea fans, spiney lobsters, and the occasional family of porpoises. The endangered hawksbill sea turtle and the brown pelican can be found swimming and foraging throughout the reef. Buck Island is one of the few places in the Caribbean protected from all forms of extractive use. Recent protective legislation will improve all forms of marine life associated with the reef.

Approved National Park Service concessionaires on St. Croix may be hired for a visit to the monument. Water and soft drinks are provided; visitors are advised to bring their own lunch for a full-day trip. A primitive hiking trail starts at the beach and traverses up and over the island for a bird's-eye view of the reef. Beware the island's vegetation: Most of it stings or has thorns. It is recommended that you wear shoes and stay on the trail at all times. The concession boats provide snorkel equipment and instruction for those wishing to explore the magnificent reef and lagoon. A guided tour of the underwater trail takes about thirty minutes; interpretive signs located on the bottom throughout the snorkel trail provide information on the marine life that you might see during your visit.

ENTRANCE FEE: No charge.

FACILITIES: No food or lodging is available on the island. The park provides picnic tables, grills, a sheltered pavilion for picnicking, and rest rooms. Meals and lodging are available on the island of St. Croix.

CAMPING: No camping is permitted on the island. The island is closed from sunset to sunrise; boats can anchor overnight in the designated anchorage at West Beach.

FISHING: All forms of fishing are prohibited in the monument. Spear guns and fishing gear are prohibited within the park boundaries.

CHRISTIANSTED NATIONAL HISTORIC SITE

2100 Church Street, #100
Christiansted, St. Croix, VI 00820-4611
(340) 773–1460
www.nps.gov/chri

Christiansted National Historic Site consists of seven acres and was designated part of the National Park System in 1952 to interpret the colonial development of the Virgin Islands through preservation of its eighteenth- and nineteenth-century structures and grounds in this former capital of the Danish West Indies. The park is located in downtown Christiansted on St. Croix.

In 1733, the Danish West Indian & Guinea Company bought St. Croix from France to develop its flatlands for sugar production. By 1760, most of the island was under sugar cultivation, which brought on a period of great wealth. A drop in sugar prices beginning in 1820 combined with emancipation of slaves in 1848 helped bring an end to the prosperity. The island was purchased by the United States in 1917 to prevent Germany from establishing a naval base in the Caribbean.

National Park Service visitor center, located in Fort Christiansvaern, a Danish fort completed in 1749, is open weekdays from 8:00 A.M. to 5:00 P.M. and weekends from 9:00 A.M. to 4:45 P.M. Here visitors may obtain information and a folder for a self-guided tour of the historic area. In addition to the fort, the site contains five other historic buildings. These include the Danish Customs House, where the government collected taxes on imports and exports; Scale House, where goods were weighed; Government House, which served as the governor's residence; Danish West Indian & Guinea Company Compound, which housed provisions and offices, warehouse, and the slave auction yard; and Steeple Building, which was built originally as a Lutheran church and later served as a bakery, hospital, and school. It now houses a museum.

ENTRANCE FEE: $2.00 per adult.

FACILITIES: No food or lodging is provided by the National Park Service, but both can be found nearby in the town of Christiansted.

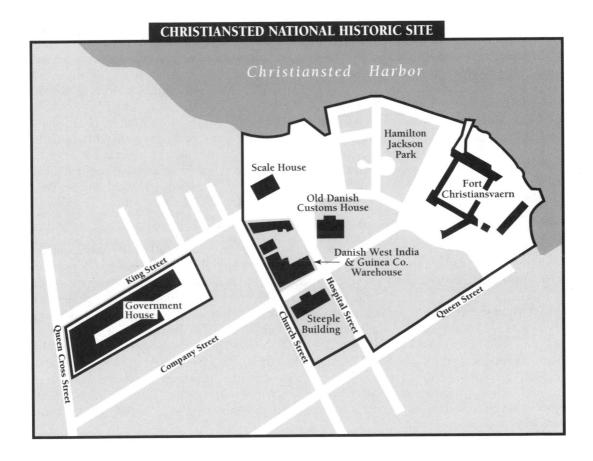

CHRISTIANSTED NATIONAL HISTORIC SITE

VIRGIN ISLANDS NATIONAL PARK

6310 Estate Nazareth
St. Thomas, VI 00802-1102
(340) 776–6201
www.nps.gov/viis

Virgin Islands National Park was authorized in 1956 to preserve nearly 14,700 acres of tropical island and water that include quiet coves, blue-green waters, and white sandy beaches fringed by lush green hills. Water and submerged lands comprise 5,650 acres of the park. The park is located on St. John Island and may be reached via daily ferry across Pillsbury Sound from Red Hook, St. Thomas. Visitors can fly to Charlotte Amalie, St. Thomas, where taxis run to Red Hook. The national park also includes Hassel Island, located in St. Thomas Harbor.

St. John Island, a former home for Indians, pirates, and slaves, is also a land of tropical seas and beautiful coral reefs, where temperatures rarely climb above 98 degrees Fahrenheit or fall below 70. Cruz Bay Visitor Contact Center on St. John is open daily 8:00 A.M. to 4:30 P.M. and provides exhibits, maps, and a schedule of park activities including hikes, programs, and guided snorkel trips. The park includes about 20 miles of trails. The Reef Bay Trail starts at 1,100 feet above sea level, winds downhill for 2.6 miles, and ends near a plantation ruin at sea level. An underwater trail with fifteen explanatory plaques for snorkelers is at Trunk Bay, which is the most popular beach. Lifeguards are on duty daily at Trunk Bay, and snorkel equipment may be rented there as well as at Cinnamon Bay.

A 15-mile tour by auto or taxi via Centerline Road and North Shore Road includes beautiful scenery and outstanding beaches. Private taxi tours of the park are operated from Cruz Bay; rental vehicles are also available here. Speed limits are 10 miles per hour in the city and 20 miles per hour in the country. Many of the roads climb and spiral at unusual angles. Points of interest in the park include the partially restored ruins of the Annaberg sugar mill complex, ancient petroglyphs, and ruins of the Reef Bay sugar mill.

ENTRANCE FEE: No charge.

FACILITIES: Cinnamon Bay Campground, on St. John's north shore, offers the only accomodations within the national park. The campground consists of forty cottages and forty-four tent-equipped campsites. Each tent comes equipped with four cots, mattresses, propane stove, charcoal grill, and gas lantern. The campground includes a restaurant, general store, and beach shop that includes boat and snorkeling equipment rentals. For information and reservations write Cinnamon Bay Campground, P.O. Box 720, Cruz Bay, St. John, U.S. Virgin Islands 00831. Call (800) 539–9998; fax (340) 776–6458. Tent-cottages on private land within the park are offered by Maho Bay Camps, Cruz Bay, St. John, U.S. Virgin Islands 00831. Call (340) 776–6240 or log onto www.mahobay.com. Other park facilities include a concessioner-operated snack bar and snorkel equipment rental at Trunk Bay. Changing rooms are at Trunk Bay and Hawksnest beaches. For additional information about St. John, check their Web site at www.stjohnisland.com.

CAMPING: See the facilities section above. Cinnamon Bay Campground also offers "Baresites," which are located in the same section of the campground as the tent-equipped sites.

FISHING: Park waters, except in designated swimming areas, are open to fishing with hand-held rods. Boats for deep-sea fishing, drift fishing, or shoreline trolling may be chartered on the island. No spearfishing is permitted in the park.

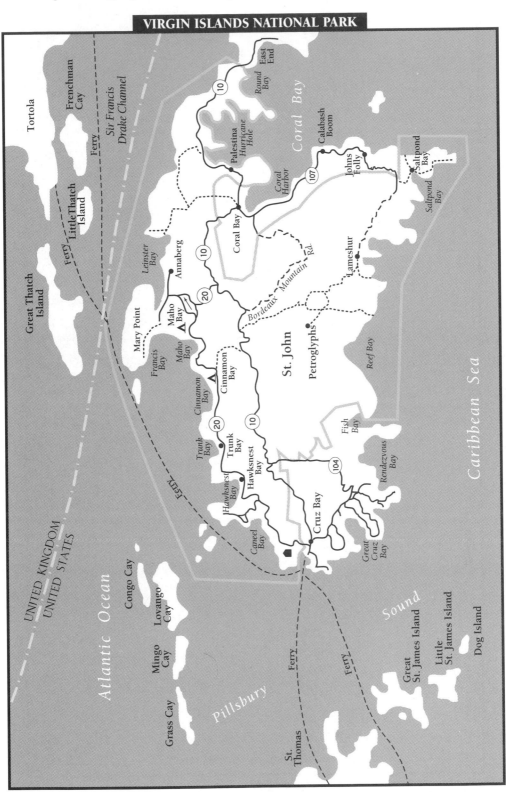

VIRGIN ISLANDS NATIONAL PARK

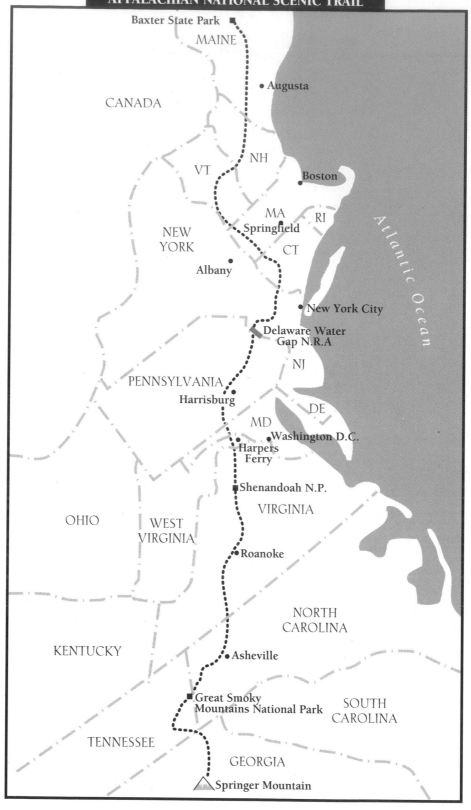

Baxter State Park

MAINE

CANADA

Augusta

NH

VT

Boston

NEW YORK

MA

Springfield

RI

CT

Albany

New York City

Delaware Water
Gap N.R.A

NJ

PENNSYLVANIA

Harrisburg

DE

MD

Washington D.C.

Harpers
Ferry

Shenandoah N.P.

OHIO

WEST
VIRGINIA

VIRGINIA

Roanoke

NORTH
CAROLINA

KENTUCKY

Asheville

Great Smoky
Mountains National Park

SOUTH
CAROLINA

TENNESSEE

GEORGIA

Springer Mountain

Atlantic Ocean

WEST VIRGINIA

STATE TOURIST INFORMATION
(800) 225–5982
www.callwva.com

APPALACHIAN NATIONAL SCENIC TRAIL
P.O. Box 807
Harpers Ferry, WV 25425
(304) 535–6331
www.appalachiantrail.org
www.nps.gov/appa

Established as a national scenic trail in 1968, the 2,160-mile Appalachian National Scenic Trail follows the Appalachian Mountains through fourteen states, connecting Mount Katahdin, Maine, with Springer Mountain, Georgia. The trail, completed in 1937, is accessible at numerous locations between its two end points. The trail passes through six national park areas, which include Great Smoky Mountains National Park (Tennessee and North Carolina), Blue Ridge Parkway (Virginia), Shenandoah National Park (Virginia), Harpers Ferry National Historical Park (West Virginia), Chesapeake and Ohio Canal National Historical Park (Maryland), and Delaware Water Gap National Recreation Area (Pennsylvania).

To view the ridges, streams, and lakes along the entire length of the Appalachian Trail, a backpacker must be willing to devote five to six months' time in an effort to accumulate approximately five million steps, either all at once or bit by bit over the years. If the goal is something less than hiking the entire length, it is possible to enjoy hikes of a few hours, a few days, or a few weeks. Those who through-hike the trail at one time usually begin at Springer Mountain in late March or early April to avoid the still relatively severe weather prevalent in the Appalachian Mountains.

The National Trails System Act of 1968, which recognized the citizen-built Appalachian Trail as one of the first national scenic trails, encouraged individual states to participate in its protection. The nonprofit Appalachian Trail Conference (ATC) coordinates the efforts of thirty-one trail clubs in maintaining volunteer stewardship over the assigned regions in cooperation with the National Park Service, U.S.D.A. Forest Service, and many state and local agencies. A list of guidebooks and maps of the trail may be obtained by writing Appalachian Trail Conference, P.O. Box 807, Harpers Ferry, WV 25425 (304–535–6331). Additional information is available from ATC or one of the member clubs.

ENTRANCE FEE: No charge.

FACILITIES: Although most of the Appalachian Trail passes through primitive backcountry areas, it occasionally comes close to developed areas, where hikers take advantage of grocery stores, restaurants, motels, hostels, showers, and the like. Guidebooks available from the ATC provide a detailed listing of facilities. Many long-distance hikers send supplies ahead to post offices along the way.

CAMPING: About 260 trailside shelters are available on a first-come basis. These shelters are generally spaced one moderate day's hiking distance apart and are to be used one night only. There are also many campgrounds near the trail, and some areas have designated campsites.

FISHING: Fishing is available at various locations along the trail. An appropriate state fishing license is required.

BLUESTONE NATIONAL SCENIC RIVER
104 Main Street
P.O. Box 246
Glen Jean, WV 25846-0246
(304) 465–0508
neri_interpretation@nps.gov
www.nps.gov/blue

Bluestone National Scenic River, encompassing 4,310 acres, was authorized as part of the National Park Service in 1988 to preserve an 11-mile section of the free-flowing Bluestone River. Access to the river is through Bluestone State Park and Pipestem Resort State Park off State Route 20 south of Hinton, West Virginia.

The Bluestone River begins on East River Mountain and flows 77 miles to its confluence with the New River at Bluestone Lake. The 11-mile section of the Bluestone River (named for the deep blue limestone stream bed) that is preserved as a national scenic river begins at the river's entry into Pipestem State Park and extends to Bluestone Lake. The ancient river has cut a gorge to depths of up to 1,200 feet. The rough terrain of this region has generally inhibited human habitation to produce a scenic, unspoiled area where visitors will find opportunities for fishing, hiking, horseback riding, mountain biking, boating, and enjoying nature. The scenic river is open year-round. Much of the Bluestone is also a wildlife management area of the West Virginia Division of Natural Resources. Hunting is permitted, except in the adjacent state parks.

Some of the finest views of the Bluestone are in Pipestem Resort State Park, where there is an overlook along the rim road. Viewpoints of the river are also at the Canyon Rim Center and the Main Lodge. An aerial tram operates from April through October from Canyon Rim to Mountain Creek Lodge. For hikers, mountain bikers, and horseback riders, an 8-mile trail that once served as a road for wagons and automobiles follows the river from Mountain Creek Lodge to Bluestone State Park.

ENTRANCE FEE: No charge.

FACILITIES: There are no federal facilities within the boundaries of the national scenic river. Mountain Creek Lodge within Pipestem Resort State Park operates from April through October.

CAMPING: No camping is permitted within the boundaries of Bluestone National Scenic River. Pipestem Resort State Park has eighty sites with flush toilets, showers, and full hookups. Bluestone State Park has eighty-five sites with flush toilets, showers, and electrical hookups.

FISHING: The Bluestone offers fishing for smallmouth bass, panfish, and catfish. A West Virginia fishing license is required.

See map on page 308.

Bluestone National Scenic River

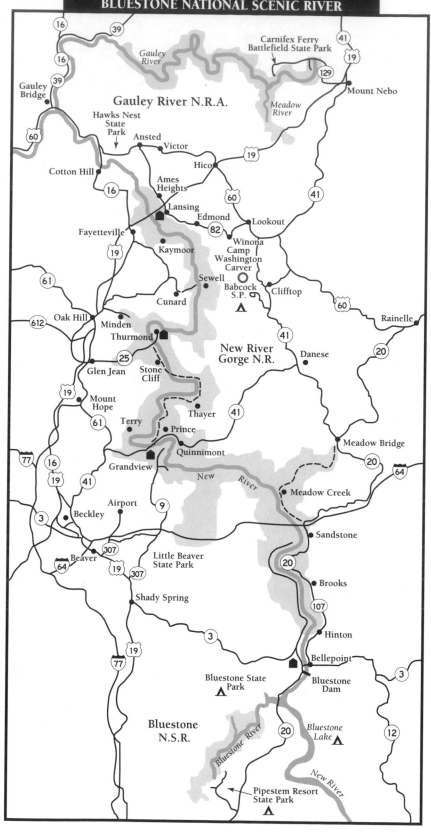

GAULEY RIVER NATIONAL RECREATION AREA
NEW RIVER GORGE NATIONAL RIVER
BLUESTONE NATIONAL SCENIC RIVER

Gauley River

Carnifex Ferry
Battlefield State Park

Gauley River N.R.A.

Meadow River

Gauley Bridge

Mount Nebo

Hawks Nest State Park

Ansted

Victor

Cotton Hill

Hico

Ames Heights

Lansing

Edmond

Lookout

Fayetteville

Kaymoor

Winona
Camp Washington Carver

Sewell

Babcock S.P.

Clifftop

Oak Hill

Cunard

Rainelle

Minden

Thurmond

New River Gorge N.R.

Danese

Glen Jean

Stone Cliff

Mount Hope

Thayer

Terry

Prince

Meadow Bridge

Quinnimont

Grandview

New   River

Meadow Creek

Airport

Beckley

Sandstone

Beaver

Little Beaver State Park

Brooks

Shady Spring

Hinton

Bellepoint

Bluestone State Park

Bluestone Dam

Bluestone N.S.R.

Bluestone River

Bluestone Lake

New River

Pipestem Resort State Park

GAULEY RIVER NATIONAL RECREATION AREA

104 Main Street
P.O. Box 246
Glen Jean, WV 25846-0246
(304) 465–0508
neri_interpretation@nps.gov
www.nps.gov/gari

Gauley River National Recreation Area comprises 11,145 acres and was authorized in 1988 to preserve portions of two of the finest white-water rivers in the eastern United States. The area is in central West Virginia between Summersville and Swiss. Vehicle access is from State Route 129 at Summersville Dam and from Swiss Road off State Route 39.

Gauley River National Recreation Area includes 25 miles of the Gauley River and 6 miles of the Meadow River. The Gauley River is one of the best white-water boating rivers in the East. The scenic gorges and valleys within and near the recreation area provide a wide variety of natural and cultural activities.

The Gauley River drops twenty-six feet per mile through a gorge with an average depth of 500 feet. More than one hundred rapids, huge volumes of water, and spectacular scenery make this one of the world's finest rivers for rafting. The upper section of the river is most demanding. White-water boating is available for six weekends, beginning the weekend after Labor Day, when the Summersville reservoir is lowered to make room for winter and early spring rains. The first four weekends provide whitewater boating on Friday through Monday and the last two weekends are just Saturday and Sunday. Water levels occasionally permit boating at other times of the year as well.

ENTRANCE FEE: No charge.

FACILITIES: Food and lodging are available nearby.

CAMPING: Primitive camping facilities are provided by the National Park Service at the Tailwaters Area. Camping is also available nearby at Babcock State Park (304–438–3004), which has fifty sites with flush toilets and showers. Summersville Lake (304–872–3459), operated by the U.S. Army Corps of Engineers, has 110 sites with flush toilets and showers.

FISHING: Both rivers provide excellent fishing. A West Virginia fishing license is required.

HARPERS FERRY NATIONAL HISTORICAL PARK

P.O. Box 65
Harpers Ferry, WV 25425-0065
(304) 535–6298
Marsha_starkey@nps.gov
www.nps.gov/hafe

Harpers Ferry National Historical Park, located at the scenic confluence of the Shenandoah and Potomac rivers, comprises about 2,500 acres. Authorized as a national monument in 1944, the area was declared a National Historical Park in 1963. Today the park has a variety of exhibits, interpretive programs and hiking trails exploring the park's six themes: industry, John Brown, Civil War, African-American history (particularly Storer College), natural history, and transportation. The park is approximately 65 miles northwest of Washington, D.C.; 20 miles southwest of Frederick, Maryland, via U.S. 340. Signs along U.S. 340 direct visitors to the visitor center and parking facility by turning at the signal light on U.S. 340.

The strategic location of Harpers Ferry resulted in its early settlement so that, by the mid-1800s, the town had a population of approximately 3,000. The area was given a shot in the arm in the 1790s when President Washington urged establishment of a national armory here. The later arrival of the railroad and the C&O Canal speeded things along. Unfortunately, the combination of the Civil War (the town changed hands eight times during the conflict) and a series of severe floods in the late 1800s resulted in abandonment of the area by many of its citizens.

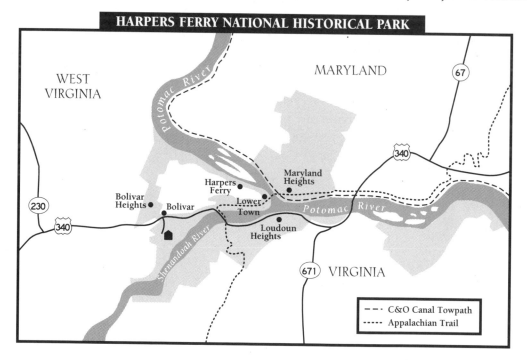

One famous visitor to Harpers Ferry in 1859 was John Brown. Brown planned to free slaves by force and establish a free Negro stronghold. His initial attack came at Harpers Ferry, a town with an arsenal of armaments in a location near the Mason-Dixon line. Brown and his twenty-one men captured the armory, which, in turn, was later stormed by troops led by Colonel Robert E. Lee. Brown was subsequently hanged for murder, treason, and slave insurrection. The building where Brown and his men sought refuge is part of the park and open for visitation.

The park area has restored buildings including a blacksmith shop, dry-goods store, provost marshal's office, clothing store, and jewelry store. An information center containing exhibits is open daily from 8:30 A.M. until 5:00 P.M. Park museums explain the six themes of Harpers Ferry National Historical Park: industry, John Brown, Civil War, natural history, transportation, and African-American history. Activities available include audiovisual presentations, guided walks, living-history programs, hiking trails, and self-guided tours.

ENTRANCE FEE: $5.00 per vehicle or $3.00 per person.

FACILITIES: No lodging is provided by the National Park Service. Visitors enter Harpers Ferry National Historical Park through the park's visitor center at the Cavalier Heights District. Shuttle buses transport visitors to other areas of the park. Private restaurants are located a few blocks from the Lower Town District. Rest rooms are next to the visitor center.

CAMPING: No camping is permitted in the historical park. Private campgrounds are nearby. Gambrill State Park (Maryland), 6 miles northwest of Frederick on Highway 40, offers camping with tables, grills, water, flush toilets, showers, and fishing (310–473–8360).

View from Maryland Heights, Harpers Ferry National Historical Park

FISHING: Fishing is permitted in the Shenandoah and Potomac rivers, which border the park. Catches include bass, catfish, crappie, and pike. An appropriate state fishing license is required.

NEW RIVER GORGE NATIONAL RIVER

104 Main Street
P.O. Box 246
Glen Jean, WV 25846-0246
(304) 465–0508
neri_interpretation@nps.gov
www.nps.gov/neri

New River Gorge National River was authorized in 1978 and comprises 70,890 acres along a rugged, white-water river running northward through deep canyons. The river is located in south-central West Virginia, between the towns of Hinton and Fayetteville. The nearest large town is Beckley.

This area of West Virginia that was once known for its coal mines, timbering, and railroads contains one of North America's oldest rivers. The 53-mile segment of the river corridor between Hinton and Fayetteville provides visitors with an abundance of natural, scenic, historic, and recreational features. Many miles of hiking, mountain biking, and horseback trails are available. The New River offers excellent white-water rafting. A list of commercial outfitters offering guide service is available from the park office.

Park headquarters is located in Glen Jean. Four visitor centers—Canyon Rim Visitor Center on U.S. 19 near Fayetteville, Hinton Visitor Center at State Route 3 By-Pass in Hinton, Thurmond Depot Visitor Center on Route 25, and Grandview Visitor Center located 6 miles north of Interstate 64 on Route 9—have exhibits, photos of the park, and a schedule of activities. The Canyon Rim Visitor Center is open year-round, while the visitor centers at Hinton, Grandview, and Thurmond are open seasonally.

ENTRANCE FEE: No charge.

FACILITIES: Water and rest rooms are at each visitor center. Picnic areas are at Canyon Rim, Dunglen, Stone Cliff, Grandview, Brooks Falls, and Sandstone Falls. Food and lodging are found in nearby communities.

CAMPING: Primitive camping areas are provided by the National Park Service at Stone Cliff, Army Camp, Grandview Sandbar, and Glade Creek. Toward the northern end of the river, Babcock State Park offers campsites with tables, grills, water, flush toilets, and showers. At the park's southern end, 9 miles south of Hinton on Highway 20, Bluestone State Park and Pipestem Resort State Park have similar facilities. Private campgrounds are near Fayetteville and Hinton.

FISHING: Fishing is excellent, with stocked brown and rainbow trout in some of the tributary streams, the New River is known for its catfish, crappie, pike, smallmouth bass, and walleye fishing. A West Virginia fishing license is required. If fishing for trout, a state trout stamp is required in addition to the regular fishing license.

See the map on page 308.

WISCONSIN

STATE TOURIST INFORMATION
(800) 432–8747
www.explorewisconsin.com

APOSTLE ISLANDS NATIONAL LAKESHORE
Route 1, Box 4
Old Courthouse Building
Bayfield, WI 54814-9599
(715) 779–3397
www.nps.gov/apis

Apostle Islands National Lakeshore, established in 1970, comprises 69,372 acres containing twenty-one islands and 12 miles of shoreline along the south side of Lake Superior. In 1986, Long Island became the twenty-first island to become part of the national lakeshore. The park is located on and near the Bayfield Peninsula in northern Wisconsin, approximately 77 miles northeast of Duluth, Minnesota. A concessioner provides excursion boat service to and among the islands from Bayfield in the summer.

The twenty-two Apostle Islands (all but one, Madeline Island, are within the park) are products of a million-year period when ice intermittently covered this region. As the glaciers receded, meltwater began to fill the basin that would eventually become Lake Superior. Evidence of earlier lake levels (old beachlines and cliffs) can still be seen on some of the islands.

By the early 1900s this area was booming, and Bayfield was a center for loggers, fishermen, shippers, and tourists. Beginning in the early 1930s, however, the combination of a bad economy and a region laid bare by fire and ax sent the area into decline. The vegetation has now returned, and the lighthouses, quarries, and fishing camps are open to the public.

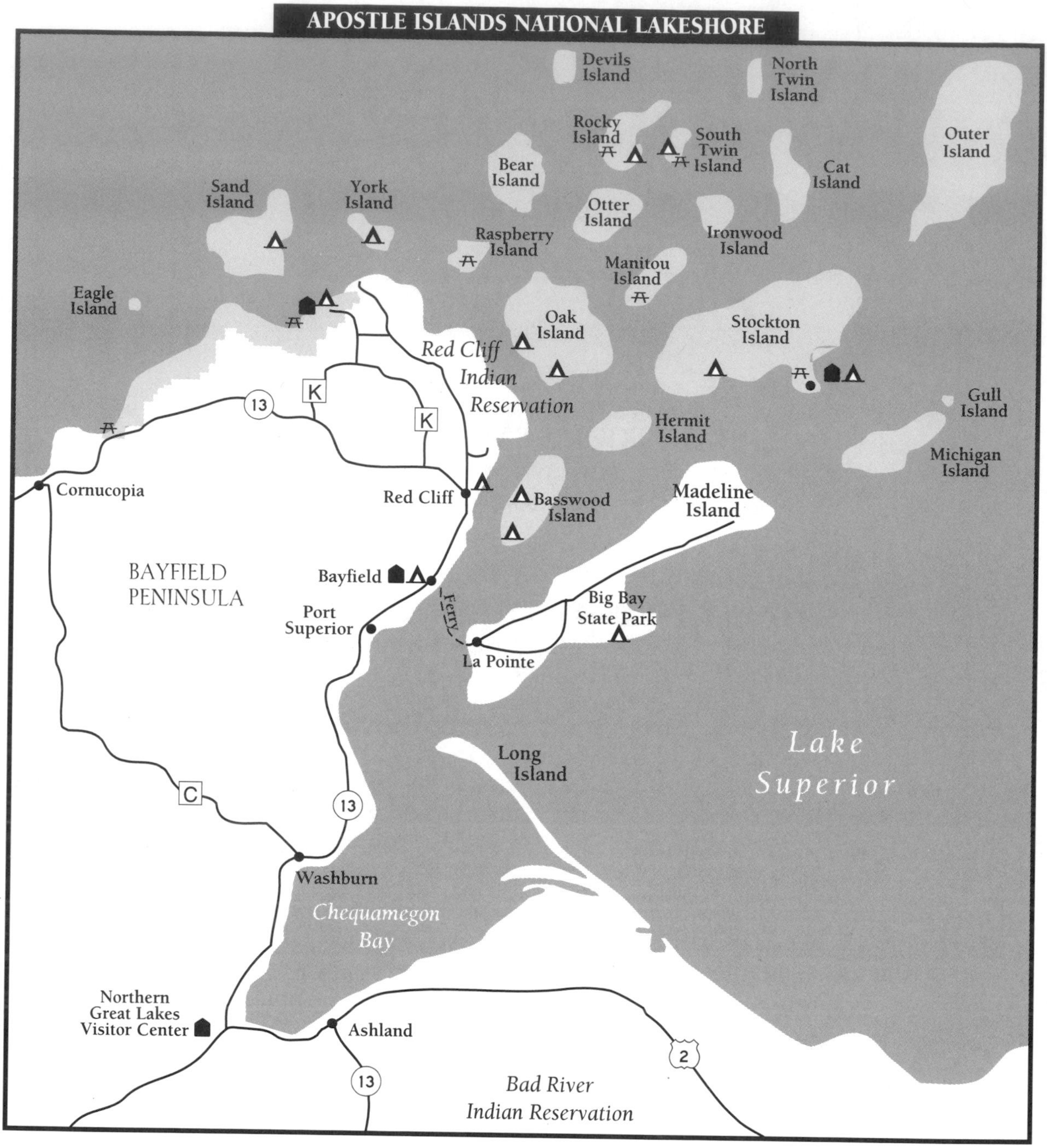

APOSTLE ISLANDS NATIONAL LAKESHORE

Devils Island

North Twin Island

Rocky Island

South Twin Island

Bear Island

Outer Island

Otter Island

Cat Island

Sand Island

York Island

Raspberry Island

Ironwood Island

Manitou Island

Eagle Island

Red Cliff Indian Reservation

Oak Island

Stockton Island

Gull Island

Hermit Island

Michigan Island

Cornucopia

13

K

K

Red Cliff

Basswood Island

Madeline Island

BAYFIELD PENINSULA

C

Bayfield

Port Superior

Ferry

Big Bay State Park

La Pointe

Long Island

Lake Superior

13

Washburn

Chequamegon Bay

Northern Great Lakes Visitor Center

Ashland

13

2

Bad River Indian Reservation

The park's visitor center in Bayfield is open daily May 1 through November 1 and Monday through Friday the remainder of the year. It contains exhibits, interpretive literature, and an audiovisual program. Information and limited amenities are available at the Little Sand Bay Visitor Center from October through May. From June through September, an information desk, exhibits, a sales area, and guided tours of an historic commercial fishing operation are also available. Little Sand Bay is 13 miles north of Bayfield. The new Northern Great Lakes Visitor Center on U.S. Highway 2 west of Ashland, Wisconsin, provides information on the Apostle Island National Lakeshore and other public lands in northern Wisconsin, northern Minnesota, and the Upper Peninsula of Michigan. It also features exhibits, an observation tower, sales area, historic archives, and a nature trail. This visitor center is open daily year-round.

Boating is one of the most popular activities in the area. Boat-ramp facilities are in Red Cliff, Bayfield, Cornucopia, and Little Sand Bay. Public docks are at Sand Island, South Twin Island, Little Sand Bay, Rocky Island, Manitou Island, Michigan Island, Stockton Island, Oak Island, Basswood Island, Outer Island, Otter Island, Raspberry Island, and Devils Island. Marinas (with boat-storage facilities) are in the Bayfield–Madeline Island area. Sea kayaks have become a very popular means of transportation among the Apostle Islands. Sailboat and sea kayak rentals and chartered fishing trips are available in Bayfield. For those without boats, daily excursion trips leave from Bayfield in summer.

One way to see the islands is by foot. More than 50 miles of hiking trails are maintained on the islands by the National Park Service. Stockton, the national lakeshore's largest island, has 14½ miles of trails. During summer, park rangers on Stockton guide nature walks and present evening programs. Rangers are also stationed on Manitou Island to conduct tours of the historic commercial fishing camp and on Raspberry Island to conduct tours of the island's light station. Volunteers provide tours of lighthouses on Sand, Devils, Michigan, and Outer Islands in summer.

ENTRANCE FEE: No charge.

FACILITIES: No overnight accommodations are provided in the park, but motels are available in Bayfield, Washburn, Cornucopia, Ashland, and on Madeline Island.

CAMPING: Camping is allowed on eighteen islands. Permits (fee charged) are required for camping and are available at the visitor stations. Call (715) 779–3398 extension 6 for details and reservations. Group campsites (for use by eight or more campers) are available on four islands. A variety of public and private campgrounds are in the surrounding communities, at Big Bay State Park on Madeline Island, and in Chequamegon National Forest. Red Cliff Indian Reservation offers modern campgrounds near Red Cliff. Be sure to boil Lake Superior water before drinking or using for cooking. Bears can be on any of the islands. Campers must store food properly to prevent bear encounters.

FISHING: The area around Apostle Islands is one of the best fish-producing habitats in Lake Superior. Sports fishing for lake, brown, and rainbow trout and for introduced species of salmon is good. Streams on the peninsula are popular for rainbow and brown trout. A Wisconsin fishing license is required.

ICE AGE NATIONAL SCENIC TRAIL;
ICE AGE NATIONAL SCIENTIFIC RESERVE

Wisconsin Department of Natural Resources
P.O. Box 7921
Madison, WI 53707
(608) 266–2181
www.nps.gov/iatr

The first national scientific reserve in the National Park Service, authorized in 1964, contains 50,000 acres of nationally significant features of continental glaciation. Ice Age National Scientific Reserve is administered by the State of Wisconsin as an affiliated area of the National Park Service. It consists of nine detached units located throughout Wisconsin. Ice Age National Scenic Trail is partially developed along its planned 1,000-mile length.

As recently as 12,000 years ago, Wisconsin—along with much of the rest of the northern United States—was covered by the last of at least four major glacial advances. During these periods, falling snow did not melt but accumulated and changed to ice under its own pressure. As the masses of ice moved southward, they leveled hills, filled valleys, and moved billions of tons of materials over the land. In Wisconsin, evidence of these huge glaciers is still clearly seen. Features known as drumlins, kames, eskers, moraines, kettles, and lake plains are preserved in the reserve.

Ice Age National Scientific Reserve consists of nine separate units located across the state, from Lake Michigan in the east to the St. Croix River on the Minnesota border. Five of these are state parks or forests (Kettle Moraine State Forest and Devil's Lake, Mill Bluff, Chippewa Moraine, and Interstate parks), and one (Horicon) is a state wildlife area. The remaining three areas are not yet developed.

Kettle Moraine, Interstate Park, and Chippewa Moraine contain interpretive centers, many miles of hiking trails, and regularly scheduled naturalist programs. Horicon and Devil's Lake also have extensive interpretive programs and facilities.

Ice Age National Scenic Trail was established in 1980. Approximately 520 miles of the 1,000-mile trail are complete and marked with signs and yellow-paint blazes providing distance and directional information. For information on the Ice Age Reserve, write Wisconsin Department of Natural Resources, Box 7921, Madison, WI 53707, or the National Park Service, 700 Ray-O-Vac Drive, Madison, WI 53711. For information on Ice Age Trail, contact the Ice Age Park and Trail Foundation, 207 East Buffalo Street, Milwaukee, WI 53202; or call (800) 227–0046.

ENTRANCE FEE: No charge.

FACILITIES: Although lodging is not available in the Ice Age units, it is available in nearby communities. Food service is available seasonally at Devil's Lake.

CAMPING: Camping is available in the Kettle Moraine, Devil's Lake, Interstate, and Mill Bluff units.

FISHING: Fishing is available in or near a number of the units, and a Wisconsin fishing license is required.

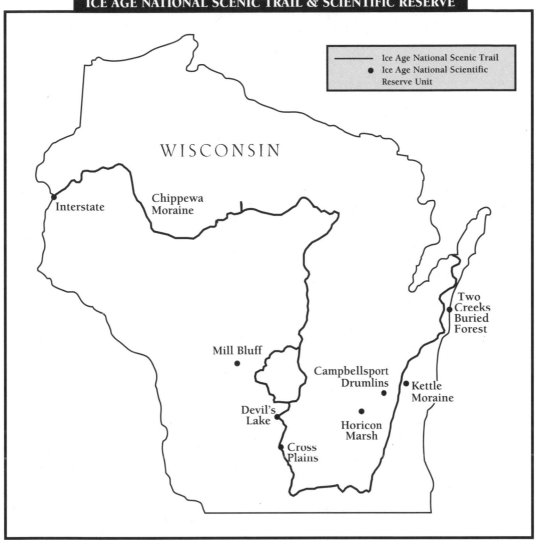

ICE AGE NATIONAL SCENIC TRAIL & SCIENTIFIC RESERVE

WISCONSIN

Ice Age National Scenic Trail
Ice Age National Scientific
Reserve Unit

Interstate

Chippewa
Moraine

Two
Creeks
Buried
Forest

Mill Bluff

Campbellsport
Drumlins

Kettle
Moraine

Devil's
Lake

Horicon
Marsh

Cross
Plains

ST. CROIX NATIONAL SCENIC RIVERWAY

P.O. Box 708
St. Croix Falls, WI 54024-0708
(715) 483-3284
www.nps.gov/sacn

The St. Croix National Scenic Riverway was established in 1968 and enlarged in 1972 to preserve approximately 250 miles of riverways that show little evidence of disturbance by man. The park begins near the sources of the St. Croix and Namekagon rivers in northern Wisconsin and follows the border between Wisconsin and Minnesota.

Thousands of years ago, this region of the United States was leveled by glacial ice flowing down from the north. As the climate warmed and the glacier melted, much of the resulting water used the St. Croix basin as an escape. The scraping of the advancing ice sheet combined with the later water runoff exposed ancient rocks and volcanic formations that are visible along the rivers.

The French were the first Europeans to venture into this region. Here they found the Dakota and Ojibwa tribes living in an area rich in both plant and wildlife. The St. Croix valley became an abundant source of beaver pelts for Europe until the early 1800s. Today, much of the riverway cuts through second-growth hardwood forests.

As one of the eight original wild and scenic rivers designated by Congress, the St. Croix Riverway protects stunning scenery and numerous recreation opportunities near a large metropolitan area. The main visitor center at St. Croix Falls, Wisconsin, is open year-round. Visitor centers are open in the summer near the towns of Grantsburg and Trego, Wisconsin.

Canoeing the rivers is one of the park's most popular activities. During late summer and fall, the water level is generally low and the lower sections of the river provide the best trips. A listing of the numerous canoe outfitters located along the riverway may be obtained by writing the park superintendent. Most visitors find that 10–20 miles of paddling downstream is a full day. Detailed maps and park rangers are available to assist visitors planning trips at all the visitor centers. The Lower St. Croix is popular for power-boating, water-skiing, and house-boating. State parks along this part of the riverway provide additional camping, picnicking, hiking, and interpretive exhibits.

ENTRANCE FEE: No charge.

FACILITIES: No food service or lodging is provided by the Park Service. Overnight accommodations and supplies are in nearby communities.

CAMPING: A number of primitive campsites are located along the riverway. Walk-in campgrounds with vault toilets and water are found at some landings. Several state parks and state forests along the riverway maintain developed campgrounds.

FISHING: Bass, muskellunge, and walleye pike are in the rivers, and the Namekagon is noted for brown, brook, and rainbow trout. A fishing license is required. Where the river forms a boundary between the two states, a license from either is valid.

See maps on pages 319 and 320.

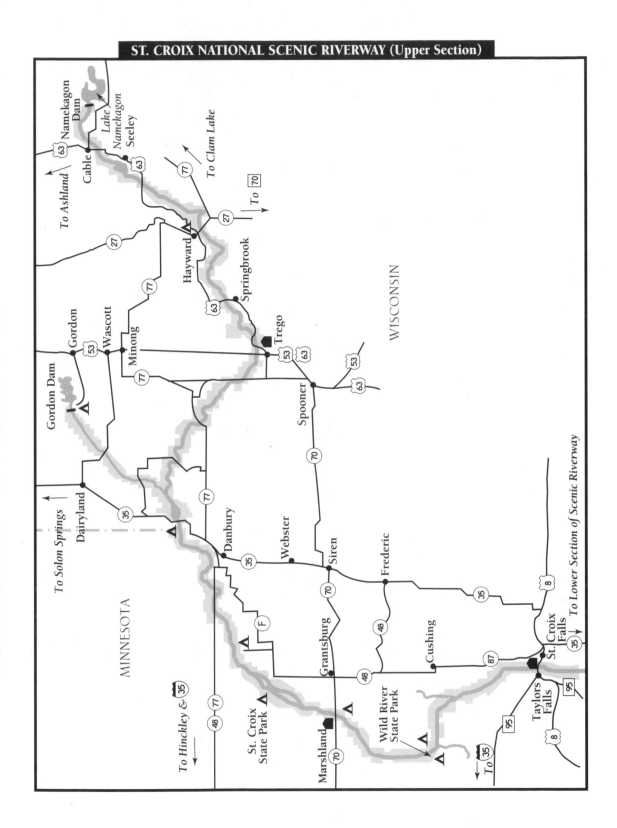

ST. CROIX NATIONAL SCENIC RIVERWAY (Lower Section)

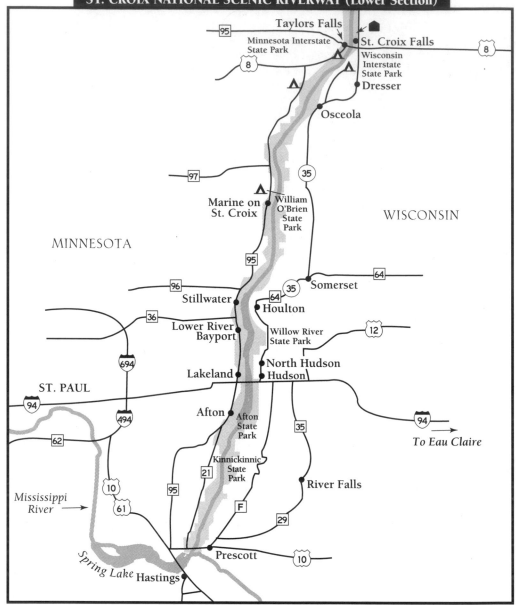

NATIONAL PARK AREAS FACILITIES AND ACTIVITIES CHART

This chart presents current information on visitor services in the areas described in this book. Generally, the services listed are those in the parks themselves. Additional services are usually available in nearby cities. Parks permitting activities such as horseback riding or boating do not necessarily rent equipment. Many parks curtail service in their off-seasons. A few park areas are not listed because they do not have the visitor services listed here.

FACILITIES AND ACTIVITIES CHART

	Fees	Visitor Center	Programs/Tours	Self-Guided Tour/Trail	Guide for Hire	Picnic Area	Campground	Group Camp Site	Backcountry Permits	Hiking	Mountain Climbing	Horse Trail	Swimming	Bathhouse	Boating	Boat Rental	Boat Ramp	Fishing	Hunting	Bicycle Trail	Snowmobile Route	Crosscountry Ski Trail	Cabin Rental	Hotel, Motel, Lodge	Groceries, Ice	Restaurant, Snacks	Campsites	Activities, Services	Visitor Center	Handicap Access
ALABAMA																														
Horseshoe Bend Natl. Military Park, 11288 Horseshoe Bend Rd., Daviston, AL 36256-9751	●	●	●	●		●				●																		●		●
Little River Canyon Natioal Preserve, 2141 Gault Ave. North, Fort Payne, AL 35967-3673		●	●	●		●	●			●			●	●	●		●	●	●	●								●		●
Natchez Trace Pkwy., 2680 Natchez Trace Pkwy., Tupelo, MS 38801		●	●	●		●	●			●			●	●	●		●	●	●	●								●		●
Russell Cave Natl. Monument, 3729 County Rd. 98, Bridgeport, AL 35740-9770		●	●	●						●																				
Tuskegee Institute Natl. Historic Site, P.O. Drawer 10, Tuskegee, AL 36087-0010		●	●	●																										
CONNECTICUT																														
Appalachian NST, P.O. Box 807, Harpers Ferry, WV 25425		●	●				●	●	●	●	●								●			●		●				●		
Weir Farm National Historic Site, 735 Nod Hill Rd., Wilton, CT 06897-1309		●	●															●												
DISTRICT OF COLUMBIA																														
Chesapeake and Ohio Canal NHP, P.O. Box 4, Sharpsburg, MD 21782	●	●	●	●		●	●			●					●			●	●	●		●		●			●	●		●
Constitution Gardens, NCP Central, 900 Ohio Dr., SW, Washington, DC 20242		●	●	●		●																								
Ford's Theatre Natl. Historic Site, NCP Central, 900 Ohio Dr., SW, Washington, DC 20242		●	●																											
Franklin Delano Roosevelt Memorial, NCP Central, 900 Ohio Dr., SW, Washington, DC 20242		●																												
Frederick Douglas Natl. Historic Site, 1411 W St., SE, Washington, DC 20020	●	●	●		●																									
George Washington Memorial Pkwy., Turkey Run Park, McClean, VA 22101	●	●	●				●		●	●	●		●		●		●	●		●				●			●	●		●
Korean War Veterans' Memorial, NCP Central, 900 Ohio Dr., SW, Washington, DC 20242		●	●																						●			●		●
Lincoln Memorial, NCP Central, 900 Ohio Dr., SW, Washington, DC 20242		●	●																						●			●		●
Lyndon B. Johnson Mem., G. W. Mem. Pkwy., Turkey Run Park, McLean, VA 22101					●																									
Mary McLeod Bethune Natl. Historic Site, 1318 Vermont Ave., NW, Washington, DC 20005		●	●	●																										
National Mall, NCP Central, 900 Ohio Dr., SW, Washington, DC 20242			●									●																●		●
Pennsylvania Avenue National Historic Site, 900 Ohio Dr., SW, Washington DC 20242		●	●																											
Old Stone House, 3051 M Street, NW, Georgetown		●	●																											
Rock Creek Park, 3545 Williamsburg Lane, NW, Washington, DC 20008		●	●			●			●	●		●							●	●								●		●
Sewall-Belmont House Natl. Historic Site, 144 Constitution Ave. NE, Washington, DC 20002		●	●			●			●																					
Theodore Roosevelt Island, G.W. Mem., Turkey Run Park, McLean, VA 22101		●	●													●	●	●									●			●
Thomas Jefferson Memorial, NCP Central, 900 Ohio Dr., SW, Washington, DC 20242		●	●														●								●			●		●
Vietnam Veterans Memorial, NCP Central, 900 Ohio Dr., SW, Washington, DC 20242		●	●																						●					
Washington Monument, NCP Central, 900 Ohio Dr, SW, Washington, DC 20242		●	●																						●			●		●
White House, President's Park NCR, 1100 Ohio Dr., SW, Washington, DC 20242	●	●	●																						●			●		●

FLORIDA

Big Cypress Natl. Preserve, HCR61, Box 110, Ochopee, FL 34141

Biscayne Natl. Park, 9700 S.W. 328th Street, Homestead, FL 33033

Canaveral Natl. Seashore, 308 Julia St., Titusville FL 32796-3521

Castillo de San Marcos Natl. Monument, 1 South Castillo Dr., St. Augustine, FL 32084-3699

De Soto Natl. Memorial P.O. Box 15390, Bradenton, FL 34280-5390

Dry Tortugas National Park, P.O. Box 6208, Key West, FL 33041

Everglades Natl. Park, 40001 State Rd. 9336, Homestead, FL 33034-6733

Fort Caroline Natl. Memorial, 12713 Fort Caroline Rd., Jacksonville, FL 32225-1240

Fort Matanzas Natl. Monument, 1 South Castillo Drive, St. Augustine, FL 32084-3699

Gulf Islands Natl. Seashore, 1801 Gulf Breeze Parkway, Gulf Breeze, FL, 32561-5000

Timucuan Ecological and Historic Preserve, 13165 Mt. Pleasant Rd., Jacksonville, FL 32225-1227

GEORGIA

Andersonville Natl. Historic Site, 496 Cemetery Road, Andersonville, GA 31711-9707

Appalachian National Scenic Trail. P.O. Box 807, Harpers Ferry, WV 25425

Chattahoochee River Natl. Recreation Area, 1978 Island Ford Parkway, Atlanta, GA 30350-3400

Chickamauga and Chattanooga Natl. Military Park, P.O. Box 2128, Fort Oglethorpe, GA 30742-0128

Cumberland Island Natl. Seashore, P.O. Box 806, St. Marys, GA 31558-0806

Fort Frederica Natl. Monument, Rt. 9, Box 286-C, St. Simons Island, GA 31522

Fort Pulaski Natl. Monument, Box 30757, Savannah, GA 31410-0757

Jimmy Carter National Historic Site, 300 North Bond Street, Plains, GA 31780-0392

Kennesaw Mountain Natl. Battlefield Park, 905 Kennesaw Mountain Dr., Kennesaw, GA 30152

Martin Luther King, Jr., Natl. Historic Site, 450 Auburn Ave., NE, Atlanta, GA 30312-0526

Ocmulgee Natl. Monument, 1207 Emery Highway, Macon, GA 31217-4399

ILLINOIS

Chicago Portage NHS, c/o Cook County Forest Preserve, 536 N. Harlem Ave., River Forest, IL 60305

Illinois and Michigan Canal National Heritage Corridor, 15709 S. Independence Blvd., Lockport, IL 60441

Lincoln Home Natl. Historic Site, 413 S. Eighth St., Springfield, IL 62701-1905

INDIANA

George Rogers Clark Natl. Historical Park, 401 S. Second St., Vincennes, IN 47591-1001

Indiana Dunes Natl. Lakeshore, 1100 N. Mineral Springs Rd., Porter, IN 46304

Lincoln Boyhood Natl. Memorial, P.O. Box 1816, Lincoln City, IN 47552-1816

KENTUCKY

Abraham Lincoln Birthplace Natl. Historic Site, 2995 Lincoln Farm Rd., Hodgenville, KY 42748-9707

Big South Fork National River and Recreation Area, 4564 Leatherwood Rd., Oneida, TN 37841

Cumberland Gap National Historical Park, P.O. Box 1848, Middlesboro, KY 40965-1848

Mammoth Cave Natl. Park, P.O. Box 7, Mammoth Cave, KY 42259-0007

	Fees	Visitor Center	Programs/Tours	Self-Guided Tour/Trail	Guide for Hire	Picnic Area	Campground	Group Camp Site	Backcountry Permits	Hiking	Mountain Climbing	Horse Trail	Swimming	Bathhouse	Boating	Boat Rental	Boat Ramp	Fishing	Hunting	Bicycle Trail	Snowmobile Route	Crosscountry Ski Trail	Cabin Rental	Hotel, Motel, Lodge	Groceries, Ice	Restaurant, Snacks	Campsites	Handicap Access: Activities, Services	Handicap Access: Visitor Center
	●	●	●	●	●	●	●	●	●	●	●	●	●	●	●	●	●	●	●	●	●	●	●	●	●	●	●	●	●
MAINE																													
Acadia Natl. Park, P.O. Box 177, Bar Harbor, ME 04609-0177	●	●	●	●	●	●	●	●		●		●	●	●	●		●	●		●	●	●				●	●	●	●
Appalachian Natl. Scenic Trail, P.O. Box 807, Harpers Ferry, WV 25425		●		●		●	●	●		●	●												●		●				
Roosevelt Campobello International Park, P.O. Box 129, Lubec, ME 04652		●		●																									●
Saint Croix Island International Historic Site, Acadia Natl. Park, P.O. Box 177, Bar Harbor, ME 04609-0177						●											●												
MARYLAND																													
Antietam Natl. Battlefield, Box 158, Sharpsburg, MD 21782-0158	●	●	●	●				●		●								●											●
Appalachian Natl. Scenic Trail, P.O. Box 807, Harpers Ferry, WV 25425		●		●		●	●	●		●	●												●		●				
Assateague Island Natl. Seashore, 7206 National Seashore Ln., Berlin, MD 21811-9742	●	●	●	●		●	●	●	●	●			●	●	●			●	●	●							●	●	●
Catoctin Mountain Park, 6602 Foxville Rd., Thurmont, MD 21788-0158		●	●	●		●	●	●	●	●		●						●				●	●				●	●	●
Chesapeake and Ohio Canal Natl. Historical Park, P.O. Box 4, Sharpsburg, MD 21782-0004	●	●	●	●		●	●	●		●		●			●	●	●	●		●		●				●	●	●	●
Clara Barton Natl. Historic Site, 5801 Oxford Rd., Glen Echo, MD 20812-1201		●	●																									●	
Fort McHenry Natl. Monument and Historic Shrine, end of E. Fort Avenue, Baltimore, MD 21230-5393	●	●	●	●		●																						●	●
Fort Washington Park, NCP East, 1900 Anacostia Dr., SE, Washington, DC 20020-6722	●	●	●			●												●											●
George Washington Memorial Pkwy., Turkey Run Park, McClean, VA 22101	●	●	●	●		●				●		●			●	●	●	●		●						●		●	
Greenbelt Park, 6565 Greenbelt Rd., Greenbelt, MD 20770-3207		●	●	●		●	●			●		●															●		●
Hampton Natl. Historic Site, 535 Hampton Ln., Towson, MD 21286-1397		●	●	●																						●			
Harpers Ferry Natl. Historic Park, P.O. Box 65, Harpers Ferry, WV 25425	●	●	●	●		●				●	●							●											●
Monocacy Natl. Battlefield, 4801 Urbana Pike, Frederick, MD 21704-7307		●	●	●																									●
Piscataway Park, NCP East, 1900 Anacostia Dr., SE, Washington, DC 20020-6722						●											●	●											●
Thomas Stone Natl. Historic Site, 6655 Rose Hill Rd., Port Tobacco, MD 20677-3400		●	●	●		●				●																			●
MASSACHUSETTS																													
Adams Natl. Historical Park, 135 Adams St., Quincy, MA 02169-1749	●	●	●																										●
Appalachian Natl. Scenic Trail, P.O. Box 807, Harpers Ferry, WV 25425		●		●		●	●	●		●	●												●		●				
Blackstone River Valley Natl. Heritage Corridor, 1 Depot Sq., Woonsocket, RI 02895				●														●											
Boston African-American Natl. Historic Site, 14 Beacon St., Suite 506, Boston, MA 02108			●	●																								●	
Boston Harbor Islands Natl. Recreation Area, 408 Atlantic Ave., Boston, MA 02210-3350			●	●		●	●	●		●			●		●			●								●		●	
Boston Natl. Historical Park, Charleston Navy Yard, Boston, MA 02129-4543	●	●	●	●		●																				●		●	●
Cape Cod Natl. Seashore, 99 Marconi Site Rd., Wellfleet, MA 02667-0250	●	●	●	●	●	●			●	●			●	●	●	●	●	●	●	●				●	●	●			●

MASSACHUSETTS *(continued)*

Frederick Law Olmsted Natl. Historic Site, 99 Warren St., Brookline, MA 02146

John Fitzgerald Kennedy Natl. Historic Site, 83 Beals St., Brookline, MA 02146-6010

Longfellow Natl. Historic Site, 105 Brattle St., Cambridge, MA 02138-3407

Lowell Natl. Historical Park, 67 Kirk St., Lowell, MA 01852-1029

Minute Man Natl. Historical Park, 174 Liberty St., Concord, MA 01742-1705

New Bedford Whaling Natl. Historic Park, 33 William St., New Bedford, MA 02740

Salem Maritime Natl. Historic Site, 174 Derby St., Salem, MA 01970-5186

Saugus Iron Works Natl. Historic Site, 244 Central St., Saugus, MA 01906-2107

Springfield Armory Natl. Historic Site, 1 Armory Square, Springfield, MA 01105-1299

MICHIGAN

Father Marquette Natl. Memorial, 720 Church Street, St. Ignace, MI 49781

Isle Royale Natl. Park, 800 E. Lakeshore Dr., Houghton, MI 49931-1895

Keweenaw Natl. Historical Park, P.O. Box 471, Calumet, MI 49913-0471

Pictured Rocks Natl. Lakeshore, P.O. Box 40, Munising, MI 49862-0040

Sleeping Bear Dunes Natl. Lakeshore, 9922 Front St., Empire, MI 49630-9797

MISSISSIPPI

Brices Cross Roads Natl. Battlefield Site, 2680 Natchez Trace Pkwy., Tupelo, MS 38801-9718

Gulf Islands Natl. Seashore, 3500 Park Rd., Ocean Springs, MS 39564-9709

Natchez National Historic Park, 640 S. Canal St., Box E, Natchez, MS 39120

Natchez Trace Parkway, 2680 Natchez Trace Pkwy., Tupelo, MS 38801-9718

Tupelo Natl. Battlefield, 2680 Natchez Trace Parkway, Tupelo, MS 38801-9718

Vicksburg Natl. Military Park, 3201 Clay St., Vicksburg, MS 39183-3495

NEW HAMPSHIRE

Appalachian Natl. Scenic Trail, P.O. Box 807, Harpers Ferry, WV 25425

Saint-Gaudens Natl. Historic Site, R.R. 3, Box 73, Cornish, NH 03745-9704

NEW JERSEY

Appalachian Natl. Scenic Trail, P.O. Box 807, Harpers Ferry, WV 25425

Delaware Water Gap Natl. Recreation Area, Bushkill, PA 18324-9999

Edison Natl. Historic Site, Main St. and Lakeside Ave., West Orange, NJ 07052-5515

Gateway Natl. Recreation Area, Floyd Bennett Field, Building 69, Brooklyn, NY 11234

Morristown Natl. Historical Park, Washington Place, Morristown, NJ 07960

Pinelands National Reserve, P.O. Box 7, New Lisbon, NJ 08064

NEW YORK

Appalachian Natl. Scenic Trail, P.O. Box 807, Harpers Ferry, WV 25425

Castle Clinton Natl. Monument, Battery Park, New York, NY 10004

NEW YORK (continued)

	Fees	Visitor Center	Programs/Tours	Self-Guided Tour/Trail	Guide for Hire	Picnic Area	Campground	Group Camp Site	Backcountry Permits	Hiking	Mountain Climbing	Horse Trail	Swimming	Bathhouse	Boating	Boat Rental	Boat Ramp	Fishing	Hunting	Bicycle Trail	Snowmobile Route	Crosscountry Ski Trail	Cabin Rental	Hotel, Motel, Lodge	Groceries, Ice	Restaurant, Snacks	Campsites	Activities, Services	Visitor Center
Eleanor Roosevelt Natl. Historic Site, 4097 Albany Post Rd., Hyde Park, NY12538-1997	●	●	●	●		●																						●	●
Ellis Island, National Park Service, Manhattan Sites, 26 Wall St., New York, NY 10005		●	●																										
Federal Hall Natl. Memorial, 15 Pine St., New York, NY10005		●	●																									●	●
Fire Island Natl. Seashore, 120 Laurel St., Patchogue, NY 11772-3596		●	●	●		●	●	●		●			●	●	●			●	●									●	●
Fort Stanwix Natl. Monument, 112 E. Park St., Rome, NY 13440-5816	●	●	●	●		●																						●	●
Gateway Natl. Recreation Area, Floyd Bennett Field, Bldg. 69, Brooklyn, NY 11234-7097		●	●			●				●			●	●	●			●		●				●	●	●		●	●
General Grant Natl. Memorial, 122nd St. and Riverside Dr., New York, NY 10024		●	●																										
Hamilton Grange Natl. Memorial, 287 Convent Ave., New York, NY 10031		●	●																										
Home of Franklin D. Roosevelt Natl. Historic Site, 4097 Albany Post Rd., Hyde Park, NY 12538-1997	●	●	●	●		●																						●	●
Martin Van Buren Natl. Historic Site, P.O. Box 545, Kinderhook, NY 12106-0545	●	●	●	●		●				●																		●	●
Sagamore Hill Natl. Historic Site, 20 Sagamore Hill Rd., Oyster Bay, NY 11771-1807	●	●	●			●																						●	●
Saint Paul's Church Natl. Historic Site, 897 S. Columbus Ave., Mount Vernon, NY 10550-5018		●	●																										
Saratoga Natl. Historical Park, 648 Route 32, Stillwater, NY 12170-1604	●	●	●			●				●												●						●	●
Statue of Liberty Natl. Monument and Ellis Island, New York, NY 10004-1467		●	●																							●		●	●
Theodore Roosevelt Birthplace Natl. Historic Site, 28 E. 20th St., New York, NY 10003	●	●	●																									●	●
Theodore Roosevelt Inaugural Natl. Historic Site, 641 Delaware Ave., Buffalo, NY 14202-1079	●	●	●	●																								●	●
Upper Delaware Scenic and Recreational River, R.R. 2, Box 2428, Beach Lake, PA 18405-9737		●	●	●		●	●			●					●			●	●			●			●			●	●
Vanderbilt Mansion Natl. Historic Site, 4097 Albany Post Rd., Hyde Park, NY 12538-1997	●	●	●			●																						●	●
Women's Rights Natl. Historical Park, 136 Fall St., Seneca Falls, NY 13148-1517		●	●	●																								●	●

NORTH CAROLINA

	Fees	Visitor Center	Programs/Tours	Self-Guided Tour/Trail	Guide for Hire	Picnic Area	Campground	Group Camp Site	Backcountry Permits	Hiking	Mountain Climbing	Horse Trail	Swimming	Bathhouse	Boating	Boat Rental	Boat Ramp	Fishing	Hunting	Bicycle Trail	Snowmobile Route	Crosscountry Ski Trail	Cabin Rental	Hotel, Motel, Lodge	Groceries, Ice	Restaurant, Snacks	Campsites	Activities, Services	Visitor Center
Appalachian Natl. Scenic Trail, P.O. Box 807, Harpers Ferry, WV 25425		●	●	●		●	●	●	●	●																	●	●	●
Blue Ridge Parkway (N.C., Va.) 199 Hemphill Knob Rd., Asheville, NC 28803		●	●	●		●	●	●	●	●		●						●						●	●	●	●	●	●
Cape Hatteras Natl. Seashore, Rt. 1, Box 675, Manteo, NC 27954-2708		●	●	●		●	●	●	●	●			●	●				●						●	●	●	●	●	●
Cape Lookout Natl. Seashore, 131 Charles St., Harkers Island, NC 28531-9702		●	●	●		●				●								●									●	●	●
Carl Sandburg Home Natl. Historic Site, 1928 Little River Rd., Flat Rock, NC 28731-9766	●	●	●	●						●														●				●	●
Fort Raleigh Natl. Historic Site, Rt. 1, Box 675, Manteo, NC 27954-2708		●	●	●																								●	●
Great Smoky Mountains Natl. Park, 107 Park Headquarters Rd., Gatlinburg, TN 37738		●	●	●		●	●	●	●	●		●						●		●				●			●	●	●
Guilford Courthouse Natl. Military Park, 2332 New Garden Rd., Greensboro, NC 27410-2355		●	●	●																●								●	●
Moores Creek Natl. Battlefield, 40 Patriots Hall Dr., Currie, NC 28435		●	●	●		●																				●		●	●
Wright Brothers Natl. Memorial, Rt. 1, Box 675, Manteo, NC 27954-2708	●	●	●	●																								●	●

OHIO

- Cuyahoga Valley Natl. Park, 15610 Vaughn Rd., Brecksville, OH 44141-3018
- Dayton Aviation Heritage Natl. Historic Park, P.O. Box 9280, Wright Bros. Station, Dayton, OH 45409-9280
- Hopewell Culture National Historic Park,, 16062 State Route 104, Chillicothe, OH 45601-8694
- James A. Garfield Natl. Historic Site, 8095 Mentor Ave., Mentor, OH 44060-5753
- Perry's Victory and International Peace Memorial, P.O. Box 549, Put-in-Bay, OH 43456-0549
- William Howard Taft Natl. Historic Site, 2038 Auburn Ave., Cincinnati, OH 45219-3025

PENNSYLVANIA

- Allegheny Portage Railroad Natl. Historic Site, 110 Federal Park Rd., Gallitzin, PA 16641
- Appalachian Natl. Scenic Trail, P.O. Box 807, Harpers Ferry, WV 25425
- Benjamin Franklin Natl. Memorial, Twentieth and Benjamin Franklin Pkwy., Philadelphia, PA
- Delaware and Lehigh Navigation Canal National Heritage Corridor, 10 E. Church St., Bethlehem, PA 18018
- Delaware Water Gap Natl. Recreation Area (Pa., N.J.), Bushkill, PA 18324-9999
- Edgar Allen Poe Natl. Historic Site, 532 N. 7th St., Philadelphia, PA 19123
- Eisenhower Natl. Historic Site, 250 Eisenhower Farm Lane, Gettysburg, PA 17325-1080
- Fort Necessity Natl. Battlefield, 1 Washington Way, Farmington, PA 15437-9514
- Friendship Hill Natl. Historic Site, 223 New Geneva Rd., Point Marion, PA 15474
- Gettysburg Natl. Military Park, 97 Taneytown Rd., Gettysburg, PA 17325-1080
- Gloria Dei (Old Swedes') Church Natl. Historic Site, Columbus Blvd. + Washington Ave., Philadelphia, PA
- Hopewell Furnace Natl. Historic Site, 2 Mark Bird Lane, Elverson, PA 19520-9505
- Independence Natl. Historical Park, 313 Walnut St., Philadelphia, PA 19106-2778
- Johnstown Flood Natl. Memorial, 733 Lake Rd., South Fork, PA 15956
- Steamtown Natl. Historic Site, 150 S. Washington Ave., Scranton, PA 18503-2018
- Thaddeus Kosciuszko Natl. Memorial, Independence NHP, 313 Walnut St., Philadelphia, PA 19106
- Upper Delaware Scenic and Recreational River, R.R.2, Box 2428, Beach Lake, PA 18405-9737
- Valley Forge Natl. Historical Park, Valley Forge, PA 19482-0953

PUERTO RICO

- San Juan Natl. Historic Site, Fort San Cristóbal, Norzagaray St., Old San Juan, PR 00901-2094

RHODE ISLAND

- Blackstone River Valley Natl. Heritage Corridor, 1 Depot Sq., Woonsocket, RI 02895
- Roger Williams Natl. Memorial, 282 N. Main St., Providence, RI 02903-1240
- Touro Synagogue Natl. Historic Site, 85 Touro St., Newport, RI 02840

SOUTH CAROLINA

- Charles Pinckney Natl. Historic Site, Ft. Sumter Natl. Mon., 1214 Middle St., Sullivans Island, SC 29482
- Congaree Swamp Natl. Monument, 100 Natl. Park Rd., Hopkins, SC 29061
- Cowpens Natl. Battlefield, P.O. Box 308, Chesnee, SC 29323-0308
- Fort Sumter Natl. Monument, 1214 Middle St., Sullivan's Island, SC 29482
- Historic Camden Revolutionary War Site, 222 Broad St., Camden, SC 29020

Facilities and Activities Chart — column headers (left to right): Fees · Visitor Center · Programs/Tours · Self-Guided Tour/Trail · Guide for Hire · Picnic Area · Campground · Group Camp Site · Backcountry Permits · Hiking · Mountain Climbing · Horse Trail · Swimming · Bathhouse · Boating · Boat Rental · Boat Ramp · Fishing · Hunting · Bicycle Trail · Snowmobile Route · Crosscountry Ski Trail · Cabin Rental · Hotel, Motel, Lodge · Groceries, Ice · Restaurant, Snacks · Campsites · Activities, Services (Handicap Access) · Visitor Center (Handicap Access)

Park	Fees	Visitor Center	Programs/Tours	Self-Guided Tour/Trail	Guide for Hire	Picnic Area	Campground	Group Camp Site	Backcountry Permits	Hiking	Mountain Climbing	Horse Trail	Swimming	Bathhouse	Boating	Boat Rental	Boat Ramp	Fishing	Hunting	Bicycle Trail	Snowmobile Route	Crosscountry Ski Trail	Cabin Rental	Hotel, Motel, Lodge	Groceries, Ice	Restaurant, Snacks	Campsites	HA: Activities, Services	HA: Visitor Center
SOUTH CAROLINA (continued)																													
Kings Mountain Natl. Military Park, 2625 Park Road, Blacksburg, SC 29702	●	●	●	●		●				●		●																●	●
Ninety Six Natl. Historic Site, P.O. Box 496, Ninety Six, SC 29666-0496		●	●	●		●				●		●						●										●	●
TENNESSEE																													
Andrew Johnson Natl. Historic Site, P.O. Box 1088, Greeneville, TN 37744-1088	●	●	●																									●	●
Appalachian Natl. Scenic Trail, P.O. Box 807, Harpers Ferry, WV 25425		●	●			●	●	●	●	●	●	●																●	●
Big South Fork Natl. River and Recreation Area, 4564 Leatherwood Rd., Oneida, TN 37841-9544	●	●	●	●		●	●	●	●	●	●	●	●		●		●	●	●			●		●			●	●	●
Chickamauga and Chattanooga Natl. Military Park, P.O. Box 2128, Fort Oglethorpe, GA 30742		●	●	●		●				●		●								●				●				●	●
Cumberland Gap Natl. Historic Park, P.O. Box 1848, Middlesboro, KY 40965	●	●	●	●		●	●	●	●	●		●															●	●	●
Fort Donelson Natl. Battlefield, P.O. Box 434, Dover, TN 37058-0434	●	●	●	●		●				●																		●	●
Great Smoky Mountains Natl. Park, 107 Park Headquarters Rd., Gatlinburg, TN 37738-4102		●	●	●		●	●	●	●	●	●	●	●					●									●	●	●
Natchez Trace Parkway, 2680 Natchez Trace Pkwy., Tupelo, MS 38801-9718		●	●	●		●	●		●	●		●	●	●	●		●	●		●							●	●	●
Obed Wild and Scenic River, P.O. Box 429, Wartburg, TN 37887-0429		●	●						●	●	●		●		●			●										●	●
Shiloh Natl. Military Park, 1055 Pittsburg Landing Rd., Shiloh, TN 38376-9704	●	●	●	●						●																		●	●
Stones River Natl. Battlefield, 3501 Old Nashville Highway, Murfreesboro, TN 37129-3094		●	●	●						●										●								●	●
VERMONT																													
Appalachian Natl. Scenic Trail, P.O. Box 807, Harpers Ferry, WV 25425		●	●			●	●	●	●	●	●	●																●	●
Marsh-Billings-Rockefeller Natl. Historical Park, P.O. Box 178, Woodstock, VT 05091	●	●	●	●						●		●										●						●	●
VIRGINIA																													
Appalachian Natl. Scenic Trail, P.O. Box 807, Harpers Ferry, WV 25425		●	●			●	●	●	●	●	●	●																●	●
Appomattox Court House Natl. Historical Park, P.O. Box 218, Route 24, Appomattox, VA 24522-0218	●	●	●	●						●																		●	●
Arlington House, The Robert E. Lee Memorial, G. W. Mem. Pkwy., Turkey Run Park, McLean, VA 22101		●	●	●																								●	●
Assateague Island Natl. Seashore, 7206 National Seashore Ln., Berlin, MD 21811-9742	●	●	●	●		●	●		●	●			●		●		●	●	●								●	●	●
Blue Ridge Parkway, 199 Hemphill Knob Rd., Asheville, NC 28803		●	●	●		●	●	●	●	●		●						●		●			●	●	●	●	●	●	●
Booker T. Washington Natl. Monument, 12130 Booker T. Washington Hwy., Hardy, VA 24101-9688		●	●	●		●				●																		●	●
Colonial Natl. Historical Park, P.O. Box 210, Yorktown, VA 23690-0210	●	●	●	●		●				●								●	●	●								●	●
Cumberland Gap Natl. Historic Park, P.O. Box 1848, Middlesboro, KY 40965-1848	●	●	●	●		●	●	●	●	●		●						●									●	●	●
Fredericksburg and Spotsylvania Natl. Military Park, 120 Chatham Lane, Fredericksburg, VA 22405-2508	●	●	●	●						●																		●	●
George Washington Birthplace Natl. Monument, 1732 Popes Creek Rd., Washington's Birthplace, VA 22443	●	●	●	●		●				●								●										●	●

VIRGINIA (continued)

George Washington Memorial Parkway, Turkey Run Park, McLean, VA 22101-0001

Green Springs Natl. Hist. Landmark Dist., c/o Shenandoah Natl. Park, 22591 Spotswood Trail, Elkton, VA 22827

Harpers Ferry Natl. Historic Park, P.O. Box 65, Harpers Ferry, WV 25425

Maggie L. Walker Natl. Historic Site, Richmond NBP, 3215 E. Broad St., Richmond, VA 23223-7517

Manassas Natl. Battlefield Park, 6511 Sudley Rd., Manassas, VA 20109

Petersburg Nat. Battlefield, 1539 Hickory Hill Rd., Petersburg, VA 23803-4721

Prince William Forest Park, 18100 Park Headquarters Rd., Triangle, VA 22172-0209

Red Hill Patrick Henry Natl. Memorial, 1250 Red Hill Road, Brookneal, VA 24528

Richmond Natl. Battlefield Park, 3215 E. Broad St., Richmond, VA 23223-7517

Shenandoah Natl. Park, 3655 US Hwy. 211 E, Luray, VA 22835-9036

Wolf Trap Farm Park for the Performing Arts, 1551 Trap Rd., Vienna, VA 22182-1643

VIRGIN ISLANDS

Buck Island Reef Natl. Monument, 2100 Church St., #100, Christiansted, St. Croix, VI 00820-4611

Christiansted Natl. Historic Site, 2100 Church St., #100, Christiansted, VI 00820-4611

Virgin Islands Natl. Park, 6310 Estate Nazareth, St. Thomas, VI 00802-1102

WEST VIRGINIA

Appalachian Natl. Scenic Trail (Me. to Ga.), P.O. Box 807, Harpers Ferry, WV 25425

Bluestone Natl. Scenic River, 104 Main St., P.O. Box 246, Glen Jean, WV 25846-0246

Chesapeake and Ohio Canal Natl. Historic Park, P.O. Box 4, Sharpsburg, MD 21782

Gauley River Natl. Recreation Area, 104 Main St., P.O. Box 246, Glen Jean, WV 25846-0246

Harpers Ferry Natl. Historical Park, P.O. Box 65, Harpers Ferry, WV 25425-0065

New River Gorge Natl. River, 104 Main St., P.O. Box 246, Glen Jean, WV 25846-0246

WISCONSIN

Apostle Islands Natl. Lakeshore, Rt. 1, Box 4, Bayfield, WI 54814-9599

Ice Age Natl. Scenic Trail; Ice Age Natl. Scientific Reserve, Wisconsin Dept. of Natural Resources, P.O. Box 7921, Madison, WI 53707

St. Croix Natl. Scenic Riverway, P.O. Box 708, St. Croix Falls, WI 54024-0708